GERMAN FIRST YEAR

GERMAN FIRST YEAR

By HARRY F. REINERT

Teacher of German
Edmonds Senior High School
Edmonds, Washington

Dedicated to serving

AMSCO

our nation's youth

When ordering this book, please specify:

either

R 95 W

or

GERMAN FIRST YEAR WORKBOOK

AMSCO SCHOOL PUBLICATIONS, Inc.

315 Hudson Street   **New York, N.Y. 10013**

ISBN 0-87720-583-3

PREFACE

The increasing popularity of audio-lingual techniques in teaching foreign languages has created a number of needs. First, there is need for a systematic presentation of the basic principles of German grammar. In addition, large numbers of pattern drills are needed. Although audio-lingualists have strongly emphasized the need for an understanding of the foreign culture, many popular introductory texts contain very little cultural information. This *Workbook in German First Year* is designed to fulfill all three of these needs.

Explanations of basic structures of German have been kept brief but made as complete as possible. Each lesson contains a large number of varied exercises to illustrate and drill the structures being taught. The final lessons give a brief overview of some of the more important aspects of German culture. Original drawings and maps that illustrate German culture are interspersed throughout the book.

The book is arranged in convenient topical units covering structure and civilization. Thus, the student can use the text as a reference source. Since each lesson is complete in itself and the lessons can be taken in any sequence, the teacher can assign individual lessons either for additional study or for review.

The explanations and vocabulary items have been presented from the viewpoint of an American who is learning German. As much as possible, German phrases and structures are rendered into idiomatic American English. A few of the reading selections in the "Reading Comprehension" unit at the back of the book are printed in *Fraktur* so that students can become acquainted with this traditional German type.

The orderly presentation of structural explanations, the number and variety of exercises, and the wide assortment of cultural materials should make this workbook invaluable both to students and teachers.

The author appreciates the valuable contributions of Mrs. Monika Dettmers Tandon, White Bear Senior High School, White Bear Lake, Minnesota; Mr. R. Donald Ford, West Springfield High School, Fairfax County, Virginia; and Mr. Willi Fischer of the University of Washington, Seattle, Washington. These three consultants read the manuscript and offered much helpful advice and criticism.

—H.R.

CONTENTS

Part I—*Verbs*

Part VI—*Civilization*

Part VII—*Exercises in Auditory and Reading Comprehension*

Part 1 — Verbs

1. PRESENT TENSE OF REGULAR VERBS

Verbs limited by personal endings are called finite verbs.

The infinitive ends in **-en** or **-n**: **sagen**, *to say*; **tun**, *to do*.

The stem of the verb is formed by dropping the **-en** or **-n** from the infinitive: **sagen** has the stem **sag-**; **tun** has the stem **tu-**. The personal endings are added to this stem. A particular personal ending is always used with each pronoun.

PRESENT-TENSE PERSONAL ENDINGS

SINGULAR	PLURAL	FORMAL SING. AND PLUR.
ich *-e* du *-st* er, sie, es *-t*	wir *-en* ihr *-t* sie *-en*	Sie *-en*

Note

Du and **ihr** are used only for speaking to children, animals, members of the family, and very close friends. The formal **Sie** (which is always spelled with a capital **S**) is used for all other persons.

PRESENT TENSE OF **sagen** (*to say*)

ich sag*e* du sag*st* er, sie, es sag*t*	wir sag*en* ihr sag*t* sie sag*en*	Sie sag*en*

Note

1. Unlike English verbs, German verbs have only one form in the present tense:

er **sagt** { he says / he is saying

er **sagt** nicht { he does not say / he is not saying

sagt er? { does he say? / is he saying?

2. Verb stems that end in **d** or **t** add **e** before the endings **-st** and **-t** to help pronunciation:

ich warte   wir warten
du wart*est*   ihr wart*et*   Sie warten
er wart*et*   sie warten

1

3. Certain other verbs also add this **e** when necessary: **es regnet**.

4. Verbs with stems ending in **ss, ß,** or **z** add only **-t** both for second and third person singular:

du grü**ßt**   **er** grü**ßt**

SOME COMMON REGULAR VERBS

arbeiten, to work	**lernen,** to learn, study	**spielen,** to play
fragen, to ask (a person)	**machen,** to make, do	**stellen,** to place
freuen, to please, make happy	**meinen,** to think, believe, mean	**suchen,** to look for, seek
glauben, to believe	**passen,** to suit, be suitable	**tanzen,** to dance
grüßen, to greet	**probieren,** to test ~taste~	**warten,** to wait
hören, to hear	**regnen,** to rain	**wohnen,** to live (in)
kaufen, to buy	**sagen,** to say	**wünschen,** to wish
kosten, to cost _to taste_	**setzen,** to set	

Note

1. **Fragen** means to ask a *person:*

  Er **fragt den Herrn.**   He asks the gentleman.

2. To ask a *question* is expressed as **eine Frage stellen:**

  Er **stellt eine Frage.**   He asks a question.

3. The verb **glauben** has its object in the dative case if the object is a person:

  Sie glaubt **dem Jungen.**   She believes the boy.

   But:

  Das glaube ich (nicht).   I (don't) believe that.

4. **Passen** also has a dative object:

  Der Hut **paßt** *mir.*   The hat suits me.

ÜBUNGEN

A. Add the personal ending to the verb stem.

1. Der Student arbeit**et**____ sehr fleißig.

2. Die Kinder wart**en**___ am Bahnhof.

3. Es regn**et**____ den ganzen Tag.

4. Du grüß**t**_____ deinen Freund.

5. Die Dame mein**t**_____, das Frühstück kostet zuviel.

6. Wir setz**en**____ die Kamera auf den Tisch.

7. Ich glaub**e**_____, er hat Glück.

8. Der Hut paß**t**_____ dem Herrn nicht.

9. Was wünsch**t**_____ ihr, Kinder?

10. Das Mädchen stell**t**_____ eine Frage.

B. Write the correct pronoun.

1. Kinder, ___ihr___ lernt Deutsch!

2. ___Ich___ höre die Musik.

3. ___Du___ spielst im Zimmer.

4. ___Sie___ tanzen sehr gut, Fräulein Müller.

5. ___Es___ freut mich, Sie kennenzulernen.

6. Was suchen ___wir, Sie, sie___? (3 answers)

7. ___Er, ihr___ wohnt in der Hauptstraße. (2 answers)

8. ___Es___ kostet fünf Mark.

9. Was machst ___du___ denn da?

10. ___Ich___ arbeite zu Hause.

C. Replace the subject in parentheses with a pronoun.

1. (Herr und Frau Müller) ___Sie___ suchen die Kinder.

2. (Gretchen) ___Sie___ wohnt in einem großen Haus.

3. (Mein Freund und ich) ___Wir___ spielen Fußball.

4. (Peter) ___Er___ macht die Arbeit.

5. (Das Buch) ___Es___ kostet zwei Mark.

6. (Du und dein Freund) ___Ihr___ hört das Konzert.

7. (Herr Bauer) Was sagen ___sie___, Herr Bauer?

8. (Die Dame) ___Sie___ fragt den Herrn.

9. (Willy) Glaubst ___du___ das, Willy?

10. (Die Gäste) ___Sie___ warten am Bahnhof.

D. Replace the subject of each sentence with the pronouns in parentheses.

1. Sie arbeitet in der Schule.
   (wir) ___arbeiten___ (ich) ___arbeite___ (ihr) ___arbeitet___

2. Der Junge tanzt gern.
   (ich) ___tanze___ (sie = they) ___tanzen___ (du) ___tanzt___

3. Ich glaube das nicht.
   (ihr) ___glaubt___ (er) ___glaubt___ (wir) ___glauben___

4. Wir probieren den Kuchen.
   (du) ___probierst___ (Sie) ___probieren___ (ich) ___probiere___

5. Sie fragen Vater.
   (du) ___fragst___ (wir) ___fragen___ (ich) ___frage___

E. Translate the italicized words into English.

1. *Sie spielen* im Garten. ___They play in the garden___

2. Was *suchst du*, Hans? ___What are you looking for, Hans?___

3. *Peter und ich lernen* Deutsch. Peter and I learn German.

4. Im Winter *regnet es* oft. It rains often in winter

5. Herr Müller *grüßt* die Gäste. Mr. Muller greets the Guests.

6. *Wohnen Sie* in Berlin, Frau Schmidt? Do you live in Berlin, Mrs. Schmidt.

7. *Er meint* das nicht. He doesn't mean that.

8. *Vater und Mutter kaufen* ein neues Auto. Mom and Dad buy a new car

9. *Ihr wartet* in einem kleinen Zimmer. You wait in a small room.

10. Der Besuch meiner Eltern *freut* mich. The visit pleased my parents

F. Translate the English into German.

1. *He wishes* Ihnen viel Glück. Er wuncht Ihnen viel Gluck.

2. *She's looking for* ihren Bruder. Sie suchten für ihren Bruder.

3. *Wieviel does that cost?* Wieviel kostet das?

4. Der Hut *suits* dir gut. Der hut steht dir gut.

5. *You are doing* es sehr gut, Herr Müller. Sie machen es sehr gut, Herr Müller

6. Die Kinder *are learning to dance.*

7. Das schöne Wetter *pleases* uns.

8. *We're hearing* ein Konzert im Park. Wir horen

9. Helmut und Hertha, *you think*, es regnet heute, nicht wahr? ihr denkt

10. *They are placing* ein Glas auf den Tisch.

abe Lincoln

Three German composers who greatly influenced European music were *Johann Sebastian Bach* (left), *Ludwig van Beethoven* (center), and *Richard Wagner* (right). Bach's music is noted for its smooth interweaving of several complex melody lines. Beethoven's works are marked by deep feeling and tremendous power. Wagner created a form of "music drama" in which the music was fitted to the actions on stage.

2. PRESENT TENSE OF IRREGULAR VERBS

Many common German verbs have irregular forms in the present tense.

PRESENT TENSE OF **sein** (*to be*)

ich **bin** I am	wir **sind** we are	
du **bist** you are	ihr **seid** you are	Sie **sind** you are
er **ist** he is	sie **sind** they are	

Note

In German, the verb **sein** is never used with a present participle. In English, we say "he *is* giv*ing*," but in German this becomes **er gibt**. The forms of **sein** are used only (1) by themselves (**Er ist zu Hause.**), (2) with a noun or adjective in the predicate (**Er ist Amerikaner. Er ist hungrig.**), or (3) with the past participle of some verbs (**Er ist gekommen.**).

PRESENT TENSE OF **haben** (*to have*) AND **wissen** (*to know*)

ich **habe**	ich **weiß**
du **hast**	du **weißt**
er **hat**	er **weiß**
wir **haben**	wir **wissen**
ihr **habt**	ihr **wißt**
sie **haben**	sie **wissen**
Sie **haben**	Sie **wissen**

Most verbs that are irregular in the present tense change the stem only in the second and third person singular. Irregular verbs with an **a** in the stem change this to **ä**.

PRESENT TENSE OF **fahren** (*to ride*)

ich fahre	wir fahren	
du f*ä*hrst	ihr fahrt	Sie fahren
er f*ä*hrt	sie fahren	

Some other verbs that form the present tense in the same way as **fahren** are: **gefallen** (*to please*), **lassen** (*to let*), **tragen** (*to carry*), **laufen** (*to run*), **schlafen** (*to sleep*), and **halten** (*to hold*).

Irregular verbs with an **e** in the stem may change the **e** to **i**.

PRESENT TENSE OF **geben** (*to give*)

ich gebe	wir geben	
du g*i*bst	ihr gebt	Sie geben
er g*i*bt	sie geben	

Some other verbs that form the present tense in the same way as **geben** are: **essen** (*to eat*), **helfen** (*to help*), **sprechen** (*to speak*), and **werfen** (*to throw*).

The verbs **nehmen** (*to take*), **sehen** (*to see*), and **werden** (*to become*) follow this general rule, but they have some differences in spelling:

PRESENT TENSE OF **nehmen, sehen,** AND **werden**

ich nehme	ich sehe	ich werde
du *nimmst*	du *siehst*	du *wirst*
er *nimmt*	er *sieht*	er *wird*
wir nehmen	wir sehen	wir werden
ihr nehmt	ihr seht	ihr werdet
sie nehmen	sie sehen	sie werden
Sie nehmen	Sie sehen	Sie werden

The verb **lesen** (*to read*) forms the present tense in the same way as **sehen**.

Note

1. Not all irregular verbs with **a** or **e** in the stem change in the present tense. **Schaffen** (*to create*) and **stehen** (*to stand*), for example, do not change in the present tense. Learning the irregular forms is part of learning the verb itself.

2. Irregular verbs with **au** in the stem change to **äu**:

    laufen   er l**äu**ft

3. Irregular verbs with **ss** in the infinitive change this to **ß** before the ending **-t**:

    essen: er i*ß*t, ihr e*ß*t

    lassen: er lä*ß*t, ihr la*ß*t

Distinguish between **ist** (*is*) and **ißt** (*eats*).

SOME COMMON IRREGULAR VERBS

essen (ißt), to eat
fahren (fährt), to travel, ride
geben (gibt), to give
gefallen (gefällt), to please
haben (hat), to have
helfen (hilft), to help

lassen (läßt), to let, leave
laufen (läuft), to run
lesen (liest), to read
nehmen (nimmt), to take
sehen (sieht), to see
sein (ist), to be

sprechen (spricht), to speak
tragen (trägt), to carry, wear
werden (wird), to become
werfen (wirft), to throw
wissen (weiß), to know

ÜBUNGEN

A. Write the sentence, changing the subject and verb to the singular.

1. Die Herren fahren mit dem Zug.

Der Herr fährt mit dem Zug

2. Wir wissen nicht den Namen.

Ich weiß

3. Ihr habt neue Kleider.

Du hast

4. Was sehen die Jungen in Deutschland?

der junge sieht

5. Die Zimmer gefallen dem Gast nicht.

Das Zimmer gefällt

6. Die Mädchen tragen die neue Frühjahrsmode.

Das mädchen trägt

7. Die Polizisten essen frische Brötchen.

Der Polizist ist

8. Wir sind schon seit sechs Monaten hier.

Ich bin

9. Sprecht ihr mit den Leuten?

Sprichst du

10. Die Kinder laufen um das Haus.

Der Kind läuft

B. Write the correct form of the verb.

1. Der junge Mann (werden) Lehrer. _werde_

2. Das Wetter (gefallen) uns gar nicht. _gefällt_

3. Was ist die Antwort? Ich (wissen) nicht. _weiß_

4. Der Junge (werfen) den Ball. _wirft_

5. Das Orchester (sein) in dem Hotel. _ist_

6. Er (lassen) die Schularbeit zu Hause. _läßt_

7. Der Kellner (tragen) Brot und Butter an den Tisch. _trägt_

8. Der Herr (helfen) dem kleinen Kind. _helfen_

9. Du (essen) zuviel Kuchen. _ist_

10. Vater (nehmen) die Hand des Kindes. _nimmt_

C. Replace the subject of each sentence with the subjects in parentheses.

1. Ich spreche mit dem Mädchen.

(wir) _sprechen_ (du) _sprichst_ (Sie) _sprechen_ (ihr) _sprecht_

2. Der Junge wird Fußballspieler.

(ich) _werde_ (wir) _werden_ (sie = they) _werden_

3. Das Café gefällt ihnen nicht.

(die Handschuhe) _gefallen_ (das Buch) _gefällt_ (die Hotels) _gefallen_

4. Wir essen Äpfel gern.

(ich) _esse_ (ihr) _esst_ (du) _ißt_ (sie = she) _ißt_

5. Ich trage einen neuen Hut.

(die Frau) _trägt_ (du) _trägst_ (er) _trägt_ (Sie) _tragen_

6. Die Schüler fahren mit dem Bus.

(wir) _fahren_ (er) _fährt_ (ihr) _fahrt_ (du) _fährst_

7. Meine Großmutter ist jetzt bei uns.

(er) _ist_ (Sie) _sind_ (ihr) _seid_

8. Sie haben Glück!

(ich) _habe_ (er) _hat_ (ihr) _habt_ (du) _hast_

9. Wir nehmen den falschen Weg.

(er) _nimmt_ (sie = they) _nehmen_ (du) _nimmst_ (ihr) _nehmt_

10. Im Kino sehen wir einen neuen Film.

(ich) _sehe_ (er) _sieht_ (Sie) _sehen_ (du) _siehst_

D. Supply the pronouns to fit the verbs.

1. Siehst _du_ den Wagen?

2. _Ihr_ seid im Park.

3. _Es_ gefällt mir, Deutsch zu sprechen.

4. Wo läuft _sie_ hin?

5. _Du_ trägst einen neuen Mantel.

6. _Ihr_ sprecht sehr gutes Deutsch.

7. _Er_ wird Amerikaner.

8. Was hast _du_ in der Hand?

9. _Er_ nimmt den Stuhl aus dem Zimmer.

10. _Er_ gibt dem Jungen einen Fußball.

E. Complete the answers to the questions.

EXAMPLE: Haben Sie das Buch? Nein, Karl _hat das Buch_.

1. Wirft Hans den Ball? Ja, Hans und sein Bruder _werfen den Ball_.

2. Hast du die Kamera? Nein, ich _habe die Kamera nicht_.

3. Helfen Sie dem Mädchen? Ja, ich _helfe dem Mädchen_.

4. Wer weiß die Antwort? Fräulein Schmidt, Sie _wissen die Antwort_.

5. Lesen Gretel und Franz ein Buch? Nur Gretel _liest_.

suit

6. Wer gibt Ihnen den Anzug? Meine Eltern _geben ihnen den Anzug._

7. Wer läuft um das Haus? Die Kinder _laufen um das Haus._

8. Hast du einen Pfennig? Nein, aber er _hat einen Pfennig._

9. Gefallen Ihnen diese Farben? Diese Farbe _gefällt mir._

10. Eßt ihr das Frühstück? Ja, wir _essen das Frühstück._

F. Translate the italicized words into English.

1. *Sie fahren* in die Stadt. _They go_

2. *Er läuft* um das Haus. _he runs_

3. *Wir sind* nicht sehr hungrig. _we are_

4. *Er weiß* die Adresse des Cafés. _he knows_

5. *Sie läßt* das Buch auf dem Tisch. _she leaves_

6. Im Herbst *wird* das Wetter kühler. _becomes_

7. *Du sprichst* mit meiner Schwester. _you speak_

8. *Ißt du* die Kartoffeln? _Are you eating_

9. *Sie fährt* mit dem Bus. _She goes_

10. Im Winter *trägt er* einen Mantel. _he wears_

G. Translate the English into German.

1. *She is traveling* nach Deutschland. _Sie fährt_

2. *Are you eating* das Frühstück, Kinder? _eßt ihr_

3. Die Verkäuferin *is giving* der Dame die Platte. _gibt_

4. *We are* sehr hungrig. _wir sind_

5. *There is* schönes Wetter heute. _Es ist ..., es gibt_

6. Zum Frühstück *he's having* nur ein paar Brötchen. _hat er_

7. *She doesn't know,* wo die Bibliothek ist. _Sie weiß nicht_

8. *They have* ein neues Klavier zu Hause. _Sie haben_

9. *Father is giving* ihr eine Kamera zu Weihnachten. _Vater gibt_

10. *Do you see* den Wald, Hans? _Siehst du_

3. PRESENT TENSE OF COMPOUND VERBS

SEPARABLE PREFIXES

Many German prepositions are also used as parts of verbs, in which case they become *separable prefixes*. The basic meaning of the preposition usually determines the meaning of the prefix. The most common separable prefixes include:

PREFIX	MEANING	EXAMPLE
ab	away from	**abfahren,** to drive away, leave
an	to, up to	**ankommen,** to come to, arrive
auf	up, on	**aufstehen,** to stand up, arise
aus	out	**ausgehen,** to go out, leave
bei	at, to	**beitragen,** to carry to, contribute
ein	into	**einsteigen,** to step into, board
her	toward speaker	**herkommen,** to come here (toward speaker from somewhere else)
hin	away from speaker	**hingehen,** to go away (to some other place)
mit	with	**mitkommen,** to come with, accompany
nach	after, according to	**nachsehen,** to see according to, look up (in a book)
vor	before, ahead	**vorschlagen,** to set before (someone), suggest
zu	together	**zumachen,** to make together, close

Note

1. The prefixes just listed are called separable because they may be separated from the rest of the verb. They always appear at the end of the clause, even when the verb root does not:

   *zu*machen—Er macht das Fenster *zu.*

2. If the infinitive is used or if the verb comes at the end of the clause, the prefix is written as part of the verb:

   Er kann das Fenster *zu*machen.

   Er sagt, daß er das Fenster *zu*machte.

3. The accent of the verb usually falls on the separable prefix.

4. If the root verb is irregular, it will remain irregular when it is part of a compound:

   die Arbeit, die er heute an*fä*ngt   the work that he begins today

Some Common Separable Verbs

abfahren, to depart
abholen, to call for, pick up (a person)
ablegen, to take off (clothing)
absetzen, to set down, let out (of a car)
anfangen, to begin
ankommen, to arrive
annehmen, to accept, receive
anrufen, to call (to someone), call up (on the telephone)
anzeigen, to report, advertise, denounce
aufhalten, to hold up, detain
aufhören, to stop (doing something)

aufpassen, to be careful, look out, pay attention
ausgehen, to go out
aussehen, to look (a certain way), appear
ausziehen, to undress, move out
einkaufen, to buy, shop
einladen, to invite
einsteigen, to get aboard, get into
fertigmachen, to prepare, get ready
herkommen, to come here
hinausfahren, to go out of
hingehen, to go there

kennenlernen, to get acquainted with
mitbringen, to bring along
mitkommen, to accompany
mitnehmen, to take along
nachschlagen, to look up (in a book)
nachsehen, to check on, look up (in a book)
vorbeikommen, to pass by, stop in (for a quick visit)
vorbereiten, to prepare
vorhaben, to intend, have in mind
vorschlagen, to suggest
zumachen, to close
zuschauen, to watch, look at

Note

1. The compounds of **halten** and **laden** do not add an **e** in the second and third person singular:

   er *hält* auf   du *lädst* ein

   All prefix -zu- words take the dative

2. **Zuschauen** has its object in the dative case:

   Ich **schaue** *dem Spiel* **zu.**   I'm watching the game.

3. **Kennenlernen** is not a true separable-prefix verb, but it follows the same rules as other verbs in this list. Notice that **kennen** is always at the end of the clause:

   Ich **lerne** ihn *kennen.*   I'm getting acquainted with him.

ÜBUNGEN

A. Change each sentence by eliminating the auxiliary.

EXAMPLE: Er kann heute nicht ausgehen. *Er geht heute nicht aus.*

1. Der Junge will den Brief mitnehmen. _Der Junge nimmt mit dem Brief_

2. Wann werden Sie bei uns vorbeikommen? _Wann kommen Sie bei uns vorbei?_

3. Sie wollen in den Bus einsteigen. _Sie steigen in den Bus ein._

4. Die Dame will ihre Freundin einladen. _Die Dame lädt ihre ein._

5. Die Amerikaner werden einige Deutsche kennenlernen. _Die Amerikaner lernen einige Deutsche kennen._

traffic

6. Der alte Wagen kann den Verkehr aufhalten. _____

_____ *Der alte Wagen hält den Verkehr auf.* _____

7. Der Junge will das Mädchen um 4 Uhr abholen. *Der Junge holt das*

_____ *Mädchen um 4 Uhr ab.* _____

8. Er muß Hut und Mantel ablegen. ___ *Er legt* _____

_____

9. Der Zug wird um 7 Uhr abfahren. *Der Zug fährt um 7 Uhr ab.*

_____

10. Der Student soll das Wort im Wörterbuch nachschlagen. *Der Student schlägt*

_____ *das Wort im Wörterbuch nach.* _____

11. Wann sollen wir Sie anrufen? *Wann rufen wir Sie an?*

_____

12. Die Eltern wollen den Kindern zuschauen. *Die Eltern schauen den*

_____ *Kindern zu.* _____

thief

13. Wir sollen den Dieb anzeigen. *Wir zeigen den Dieb an*

_____

14. Wir sollen heute nachmittag anfangen. *Wir fangen heute nachmittag*

_____ *an.* _____

15. Ihr sollt gut aufpassen. *Ihr paßt gut auf*

_____

B. Write the sentence, changing the subject from the singular to the plural.

1. Er sieht sehr müde aus.

_____ *Sie sehen* _____

2. Ich komme morgen früh an.

_____ *Wir kommen* _____

3. Sie fährt aus der Stadt hinaus.

_____ *Sie fahren* _____

4. Welches Buch bringst du mit?

_____ *Welche Bücher bringen* _____

5. Er nimmt das Geschenk an.

_____ *Sie nehmen* _____

Change the subject of the sentence from the plural to the singular.

6. Ihr hört mit dem Lärm auf.

_____ *Du hörst* _____

7. Die Studenten schlagen das Wort nach.

_____ *Der Student schlägt* _____

8. Wir haben das vor.

_____ _Ich habe_ _____

9. Die Züge kommen spät an.

_____ _Der Zug_ _kommt_ _____

10. Wann fangen die Programme an?

_____ _fangt das Program_ _____

C. Write the sentence, replacing the compound verb with the correct form of each verb in parentheses.

1. Sie holt meine Schwester ab.

pick up (einladen)   _____ _lädt_ _ein_ _____

(anrufen)   _____ _ruft_ _an_ _____

(kennenlernen)   _____ _lernt_ _kennen_ _____

2. Er lädt seinen Freund ein.

(abholen)   _____ _holt_ _ab_ _____

take along (mitnehmen)   _____ _nimmt_ _mit_ _____

(anrufen)   _____ _ruft_ _an_ _____

3. Wir halten den Bauern auf.

set down / let out (absetzen)   _____ _setzen_ _ab_ _____

(einladen)   _____ _laden_ _ein_ _____

4. Sie hat ein besonderes Buch vor.

(mitnehmen)   _____ _nimmt_ _mit_ _____

(vorschlagen)   _____ _schlägt_ _vor_ _____

5. Mein Freund fährt um 8 Uhr ab.

(ankommen)   _____ _kommt_ _an_ _____

(vorbeikommen)   _____ _kommt_ _vorbei_ _____

D. Complete the answers to the questions.

EXAMPLE: Bringen Sie das Glas mit? Ja, ich _____ _bringe das Glas mit_ _____

1. Schlägt Karl einen Ausflug vor?

Ja, Karl _____ _schlägt einen Ausflug vor_ _____.

2. Sagen Sie, daß sieben Gäste mitkommen?

Ja, sieben Gäste _____ _kommen mit_ _____.

3. Schlagen Sie die Antwort in dem großen Buch nach?

Ja, ich _____ _schlage die Antwort in dem großen Buch nach_ _____

4. Was ist mit ihm los? Sieht er nicht müde aus?

Ja, und nicht nur er; wir alle _____ _sehen müde aus_ _____.

5. Nimmst du den Hund in die Schule mit?

Nein, mein Bruder _nimmt den Hund in die Schule mit._

6. Laden Sie Ihre Freunde zum Abendessen ein?

Ja, ich _lade meine Freunde zum Abendessen ein_

7. Wann kommt das Schiff an?

Heute abend um 8 Uhr _kommt das Schiff an_

8. Lernst du das blonde Mädchen kennen?

Ja, ich _lerne das blonde Mädchen kennen_

9. Wann holen Sie mich ab?

Gegen 7 Uhr _hole ab_

10. Wer macht das Fenster zu?

Die Dame _macht das Fenster zu._

E. Translate into English.

1. Ich nehme den Brief mit. _I take the letter along._

2. Er ruft mich an. _He calls me up_

3. Sie setzen ihn am Bahnhof ab. _They drop him off at the train station_

4. Sie bereitet die Aufgabe vor. _She prepares the task_

5. Hier steigen wir ein. _We get on here_

6. Du siehst sehr froh aus. _You look very happy._

7. Ich schlage eine Reise vor. _I suggest a trip_

8. Der Bus fährt nicht ab. _The bus doesn't leave_

9. Er paßt gut auf. _He is careful_

10. Wir fangen jetzt an. _We begin now._

F. Translate into German.

1. They're picking me up later this afternoon. _Sie holen mich heute Nachmittag ab_

2. How do I call you up? _Wie rufe ich dich an_

3. He looks very hungry. _Er sieht sehr hungrig aus._

4. Karl, you're leaving soon. _Karl, du fährst bald ab_

5. Mother is arriving early today. _Mutter kommt früh heute an_

6. We're advertising on the radio (**im Radio**). _Wir zeigen im Radio an_

7. The students are preparing the lesson. _Die Studenten machen die Lektion fertig_

8. She is moving out tomorrow. _Sie zieht morgen aus_

9. What do you intend, children? _Was habt ihr vor, Kinder?_

10. He is closing the door now. _Er macht jetzt die Tür zu_

INSEPARABLE PREFIXES

Several prefixes are never separated from the verb stem: **be-, emp-, ent-, er-, ge-, miß-, ver-,** and **zer-.** The prefixes **über-** and **unter-** are sometimes separable, sometimes inseparable, depending on the particular verb.

Note

1. The inseparable prefixes do not have specialized meanings in the same way as the separable prefixes, but they often change the meaning of a verb. For example, **suchen** means *to seek* but **besuchen** means *to visit*.

2. The prefix **be-** sometimes means *at, with*, as in **bearbeiten**, *to work at*.

3. The prefixes **er-** and **ent-** indicate some goal: **erreichen**, *to reach*.

4. **Ver-** and **zer-** are often used for emphasis, and **zer-** often indicates destruction. For example, **verantworten** means *to be completely answerable, responsible*; **zerbrechen**, *to break into pieces*.

5. When **über-** and **unter-** are separable, they keep their basic meanings as prepositions. When they are inseparable, they do not have their literal meanings: **übersetzen**, *to translate*; **unternehmen**, *to undertake*.

6. Irregular verbs keep the same irregularities they would have without the prefix: **unternehmen, unter*nimmt*.**

7. Verbs with inseparable prefixes are stressed on the stem, not on the prefix: **über-sétz-en, unter-néhm-en.**

Some Common Inseparable Verbs

antworten, to answer (a person)
beachten, to pay attention to, notice
bedeuten, to mean
behandeln, to deal with, handle (something)
bekommen, to get, acquire, receive
bestellen, to order
besuchen, to visit
bezahlen, to pay (for)
entleihen, to borrow

entschuldigen, to excuse
erklären, to explain
erledigen, to complete
erreichen, to reach (a place)
erwarten, to await, expect
erzählen, to tell, relate
frühstücken, to have breakfast
gebrauchen, to use
gehören, to belong to (a person)
überraschen, to surprise
übersetzen, to translate
unternehmen, to undertake

unterscheiden, to distinguish, tell apart
verbrennen, to burn (= to set on fire)
verdienen, to earn
verkaufen, to sell
vermeiden, to avoid
versuchen, to try
verwalten, to manage, supervise
wiederholen, to repeat
zerbrechen, to break (into pieces)

Note

1. The verbs **antworten** and **gehören** are followed by objects in the dative case:

| Er **antwortet** *dem* **Lehrer.** | He answers the teacher. |
| Es **gehört** *ihm.* | It belongs to him. |

2. Do not confuse **bekommen** with "to become." In German, *to become* is **werden.** The verb **bekommen** means *to get, receive*:

| Er **bekommt** die Karte. | He gets the card. |

When "get" means "become," **werden** must be used: *It is getting colder* = **Es wird kälter.** To remember this, bear in mind that **bekommen** must be used with an object, but **werden** may be used with an adjective.

ÜBUNGEN

A. Change each sentence by eliminating the auxiliary.

EXAMPLE: Was kann das bedeuten? *Was bedeutet das?*

1. Er will um 7 Uhr frühstücken. _____ *Er frühstück um 7 Uhr* _____

2. Sie sollen uns nicht überraschen. _____ *Sie überrasch uns nicht.* _____

3. Wieviel Geld soll er im Monat verdienen? _____ *Wieviel Geld verdien er im Monat?*

4. Soll ich die Frage wiederholen? _____

5. Wieviel muß sie dafür bezahlen? _____

6. Der Mann darf zwei Bücher entleihen. _____

7. Wann werden wir die Post bekommen? _____

8. Wie soll ich ihm antworten? _____

9. Er will das Problem vermeiden. _____

10. Ihr könnt das Geld gebrauchen. _____

B. Change the following sentences from the plural to the singular:

1. Wir übersetzen die Sätze. _____

2. Die Teller zerbrechen. _____

3. Wir unternehmen die Reise. _____

4. Ihr verkauft einige Bücher. _____

5. Die Studenten erzählen die Geschichte. _____

6. Nie erreichen wir rechtzeitig die Schule. _____

7. Die Herren bestellen ein gutes Essen. _____

8. Diese Schuhe gehören meinem Vater. _____

9. Ihr antwortet auf die Frage. _____

10. Wir unterscheiden die zwei Teile Deutschlands. _____

_____

C. Complete the answers to the questions.

EXAMPLE: Antwortest du dem Lehrer? Ja, ich _____ *antworte dem Lehrer* _____.

1. Erledigen sie jetzt die Arbeit?

   Nur Anna _____.

2. Ich habe kein Geld mit. Kannst du die Rechnung bezahlen?

   Ja, ich _____.

3. Wer gebraucht das Papier?

   Meine Brüder _____.

4. Übersetzen Sie dieses Wort, Herr Meyer?

Nein, Herr Schmidt _____.

5. Wer verkauft den Wagen?

Meine Eltern _____.

6. Erwartet Hans eine Karte?

Beide, Hans und Werner, _____.

7. Wieviele Leute entleihen Bücher?

Nur eine Dame _____.

8. Wiederholst du die Antwort?

Nein, Gretchen _____.

9. Gehört dem Jungen die Uhr?

Ja, sie _____.

10. Bekommst du die Karten für das Konzert?

Nein, mein Bruder _____.

D. Replace the subject of each sentence with the subjects in parentheses.

1. Wir erledigen heute abend die neue Aufgabe.

(er) _____

(ich) _____

(die Kinder) _____

2. Der Lehrer erklärt die Frage.

(ich) _____

(ihr) _____

(Anna) _____

3. Mein Vater verwaltet ein Warenhaus in der Stadt.

(meine Eltern) _____

(du) _____

(wir) _____

4. Ich zerbreche das Glas.

(ihr) _____

(er) _____

(wir) _____

5. Wir unterscheiden zwischen guten und schlechten Programmen.

(der Herr) _____

(ich) _____

(die Jungen) _____

6. Das Geschäft gehört dem Herrn.

(die Handschuhe) ---

(die Wohnung) ---

(der Hut) ---

7. Ihr verdient das Geld.

(du) ---

(die Männer) ---

(er) ---

8. Er vermeidet den Verkehr.

(wir) ---

(ich) ---

(die Eltern) ---

9. Wir besuchen die Eltern heute abend.

(du) ---

(er) ---

(sie = they) ---

10. Sie beachten die Warnungen.

(er) ---

(wir) ---

(du) ---

E. Translate the italicized words into English.

1. Mein Bruder *verwaltet* das neue Geschäft.   m

2. Was *bedeutet* dieses Wort?   means

3. *Wir versuchen* unsere Eltern *zu überraschen.*

4. Der Fußball *gehört* den drei Jungen.

5. *Unterscheiden Sie* die Klaviere?

6. *Ihr beachtet* den Plan *nicht.*   don't notice

7. *Ich übersetze* die Aufgabe ins Englische.   translate

8. Mein Freund *wiederholt* den Plan.   repeats

9. Ihre Schwester *erledigt* den Brief.   completes

10. Die Gäste *bestellen* einen billigen Nachtisch.   orders

F. Translate the English into German.

1. Die Polizisten *are having breakfast* im Café.   frühstücken

2. Hans *is trying* das Rad *to sell.*   besucht zu verkaufen

3. Wo *do we get* die Post?   bekommen wir

4. *Are you answering* dem Herrn, Werner? _____ antwortest du _____

5. Der Tisch *belongs* meiner Mutter. _____ gehört _____

6. Die Schüler *are waiting for* die Sommerferien. _____ warten auf _____

7. Wir *reach* den Park bald. _____ erreichen _____

8. Der Ball *breaks* das Fenster. _____ zerbricht _____

9. *Are you avoiding* den Regen, Herr Weber? _____ Vermeiden sie _____

10. Was *is she borrowing?* _____ entleiht sie _____

The gable roof and the timbered paneling, called *Fachwerk*, are typical features of the German *Rathaus*, or city hall.

4. REFLEXIVE VERBS

A reflexive verb is a verb that is used with a reflexive pronoun to show that the subject and the object of the verb are the same person or thing. The reflexive pronoun may be either a direct or an indirect object. For example, in English we may say:

I saw myself in the mirror. *Or:* I bought myself a new suit.
    direct   indirect
    object   object

The German reflexive pronoun is the same as the regular object pronoun for the first and second person, but the pronoun **sich** is used for all third-person reflexives and for the formal **Sie.**

GERMAN REFLEXIVE PRONOUNS

PERSONAL PRONOUN	REFLEXIVE PRONOUN	
	DATIVE	ACCUSATIVE
ich	**mir**	**mich**
du	**dir**	**dich**
er, sie, es	**sich**	**sich**
wir	**uns**	**uns**
ihr	**euch**	**euch**
sie	**sich**	**sich**
Sie	**sich**	**sich**

Note

The English reflexive pronouns *myself, yourself, themselves, etc.* are also used non-reflexively to show emphasis: "He did it *himself.*" Do not confuse these two uses. The emphatic form in German is **selbst:**

Ich kaufte **mir** einen Hut.   I bought myself a hat.

    But:

Ich kaufte *selbst* den Hut.   I bought the hat myself.

Although almost any verb can sometimes be used reflexively, some German verbs are always reflexive—even though the English equivalent may not have a reflexive pronoun.

SOME COMMON REFLEXIVE VERBS

sich anhören, to listen to
sich ansehen, to look at, watch
sich anziehen, to dress (oneself)
sich aufhalten, to delay, sustain
sich ausziehen, to undress, take off (clothing)
sich beeilen, to hurry
sich erinnern (an), to remember

sich freuen (an, auf, über), to be happy about, look forward to
sich fühlen, to feel (a certain way)
sich interessieren (für), to be interested (in)
sich kämmen, to comb
sich melden, to announce oneself

sich merken, to bear in mind, remember
sich rasieren, to shave (oneself)
sich setzen, to sit down
sich überlegen, to think over
sich unterhalten, to converse
sich verlassen (auf), to depend (on)
sich vorstellen, to imagine

Note

1. Many of these verbs are also used without the reflexive pronoun: **erinnern,** *to remind.* (Hence, **sich erinnern** means "to remind oneself," *to remember.*) Other verbs that may be used with or without a reflexive pronoun could have been included in this list:

Ich **wasche** dem Kind die Hände.	I wash the child's hands.
Ich **wasche** *mir* die Hände.	"I wash for myself the hands" = I'm washing my hands.

2. If the reflexive verb has no other object, the reflexive pronoun will always be the direct object:

Ich ziehe **mich** an.   I'm getting dressed.

If the reflexive verb has some other noun or pronoun for the direct object, the reflexive pronoun becomes the indirect object:

Ich ziehe **mir** den Mantel an.   I'm putting on my coat.

ÜBUNGEN

A. Supply the reflexive pronoun.

1. Ich muß _____ beeilen.

2. Interessiert er _____ dafür?

3. Kinder, setzt _____!

4. Das werden wir _____ überlegen.

5. Wie fühlst du _____ heute?

6. Vater rasiert _____ jeden Morgen.

7. Sie haben _____ daran erinnert.

8. Die Studenten im Zimmer unterhalten _____ leise.

9. Ich will _____ diese Platte anhören.

10. Immer hat _____ Werner mit lauter Stimme gemeldet.

11. Das Mädchen steht vor dem Spiegel und kämmt _____ das Haar.

12. Wir ziehen _____ jeden Morgen vor dem Frühstück an.

13. Solche Dinge sollen Sie _____ merken.

14. Das kann ich _____ vorstellen.

15. Ich freue _____ sehr darüber.

B. Replace the subject of each sentence with the subjects in parentheses.

1. Wir unterhalten uns auf Deutsch.

(die Jungen) _____

(meine Eltern) _____

(ihr) _____

2. Mein Bruder zieht sich schnell aus.

(du) _____

(die Kinder) _____

(ich) _____

3. Die Studenten interessieren sich für neue Bücher.

(wir) _____

(du) _____

(Herr Weber) _____

4. Ich stelle mir ein schönes Lied vor.

(meine Schwester) _____

(Sie) _____

(ihr) _____

5. Sie freuen sich darauf.

(meine Eltern) _____

(du) _____

(wir) _____

6. Wir sehen uns den neuen Film an.

(ich) _____

(die Dame) _____

(ihr) _____

7. Er beeilt sich mit der Arbeit.

(die Leute) _____

(ich) _____

(wir) _____

8. Sie zieht sich ein Kleid an.

(das Mädchen) _____

(ich) _____

(Sie) _____

9. Ich überlege mir die Antwort.

(er) _____

(wir) _____

(ihr) _____

10. Heute fühlt er sich wohl.

(ich) _____

(wir) _____

(du) _____

C. Change each sentence by using a reflexive pronoun.

EXAMPLES: Ich kaufe einen Anzug.   Ich kaufe *mir* einen Anzug.

Ich kämme *dem Kind* das Haar.   Ich kämme *mir* das Haar.

1. Er macht sein Auto fertig.

----

2. Wir hören die Musik an.

----

3. Die Mutter wäscht *dem Kind* das Gesicht.

----

4. Ich setze *den Jungen* aufs Pferd.

----

5. Du machst das Frühstück.

----

6. Sie bereitet *den Studenten* auf dei Prüfung vor.

----

7. Ich bestelle eine Karte für das Konzert.

----

8. Die Männer kaufen viele Bücher.

----

9. Er rasiert *den Herrn.*

----

10. Der Herr erinnert *die Dame* an das Konzert.

D. Complete the answers to the questions.

1. Was hören Sie sich an?

Das Programm ---------------------------------.

2. Freust du dich auf die Reise?

Ja, ---.

3. Überlegen sich die Kinder die Antwort?

Nur Hans ---------------------------------------.

4. Wie fühlt sich Ihre Mutter heute?

Sie --.

5. Kann er sich an das Wort erinnern?

Nein, er ---.

6. Unterhält er sich mit seinem Bruder?

Ja, er ---.

7. Hast du dir ihren Namen gemerkt?

Leider nicht, aber Günther _____.

8. Sollen wir uns an den Tisch oder auf die Bank setzen?

Kinder, _____.

9. Interessiert sich Herr Müller für den Sport?

Ja, er _____.

10. Wie oft melden sich die Schüler?

Zweimal in einer Stunde _____.

E. Translate into English.

1. Wir fühlen uns müde. _____

2. Ich ziehe mich an. _____

3. Er wäscht sich die Hände. _____

4. Der Bauer rasiert sich früh am Morgen. _____
_____

5. Interessieren Sie sich für Fußball? _____

6. Du sollst dir die Adresse merken. _____

7. Ich werde mir die Sache überlegen. _____

8. Die Gäste wollen sich das Konzert anhören. _____

9. Die Dame freut sich über das Geschenk. _____

10. Das kann ich mir vorstellen. _____

F. Translate into German.

1. The boy sits down on the chair. _____
_____

2. We do not converse in German. _____
_____

3. The gentleman imagines a beautiful garden. _____
_____

4. The children are getting dressed. _____

5. I'm combing my hair. _____

6. The pupils say their names (= announce themselves). _____

7. The people are rushing. _____

8. Gretchen is taking off her coat. _____

9. We're keeping the time in mind. _____

10. They are looking at the pictures. _____

5. MODAL AUXILIARIES

A *modal auxiliary verb* is used with the infinitive of the main verb to indicate obligation, necessity, ability, or preference. German has six modal auxiliaries.

> **dürfen, durfte, gedurft,** may, to be permitted
> **können, konnte, gekonnt,** can, to be able
> **mögen, mochte, gemocht,** to like
> **müssen, mußte, gemußt,** must, to have to
> **sollen, sollte, gesollt,** should, ought, supposed to
> **wollen, wollte, gewollt,** to want to, to will

Note

1. In the simple past, the modals have the regular past-tense endings.
2. The present perfect tense of the modals is conjugated with **haben** as the auxiliary:

Ich habe es gekonnt.   I was able to do it.

However, since the modals seldom occur in this construction, the past participle of the modal is rarely used.

The modal auxiliaries are irregular in the present tense.

MODAL VERBS: PRESENT TENSE					
dürfen	**können**	**mögen**	**müssen**	**sollen**	**wollen**
ich **darf**	**kann**	**mag**	**muß**	**soll**	**will**
du **darfst**	**kannst**	**magst**	**mußt**	**sollst**	**willst**
er **darf**	**kann**	**mag**	**muß**	**soll**	**will**
wir **dürfen**	**können**	**mögen**	**müssen**	**sollen**	**wollen**
ihr **dürft**	**könnt**	**mögt**	**müßt**	**sollt**	**wollt**
sie **dürfen**	**können**	**mögen**	**müssen**	**sollen**	**wollen**
Sie **dürfen**	**können**	**mögen**	**müssen**	**sollen**	**wollen**

Note

Like most irregular verbs in German, only the singular forms of the modal verbs are irregular; the plurals are regular.

USES OF THE MODAL VERBS

A. **Können,** *to be able,* can also mean *to know how to do something:*

Er kann Deutsch.   He knows (how to speak) German.

(Otherwise, *to know* is expressed by **kennen** or **wissen.** See Lesson 8, page 46.)

B. A German clause never has more than one finite verb. Whenever a modal is used with another verb, the other verb will be an infinitive at the end of the clause:

Ich **kann** ihn *hören.*   I can hear him.

C. When the meaning is clear, the modals are sometimes used without an infinitive:

Das kann ich nicht.   I can't [do] that.

Ich muß in die Stadt.   I must [go] to the city.

D. In English, *must* is also expressed by *have to* and *have got to*. Note how the present and past tenses of these English modal auxiliaries are expressed in German:

I must stay here. ⎫
I have to stay here. ⎬   Ich **muß** hier bleiben.
I've got to stay here. ⎭

I had to stay here.   Ich **mußte** hier bleiben.

E. The present tense of **mögen** is used in the sense of *to like:*

Das **mag** sie nicht.   She doesn't like that.

Most often the subjunctive form, meaning *would like,* is used.

SUBJUNCTIVE OF **mögen**

ich **möchte**	wir **möchten**	
du **möchtest**	ihr **möchtet**	Sie **möchten**
er **möchte**	sie **möchten**	

Note

1. **Wollen** means *to want* in a more demanding tone than **möchte:**

    Ich **will** ein neues Kleid kaufen.   I want to buy a new dress!

    Ich **möchte** ein neues Kleid kaufen.   I'd like to buy a new dress.

2. To show politeness, **möchte** is always used:

    Ich **möchte** eine Tasse Kaffee, bitte.   I'd like a cup of coffee, please.

3. **Gern** with a verb means *I enjoy:*

    Ich **trinke** Kaffee **gern.**   I like to drink coffee.

    Möchte means *I'd like to get:*

    Ich **möchte** Kaffee.   I'd like some coffee.

ÜBUNGEN

A. Write the correct form of the present tense of the modal auxiliary.

1. (müssen)   Ich _____ mich beeilen.

2. (sollen)   Du _____ früh aufstehen.

3. (dürfen)   _____ wir das Auto hier parken?

4. (sollen)   Ihr _____ die Arbeit fertigmachen.

5. (wollen)   Was _____ Hans damit machen?

6. (können)   Du _____ die Schule sehen.

7. (mögen)   Er _____ ihn nicht.

8. (wollen)   Ich _____ mir einen neuen Anzug kaufen.

9. (müssen)   Ihr _____ die Aufgabe lernen.

10. (dürfen)   Die Gäste _____ hier sitzen.

B. Change the tense of the modal auxiliary to the simple past tense.

1. Er kann dem Jungen helfen.   _____

2. Wir müssen uns das gut anhören.   _____

3. Sie soll ihre Mutter anrufen.   _____

4. Du darfst nicht einsteigen.   _____

5. Ihr wollt eine Reise machen.   _____

6. Können Sie den Herrn verstehen?   _____

7. Darf ich das Buch mitnehmen?   _____

8. Hans will eine Frage stellen.   _____

9. Wir können Deutsch.   _____

10. Du mußt dir einen Mantel anziehen.   _____

C. Replace the subject of each sentence with the pronouns in parentheses.

1. Wir wollen ins Konzert gehen.

(du) _____   (er) _____   (Sie) _____

2. Ich möchte ein großes Glas Wasser.

(sie = she) _____   (wir) _____   (du) _____

3. Sie kann mit dem Auto fahren.

(ihr) _____   (sie = they) _____   (ich) _____

4. Du darfst drei Bücher entleihen.

(wir) _____   (Sie) _____   (ich) _____

5. Wo soll er suchen?

(ich) _____   (ihr) _____   (du) _____

6. Womit müssen wir anfangen?

(er) _____   (sie = they) _____   (ich) _____

7. Ich will nach Berlin fahren.

(du) _____   (Sie) _____   (ihr) _____

8. Wir dürfen nicht hier bleiben.

(er) _____   (ihr) _____   (ich) _____

9. Sie möchten frische Brötchen kaufen.

(ich) _____   (wir) _____   (er) _____

10. Ich muß in die Stadt.

(wir) _____   (ihr) _____   (du) _____

D. Replace the modal auxiliary with the correct form of each modal in parentheses, keeping the same tense as in the original.

1. Ich kann diesen Mantel tragen.   (dürfen, wollen, sollen)

_____

2. Wir möchten Herrn Schneider sprechen.   (sollen, dürfen, können)

_____

3. Du darfst in diesem Restaurant essen.   (möchten, wollen, sollen)

_____

4. Ihr müßt nach Hause.   (sollen, wollen, können)

_____

5. Er soll das Buch lesen.   (können, mögen, wollen)

_____

6. Sie mußten in die Bibliothek gehen.   (wollen, können, sollen)

_____

7. Wen wollte er besuchen?   (dürfen, müssen, sollen)

_____

8. Womit konnten die Kinder spielen?   (wollen, dürfen, müssen)

_____

9. Ich sollte die Sprache lernen.   (müssen, können, wollen)

_____

10. Du mußtest mit der Straßenbahn fahren.   (sollen, können, dürfen)

_____

E. Complete the answers to the questions.

1. Wir sind Studenten. Dürfen wir in der Bibliothek arbeiten?

Ja, alle Studenten _____.

2. Sie wollen ein paar Briefe schreiben, nicht wahr?

Ja, ich _____.

3. Möchtest du Tee oder Kaffee?

Ich _____.

4. Können Sie um 7 Uhr kommen?

Ja, wir _____.

5. Darf ich die Bilder sehen?

Ja, Sie _____ .

F. Translate into English.

1. Er möchte Sie kennenlernen. _____

2. Wir dürfen nicht in den Park gehen. _____

_____

3. Ihr sollt nicht soviel Lärm machen. _____

_____

4. Ich mußte ein Heft kaufen. _____

5. Dürfen wir ins Kino gehen? _____

6. Wollten Sie eine Reise machen? _____

7. Ich kann dem Herrn helfen. _____

8. Sie mußte in die Stadt. _____

9. Können Sie Deutsch? _____

10. Ich möchte Fräulein Schmidt sprechen. _____

_____

G. Translate into German.

1. We want to go to the concert. _____

2. We had to leave this morning. _____

3. She should read this book. _____

4. Can't you see me, Fritz? _____

5. I was supposed to call my brother. _____

6. She'd like a cup of tea. _____

7. May we visit the cathedral? _____

8. How's one supposed to do that? _____

9. What did they want? _____

10. I must go into the city. _____

6. INTERROGATIVES; IMPERATIVES

In German, questions and commands are formed by placing the verb first in the statement:

Wiederholen Sie den Satz?	Are you repeating the sentence?
Wiederholen Sie den Satz!	Repeat the sentence!

In speaking, the voice rises at the end of the question and falls at the end of the command.

INTERROGATIVES

Questions can also be formed by using special interrogative words.

INTERROGATIVE WORDS

wann? when?	**wie lange?** how long?
warum? why?	**wieviel?** how much?
was? what?	**wieviele?** how many?
was für ein? what sort of?	**wo?** where?
welcher? which?	**woher?** from where?
wer? who?	**wohin?** to where?
wie? how?	

IDIOMS

nicht wahr? isn't it true?
Wie geht's? How are you?
Wie heißen Sie? What's your name?

Note

1. In questions formed with reflexive verbs, the reflexive pronoun precedes the subject if the subject is a noun, and follows the subject if it is a pronoun:

Interessieren *sich* die **Leute** dafür?	Are the people interested in it?
Interessiert **er** *sich* dafür?	Is he interested in it?

2. The pronouns **wer** and **was** are declined (see Lesson 14, page 99).

3. The interrogative adjective **welcher** has the same endings as **dieser** (see Lesson 17, page 127).

4. **Wann** is used only to ask a question:

Wann kommt der Zug?	When does the train come?

Wenn is used for *whenever*:

Ich werde ihn fragen, **wenn** er kommt.	I'll ask him when(ever) he comes.

5. **Wo** indicates that a thing is located in a specific place:

> **Wo** ist das Buch?   Where is the book?

Woher must be used to indicate movement *toward* the speaker:

> **Woher** kommen Sie? ⎱
> **Wo** kommen Sie **her?** ⎰   Where do you come from?

Wohin must be used to indicate movement *away from* the speaker:

> **Wohin** gehen Sie? ⎱
> **Wo** gehen Sie **hin?** ⎰   Where are you going (to)?

6. In the expression **was für ein,** the **für** does not govern the accusative case of **ein.** The article **ein** has whatever case is required by the rest of the sentence:

> Ich weiß, **was für** *einen*   I know what kind of car he has.
>   Wagen er hat.

> **Was für** *einer* Dame haben   To what sort of lady did you
>   Sie das Buch gegeben?   give the book?

In the plural, **ein** is omitted:

> **Was für Karten** suchen Sie?   What kind(s) of cards are you
>   looking for?

7. The expression **nicht wahr?** can be added to any statement to make a negative question. The speaker expects a "yes" answer:

> Das Wetter ist schön, **nicht wahr?**   The weather is beautiful, isn't it?

8. To form questions in English, some form of *be* or *do* is placed before the subject: "*Are* they coming?"; "*Does* he have …?" Since such auxiliaries are not used in German, a question is formed by placing the main verb first: *Kommen* **sie?** *Hat* **er …?**

ÜBUNGEN

A. Change the following statements to questions:

1. Der Bus fährt sehr langsam. _____

2. Er will das Rathaus sehen. _____

3. Die Dame sieht den Garten. _____

4. Wir machen eine Reise nach Deutschland. _____
   _____

5. Sie spricht gut Deutsch. _____

6. Die Kinder waschen sich die Hände. _____
   _____

7. Du hast das Radio mitgebracht. _____

8. Sie werden ins Kino gehen. _____

9. Er muß sich beeilen. _____

10. Wir hören uns das Programm an. _____

Change the following sentences to questions by adding **nicht wahr?** Then translate the new sentences into English.

11. Wir stehen früh auf. _____

_____

12. Mutter ruft dich. _____

_____

13. Es ist ein kalter Tag. _____

_____

14. Frau Schmidt trägt einen neuen Hut. _____

_____

15. Du hast genug Geld. _____

_____

B. Complete each question with the German equivalent of the word in parentheses.

1. (Which) _____ Buch haben Sie gelesen?

2. (How) _____ macht man das?

3. (When) Wissen Sie, _____ der Zug kommt?

4. (From where) _____ kommt der Brief?

5. (What sort of) _____ Kamera kauft Herr Braun?

6. (Which) Mit _____ Schiff wollen Sie fahren?

7. (Where) _____ fahren Sie morgen?

8. (What) _____ sagt er?

9. (How) _____ geht es Ihnen?

10. (Where) _____ haben Sie das gefunden?

11. (When) _____ hat das Orchester gespielt?

12. (Who) _____ spricht jetzt?

13. (What sort of) _____ Bücher lesen Sie gern?

14. (Which) _____ Haus gehört Ihnen?

15. (How) _____ kommt man zum Hotel?

C. Construct a question that could be answered by the sentence.

EXAMPLES: Ich kenne ihn nicht.   *Kennen Sie ihn?*

Ich habe Sie gerufen.   *Wer hat mich gerufen?*

1. Ja, heute ist das Wetter sehr schön. _____

2. Er fährt einen Volkswagen. _____

3. Wir kommen um 7 Uhr in Berlin an. _____

4. Frau Schmidt geht in die Stadt. _____

5. Er sagte, daß er nicht kommen kann. _____

6. Die Karten kosten 30 DM. --

7. Den Kölner Dom haben wir besucht. --

8. Ich komme aus Amerika. --

9. Sie heißt Luise Müller. --

10. Wir sind schon seit sechs Wochen hier. --

IMPERATIVES

The *formal* imperative (command or request) is formed by placing the verb first, followed by the pronoun **Sie.** The *singular informal* imperative (corresponding to **du**) is formed by adding **-e** to the stem of the verb. The *plural informal* imperative (corresponding to **ihr**) is the same as the second person plural form of the verb. The English equivalent is the same for all three German forms:

Bleibe hier, Hans!   ⎫
Bleibt hier, Kinder!   ⎬   Stay here!
Bleiben Sie hier, Herr Schmidt! ⎭

Note

1. Unlike English, the formal imperative *always* uses the pronoun.

2. English imperatives beginning with "Let's" are expressed in German by putting the verb first, followed by **wir:**

    Gehen wir nach Hause!   Let's go home!

Note that **lassen** is not used in this construction in German.

3. A general command that is not addressed to a specific person may use the infinitive:

    Einsteigen!   All aboard!

    Nicht zumachen!   Do not close!

4. Every imperative in German is followed by an exclamation point (!), even though it may not be emphatic:

    Setzen Sie sich, bitte!   Please have a seat.

    Bitte, **bedienen Sie sich!**   Please help yourself.

5. Commonly used verbs usually drop the **-e** in the informal singular imperative. A few such verbs are **erzählen, hören, kommen, machen, sagen,** and **stehen:**

    Sag' mir etwas!   Tell me something.

    Komm mit!   Come with me (us).

    Steh auf!   Get up!

(The use of the apostrophe when the **-e** is dropped is optional.)

Many other verbs may also occasionally drop the **-e** in the informal singular.

6. Irregular verbs that change the **e** of the stem to **i** or **ie** in the singular use the irregular stem for the informal singular imperative and never add **-e:**

    Sieh den Wagen da **an!**   Look at that car!

    Nimm dein Heft **mit!**   Take your notebook with you!

7. Irregular verbs that have **ä** in the singular do *not* have **ä** in the singular imperative:

Schlaf wohl!   Sleep well!

Schlag es **nach**!   Look it up!

ÜBUNGEN

D. Change to the imperative.

1. Sie bringen Ihren Bruder mit. --

2. Du nimmst die Karte mit. --

3. Sie wiederholen die Frage. --

4. Ihr holt die Zeitung. --

5. Du vergißt mich nicht. --

6. Sie setzen sich an den Tisch. --

7. Ihr sagt uns nichts. --

8. Du läufst durch das Haus. --

9. Sie antworten nicht auf die Frage. --

10. Du bleibst nicht zu Hause. --

11. Ihr helft dem Jungen. --

12. Sie grüßen die Dame. --

13. Du gibst ihm die Hand. --

14. Ihr zeigt uns das Hotel. --

15. Wir unterhalten uns auf Deutsch. --

E. Change the following questions to imperatives:

1. Seht ihr das Haus an? --

2. Übersetzt du ins Deutsche? --

3. Machen Sie das Fenster zu? --

4. Verläßt du dich darauf? --

5. Kommen Sie mit? --

Change the following imperatives to questions:

6. Warten Sie auf mich! --

7. Lerne die neuen Wörter! --

8. Trinkt die Milch! --

9. Ziehen Sie sich den Mantel an! --

10. Paß auf! --

F. Write each sentence, replacing the verb with the correct forms of the verbs in parentheses.

1. Kauft er eine Platte?

(haben) --

(zerbrechen) --

(spielen) --

2. Rufe den Herrn!

(holen) --

(mitnehmen) --

(fragen) --

3. Laden Sie die Dame ein?

(kennenlernen) --

(besuchen) --

(sich erinnern an) --

4. Sagen Sie mir etwas!

(erzählen) --

(zeigen) --

(schenken) --

5. Vergiß das nicht!

(wiederholen) --

(sich überlegen) --

(versprechen) --

6. Er kann den Satz übersetzen, nicht wahr?

(schreiben) --

(lesen) --

(verstehen) --

7. Setze dich!

(sich melden) --

(mitkommen) --

(sich unterhalten) --

8. Singen sie ein Lied?

(sich vorstellen) --

(nennen) --

(hören) --

9. Kommt der Großvater heute?

(abfahren) _____

(arbeiten) _____

(tanzen) _____

10. Nicht herumstehen!

(anfangen) _____

(einsteigen) _____

G. Translate into English.

1. Kaufen Sie eine Krawatte? _____

2. Lade deinen Freund ein! _____

3. Beginnt der Unterricht um 11 Uhr? _____

4. Wo kommen die Leute her? _____

_____

5. Kämmt euch das Haar! _____

6. Was für Musik spielt das Orchester? _____

_____

7. Wieviel kostet das Hotelzimmer? _____

8. Kommen Sie nicht zu spät! _____

9. Welches Lied singen sie? _____

10. Anna, sprich lauter, bitte! _____

11. Wissen Sie die Antwort? _____

12. Warum interessiert er sich dafür? _____

13. Wann fährt sie ab? _____

14. Sie haben meine Schwester kennengelernt, nicht wahr? _____

_____

15. Vergiß seinen Geburtstag nicht! _____

H. Translate into German.

1. What kind of tree is that? _____

2. Children, wash your face! _____

3. Is Grandmother coming today? _____

4. What's your name? _____

5. They're calling you, aren't they? _____

6. Where is the mail from? _____

7. Which hospital is she looking for? _____

8. Don't forget your gloves, Mrs. Müller. _____

_____

9. Look at the picture, Hans! _____

10. When do you study? _____

11. How many people live in Hamburg? _____

_____

12. Are they conversing in German? _____

13. Let's look it up. _____

14. Why is he opening the door? _____

15. What color is this ink? _____

The postage stamp on the left, issued by the Hitler regime in 1936, commemorates the German reoccupation of the Saarland. Note the Nazi swastika. The other two stamps were issued by the Federal Republic in recent years. The postage stamp in the center celebrates the Christmas season. The stamp on the right honors Pope John XXIII, who was widely acclaimed for his liberal views on social questions and his humane influence in world affairs.

7. SIMPLE PAST AND PRESENT PERFECT OF REGULAR VERBS

THE SIMPLE PAST

Regular verbs (also called *weak verbs*) form the simple past tense by adding **-t-** to the stem and using a special set of endings.

SIMPLE PAST OF **fragen**

ich		e
du		est
er		e
wir	**fragt-**	en
ihr		et
sie		en
Sie		en

Note

1. The simple past can be used much as it is used in English: **ich fragte,** *I asked.*

   However, it is used mostly in writing and in sentences with several verbs close together. In conversation, the Germans prefer to use the present perfect tense.

2. Verbs with stems ending in **-d, -t,** or two or more separately pronounced consonants (**reg/nen**) add an extra **-e-** before the **-t-** in the simple past:

   ich antwortete   es regnete

3. Note that the simple past can be translated by several English past-tense forms:

er fragte { he asked / he used to ask / he was asking }   **er fragte nicht** { he did not ask / he was not asking }

THE PRESENT PERFECT

The present perfect tense in German is formed by the present tense of the auxiliary verb and the past participle.

PRESENT PERFECT OF **fragen**

ich **habe**	
du **hast**	
er **hat**	
wir **haben**	**gefragt**
ihr **habt**	
sie **haben**	
Sie **haben**	

The present perfect of most regular German verbs uses **haben** as the auxiliary verb. All regular verbs form the past participle by adding the prefix **ge-** and the ending **-t** to the verb stem:

fragen—**ge**frag**t**   **such**en—**ge**such**t**

(The past participle can also be formed by adding **ge-** before the third person singular, present tense: **fragt**—**gefragt.**)

Note

1. The **ge-** is *not* added if:

   a. the verb has an inseparable prefix:

   versuchen—*versucht*   **erwarten**—*erwartet*

   b. the verb is of Latin origin (especially with the ending **-ieren**):

   interessieren—*interessiert*   **probieren**—*probiert*

2. If the verb has a separable prefix, the **ge-** is inserted between the prefix and the stem:

   ablegen—ab**ge**legt   **zu**machen—zu**ge**macht

3. The German present perfect tense can be translated by several forms of the past tense in English:

ich habe gefragt $\begin{cases} \text{I asked} \\ \text{I was asking} \\ \text{I have asked} \end{cases}$ **ich habe nicht gefragt** $\begin{cases} \text{I didn't ask} \\ \text{I wasn't asking} \\ \text{I haven't asked} \end{cases}$

SOME VERBS THAT ARE REGULAR IN THE PRESENT PERFECT

bauen, to build	**hoffen,** to hope	**öffnen,** to open
danken, to thank	**holen,** to get, fetch	**schenken,** to give a present
dauern, to last, endure	**kochen,** to cook (especially, to boil)	**schicken,** to send
fehlen, to lack, be missing		**studieren,** to study (at a university or a school subject)
sein **folgen,** to follow	**leben,** to live	
fühlen, to feel	**legen,** to lay, set	**zeigen,** to point out, to show
hassen, to hate	**lieben,** to love	

Note

1. The object of **danken, fehlen,** and **folgen** is in the dative case:

   Danken Sie *der* Dame!   Thank the lady.

   Ein Buch **fehlt** *dem* Studenten.   The student needs a book. ("A book is lacking to the student.")

   Ich **folge** *dem* Mann.   I'm following the man.

2. **Folgen** is used with **haben** to mean *to obey* and with **sein** to mean *to follow*:

   Ich **habe** ihm gefolgt.   I obeyed him.

   Ich **bin** ihm gefolgt.   I followed him.

ÜBUNGEN

A. Add the simple past-tense ending to the verb stem.

1. Wer fehl*te* _____ heute? *Who wasnt here today*

2. Mutter koch*te* _____ heute morgen eine Suppe.

3. Zeig*te* _____ er Ihnen das Hotel?

4. Wie öffn*ete* ____ man das?

5. Wir bau*ten* ____ ein neues Haus.

6. In welchem Jahrhundert leb*te* _____ Friedrich der Große? *King of Prussia Alte Fritz*

7. Wir dank*ten* ____ den Kindern dafür.

8. Der Student erledig*te* _____ die Aufgabe.

9. Vater arbeit*ete* ____ gestern im Büro. *office*

10. Die jungen Leute tanz*ten* ____ gern.

B. Write the correct form of the present perfect tense of the verb in parentheses.

EXAMPLE: (machen) Was ___*hat*___ er gestern ___*gemacht*___?

1. (zeigen) Welches Buch ___*hat*___ er Ihnen ___*gezeigt*___?

2. (holen) Hans ___*hat*___ die Zeitung ___*geholt*___.

3. (aufhören) *Stop* Wann ___*hat*___ der Lärm endlich ___*aufgehört*___?

4. (fragen) ___*Hast*___ du Vater ___*gefragt*___?

5. (kosten) Wieviel ___*haben*___ die Handschuhe ___*gekostet*___?

6. (hoffen) Wir _____, Sie zu besuchen.

7. (öffnen) Der Kellner ___*hatten*___ das Restaurant genau um 9 Uhr ___*geöffnet*___.

8. (erklären) Wie ___*haben*___ die Eltern das Problem ___*erklärt*___?

9. (folgen) Du _____ dem Zug _____.

10. (schenken) Er _____ mir einen Pfennig _____.

C. Change the tense of the verb to the simple past.

1. Er schickt seinem Bruder ein Geburtstagsgeschenk. ____*schickte*____

2. Du machst das Fenster zu. ____*machtest*____

3. Ich lerne fleißig Deutsch. ____*lernte*____

4. Wir lieben unsere Freunde. ____*liebten*____

5. Ihr spielt auf dem Spielplatz. ____*spielt*____

6. Er öffnet das Paket. ____*öffnete*____

7. Sie holen drei Bücher. ____*holten*____

8. Du legst den Apfel auf den Tisch. ____*legtest*____

9. Diese Antwort bedeutet nichts. ____*bedeutete*____

10. Sie schenkt ihrem Bruder eine Kamera. ____*schenkte*____

11. Man baut eine neue Schule in dieser Stadt. ____*baute*____

12. Wir fühlen den kalten Wind. ----- *fühlten* -----------

13. Sie haßt solchen großen Lärm. ----------------------

14. Ich wünsche mir ein neues Fahrrad zum Geburtstag. ----- *wünsche* -----

15. Der Familie fehlt ein gutes Auto. ----- *fehlte* -----

D. In exercise *C*, write each sentence, changing the verb to the present perfect tense.

1. ----- *hat , geschickt* -----
2. ----- *hast , zugemacht* -----
3. ----- *habe , gelernt* -----
4. ----- *haben , geliebt* -----
5. ----- *habt , gespielt* -----
6. ----- *hat , geöffnet* -----
7. ----- *haben , geholt* -----
8. ----- *hast gelegt* -----
9. ----- *hat , bedeutet* -----
10. ----- *hat , geschehlt* -----
11. ----- *hat , gebaut* -----
12. ----- *haben , gefühlt* -----
13. ----- *hat , ~~gehabt~~ gehaßt* -----
14. ----- *habe , ~~ge~~ gewünscht* -----
15. ----- *hat , gefehlt* -----

E. Write each sentence, changing the verb from the simple past to the present perfect tense.

1. Ich dankte dem Herrn dafür.
----- *habe , gedankt* -----

2. Die Kinder spielten auf dem Hof.
----- *haben , gespielt* -----

3. Wir besuchten einige Städte in Deutschland.
----- *haben , besucht* -----

4. Ihr machtet schöne Kleider.
----- *habt , gemachte* -----

5. Du stelltest eine Frage. *ask a question*
----- *hast , gestellte* -----

6. Der neue Anzug paßte dir gut.
----- *hat , gepaßt* -----

7. Gestern besuchte ich meinen Onkel.
----- *habe , besucht* -----

8. Herr und Frau Weber kauften ein neues Auto.
----- *haben , gekauft* -----

9. Er sagte nichts.

_____ *hat, gesagt* _____

10. Meine Eltern wohnten einmal in diesem Haus.

_____ *haben, gewohnt* _____

F. Replace the verb in each sentence with the verbs in parentheses, using the same tense. (If the present perfect is used, write the entire sentence.)

1. Im September bestellte er das Buch.   (kaufen, schenken, suchen)

_____ *kaufte, schenkte, suchte* _____

2. Einige Leute arbeiteten in diesem Zimmer.   (spielen, tanzen, leben)

_____ *spielten, tanzten, lebten* _____

3. Wir besuchten den Herrn.   (holen, fragen, hassen)

_____ *holten, fragten, hassten* _____

4. Ich erklärte die Geschichte.   (hören, erzählen, lernen)

_____ *hörte, erzählte, lernte* _____

5. Der Junge dankte uns nicht.   (folgen, glauben, grüßen)

_____ *folgte, glaubte, grüßte* _____

6. Du hast das Restaurant gesucht.   (öffnen, bauen, kaufen)

_____ *hast geöffnet, gebaut, gekauft* _____

7. Wir haben dem Lehrer geantwortet.   (danken, folgen, zuschauen)

_____ *haben gedankt, or sind gefolgt, zugeschaut* _____

8. Ich habe die neuen Wörter gelernt.   (beachten, wiederholen, erklären)

_____ *habe beachtet, wiederholt erklärt* _____

9. Sie hat den Kuchen gekauft.   (probieren, holen, zeigen)

_____ *hat probiert, geholt, gezeigt* _____

10. Haben Sie die Aufgabe gemacht?   *übersetzt*   (übersetzen, vorbereiten, hören)

_____ *übersetzt, vorbereitet, gehört* _____

G. Replace the subject of each sentence with the subjects in parentheses.

1. Wir besuchten viele Städte in Deutschland.   (ich, er, ihr)

*ich besuchte, er besuchtest, ihr besucht*

2. Vater bezahlte das Fenster.   (wir, ich, du)

*wir bezahlten, ich bezahlte, du bezahltest*

3. Ich legte Hut und Mantel ab.   (wir, der Herr, die Gäste)

*wir legten, der Herr legte, die Gäste legten*

4. Sie frühstückten um 8 Uhr.   (ich, wir, meine Schwester)

*ich frühstückte, wir frühstückten, frühstückte*

5. Die Studenten machten die Tür zu.   (ihr, er, du)

*ihr machtet, er macht, du machtest*

6. Wir haben ihm unser Haus gezeigt. (Vater, ich, du)

Vater hat gezeigt, habe, du

7. Die Kinder haben nicht mit dem Lärm aufgehört. (mein Bruder, wir, du)

8. Ein Paar Handschuhe hat 10 Mark gekostet. (die Handschuhe, das Kleid, drei Bücher)

9. Wir haben zwei Plätze im Theater bestellt. (ich, die Gäste, er)

10. Was hast du denn erwartet? (er, ihr, sie = they)

H. Complete the answers to the questions, using the present perfect tense.

1. Arbeiteten Sie gestern?
Nein, _ich habe gestern nicht gearbeitet._

2. Haben die beiden Jungen das Fenster bezahlt?
Nein, nur Fritz _hat das Fenster bezahlt._

3. Haben Sie ihm einen Ball zum Geburtstag geschenkt?
Ja, ich _habe ihm einen Ball zum Geburtstag geschenkt_

4. Wer machte die Tür auf?
Ich _habe die Tür auf gemacht._

5. Wie lange lernen Sie heute?
Ich weiß nicht; aber gestern abend _habe ich lange gelernt_

6. Hast du heute eine Geschichte gehört?
Ja, der Lehrer _hat mir eine Geschichte_

7. Welches Gebäude zeigte er Ihnen?
Die Schule _hat er mir gezeigt_

8. Wie oft wiederholte Herr Schmidt die Frage?
Zweimal _hat Herr Schmidt wiederholt._

9. Was kaufte er gestern?
Ein schönes Buch _____.

10. Was ist das? Hörten Sie etwas?
Nein, _ich habe nichts gehört_

I. Translate into English.

1. Was haben Sie gehört? _What have you heard?_

2. Das machte Spaß! _That was fun._

3. Mutter hat ein wunderbares Essen gekocht. _Mother has cooked a wonderful dinner._

4. Der Brief freute uns sehr. _The letter pleased me was._

5. 1965 haben wir in dieser Straße gewohnt. _We have lived on this street since 1965._

6. Die Kinder haßten kaltes Wasser. _____

7. Er hat das Paket geöffnet. _He opened the package._

8. Wir schickten eine Karte an unsere Tante. _____

_____

9. Die Schüler folgten dem Lehrer durch die Stadt. _____

_____

10. Herr Müller hat ein großes Haus gebaut. _Mr. Müller has built a large house._

J. Translate into German.

1. The teacher explained the lesson. _Der Lehrer erklärte die Lektion_

_____

2. What did he build? _____

_____

3. We didn't hear the music. _____

_____

4. She's already thanked the lady. _Sie hat schon der Dame gedankt._

_____

5. I laid the card on the table. _____

_____

6. We haven't opened the window. _____

_____

7. The children were playing in the park. _Die Kinder haben in der Park gespielt_

_____

8. I have shown the letter to Mother. _____

_____

9. We bought it today. _____

_____

10. Hans asked Miss Schmidt. _____

_____

8. SIMPLE PAST AND PRESENT PERFECT OF IRREGULAR VERBS

Irregular verbs (also called *strong verbs*) change the vowel in the stem to form the simple past and the perfect participle. Irregular verbs can be divided into two groups: (*a*) mixed and (*b*) pure.

MIXED FORMS

Mixed forms of irregular verbs change the stem in the past, but they have the same endings as regular verbs.

PAST TENSES OF **bringen**

SIMPLE PAST	PRESENT PERFECT
ich **brachte**	ich **habe gebracht**
du **brachtest**	du **hast gebracht**
er **brachte**	er **hat gebracht**
wir **brachten**	wir **haben gebracht**
ihr **brachtet**	ihr **habt gebracht**
sie **brachten**	sie **haben gebracht**
Sie **brachten**	Sie **haben gebracht**

Note

The mixed forms of such verbs are combinations of two verb roots (**bring**en, **brach**te, ...), but the past tenses are like those of all other regular verbs—their stem ends in **-t-** and they have the regular endings of the past. (Mixed forms also occur in English: compare the verb *think, thought, thought* with *drink, drank, drunk*.)

SOME COMMON MIXED IRREGULAR VERBS

brennen, brannte, gebrannt, to burn (be ablaze)
    verbrennen, verbrannte, verbrannt, to burn (set on fire)
bringen, brachte, gebracht, to bring
    mitbringen, brachte mit, mitgebracht, to bring along
    verbringen, verbrachte, verbracht, to spend (time)
denken, dachte, gedacht, to think
haben, hatte, gehabt, to have
kennen, kannte, gekannt, to be acquainted with, know
nennen, nannte, genannt, to call (give a name to)
wissen, wußte, gewußt, to know (a fact)

Note

1. The principal parts of irregular verbs must be memorized for each verb individually. There are no general rules for forming them.

2. The verb **kennen** means *to know* in the sense of *to be acquainted with*, that is, *to know a person, book, play,* etc.:

Ich **kenne Herrn Weber.**	I know Mr. Weber.
Ich **kenne Goethes „Faust."**	I know Goethe's *Faust.*

1749 – 1839

3. **Können** is used to mean *to know how to do something*: **Ich kann Deutsch,** *I know (how to speak) German.* (See Lesson 5, page 25.)

4. **Wissen** means *to know information,* and is often followed by a phrase or clause that explains what is known:

Ich **weiß die Adresse.**	I know the address.
Ich **weiß, wo er ist.**	I know where he is.

PURE FORMS

Pure irregular verbs change the vowel of the stem in the simple past and usually in the past participle. They also have some different endings in the simple past.

SIMPLE PAST TENSE OF
sprechen, sprach, gesprochen

	ENDINGS
ich **sprach**	—
du **sprachst**	*-st*
er **sprach**	—
wir **sprachen**	*-en*
ihr **spracht**	*-t*
sie **sprachen**	*-en*
Sie **sprachen**	*-en*

THE PAST PARTICIPLE

A. The past participle of pure irregular verbs has the prefix **ge-** and the ending **-en.** (The past participles of regular verbs end in **-t.**)

B. There is no **ge-** prefix if the verb has an inseparable prefix:

vergessen   vergaß   **vergessen**

C. If the verb has a separable prefix, **ge-** is inserted between the prefix and the stem:

aussehen—aus**ge**sehen   **mit**nehmen—mit**ge**nommen

D. If the verb root is irregular, all compounds of that verb will be irregular in the same way:

schr**ei**ben	schr**ie**b	geschr**ie**ben
beschr**ei**ben	beschr**ie**b	beschr**ie**ben

SOME COMMON PURE IRREGULAR VERBS

The pure irregular verbs may be grouped according to the pattern of vowel change.

Group A: $a \rightarrow u \rightarrow a$

einladen (lädt ein), lud ein, eingeladen, to invite
schlagen (schlägt), schlug, geschlagen, to strike, beat
    nachschlagen, schlug nach, nachgeschlagen, to look up
    vorschlagen, schlug vor, vorgeschlagen, to suggest
tragen (trägt), trug, getragen, to carry; to wear
waschen (wäscht), wusch, gewaschen, to wash

Group B: $a \rightarrow \begin{Bmatrix} ie \\ i \end{Bmatrix} \rightarrow a$

fangen (fängt), fing, gefangen, to catch
    anfangen, fing an, angefangen, to begin
gefallen (gefällt), gefiel, gefallen, to please
halten (hält), hielt, gehalten, to hold; to stop
    aufhalten, hielt auf, aufgehalten, to detain
lassen (läßt), ließ, gelassen, to let, leave, allow
schlafen (schläft), schlief, geschlafen, to sleep

Group C: $\begin{Bmatrix} e \\ i \end{Bmatrix} \rightarrow a \rightarrow o$

beginnen, begann, begonnen, to begin
brechen (bricht), brach, gebrochen, to break
    zerbrechen, zerbrach, zerbrochen, to break to pieces
helfen (hilft), half, geholfen, to help
nehmen (nimmt), nahm, genommen, to take
    annehmen, nahm an, angenommen, to accept
    mitnehmen, nahm mit, mitgenommen, to take along
    unternehmen, unternahm, unternommen, to undertake
sprechen (spricht), sprach, gesprochen, to speak
    versprechen, versprach, versprochen, to promise
werfen (wirft), warf, geworfen, to throw

Group D: $ei \rightarrow ie \rightarrow ie$

entleihen, entlieh, entliehen, to borrow
schreiben, schrieb, geschrieben, to write
unterscheiden, unterschied, unterschieden, to distinguish, tell apart
vermeiden, vermied, vermieden, to avoid

Group E: $\begin{Bmatrix} e \\ i \\ ie \end{Bmatrix} \rightarrow a \rightarrow e$

bitten, bat, gebeten, to ask, plead
essen (ißt), aß, gegessen, to eat
geben (gibt), gab, gegeben, to give
    ausgeben, gab aus, ausgegeben, to spend (money)
lesen (liest), las, gelesen, to read
liegen, lag, gelegen, to lie

sehen (sieht), sah, gesehen, to see
  aussehen, sah aus, ausgesehen, to seem, look (like)
  nachsehen, sah nach, nachgesehen, to check on, look after
sitzen, saß, gesessen, to sit
vergessen (vergißt), vergaß, vergessen, to forget

Group F : *ie → o → o*

schließen, schloß, geschlossen, to close
verlieren, verlor, verloren, to lose
ziehen, zog, gezogen, to pull, draw

Group G : *i → a → u*

finden, fand, gefunden, to find
singen, sang, gesungen, to sing
trinken, trank, getrunken, to drink

Group H : *verbs with unique patterns of vowel change*

bekommen, bekam, bekommen, to get, receive
empfehlen (empfiehlt), empfahl, empfohlen, to recommend
heißen, hieß, geheißen, to be called (named)
rufen, rief, gerufen, to call (to someone)
  anrufen, rief an, angerufen, to call (on the telephone)
schneiden, schnitt, geschnitten, to cut
stehen, stand, gestanden, to stand
  verstehen, verstand, verstanden, to understand
tun, tat, getan, to do

Note

1. In addition to vowel changes, many irregular verbs have other spelling changes that must be learned individually:

nehmen—genommen   essen—gegessen

2. The objects of **helfen** and **gefallen** are in the dative case:

Ich **helfe** *der* Dame.	I'm helping the lady.
Die Karte **gefällt** *mir*.	"The card pleases me" = I like the card.

ÜBUNGEN

A. Fill in the endings of the simple past.

1. Die Kinder schlief _en_ _____ lange.

2. Ich sang _____ ein neues Lied. song

3. Er nannte _____ den Hund „Basil."

4. Die Leute gab _en_ _____ viel Geld aus. spend

5. Der Unterricht fing _____ um 8 Uhr an. instruction

6. Vater nahm _____ Hänschen mit. Johnny

7. Du warf _st_ _____ den Ball.
    threw

8. Ihr schrieb_t_____ lange Briefe.

9. Wir saß_en_____ auf der Bank.

10. Ich kann_____ den Herrn.

11. Das Mädchen vergaßt_____ die Adresse. *forgot*

12. Wir brach_ten_____ unsere Kamera mit. *brought*

13. Der Schüler las_____ viele Bücher.

14. Er wuß_te_____ nicht, von wem der Brief war. *from whom*

15. Peter schlug_____ eine Reise vor. *suggest*

B. Change the verb in each sentence to the simple past tense.

1. Er spricht mit seiner Mutter. — ~~spricht~~ sprach

2. Sie vermeidet es, ihm die Hand zu geben. — vermeide

3. Wir beginnen mit einer neuen Aufgabe. — begasen

4. Sie hilft ihm mit der Arbeit. — ~~helfe~~ half

5. Der Lehrer heißt Herr Meier. — ~~heiße~~ hieß

6. Der Kellner zerbricht den Teller. — ~~zerbreche~~ zerbrach

7. Das Papier brennt. — ~~brenn~~ brannte

8. Das alte Auto hält den Verkehr auf. — hielt

9. Wir schließen das Fenster. — schlossen

10. Ihr bekommt Post von Vater. — bekamt

11. Du siehst sehr müde aus. — sahst

12. Wir bringen unsere Freunde mit. — brachten

13. Er läßt das Heft zu Hause. *notebook* — ließ

14. Die meisten Kinder trinken Milch. — tranken

15. Er ißt die Brötchen. — aß

16. Das kranke Kind liegt im Bett. — ~~liege~~ lag

17. Ich weiß nicht, wer mich anruft. — ~~ruofte~~ anrief

18. Mutter wäscht die Kleider. — wusch

19. Du entleihst drei Bücher. — entliehst

20. In dem alten Haus finden sie alte Zeitungen. — fanden

C. Change the sentences in exercise *B* to the present perfect tense.

1. hat, gesprochen

2. hat, vermieden

3. haben, begonnen

4. hat, geholfen

5. hat, ~~hat~~ geheißen

6. hat, zerbrochen

7. _____ hat, ~~gebrochen~~ rannt auf _____
8. _____ hat, gehalten _____
9. _____ haben, geschlossen _____
10. _____ habt, begonnen _____
11. _____ hast, ausgesehen _____
12. _____ haben, ~~ge~~ mitgebracht _____
13. _____ hat, gelassen _____
14. _____ haben, getrunken _____
15. _____ hat gegessen _____
16. _____ hat gelegen _____
17. _____ habe gewußt _____
18. _____ hat gewaschen _____
19. _____ hast entliehen _____
20. _____ haben gefunden _____

D. Write each sentence, replacing the verb with the verbs in parentheses, using the same tense.

1. Ich rief meinen Bruder an.

   (einladen)   Ich lud meinen Bruder ein.
   (finden)   fand
   (mitnehmen)   nahm   mit

2. Er vergaß das Buch.

   (annehmen)   Er nahm das Buch an.
   (lesen)   las
   (bekommen)   bekam

3. Sie schlief im großen Zimmer.

   (sitzen)   Sie saß im großen Zimmer.
   (liegen)   lag
   (singen)   sang

4. Wir hatten ein neues Radio.

   (empfehlen)   reccomend Wir empfahlen ein neues Radio.
   (bekommen)   bekamen
   (finden)   fanden

5. Sie sprach drei Sprachen.

   (unterscheiden) distinguish Sie unterschied drei Sprachen
   (schreiben)   schrieb
   (vergessen)   vergaß

6. Ich habe ein neues Bild *picture* bekommen.

(annehmen) Ich habe ein neues Bild angenommen.

(finden) habe gefunden

(beginnen) habe begonnen

7. Ihr habt die Karte getragen.

(entleihen) Ihr habt die Karte entliehen

(verlieren) habt verloren

(lesen) habt gelesen

8. Du hast den Stock gesehen.

(verbrennen) Du hast den Stock verbrannt

(zerbrechen) hast zerbrochen

(werfen) hast geworfen

9. Sie hat das neue Kleid *dress* mitgenommen.

(waschen) Sie hat das neue Kleid gewaschen

(finden) hat gefunden

(empfehlen) hat empfohlen

10. Er hat gar nichts vergessen.

(tun) *to do* Er hat gar nichts getan.

(anfangen) hat angefangen

(versprechen) hat versprochen

E. Replace the subject of each sentence with the subjects in parentheses.

1. Der Anzug gefiel mir nicht.

(es) Es gefiel

(die Kleider) gefielen

(das Hotel) gefiel

2. Ich saß im dunklen Zimmer.

(wir) saßen

(er) saß

(du) saßt oder sasst

3. Wir warfen Schneebälle.

(die Jungen) warfen

(ich) warf

(ihr) warft

4. Was schlug sie vor? *suggest*

(du) schlugst

(Sie) schlugen

(die Männer) ----- *schlugen* --------------------------

5. Ich kannte den Herrn nicht.

(Hans) ------- *kannte* ---------------------

(wir) -------- *kannten* -------------------

(er) ---------- *kannte* --------------------

6. Wir haben drei Stücke unterschieden.

(ich) ----- *habe* ----- *unterschieden* -----

(er) --------- *hat* ----------- " ------------

(ihr) --------- *habt* ----------- " -----------

7. Mutter hat viele Freundinnen eingeladen.

(wir) ----- *haben* ----------- " ------------

(Sie) -------- *haben* ----------- " -----------

(ich) --------- *habe* ----------- " -----------

8. Ich habe dem Studenten geholfen.

(der Professor) ----- *hat* ----------- " ------------

(wir) --------- *haben* ----- " -----------

(die anderen Jungen) -- *haben* ----- " -----------

9. Ihr habt zuviel gegessen.

(ich) --------- *habe* ----- " ------------

(die Gäste) ----- *haben* ----- " -----------

(du) --------- *hast* ----- " ------------

10. Ich habe das Wort schon nachgeschlagen.

(der Student) ------ *hat* ----------- " ------------

(wir) --------------- *haben* ----- " -----------

(die Schüler) --------- *haben* ----- " -----------

SEIN AS AUXILIARY

Many irregular verbs have **sein** as an auxiliary in the present perfect tense: **er *ist* gekommen; wir *sind* gelaufen.** The verbs in this group are those that are intransitive (have no direct object) and also show a change of place or condition. The verbs **bleiben** and **sein** (and sometimes **stehen**) also are conjugated with **sein.** Note that the use of **sein** rather than **haben** as auxiliary verb does not affect the English translation of the present perfect tense.

Ich **bin** gekommen. $\begin{cases} \text{I have come.} \\ \text{I came.} \end{cases}$

Some Common Verbs Conjugated with **sein**

aufstehen, stand auf, ist aufgestanden, to get up
ausziehen, zog aus, ist ausgezogen, to move out
bleiben, blieb, ist geblieben, to remain, stay

fahren (fährt), fuhr, ist gefahren, to go, ride, travel
   abfahren, fuhr ab, ist abgefahren, to depart
   hinfahren, fuhr hin, ist hingefahren, to go away
fallen (fällt), fiel, ist gefallen, to fall
gehen, ging, ist gegangen, to go
kommen, kam, ist gekommen, to come
   ankommen, kam an, ist angekommen, to arrive
   mitkommen, kam mit, ist mitgekommen, to accompany, come along
laufen (läuft), lief, ist gelaufen, to run
sein (ist), war, ist gewesen, to be
steigen, stieg, ist gestiegen, to climb, rise
   aussteigen, stieg aus, ist ausgestiegen, to get off, disembark
   einsteigen, stieg ein, ist eingestiegen, to get aboard
sterben (stirbt), starb, ist gestorben, to die
wachsen (wächst), wuchs, ist gewachsen, to grow
werden (wird), wurde, ist geworden, to become

Note

1. **Stehen** may have either **haben** or **sein** as its auxiliary. (**Sein** is the older form and more common in southern Germany.) The preferred auxiliary today is **haben:**

   Ich *habe* im Garten **gestanden.**   I stood in the garden.

   The verb **verstehen** *always* takes the auxiliary **haben.**

2. When **fahren** has a direct object, the auxiliary **haben** (rather than **sein**) is used:

   Ich *habe* den Wagen **gefahren.**   I drove the car.

     But:

   Ich *bin* mit dem Wagen **gefahren.**   I went by car.

3. **Gehen** generally implies going on foot:

   Ich **gehe** zu Fuß.   I'm walking.

     But:

   Ich **fahre** mit dem Bus (Fahrstuhl, Zug,   I'm going by bus (elevator, train, etc.).
   usw.).

ÜBUNGEN

A. Complete each sentence with the correct form of the simple past tense of the verb in parentheses.

  1. (laufen)   Die Jungen _____ durch das Zimmer.

  2. (sterben)   Mehrere Tiere _____ während des Winters.

  3. (ankommen) Meine Mutter _____ heute früh um 7 Uhr _____.

  4. (wachsen)   Schöne Blumen _____ im Garten.

  5. (werden)   Mein Bruder _____ Arzt.

  6. (fahren)   Ich _____ mit dem Bus.

  7. (bleiben)   Wir _____ zwei Tage in München.

8. (ausziehen)   Meine Schwester _____ am Montag _____.

9. (einsteigen)   Der Herr _____ in den Zug _____.

10. (gehen)   Gestern abend _____ wir früh nach Hause.

B. In exercise *A*, change each sentence by using the present perfect tense of the verb in parentheses.

1. _____

2. _____

3. _____

4. _____

5. _____

6. _____

7. _____

8. _____

9. _____

10. _____

C. Write the correct form of **haben** or **sein**.

1. Der Anzug _____ mir sehr gefallen.

2. Er _____ gestern abend angekommen.

3. Wir _____ die Arbeit unternommen.

4. Die Leute _____ mit dem Fahrstuhl gefahren.

5. Wir _____ hier sechs Monaten geblieben.

6. Das Kind _____ den kleinen Wagen gezogen.

7. Die Gäste _____ am Stammtisch gesessen.

8. Die Jungen _____ sehr schnell gelaufen.

9. Ihr _____ unter dem Baum gelegen.

10. Die Reise _____ am Mittwoch angefangen.

11. Bäume aller Art _____ im Park gewachsen.

12. Am Montag _____ ich aus dem alten Haus ausgezogen.

13. Die Jungen _____ den Fußball geworfen.

14. Ich _____ früh aufgestanden.

15. Das schlechte Wetter _____ wir vermieden.

16. Vorigen Sommer _____ wir hingefahren.

17. Du _____ das Geld verloren.

18. Das Wetter _____ schön geworden.

19. Ich _____ der Dame geholfen.

20. Was _____ du getan, Hänschen?

D. Write each sentence, replacing the verb with the verbs in parentheses, using the same tense.

1. Er ist am Montag abgefahren.

(sprechen)   _____

(ankommen)   _____

(gehen)   _____

2. Ihr habt früh gewaschen.

(aussteigen)   _____

(anrufen)   _____

(hinfahren)   _____

3. Sind sie dort geblieben?

(schlafen)   _____

(sein)   _____

(stehen)   _____

4. Ist das Tier gefallen?

(sterben)   _____

(trinken)   _____

(wachsen)   _____

5. Ich bin gestern eingestiegen.

(mitkommen)   _____

(aufstehen)   _____

(singen)   _____

E. Write each sentence, changing the verb to the present tense.

1. Ich trug das Geschenk nach Hause. _____

2. Er ist mit dem Wagen gefahren. _____

3. Du sahst in dem Wörterbuch nach. _____

4. Der Plan hat dem Herrn nicht gefallen. _____

_____

5. Der Junge ist über die Straße gelaufen. _____

6. Sie verloren die Zeitungen. _____

7. Die Dame lud einige Freundinnen ein. _____

_____

8. Das Wetter ist sehr warm geworden. _____

9. Du warst in der Schule. _____

10. Er hat einen großen Fehler vermieden. _____

_____

11. Sie hat den Schlüssel angenommen. _____

12. Wir lasen mehrere Briefe. _____

13. Leider hat Jürgen nicht die richtige Antwort gewußt. _____
_____

14. Ein großer Baum ist im Hof gewachsen. _____
_____

15. Mein Freund hieß Hans Müller. _____

F. Complete the answers to the questions, using the simple past or the present perfect tense.

1. Wann fängt der Unterricht an?

Heute _____.

2. Was haben Sie in der Bibliothek getan?

Gestern _____.

3. Lebt Ihr Großvater noch?

Nein, er _____.

4. Hatten Sie alles mit?

Nein, die Karten _____.

5. Wie hieß dein Hund?

Ich _____.

6. Stehen Sie morgens früh auf?

Heute um 7 Uhr _____.

7. Wann fährt der Zug ab?

Schon vor einer Stunde _____.

8. Ist Post für Vater da?

Ja, er _____.

9. Haben die Kinder viel Lärm gemacht?

Nein, sie _____.

10. Wer machte die Tür zu?

Gretchen _____.

G. Translate into English.

1. Wer hat dieses Buch verloren? _____

2. Um wieviel Uhr sind Sie angekommen? _____
_____

3. Der Hund ist schnell gelaufen. _____

4. Vater hat eine Reise vorgeschlagen. _____

5. Der Herr ist im großen Zimmer geblieben. _____

_____

6. Wen haben Sie heute mitgebracht? _____

_____

7. Wir haben den Weg vergessen. _____

8. Meine Schwester hat drei Briefe geschrieben. _____

_____

9. Der Zug ist um 7 Uhr abgefahren. _____

10. Mit welchem Buch haben Sie angefangen? _____

_____

H. Translate into German.

1. She didn't see the water. _____

_____

2. We spoke with the policeman. _____

_____

3. Have the children gotten up yet? _____

_____

4. What were they thinking? _____

_____

5. Did he come along? _____

_____

6. The snow got very deep there. _____

_____

7. You were writing a letter. _____

_____

8. I did not hit the boy. _____

_____

9. Why hasn't he called us? _____

_____

10. Where were you staying yesterday? _____

_____

9. THE FUTURE TENSE

The future tense in German is formed by using the present tense of the auxiliary verb **werden** with the infinitive of the main verb.

FUTURE TENSE OF **sehen**

ich **werde sehen** du **wirst sehen** er **wird sehen**	wir **werden sehen** ihr **werdet sehen** sie **werden sehen**	Sie **werden sehen**

Note

1. The verb **werden** has three distinct and unrelated uses:

   a. By itself, meaning *to become*:

   Der Junge **wird** hungrig.   The boy is becoming (getting) hungry.

   b. With an infinitive, to form the future tense:

   Er **wird** bald **essen.**   He will eat soon.

   c. With the past participle, to form the passive voice:

   Die Tür **wird aufgemacht.**   The door is being opened.

2. Both in German and in English, the present-tense verb is often used when the future is intended, especially with an adverb indicating the future:

   Ich **fahre** morgen um 7 Uhr ab.   I'm leaving at 7 o'clock tomorrow morning.

3. In English, the future tense is formed with *shall* or *will*, but these auxiliaries are often replaced with "going to": *He's going to leave tomorrow.* When "going" is used in this way—to express the future—it is translated by **werden,** *not* **gehen:**

   I'm going to the city.   Ich **gehe** in die Stadt.

   But:

   I'm going to write a letter.   Ich **werde** einen Brief schreiben.

ÜBUNGEN

A. Change each sentence to the future tense.

1. Der Lehrer erzählt uns eine Geschichte.

----

2. Wir kaufen Brot in der Stadt.

----

3. Meine Eltern fahren in zwei Wochen ab.

----

4. Der Zug kommt um 5 Uhr an.

_____

5. Kurt nimmt seinen Bruder mit.

_____

6. Das Wetter wird kälter.

_____

7. Ich überlege mir die Sache.

_____

8. Sie frühstückt im Café.

_____

9. Du interessierst dich für den Dom.

_____

10. Bleibt ihr zu Hause?

_____

11. Mutter ist in der Küche.

_____

12. Ich erinnere mich an die Ferien.

_____

13. Verlassen sich die Herren darauf?

_____

14. Er will Fräulein Maier sprechen.

_____

15. Du schlägst die Antwort nach.

_____

B. Change the following sentences from plural to singular:

1. Wir werden morgen früh abfahren. _____

2. Ihr werdet Tante Frieda besuchen. _____

3. Die Kinder werden auf dem Hof spielen. _____

4. Wann werden wir in München ankommen? _____

5. Werdet ihr die Arbeit machen müssen? _____

Change the following sentences from singular to plural:

6. Er wird mit dem Bus fahren. _____

7. Ich werde im See schwimmen. _____

8. Du wirst dir ein schönes Konzert anhören. _____

9. Sie wird die Sprache lernen können. _____

10. Ich werde mir einen Mantel anziehen. _____

C. Answer each question in the future tense, using the words in parentheses in the answer.

1. Wann fährt Ihr Schiff nach Deutschland?   (am Mittwoch)

Unser Schiff _____.

2. Wie lange werden Sie in München bleiben?   (zwei Wochen)

Wir _____.

3. Ist Ihre Großmutter schon bei Ihnen?   (morgen)

Nein, sie _____.

4. Was sollen die Leute als erstes tun?   (sich setzen)

Als erstes _____.

5. Was müssen wir für morgen machen?   (die Sätze übersetzen)

Wir _____.

6. Wann wirst du mich anrufen?   (heute abend)

Ich _____.

7. Wie wird das Wetter morgen sein?   (Regen geben)

Es _____.

8. Werden Sie die Adresse vergessen?   (nicht)

Nein, ich _____.

9. Mit welcher Eisenbahn werden sie fahren?   (mit der Bundesbahn)

Sie _____.

10. Was wollen die Gäste tun?   (eine Reise machen)

Die Gäste _____.

D. Replace the subject of each sentence with the subjects in parentheses.

1. Er wird das Buch lesen.

(wir)_____

(Sie) _____

(das Mädchen) _____

2. Die Kinder werden sich waschen.

(Hans) _____

(ich) _____

(ihr) _____

3. Wir werden alte Lieder singen.

(Frl. Müller) _____

(die Gäste) _____

(du) _____

4. Das wird uns nicht überraschen.

(ihr) _____

(Sie) ---

(du) ---

5. Das wirst du dir merken.

(ich) ---

(die Leute) ---

(wir) ---

E. Translate into English.

1. Die Herren werden nach dem Programm fragen. ---

----

2. Als erstes wirst du dich melden. ---

----

3. Wir werden unser Auto verkaufen. ---

4. Ich werde zu Fuß gehen. ---

5. Alle Damen werden einen neuen Hut tragen. ---

----

6. Der Herr wird uns den richtigen Weg zeigen. ---

----

7. Wie werdet ihr das vermeiden können? ---

----

8. Sie werden einen Schlüssel bekommen. ---

9. Welche Tiere werden die Kinder im Wald sehen? ---

----

10. Woran werden sich die Studenten erinnern müssen? ---

F. Translate into German.

1. He will invite us. ---

2. We'll have to hurry. ---

3. She will explain it to us. ---

4. When is the farmer going to build the wall? ---

----

5. Children, you will thank the lady, won't you? ---

----

6. I'm going to buy a newspaper later. ---

----

7. My sister is going to cook supper. ---

----

8. Hans, you'll be able to work tomorrow, won't you? _____

_____

9. The gentleman will greet the guests. _____

10. When will they know the answer? _____

_____

Johannes Gutenberg (1397–1468) invented movable metallic type. He derived his concept of the printing press from the operation of a wine press. The famous Gutenberg Bible was the first book to be printed with movable type.

10. REVIEW OF PART 1—VERBS

WORTSCHATZ

Im Klassenzimmer

abwischen, to erase (a chalkboard), wipe off

(das Licht) **anmachen,** to turn on (the light)

die **Aufgabe, -n,** assignment

aufmachen, to open

aufstehen, to stand up, get up

(das Licht) **ausmachen,** to turn off (the light)

ausradieren, to erase (on paper)

(Blätter) **austauschen,** to exchange (papers)

auswendig lernen, to learn by heart

der **Bericht, -e,** report

das **Blatt, ⸚er,** sheet (of paper)

der **Bleistift, -e,** pencil

die **Bücherei, -en,** library (= die **Bibliothek**)

das **Büro, -s,** office

der **Direktor, -en,** principal (male)

die **Direktorin, -nen,** principal (female)

durchfallen, to fail, flunk (an exam)

der **Eßsaal, -säle,** dining hall, messhall

das **Examen,** exam

falsch, incorrect

fehlen, to be absent

das **Fenster, -,** window

der **Füll(feder)halter, -,** fountain pen

für sich lesen, to read to oneself

die **Garderobe, -n,** coat closet, cloakroom

die **Geographie,** geography

die **Geschichte, -n,** history, story

der **Gummi, -s,** eraser

  Radiergummi, pencil-eraser

das **Heft, -e,** notebook

die **Klasse, -n,** class (= subject), grade level (in school)

das **Klassenzimmer, -,** classroom

der **Korridor, -e,** hall

korrigieren, to correct

die **Kreide,** chalk

der **Kugelschreiber, -,** ballpoint pen

das **Laboratorium, -ien,** laboratory

die **Landkarte, -n,** map

(**laut**) **vorlesen,** to read aloud

der **Lehrer, -,** teacher (male)

die **Lehrerin, -nen,** teacher (female)

die **Lektion, -en,** lesson

lernen, to learn, study

die **Literatur,** literature

die **Mathematik,** mathematics

noch (ein)mal, once more

die **Note, -n,** grade (on a test, report card, etc.)

das **Papier,** paper

der **Papierkorb, ⸚e,** wastepaper basket

der **Plattenspieler, -,** record player

der **Projektionsapparat, -e,** movie projector

die **Prüfung, -en,** test, quiz

das **Pult, -e,** (student) desk

der **Punkt, -e,** point (in scoring)

richtig, correct

Ruhe!, Quiet!

die **Schallplatte, -n,** phonograph record

die **Schularbeit, -en,** homework

der **Schüler, -,** pupil (boy)

die **Schülerin, -nen,** pupil (girl)

der **Schulrat, ⸚e,** school superintendent, inspector

die **Seite, -n,** page

sich setzen, to sit down

sorgfältig schreiben, to write carefully

das (der) **Spind, -e,** locker

spitzen, to sharpen (a pencil)

der **Student, -en,** student (male)

die **Studentin, -nen,** student (female), "coed"

studieren, to study (at a university)

die **Stufe, -n,** level (of a program), step

die **Stunde, -n,** (class) period, hour

die **Tafel, -n,** chalkboard, blackboard

der **Tisch, -e,** (teacher's) desk

das **Tonband, ⸚er,** (magnetic) tape

der **Tonbandapparat, ⸚e,** tape recorder

das **Tonbandgerät, -e,** tape recorder

die **Tür, -en,** door

die **Übung, -en,** exercise

das **Übungsbuch, ⸚er,** exercise book

das **Übungsheft, -e,** workbook

der **Unterricht,** instruction, teaching

unterrichten, to teach

verbessern, to correct

die **Wand, ⸚e,** wall (of a room)

wiederholen, to repeat

die **Zensur, -en,** grade (on schoolwork)

das **Zeugnis, -se,** report card

zuhören, to listen, pay attention

zumachen, to close

1. *a.* Both **aufstehen** and **durchfallen** use the auxiliary **sein** for the present perfect tense:

Er *ist* **aufgestanden.**   He stood up.

   b. **Durchfallen** may be used with the preposition **in:**

Er ist **durch** die Prüfung
gefallen.

    Or: He flunked the test.

Er ist *in* der Prüfung
durchgefallen.

2. Observe the distinctions between **die Klasse, die Stunde,** and **der Unterricht:**

   a. **Die Klasse** refers to a particular school subject (**Deutsch, Geschichte,** etc.) or to the members of a class:

Es sind 25 Schüler in dieser **Klasse.**   There are 25 pupils in this class.

   b. **Die Stunde** refers to the period when a class meets:

In der ersten **Stunde** lernen wir Deutsch.   We have German in the first period.

   c. **Der Unterricht** refers to the classroom activity itself:

Der **Unterricht** fängt um 9 Uhr an.   Class starts at 9 o'clock.

3. *a.* **Student** (*f.,* **Studentin**) and **studieren** properly refer to students at the university level, although high school students may sometimes be referred to as **Studenten.** At the lower levels, **Schüler** (*f.,* **Schülerin**) and **lernen** are used: **der Student** *studiert* but **der Schüler** *lernt.*

   b. Since **lernen** means both *to learn* and *to study,* **der Schüler lernt Deutsch** means both *the pupil is learning German* and *the pupil is studying German.*

4. **Unterrichten, verbessern,** and **wiederholen** are inseparable; all the other compound verbs in the list on page 63 have separable prefixes.

5. **Zuhören** has an object in the dative case:

Ich hörte *dem* **Lehrer** zu.   I listened to the teacher.

Ich hörte *der* **Musik** zu.   I listened to the music.

ÜBUNGEN

  A. Supply the verb endings.

1. Die Schüler geh_____ ins Klassenzimmer.

2. Der Lehrer sagt: „Kinder, mach_____ das Buch zu!"

3. Heute bleib_____ wir eine halbe Stunde im Laboratorium.

4. In einer deutschen Schule steh_____ ein Schüler auf, wenn er auf eine Frage antwort_____.

5. Wieviele Studenten fehl_____ heute?

6. Man soll_____ die Aufgabe sorgfältig schreiben.

7. Die Schülerin komm_____ an den Tisch.

8. Wir könn_____ nicht heute den Film sehen, denn der Projektionsapparat geh_____ nicht.

9. Alle Schüler schreib_____ ins Übungsheft.

10. Nach der Prüfung, sagt der Lehrer: „Tausch_____ die Blätter aus!"

11. Mit lauter Stimme ruf_____ der Direktor: „Ruhe!"

12. Anna mach_____ heute einen Bericht.

13. Zu Mittag ess_____ die meisten Studenten im Eßsaal.

14. Peter bekomm_____ heute eine schlechte Note.

15. Ihr dürf_____ entweder mit Bleistift oder mit Kugelschreiber schreiben.

B. Reconstruct the sentence by inserting the correct form of the modal auxiliary in parentheses.

EXAMPLE: (müssen)   Ich mache heute abend die Schularbeit.
Ich *muß* heute abend die Schularbeit *machen.*

1. (sollen)   Er bringt das Heft mit.

----

2. (wollen)   Hans schreibt an die Tafel.

----

3. (müssen)   Wir setzen uns ans Pult.

----

4. (können)   Du wischt die Tafel ab.

----

5. (dürfen)   Ihr geht ins Büro.

----

6. (müssen)   Der Student bereitet sich auf die Prüfung vor.

----

7. (sollen)   Ich verbessere meine Schularbeit.

----

8. (wollen)   Die Schüler laufen um die Schule.

----

9. (können)   Ich verstehe diese Aufgabe nicht.

----

10. (dürfen)   Macht er die Tür zu?

C. Change the verb in each sentence to the simple past:

1. Ich lasse das Heft in meinem Spind.   -----------------------------

2. Kommt der Schulrat zu Besuch?   -----------------------------

3. Der Lehrer ist in der Bücherei. _____

4. Wir korrigieren unsere Fehler. _____

5. Sind viele Schüler im Korridor? _____

6. Wann haben wir Unterricht? _____

7. Du vergißt den Bleistift. _____

8. Fangen wir mit einer neuen Lektion an? _____

9. Jeder Student wiederholt den Satz. _____

10. Ich bringe einen Füllfederhalter mit. _____

11. Er interessiert sich für die Geschichte. _____

12. Die Schüler sitzen am Pult. _____

13. Wir machen das Buch auf. _____

14. Der Lehrer macht das Licht an. _____

15. Er lernt den Dialog auswendig. _____

16. Ihr schreibt die Übungen sorgfältig. _____

17. Man ißt im Eßsaal. _____

18. Uns fehlt ein gutes Tonbandgerät. _____

19. Die Studenten unterhalten sich auf Deutsch. _____

20. Der Lehrer steht an der Tür des Klassenzimmers. _____

D. Change the sentences in exercise *C* to the (*a*) present perfect tense and (*b*) future tense.

1. *a.* _____

 b. _____

2. *a.* _____

 b. _____

3. *a.* _____

 b. _____

4. *a.* _____

 b. _____

5. *a.* _____

 b. _____

6. *a.* _____

 b. _____

7. *a.* _____

 b. _____

8. *a.* _____

 b. _____

9. *a.* _____

 b. _____

10. *a.* _____

    b. _____

11. *a.* _____

    b. _____

12. *a.* _____

    b. _____

13. *a.* _____

    b. _____

14. *a.* _____

    b. _____

15. *a.* _____

    b. _____

16. *a.* _____

    b. _____

17. *a.* _____

    b. _____

18. *a.* _____

    b. _____

19. *a.* _____

    b. _____

20. *a.* _____

    b. _____

E. Change the following sentences to the present perfect tense:

1. Ich hatte keine Tinte für meinen Füllhalter. _____

_____

2. Die Schüler gingen an die Tafel. _____

_____

3. In der Schule lernten wir Geographie und Mathematik. _____

_____

4. Mein Klassenzimmer war am Ende des Korridors. _____

_____

5. Der Lehrer zeigte auf die Landkarte. _____

_____

6. Er spitzte seinen Bleistift. _____

_____

7. Im Laboratorium hörten wir einem Tonband zu. _____

_____

8. Gretchen verlor ihr Heft. _____

_____

9. Der Schüler warf das Buch in den Papierkorb. _____

_____

10. Die Schüler legten Hut und Mantel in der Garderobe ab. _____

_____

11. Dieter wischte die Tafel ab. _____

_____

12. Leider fiel er durch die Prüfung. _____

_____

13. Auf welcher Seite fingen wir an? _____

_____

14. Die schlechte Zensur gefiel ihr nicht. _____

_____

15. Die Studenten fuhren mit dem Bus. _____

_____

F. Change the following sentences to the future tense:

1. Ich habe die Aufgabe gut gemacht. _____

_____

2. Er hat die Lektion noch einmal gelesen. _____

_____

3. Wir haben die Geschichte für uns gelesen. _____

_____

4. Du hast mit Kreide auf die Tafel geschrieben. _____

_____

5. Die Jungen haben das Fenster im Klassenzimmer zerbrochen. _____

_____

6. Die Schüler haben im Eßsaal gegessen. _____

_____

7. Alle Schüler haben die Blätter ausgetauscht. _____

_____

8. Du hast die Übung auswendig gelernt. _____

_____

9. Sie hat dem Lehrer richtig geantwortet. _____

_____

10. Die Schüler haben sich für die neuen Schallplatten interessiert. _____

_____

G. Write each sentence, replacing the verb with the verbs in parentheses, using the same tense.

1. Er ist durch die Schule gelaufen.

(gehen) ---

(tanzen) ---

(kommen) ---

2. Sie wird ihren Bleistift gebrauchen.

(finden) ---

(spitzen) ---

(verlieren) ---

3. Ich entlieh drei Bücher.

(kaufen) ---

(mitnehmen) ---

(bringen) ---

4. Wir haben die Schularbeit korrigiert.

(verbessern) ---

(sorgfältig schreiben) ---

(vorlesen) ---

5. Dieses Heft hat mir nicht gefallen.

(gehören) ---

(helfen) ---

6. Alle Studenten mußten die Aufgabe auswendig lernen.

(sollen) ---

(wollen) ---

(können) ---

7. Ich werde die Antwort wiederholen.

(nachschlagen) ---

(erwarten) ---

(zuhören) ---

8. Der Student hat sich gesetzt.

(aufstehen) ---

(für sich lesen) ---

(durchfallen) ---

9. Sie verbesserte die Fehler.

(ausradieren) ---

(vermeiden) ---

(korrigieren) ---

10. Machen Sie das Buch auf!

(austauschen)   --

(zumachen)   --

(mitbringen)   --

H. Translate into English.

1. Wir radierten die Fehler auf dem Papier aus. ----------------------

----

2. Sollte er das Übungsheft mitbringen? ----------------------------

----

3. Wann wird der Unterricht anfangen? --------------------------

4. Ich lerne Deutsch gern. --------------------------------------

5. Man darf im Eßsaal nicht spielen. ----------------------------

----

6. Alle Schüler setzen sich ans Pult. ----------------------------

----

7. Maria hat an die Tafel geschrieben. --------------------------

8. Machen Sie bitte das Licht an, sobald Sie ins Klassenzimmer kommen! -------

----

9. Unser Lehrer fehlt heute. ------------------------------------

10. Herr Müller fragt: „Soll ich die Antwort wiederholen?" ---------------

----

11. Hertha hat die Tafel abgewischt. ----------------------------

12. Die Studenten müssen im Laboratorium dem Tonband sorgfältig zuhören. ------

----

13. In welcher Stunde haben wir Deutschunterricht? --------------------

----

14. Er schrieb mit einem Kugelschreiber. ------------------------

----

15. Nicht alle Schüler interessieren sich für Mathematik. -----------------

----

I. Translate into German.

1. Do you have any paper, Hans? --------------------------------

2. Yesterday we listened to records. ----------------------------

----

3. Tomorrow all the pupils will read aloud. _____

4. On the wall of our classroom is a large map. _____

5. The teacher wrote the assignment on the blackboard. _____

6. We're supposed to sharpen our pencils before class begins. _____

7. She lost her notebook and fountain pen in the hall. _____

8. The principal called several pupils into the office. _____

9. May I borrow your eraser? _____

10. We had to write the exercises with a fountain pen. _____

11. In the library you keep hearing "Quiet!" _____

12. You didn't flunk, did you? _____

13. The class is interesting, isn't it? _____

14. The weather was so bad today, we had to turn on the light. _____

15. We will repeat the assignment tomorrow. _____

Johann Wolfgang von Goethe (1749–1832), a master poet, playwright, and novelist, ranks among the greatest writers of all time.

Part II—Nouns and Pronouns

11. ARTICLES AND CASES; *KEIN*

German nouns fall into three groups called genders. The gender of a noun—masculine, feminine, or neuter—is identified by the form of the definite article that is used with the noun. The indefinite article is **ein** or **eine.**

GERMAN ARTICLES

	DEFINITE	INDEFINITE
MASCULINE	**der**	**ein**
FEMININE	**die**	**eine**
NEUTER	**das**	**ein**

Note

1. In most instances, the gender of a noun has little to do with biological (or natural) gender: **Mädchen** is neuter although it means *girl*. Regardless of gender, the German definite article is always translated as *the*, the indefinite article as *a* or *an*.

2. Every German noun is always capitalized. When other parts of speech are used as nouns, they are also capitalized:

das Gute, the good   **das Singen,** the singing

der NOUNS

Abend, evening
Anzug, suit
Apfel, apple
Arzt, physician, doctor
Ausflug, excursion, outing
Bahnhof, (train) station
Ball, ball
Bauer, farmer
Baum, tree
Berg, mountain
Besuch, visit
Boden, ground, floor
Brief, letter
Bruder, brother
Bus, bus
Dank, thanks
Dieb, thief
Doktor, doctor
Eimer, pail, bucket
Esel, donkey
Fehler, mistake, error

Film, film, movie
Flugplatz, airport
Fluß, river
Freund, friend (male)
Fuß, foot
Fußball, soccer
Gang, motion; pace; path
Garten, garden, yard
Gast, guest
Geburtstag, birthday
Gott, God
Gruß, greeting
Handschuh, glove
Herr, gentleman, Mr.
Himmel, heaven, sky
Hof, yard, courtyard
Hund, dog
Hut, hat
Junge, boy
Kaffee, coffee
Keller, cellar

Kellner, waiter
König, king
Kuchen, cake
Laden, shop, store
Lärm, noise
Lehrer, teacher
Mann, man (adult male)
Mantel, coat
Meister, master
Mensch, man (human being)
Monat, month
Mond, moon
Morgen, morning
Nachbar, neighbor
Nachtisch, dessert
Name, name
Ofen, oven
Ohrring, earring
Onkel, uncle
Park, park
Pfennig, penny

Plan, plan
Plattenspieler, record player
Platz, place
Polizist, policeman
Preis, price; prize
Regen, rain
Ring, ring
Rücken, back
Satz, sentence
Schlafsack, sleeping bag
Schlüssel, key
Schnee, snow
Schuh, shoe

See, lake
Sohn, son
Spaß, fun
Spaziergang, walk, stroll
Sport, sport(s)
Staat, state
Stein, stone
Stock, stick; floor (of building)
Student, student
Stuhl, chair
Tag, day
Tanz, dance
Tee, tea

Teil, part, portion
Teller, plate
Tisch, table
Vater, father
Verkäufer, salesman
Verkehr, traffic
Vetter, (male) cousin
Wagen, car
Wald, woods, forest
Weg, road, way
Wind, wind
Zug, train

Note

1. **Garten** means both *garden* and *backyard* (of a private house):

Sind die Kinder zu Hause? | Are the children at home?
Ja, sie spielen im **Garten.** | Yes, they're playing in the (back)yard.

2. A **Hof** is the enclosed courtyard of an apartment house, school building, or farmhouse:

Die Kinder spielen auf dem **Hof.** | The children are playing in the (school) playground.

die Nouns

Adresse, address
Antwort, answer
Arbeit, work, job
Aufgabe, exercise, homework assignment
Bank, (money) bank; bench
Bibliothek, library
Blume, flower
Butter, butter
Dame, woman, lady
Ecke, corner
Eisenbahn, railway
Erde, earth
Familie, family
Farbe, color
Feder, feather, pen
Frage, question
Frau, woman, wife, Mrs.
Freude, joy
Geschichte, story, history
Grenze, boundary, limit
Großmutter, grandmother
Hand, hand
Hütte, cabin, hut
Kamera, camera
Karte, card, map, ticket
Kartoffel, potato
Kirche, church

Klasse, class
Krawatte, necktie
Küche, kitchen
Lektion, lesson
Limonade, lemonade
Luft, air
Mark, mark (28 cents)
Mauer, wall (outside, boundary)
Medizin, medicine, medication
Milch, milk
Minute, minute
Musik, music
Mutter, mother
Nähe, vicinity
Post, mail, post office
Prüfung, test
Rechnung, bill (for services or materials)
Reise, trip, journey
Sache, thing, matter, affair
Schallplatte, (phonograph) record
Schule, school
Schwester, sister
See, sea, ocean
Seite, side, page

Speisekarte, menu
Sprache, language
Stadt, city
Stelle, place
Stimme, voice
Straße, street
Straßenbahn, streetcar
Stunde, hour (60 minutes)
Tafel, blackboard
Tante, aunt
Tasche, pocket
Tasse, cup
Tinte, ink
Tochter, daughter
Tür, door
Uhr, clock, watch, o'clock
Verkäuferin, saleslady
Verzeihung, pardon
Vorsicht, caution
Wand, wall (of room)
Welt, world
Woche, week
Wohnung, dwelling, apartment
Wurst, sausage
Zahl, number
Zeit, time
Zeitung, newspaper
Zigarette, cigarette

das Nouns

Auto, car
Bein, leg
Bett, bed
Bild, picture
Brot, bread
Brötchen, roll
Buch, book
Café, cafe, coffee house
Dach, roof
Datum, date (calendar)
Ding, thing
Dorf, village
Ende, end
Fahrrad, bicycle
Feld, field
Fenster, window
Fest, festival, banquet
Feuer, fire
Fleisch, meat
Flugzeug, airplane
Fräulein, young lady, Miss
Frühstück, breakfast
Geld, money
Geschäft, business

Geschenk, gift, present
Gesicht, face, countenance
Glas, glass
Glück, luck
Haus, house
Heft, notebook
Herz, heart
Holz, wood
Hotel, hotel
Jahr, year
Kind, child
Kino, movie theater
Klavier, piano
Kleid, dress
Konzert, concert
Krankenhaus, hospital
Land, country
Lied, song
Mädchen, girl
Meer, sea, ocean
Obst, fruit
Orchester, orchestra
Paar, pair

Paket, package
Papier, paper
Pech, trouble, bad luck
Pferd, horse
Programm, program
Rad, wheel, bicycle
Radio, radio
Rathaus, courthouse
Restaurant, restaurant
Schiff, ship
Schlafzimmer, bedroom
Schwein, hog
Stück, piece
Telefon, telephone
Theater, theater
Tier, animal
Tonband, (magnetic) tape
Vergnügen, pleasure
Wasser, water
Weh, pain
Wetter, weather
Wort, word
Zimmer, room

Note

1. It is essential to learn which article goes with each German noun.

2. In compound nouns, the article is determined by the last noun in the compound:

$$\textbf{das Auto} + \textit{\textbf{der}} \textbf{ Bus} = \textit{\textbf{der}} \textbf{ Autobus}$$

$$\textbf{der Ton} + \textit{\textbf{das}} \textbf{ Band} = \textit{\textbf{das}} \textbf{ Tonband}$$

Thus, all compounds of a root are usually the same gender: **der Zug, der Anzug.** (*Exception*: **das Wort,** *die* **Antwort.**)

3. **Der Mann** refers to an adult human male; **man** is a general pronoun meaning *one* or *someone*.

4. **Das Paar** is a *pair, set of two*; **ein paar** (with a small **p**) means *a few*.

5. Most nouns that refer to males are **der** nouns: **der Vater, der Freund, der Hund.**

6. Most nouns that refer to females are **die** nouns: **die Mutter, die Schwester, die Kuh.** (*Exceptions*: **das Mädchen, das Fräulein.**)

7. Masculine nouns can be made feminine by adding the ending **-in:** *die* **Freundin,** *girl (or woman) friend*; *die* **Lehrerin,** *woman teacher*. When **-in** is added, some nouns acquire an umlaut: **der Arzt,** *die* **Ärztin** (*woman physician*); **der Hund,** *die* **Hündin.**

8. Most nouns ending in **-e** are feminine: **die Frage.** (*Exceptions*: **der Name, das Ende, der Junge,** and most nouns ending in **-ee.**)

9. Nouns ending in **-ung, -tät, -ion,** and **-ik** are feminine: **die Zeitung, die Universität, die Lektion, die Grammatik.**

10. All nouns ending in **-lein** or **-chen** are **das** nouns: **das Mädchen, das Fräulein, das Brötchen, das Schwesterchen.** (Some nouns acquire an umlaut when **-chen** or **-lein** is added: **der Fuchs,** *das* **Füchs***lein;* **Hans, Häns***chen* or **Häns***el.*)

ÜBUNGEN

A. Replace the definite article with the indefinite article.

1. Sehen Sie *das* Haus?

   Sehen Sie _____ Haus?

2. *Der* Herr kommt durch *die* Tür.

   _____ Herr kommt durch _____ Tür.

3. Wir grüßen *das* Mädchen.

   Wir grüßen _____ Mädchen.

4. Hier ist *der* Brief von Mutter.

   Hier ist _____ Brief von Mutter.

5. *Die* Dame kauft ein Paar Handschuhe.

   _____ Dame kauft ein Paar Handschuhe.

6. *Der* Tisch steht in der Ecke.

   _____ Tisch steht in der Ecke.

7. *Der* Lehrer spielt *die* Schallplatte.

   _____ Lehrer spielt _____ Schallplatte.

8. *Der* Junge sucht *das* Schwein.

   _____ Junge sucht _____ Schwein.

9. *Die* Karte kostet 1 Mark.

   _____ Karte kostet 1 Mark.

10. *Der* Freund bringt die Post.

    _____ Freund bringt die Post.

11. *Das* Stück Butter ist teuer.

    _____ Stück Butter ist teuer.

12. *Der* Zug kommt spät an.

    _____ Zug kommt spät an.

13. *Der* Bauer baut *die* Mauer.

    _____ Bauer baut _____ Mauer.

14. Wir lernen *die* Sprache sprechen.

    Wir lernen _____ Sprache sprechen.

15. *Der* Arzt bringt *die* Medizin.

    _____ Arzt bringt _____ Medizin.

16. *Der* Student hört sich *das* Tonband an.

    _____ Student hört sich _____ _____ Tonband an.

17. Wir haben *das* Schiff gesehen.

    Wir haben _____ Schiff gesehen.

18. *Der* Kellner bringt *das* Glas Wasser.

    _____ Kellner bringt _____ Glas Wasser.

19. *Der* Park ist nicht weit von hier.

    _____ Park ist nicht weit von hier.

20. *Der* Dieb öffnete langsam den Keller.

    _____ Dieb öffnete langsam den Keller.

B. Replace the indefinite article with the definite article.

1. *Ein* Garten liegt hinter unserem Haus.

   _____ Garten liegt hinter unserem Haus.

2. *Ein* Gast hat *eine* Wurst gegessen.
            _____ Gast hat _____ Wurst gegessen.

3. *Ein* Pferd kann nicht *eine* Zeitung lesen.
            _____ Pferd kann nicht _____ Zeitung lesen.

4. Ich habe *ein* Wort nicht verstanden.
            Ich habe _____ Wort nicht verstanden.

5. *Ein* Vater kauft *ein* Fahrrad.
            _____ Vater kauft _____ Fahrrad.

6. Im Schlafzimmer steht *ein* Bett.
            Im Schlafzimmer steht _____ Bett.

7. *Ein* Haus muß *ein* Dach haben.
            _____ Haus muß _____ Dach haben.

8. *Ein* König kauft *ein* Bild.
            _____ König kauft _____ Bild.

9. *Eine* Frau spielt Klavier.
            _____ Frau spielt Klavier.

10. *Ein* Mädchen will *eine* Frage stellen.
            _____ Mädchen will _____ Frage stellen.

C. Replace the italicized words with each of the nouns in parentheses, using the indefinite article.

1. Der Herr kauft *eine Krawatte*.   (die Zeitung, das Auto, die Kamera)

----

2. *Ein Hund* läuft über die Straße.   (das Kind, die Mutter, der Junge)

----

3. Karl bringt *ein Buch*.   (die Schallplatte, das Heft, die Tasse)

----

4. *Eine Dame* ruft uns.   (der Freund, das Mädchen, der Bauer)

----

5. *Ein Bus* kommt bald.   (das Schiff, der Zug, die Verkäuferin)

Replace the italicized words with each of the nouns in parentheses, using the definite article.

6. Da drüben ist *das Hotel*.   (ein Krankenhaus, eine Bibliothek, ein Wald)

----

7. Wir suchen *die Hütte*.   (eine Bank, ein Theater, ein Dorf)

----

8. *Das Buch* ist interessant.   (ein Film, ein Programm, eine Geschichte)

----

9. Haben Sie *das Lied* gehört?   (ein Konzert, eine Stimme, ein Tier)

----

10. *Der Apfel* ist rot.   (eine Tinte, ein Kleid, ein Handschuh)

D. Translate the articles in parentheses into German.

1. _____ Polizist hat _____ Telefon.
  (The)   (a)

2. _____ Wagen kommt um _____ Ecke.
  (A)   (the)

3. _____ Mädchen kauft _____ Geschenk.
  (The)   (a)

4. _____ Gruß war herzlich.
  (The)

5. _____ Kellner hat _____ Adresse vergessen.
  (The)   (the)

6. _____ Orchester spielt im Park.
  (An)

7. Herr Schmidt hat _____ Sohn und _____ Tochter.
                    (a)   (a)

8. Es gibt _____ Bibliothek hier in der Nähe.
           (a)

9. _____ Junge spielt _____ Stück auf dem Klavier.
  (The)   (a)

10. _____ Gast möchte _____ Glas Wasser.
   (The)   (a)

CASES

The case ending of the article shows how the noun is being used in a particular sentence. Since German has four cases, each article has four forms:

DECLENSION OF THE DEFINITE ARTICLE

	SINGULAR		
Case	*Masculine*	*Feminine*	*Neuter*
NOMINATIVE	**der**	**die**	**das**
ACCUSATIVE	**den**	**die**	**das**
DATIVE	**dem**	**der**	**dem**
GENITIVE	**des**	**der**	**des**

(For the plural forms of the definite article, see Lesson 12, page 84).

DECLENSION OF NOUNS THAT ADD -n OR -en

An **-n** or **-en** is added to some **der** and **das** nouns in all cases except the nominative singular.

A. Nouns that add **-n:**

  der Bauer—(den, dem, des) Bauer*n*
  der Herr—(den, dem, des) Herr*n* (The plural adds **-en:** die Herr*en*.)
  der Junge—(den, dem, des) Jung*en*
  der Nachbar—(den, dem, des) Nachbar*n* (gen. sometimes Nachbar*s*)
  der Name—(den, dem) Name*n*; gen. sing., des Name*ns*

B. Nouns that add **-en**:

das Herz—dat., dem Herz**en**; gen. sing., des Herz**ens**; plural, die Herz**en**
der Mensch—(den, dem, des) Mensch**en**
der Polizist—(den, dem, des) Polizist**en**
der Student—(den, dem, des) Student**en**

Note

1. Most **der** and **das** nouns add **-s** or **-es** in the genitive singular.

   a. Nouns of one syllable add **-es: das Haus, des Haus*es.***
   Der Bus doubles the **s** in the genitive: **des Bus*ses.***

   b. Nouns with more than one syllable add **-s: der Vater, des Vater*s.***

   c. Nouns that add **-(e)n** in all forms do not add the **-s**. Exceptions are **des Herzens** and **des Namens.**

2. In an older form, an **-e** was added to the dative form of all **der** and **das** nouns. This is found today mostly in idioms: **nach Haus*e.***

Uses of the Cases

Nominative: subject; predicate noun (after **sein** or **werden**).

Accusative: direct object; object of certain prepositions; duration (length of time).

Dative: indirect object; object of the verbs **antworten, fehlen, folgen, gefallen, gehören, glauben, helfen, passen;** object of certain prepositions.

Genitive: possession; object of certain prepositions.

Note

1. The accusative case without a preposition is used to indicate a length of time:

Ich habe drei **Tage** gewartet.	I waited (for) three days.
Er hat **den ganzen Tag** gearbeitet.	He worked all day long.

2. a. Possession is shown by using the genitive case of the possessor:

der Hut **der Dame**	the lady's hat ("the hat of the lady")
ein Fenster **des Hauses**	a window of the house

   b. If the possessor is a proper noun, possession may be shown by adding **-s** to the noun, but *without* an apostrophe:

Beethovens Musik ist sehr schön.	Beethoven's music is very beautiful.
Emils Vater ist Lehrer.	Emil's father is a teacher.

   c. Although most "of" phrases in English are translated with the genitive case in German, the genitive case is not used in expressions that indicate servings or portions:

ein Glas Wasser	a glass of water
ein Stück Fleisch	a piece of meat

3. When nouns used as direct and indirect objects both appear in the same sentence, the indirect object comes first:

Er gibt *dem Mann* das Buch.	He gives the book to the man.

DECLENSION OF THE INDEFINITE ARTICLE

Case	Masculine	Feminine	Neuter
NOMINATIVE	ein	eine	ein
ACCUSATIVE	einen	eine	ein
DATIVE	einem	einer	einem
GENITIVE	eines	einer	eines

Note

The indefinite article has the same endings as the definite article except when it replaces **der** and **das;** in those three forms, **ein** has *no* ending.

KEIN

The adjective **kein,** meaning *no* (= *not any*), is declined in the same way as **ein.**

Note

German has three negative forms:

1. **nein,** the opposite of **ja,** which can be used only at the beginning of an answer to a question.

2. **nicht,** an adverb meaning *not*, which negates the verb (or an adjective):

> Ich **gehe** *nicht.*   I'm not going.
> Das ist *nicht* **gut.**   That is not good.

3. **kein,** which negates a noun or pronoun:

> Ich habe *kein* **Geld.**   I have no money.

Whenever *no* in English refers to a noun and means "not any," **kein** (never **nein!**) must be used.

ÜBUNGEN

E. Replace the indefinite article with the definite article.

1. *Ein* Hut paßt *einem* Herrn nicht.   _____ Hut paßt _____ Herrn nicht.

2. *Ein* Mädchen mit *einem* Brief sucht *einen* Platz.   _____ Mädchen mit _____ Brief sucht _____ Platz.

3. *Ein* Wir hören die Musik *eines* Orchesters.   Wir hören die Musik _____ Orchesters.

4. *Einem* Tisch fehlt *ein* Bein.   _____ Tisch fehlt _____ Bein.

5. In *einer* Ecke *eines* Zimmers steht *ein* Rad.   In _____ Ecke _____ Zimmers steht _____ Rad.

6. *Ein* Junge dankt *einem* Polizisten.   _____ Junge dankt _____ Polizisten.

7. *Ein* Herr sucht *einen* neuen Weg.   _____ Herr sucht _____ neuen Weg.

8. *Eine* Tür *einer* Schule fehlt.
_____ Tür _____ Schule fehlt.

9. *Ein* Junge in *einem* Park sucht *einem* Schuh.
_____ Junge in _____ Park sucht _____ Schuh.

10. *Ein* Besuch *eines* Freundes gefällt *einem* Herrn.
_____ Besuch _____ Freundes gefällt _____ Herrn.

F. Replace the definite article with the indefinite article.

1. *Der* Kellner bringt *dem* Herrn *die* Speisekarte.
_____ Kellner bringt _____ Herrn _____ Speisekarte.

2. *Das* Zimmer *des* Hotels ist nicht groß.
_____ Zimmer _____ Hotels ist nicht groß.

3. *Der* Gast hilft *dem* Mädchen.
_____ Gast hilft _____ Mädchen.

4. Sie tragen *das* Bett in *das* Krankenhaus.
Sie tragen _____ Bett in _____ Krankenhaus.

5. Ich suche *den* Arzt.
Ich suche _____ Arzt.

6. In *dem* Garten steht *der* Baum.
In _____ Garten steht _____ Baum.

7. *Das* Haus *des* Bauern heißt *das* Bauernhaus.
_____ Haus _____ Bauern heißt _____ Bauernhaus.

8. Er hat *den* Ring in *der* Straßenbahn gefunden.
Er hat _____ Ring in _____ Straßenbahn gefunden.

9. *Der* Junge schreibt an *die* Tafel.
_____ Junge schreibt an _____ Tafel.

10. *Der* Vater hat *den* Anzug gekauft.
_____ Vater hat _____ Anzug gekauft.

G. Use **kein** to change the sentence to the negative.

EXAMPLE: Ich habe das Buch. *Ich habe kein Buch.*

1. Er hat das Mädchen gesehen. _____

2. Ich höre die Musik. _____

3. Das gehört dem Herrn. _____

4. Sie schreibt den Brief. _____

5. Dieser Preis gefällt der Familie. _____

6. Wir machen einen Fehler. _____

7. Ich habe das Brot gekauft. _____

8. Sie hat die Adresse des Arztes. _____

9. Es gibt eine Prüfung heute. _____

10. Hier ist ein Platz. _____

H. Supply the definite article.

1. Ich zeige _____ Gast _____ Brief.

2. Er holt _____ Hut.

3. Der Student antwortet _____ Lehrer.

4. Er liest _____ Buch.

5. _____ Wetter heute ist schlecht.

6. Die Kamera gefällt _____ Dame.

7. _____ Rad kostet 100 Mark.

8. Paul ißt _____ Apfel mit großem Appetit.

9. Die Ecken _____ Schulzimmers sind dunkel.

10. Das Fußballspiel ist _____ beliebteste Sport Deutschlands.

I. Replace the noun in italics with each of the nouns in parentheses, using the correct form of the italicized article.

1. Wir zeigen *dem Mann* das Haus.   (die Dame, der Junge, das Kind)

    ----

2. Sie kaufen *ein Klavier*.   (das Haus, der Apfel, die Schallplatte)

    ----

3. Er fragt *den Polizisten*.   (der Freund, das Mädchen, die Frau)

    ----

4. Ich suche *eine Wohnung*.   (der Fluß, das Zimmer, die Karte)

    ----

5. Du hilfst *der Verkäuferin*.   (der Herr, das Fräulein, die Schwester)

    ----

6. Wir haben *kein Café* gesehen.   (der Schnee, der Berg, die Mauer)

    ----

7. Die Tür *des Hauses* ist geschlossen.   (das Auto, die Bank, der Bus)

    ----

8. Ich folgte *dem Herrn*.   (der Student, die Dame, das Kind)

    ----

9. Wir sitzen in *dem Keller*.   (die Hütte, das Zimmer, die Bibliothek)

    ----

10. Er hat *kein Papier*.   (das Glück, der Schlüssel, die Milch)

J. The answers to the following questions appear in parentheses. Answer each question with a complete sentence in German.

1. Wem dankt der Herr?   (the lady)

----

2. Was liest die Dame?   (a letter)

----

3. Wessen Mantel trägt Luise?   (Olga's)

----

4. Wem folgt der Hund?   (the child)

----

5. Wer macht einen Spaziergang?   (the family)

----

6. Wem bringt der Kellner die Rechnung?   (the guest)

----

7. Wieviel kostet das?   (1 Mark)

----

8. Was bringt der Gast mit?   (a gift)

----

9. Was haben Sie im Park gehört?   (a concert)

----

10. Wessen Zimmer ist das?   (the brother's)

K. Translate the English into German.

1. Er zeigt mir die Tür *of the room.*   --

2. Wir suchen *a place,* wo wir parken können. --

3. Ich gebe *the friend* die Adresse.   --

4. Das kostet nur *one* Pfennig.   --

5. Es tut *the policeman* Weh, solche bösen Worte zu hören.   --

6. Die Wand *of the bedroom* ist grün.   --

7. Wir möchten *a glass of water* trinken.   --

8. Zeigen Sie mir *the road,* bitte!   --

9. Wo ist *the park*?   --

10. Die Mutter gibt *the girl an apple.*   --

11. *Miss Weber's* Muttersprache ist Deutsch.   --

12. Ich habe *a glove* verloren.   --

13. Diese Mauer ist *the boundary of the yard.* --

14. Nächste Woche machen wir *an outing*. --

15. Wo haben Sie *the animal* gesehen? --

16. Herr Müller gab *the dog a piece of meat*. --

17. *The sky* ist blau. --

18. *The plane* kommt jetzt an. --

19. Auf dem Rücken trägt er *a sleeping bag*. --

20. Vater hilft *a neighbor*. --

The *Kaiser Wilhelm Memorial Church*, in West Berlin, was badly damaged during World War II. It now stands like a Gothic relic beside the new church—a modern structure—that was built to replace it.

12. PLURALS

The plural forms of German nouns fall into five groups. They are formed from the singular as follows:

I. By adding **-n** or **-en**:

der Bauer—die Bauer**n**   der Herr—die Herr**en**

II. By adding **-e** (and, sometimes, an umlaut on the root):

der Abend—die Abend**e**   der Ball—die Bäll**e**

III. By adding **-er** (and, sometimes, an umlaut on the root):

das Bild—die Bild**er**   das Dorf—die Dörf**er**

IV. No ending is added (but sometimes an umlaut is added to the root):

der Fehler—die Fehler   der Vater—die Väter

V. by adding **-s**:

das Auto—die Auto**s**   der Park—die Park**s**

One set of definite articles is used for *all* plurals, no matter whether the noun has **der, die,** or **das** in the singular:

DECLENSION OF THE DEFINITE ARTICLE

Case	PLURAL *All Genders*
NOMINATIVE	**die**
ACCUSATIVE	**die**
DATIVE	**den**
GENITIVE	**der**

Note

The plural forms of nouns in groups II, III, and IV also add **-n** in the dative:

Plural

NOMINATIVE	DATIVE
die Gäste	den Gäste**n**
die Bilder	den Bilder**n**
die Zimmer	den Zimmer**n**

GROUP I: *Some Common Nouns that Add* -(*e*)*n*

die **Adresse,** address	der **Bauer,** farmer	die **Dame,** lady, woman
die **Antwort,** answer	das **Bett,** bed	der **Doktor,** doctor
die **Aufgabe,** assignment	die **Bibliothek,** library	die **Ecke,** corner
die **Bank,** bank (money)	die **Blume,** flower	die **Eisenbahn,** railroad

das **Ende,** end
die **Familie,** family
die **Farbe,** color
die **Feder,** feather, pen
die **Frage,** question
die **Frau,** lady
die **Geschichte,** story
die **Grenze,** boundary
der **Herr,** gentleman
das **Herz,** heart
die **Hütte,** hut, cabin
der **Junge,** boy
die **Karte,** card
die **Kartoffel,** potato
die **Kirche,** church
die **Klasse,** class
die **Krawatte,** necktie
die **Küche,** kitchen
die **Lektion,** lesson
die **Mauer,** (outside) wall
die **Medizin,** medicine

der **Mensch,** man, human being
die **Minute,** minute
der **Nachbar,** neighbor
der **Name,** name
die **Platte,** (phonograph) record, disc
der **Polizist,** policeman
die **Prüfung,** test
die **Rechnung,** bill (for payment)
die **Reise,** trip
die **Sache,** thing, matter, affair
die **Schule,** school
die **Schwester,** sister
der/die **See,** lake, sea
die **Seite,** page
die **Sprache,** language
der **Staat,** state, country
die **Stelle,** place

die **Stimme,** voice
die **Straße,** street
die **Straßenbahn,** streetcar
der **Student,** student
die **Stunde,** hour
die **Tafel,** blackboard
die **Tante,** aunt
die **Tasche,** pocket
die **Tasse,** cup
die **Tinte,** ink
die **Tür,** door
die **Uhr,** clock
die **Verkäuferin,** saleslady
der **Vetter,** (male) cousin
die **Woche,** week
die **Wohnung,** dwelling
die **Zahl,** number
die **Zeit,** time
die **Zeitung,** newspaper
die **Zigarette,** cigarette

Note

1. In Group I, nouns that end in **-e** in the singular have plurals ending in **-n:**

das Ende—die End**e**n

2. Nouns that do not end in **-e** in the singular have plurals ending in **-en:**

das Bett—die Bett**en**

Exceptions: The plurals of the following nouns end in **-n:**

der Bauer—die Bauer**n**
die Feder—die Feder**n**
die Kartoffel—die Kartoffel**n**
die Mauer—die Mauer**n**

der Nachbar—die Nachbar**n**
die Schwester—die Schwester**n**
die Tafel—die Tafel**n**

3. Nouns that end in **-ung** in the singular have plurals ending in **-en:**

die Prüfung—die Prüfung**en**

4. The ending **-in** doubles the **n** in the plural:

die Verkäuferin—die Verkäuferi**nn**en

Group II: *Some Common Nouns that Add* **-e**

A. *without adding an umlaut*

der **Abend,** evening
das **Bein,** leg
der **Berg,** mountain
der **Besuch,** visit
der **Bleistift,** pencil
der **Brief,** letter
das **Brot,** (loaf of) bread
der **Bus,** bus

der **Dieb,** thief
das **Ding,** thing
das **Fest,** festival, banquet
der **Film,** film, movie
das **Flugzeug,** airplane
der **Freund,** friend
das **Frühstück,** breakfast
das **Geschäft,** business

das **Geschenk,** gift
das **Heft,** notebook
der **Hund,** dog
das **Jahr,** year
das **Klavier,** piano
der **König,** king
das **Konzert,** concert
das **Meer,** sea, ocean

der **Monat,** month
das **Paar,** pair
das **Paket,** package
das **Papier,** paper
der **Pfennig,** penny
das **Pferd,** horse
der **Preis,** price

das **Programm,** program
der **Ring,** ring
das **Schiff,** ship
der **Schuh,** shoe
das **Schwein,** hog
der **Stein,** stone
das **Stück,** piece

der **Tag,** day
der **Teil,** part
das **Telefon,** telephone
das **Tier,** animal
der **Tisch,** table
der **Weg,** road, way
der **Wind,** wind

B. *with an added umlaut*

der **Arzt,** physician, doctor
der **Ausflug,** excursion, outing
der **Ball,** ball
die **Bank,** bench
der **Baum,** tree
der **Fluß,** river
der **Fuß,** foot
der **Gang,** motion, path
der **Gast,** guest

der **Gruß,** greeting
die **Hand,** hand
der **Hof,** yard, courtyard
der **Hut,** hat
der **Plan,** plan
der **Platz,** place
der **Satz,** sentence
der **Schlafsack,** sleeping bag
der **Sohn,** son

die **Stadt,** city
der **Stock,** stick, floor (= story)
der **Strumpf,** stocking, sock;
    pl., hosiery
der **Stuhl,** chair
der **Tanz,** dance
die **Wand,** wall (of a room)
die **Wurst,** sausage
der **Zug,** train

Note

1. **Bus** and **Fluß** form the plural with **-ss-:**

$$Busse \qquad Flüsse$$

2. **Fuß** and **Gruß** keep the **ß** in the plural:

$$Füße \qquad Grüße$$

3. **Preis** does *not* double the **s:**

$$die \ Preise$$

GROUP III: *Some Common Nouns that Add* **-er**

A. *without adding an umlaut*

das **Bild,** picture
das **Feld,** field

das **Gesicht,** face
das **Kind,** child

das **Kleid,** dress, clothing
das **Lied,** song

B. *with an added umlaut*

das **Buch,** book
das **Dach,** roof
das **Dorf,** village
das **Glas,** glass

der **Gott,** God
das **Haus,** house
das **Land,** country
der **Mann,** man

das **Rad,** wheel
das **Tonband,** (magnetic) tape
der **Wald,** woods
das **Wort,** word

Note

1. The plural of **Wort** may also be **Worte.**

2. Generally, nouns in this group that can have an umlaut (with **a, o,** or **u** in the stem) add an umlaut in the plural.

GROUP IV: *Some Common Nouns that Do Not Add an Ending*

A. *the singular and plural forms are the same*

das **Brötchen,** roll
der **Eimer,** pail
der **Esel,** donkey
der **Fehler,** mistake
das **Fenster,** window
das **Fräulein,** young lady
der **Keller,** cellar
der **Kellner,** waiter

der **Kuchen,** cake
der **Lehrer,** teacher
das **Mädchen,** girl
die **Mark,** mark (29¢)
der **Meister,** master
der **Onkel,** uncle
das **Orchester,** orchestra

der **Plattenspieler,** record
 player
der **Schlüssel,** key
der **Teller,** plate
das **Theater,** theater
der **Wagen,** car
das **Zimmer,** room

B. *an umlaut is added*

der **Apfel,** apple
der **Boden,** floor, ground
der **Bruder,** brother
der **Garten,** garden

der **Laden,** store, shop
der **Mantel,** coat
die **Mutter,** mother

der **Ofen,** oven
die **Tochter,** daughter
der **Vater,** father

Note

1. Words ending in **-chen** and **-lein** usually are in this group.

2. The plural of **Fräulein** may also be **Fräuleins.**

3. The older plural of **Boden** does not add the umlaut. Now the plural is more commonly **die Böden.**

GROUP V: *Some Common Nouns that Add -s*

das **Auto,** car
das **Café,** cafe
das **Hotel,** hotel

die **Kamera,** camera
das **Kino,** movie theater
der **Park,** park

das **Radio,** radio
das **Restaurant,** restaurant

Note

1. The plural of **Park** may also be **Parke.**

2. The nouns in this group are generally of non-Germanic origin.

3. The plurals of family names also add **-s: die Müllers, die Schmidts.**

Some Common Nouns that Have Only Plural Forms

die **Eltern,** parents
die **Ferien,** vacation

die **Geschwister,** brother(s)
 and sister(s)

die **Leute,** people
die **Weihnachten,** Christmas

Note

1. A few nouns have plurals that do not belong to any of these groups: **das Datum—die *Daten*** (*data*); **das Obst—die *Obstarten*** (*fruits*).

2. The plural of a compound noun is always the same as the plural of the last root:

der **Zug**, die *Züge*   das **Rad**, die *Räder*

der **An**zug, die An*züge*   das Fahr**rad**, die Fahr*räder*

ÜBUNGEN

A. Complete the sentence by using the plural form of the noun in parentheses. (Use the definite article with the noun where possible.)

1. (der Gast)   ---------------------- kommen jetzt.

2. (das Kind)   Das Lied gefällt ----------------------.

3. (das Tonband)   Haben Sie ---------------------- mit?

4. (die Zeitung)   Wieviele ---------------------- kauft der Herr?

5. (die Geschichte)   Die Schüler hören ---------------------- gern.

6. (das Feld)   Wir fahren durch ----------------------.

7. (das Mädchen)   Vier ---------------------- kommen ins Haus.

8. (die Frage)   Kann Jürgen Antwort auf ---------------------- geben?

9. (das Hotel)   ---------------------- in dieser Stadt sind elegant.

10. (die Kartoffel)   Es gibt Schweinebraten und ---------------------- zum Abendessen.

11. (der Laden)   In ---------------------- gibt es viele schöne Sachen zu kaufen.

12. (der Berg)   In Süddeutschland sieht man viele ----------------------.

13. (die Wand)   Zu Hause haben wir viele Bilder an ----------------------.

14. (der Mann)   Wir sprechen mit ----------------------.

15. (der Baum)   Im Wald stehen große ----------------------.

16. (die Blume)   ---------------------- im Garten sind sehr schön.

17. (der Wagen)   Er interessiert sich für ----------------------.

18. (das Land)   Die Grenzen dieser ---------------------- sind nicht ganz sicher.

19. (der Bruder)   Er zeigt ---------------------- den Weg.

20. (das Brötchen)   Sind ---------------------- gut?

B. Revise the sentence by changing all singular nouns to the plural.

1. Die Tür der Kirche ist groß. ----------------------

----

2. Der Bauer geht über das Feld. ----------------------

----

3. Die Farbe des Kleides gefällt der Dame. ----------------------

----

4. Meine Eltern wollen sich das Bild ansehen. ----------------------

----

5. Die Verkäuferin grüßt den Herrn. _____

_____

6. Der Wagen fährt schnell durch die Stadt. _____

_____

7. Der Dame gefällt die Farbe des Handschuhs nicht. _____

_____

8. Der Gast hört keine Stimme in der Schule. _____

_____

9. Der Kellner bringt die Rechnung. _____

_____

10. Das Geschäft dieses Dorfes ist klein. _____

_____

11. Im Park kann man sich auf die Bank setzen. _____

_____

12. Einmal im Jahre macht mein Bruder einen interessanten Ausflug. ____

_____

13. Das Mädchen will den Stuhl kaufen. _____

_____

14. Die Mutter ruft das Kind. _____

_____

15. Das Fenster der Wohnung ist geschlossen. _____

_____

C. Revise the sentence by changing all plural nouns to the singular.

1. Die Jungen haben die Teller zerbrochen. _____

_____

2. Die Kinder essen Äpfel gern. _____

_____

3. Die Böden dieser Häuser sind kalt. _____

_____

4. Meine Onkel kommen morgen zu Besuch. _____

_____

5. Die Esel laufen über die Felder und durch die Wälder. _____

_____

6. Die Frauen sprechen mit deinen Schwestern. _____

_____

7. In den Läden haben die Herren diese Karten gekauft. _____

_____

8. Die Geschichte dieser Staaten ist sehr interessant. _____

_____

9. Meine Freunde haben sich neue Mäntel gekauft. _____

_____

10. Pferde tragen keine Hüte. _____

_____

D. Replace the noun in italics with the plural forms of the nouns in parentheses, changing the form of the article where necessary.

EXAMPLE: Hast du deine *Bücher*? (der Bleistift, . . .)
Hast du deine *Bleistifte*?

1. Welche *Züge* fahren nach Hamburg?   (das Schiff, der Bus, das Flugzeug)

_____

2. Vor einigen *Minuten* habe ich das gehört.   (die Woche, der Tag, das Jahr)

_____

3. Wir haben die Stimmen der *Jungen* gehört.   (der Arzt, der Mensch, der Meister)

_____

4. Er will sich die *Platten* anhören.   (das Programm, das Tonband, das Klavier)

_____

5. Haben Sie meine *Briefe*?   (das Buch, der Schlüssel, die Tasse)

_____

6. Können Sie die *Plätze* finden?   (der Fehler, das Café, der Dieb)

_____

7. Welche *Herren* haben Sie kennengelernt?   (das Kind, die Dame, das Fräulein)

_____

8. An den *Wänden* hängen viele Bilder.   (die Tür, das Auto, der Zug)

_____

9. Im Radio hört man viele *Programme*.   (die Stimme, die Sprache, das Lied)

_____

10. Er singt ein Lied für die *Herren*.   (der König, der Nachbar, der Polizist)

_____

E. Complete the answers to the questions.

1. Sprechen deine Geschwister Englisch? Meine Schwester spricht nur Deutsch, aber mein Bruder kann mehrere _____.

2. Sind Sie vorher in diesem Dorf gewesen? Vielleicht. Mir aber sind alle _____ gleich.

3. Haben Sie das Buch mitgebracht? Welches Buch? Ich habe hier drei _ _ _ _ _ _ _ _ _ _ _ _ _ _ _ _ _ .

4. Was machen Sie heute abend? Ich muß ein paar _ _ _ _ _ _ _ _ _ _ _ _ schreiben.

5. Was sind Berlin, Hamburg, und München? Sie sind alle _ _ _ _ _ _ _ _ _ _ _ _ .

6. Wo ist das Hotel? Welches wollen Sie finden? Es sind zwei _ _ _ _ _ _ _ _ _ _ _ _ in der Nähe.

7. Wie lange sind Sie schon hier? Wir wohnen seit sechs _ _ _ _ _ _ _ _ _ _ _ _ hier.

8. Hat Vater sich einen neuen Anzug gekauft? Nein, die _ _ _ _ _ _ _ _ _ _ _ waren zu teuer.

9. Mit welchem Gast spricht der Herr? Er spricht mit allen _ _ _ _ _ _ _ _ _ _ _ .

10. Wie lange dauert die Reise? Sie dauert sechs _ _ _ _ _ _ _ _ _ _ _ _ _ .

F. Translate the English into German.

1. Er gibt *the men* das Geld. _

2. Können Sie *the girls* sehen? _

3. Wieviele *rivers* gibt es in Deutschland? _

4. *The children* spielen mit *the dogs*. _

5. Im Zoo sieht man seltene *animals*. _

6. Hoher Schnee liegt auf *the mountains*. _

7. *The children's hands* werden kalt. _

8. Viele Deutsche sprechen zwei *languages*. _

9. Die Studenten sollen zwanzig *sentences* übersetzen. _

10. Die Leute kommen aus vielen *countries*. _

13. PERSONAL PRONOUNS

Personal pronouns are special words used only to replace nouns: "Where is the *book*? Here *it* is." The nouns that are replaced need not be expressed: "(*John and Mary*,) are *you* coming?"

PERSONAL PRONOUNS (NOMINATIVE CASE)

Person	Singular	Plural
FIRST	**ich,** I	**wir,** we
SECOND	**du,** you	**ihr,** you
THIRD	**er,** he **sie,** she **es,** it	**sie,** they

Second person formal, sing. and plur.
Sie, you

Note

1. Bear in mind that the pronoun used to replace the noun depends on the article:

der—*er*   **die**—*sie*   **das**—*es*

Every **der** noun is always referred to with some form of **er,** every **die** noun with some form of **sie,** and every **das** noun with some form of **es:**

Wo ist **das** Schwesterchen? *Es* ist im Garten.	Where is the little sister? She is in the garden.
Wann kommt **der** Zug? *Er* kommt um 11 Uhr.	When is the train coming? It is coming at 11 o'clock.

2. When the true subject of the sentence follows the verb, an **es** at the beginning of the sentence is usually translated as *there:*

Es sind fünf Stühle im Zimmer.	There are five chairs in the room.
Es gibt viele Bücher hier.	There are many books here.
Es gibt schönes Wetter heute.	The weather is nice today. ("There is nice weather . . .")

(For the difference between the use of **es sind** and **es gibt,** see Lesson 18, page 133, Note 2.)

3. *a.* **Du** and **ihr** are used when speaking to children, classmates, members of one's own family, intimate friends, and animals; **du** is used when speaking to God, as in prayer. All other persons are generally addressed as **Sie,** which is always capitalized.

   b. When used in a letter, **Du** and **Ihr** and their possessive forms **Dein** and **Euer** are capitalized.

   c. Students, soldiers, and some groups of workers often use **du** with one another. Usually, the first name is used with **du,** and a title (**Herr, Frau, Professor,** etc.) accompanies **Sie.** However, persons in authority who are on friendly terms with those under them—teachers and employers, for example—may use the first name along with **Sie.**

4. The pronoun **sie** can be either singular (*she*) or plural (*they*). The ending on the verb shows which is meant. With a capital **S, Sie** means *you* both singular and plural:

„Wann **kommen Sie,** Herr Schmidt (meine Herren)?“ „Ich komme (Wir kommen) morgen.“

"When are you coming, Mr. Smith (gentlemen)?" "I'm (We're) coming tomorrow."

Declension of Personal Pronouns

NOMINATIVE	ich	du	er	sie	es	wir	ihr	sie	Sie
ACCUSATIVE	mich	dich	ihn	sie	es	uns	euch	sie	Sie
DATIVE	mir	dir	ihm	ihr	ihm	uns	euch	ihnen	Ihnen

Note

1. A genitive form of the personal pronouns does exist, but its use is so rare that it need not be learned now.

   To express possession, the personal pronouns are replaced by the corresponding possessive adjectives. (See Lesson 17.)

   Ich lese **mein** Buch. I'm reading my book.

   Sie trägt **ihren** Mantel. She is wearing her coat.

2. *a.* Whenever a preposition is used with a pronoun referring to an inanimate object, the pronoun is replaced by the prefix **da-,** which is attached to the preposition:

   Ich weiß nichts **davon.** I know nothing about it.

   b. When the preposition begins with a vowel, an **r** is inserted to help pronunciation: **daraus, darüber,** etc.

   c. The **da-** compounds are the same for both singular and plural:

   Ich habe die Frage(n) gehört, aber ich kann nicht **darauf** antworten. I heard the question(s), but I can't answer it (them).

   d. The prepositions **ohne, seit,** and **außer** cannot be combined with **da-: Ohne es kann er nicht fahren.**

   e. When not referring to a specific object, adverbial forms of the prepositions are used in place of the **da-** compounds. (See Lesson 18, page 133.)

   Er sitzt **dahinter.** He's sitting behind it.

   But:

   Er sitzt da *hinten.* He's sitting there in the back.

   f. If reference is to a person, the pronoun *must* be used:

   Wir warten **auf** *sie.* We are waiting for her.

3. *a.* Whenever a pronoun is used for the direct object, it comes before the indirect object, if there is one:

   Er gab *es* **dem Mann;** er gab *es* **ihm.** He gave it to the man; he gave it to him.

   b. If the direct object is a noun, it comes *after* the indirect object:

   Sie gab **ihm** *das Buch.* She gave him the book.

   Sie gab **dem Kind** *das Buch.* She gave the book to the child.

In addition to these personal pronouns of specific reference, German also has several pronouns of general reference. Among these are **man** (*one*), **jemand** (*someone*), and **niemand** (*no one*).

DECLENSION OF INDEFINITE PRONOUNS

NOMINATIVE	**man**	**jemand**	**niemand**
ACCUSATIVE	**einen**	**jemand**(en)	**niemand**(en)
DATIVE	**einem**	**jemand**(em)	**niemand**(em)
GENITIVE	**eines**	**jemandes**	**niemandes**

Note

1. **Jemand** and **niemand** may add the endings **-en** and **-em** for the accusative and dative, respectively, but it is not necessary:

   Ich habe **jemand** (or **jemanden**) gesehen.   I've seen someone.

2. The word **man** (not to be confused with **der Mann**) is used for vague or general reference, meaning "someone or other" or "they," "one," "everybody," etc. In English, this is often expressed with *you* when not referring to a specific person:

   Man soll nicht zu schnell fahren.   You shouldn't drive too fast.

ÜBUNGEN

A. Replace each noun with the appropriate pronoun.

EXAMPLE: Die Dame sah den Herrn. *Sie sah ihn.*

1. Der Herr will den Wagen kaufen. _____

2. Das Kleid gefällt der Dame. _____

3. Die Studenten lernen die Sprache. _____

4. Die Verkäuferin muß die Preise auswendig lernen. _____

5. Die Schallplatte kostet zu viel. _____

6. Das Mädchen schreibt das Wort an der Tafel. _____

7. Der Kellner bringt dem Gast die Speisekarte. _____

8. Die Familie wird mit dem Bus fahren. _____

9. Mutter spricht mit meinem Bruder. _____

10. Der Polizist hilft dem Kind. _____

11. Meine Tante hat den Handschuh verloren. _____

12. Die Blumen sind für die Dame. _____

13. Dem Haus fehlt das Dach. _____

14. Der Dieb ging ans Haus. _____

15. Der Junge liegt in dem Bett. _____

B. Write the correct form of the pronoun in parentheses.

1. (wir)   Das macht _____ Spaß!

2. (du)   Vater will mit _____ sprechen.

3. (ihr)   Der Lehrer sucht _____.

4. (er)   Wer hat _____ das Geld gegeben?

5. (Sie)   Wie geht es _____?

6. (sie = she)   Ich werde _____ antworten.

7. (ich)   Ursel sitzt hinter _____.

8. (niemand)   Die Leute haben _____ gesehen.

9. (du)   Hier ist ein Geschenk für _____.

10. (man)   Das kann _____ nicht tun!

11. (sie = they) Frau Schmidt hat _____ gerufen.

12. (es)   Wir haben _____ gestern gesehen.

13. (ihr)   Der Mann zeigt _____ den Weg.

14. (jemand)   Der Bauer spricht mit _____.

15. (wir)   Was wollen Sie _____ sagen?

C. Complete each sentence by writing a pronoun in the proper form to represent the noun in parentheses.

1. (der Tanz)   _____ war interessant.

2. (der Sport)   Was hält er (von) _____?

3. (das Pferd)   _____ läuft über das Feld.

4. (der Schlüssel)   Der Gast sucht _____.

5. (der Eimer)   Der Bauer stellt _____ unter die Kuh.

6. (das Feld)   Eine Mauer geht (um) _____.

7. (die Geschichte)   Wir haben _____ schon gehört.

8. (die Großmutter)   Die Karte ist von _____.

9. (die Ferien)   Wir freuen uns (auf) _____.

10. (die Eltern)   Er bleibt bei _____.

11. (das Fenster)   Paul macht _____ zu.

12. (die Rechnung)   Der Kellner gab _____ dem Herrn.

13. (der Schnee)   Wir sehen _____ gern.

14. (der Tisch)   Die Gäste im Restaurant setzen sich (an) _____.

15. (der Vater)   Ich schreibe einen Brief an _____.

D. Replace the pronoun in each sentence with the correct forms of the pronouns in parentheses, making other changes in the sentence where necessary.

1. Die Dame sah uns in der Stadt.

(Sie) ------------------- (er) --------------------- (du) ----------------------

2. Hier ist eine Tasse Kaffee für sie.

(ich) ------------------ (ihr) --------------------- (wir) ---------------------

3. Mutter gab mir ein Stück Brot.

(er) ------------------- (du) --------------------- (sie = she) ----------------

4. Die Leute können sich darauf verlassen.

(ich) ------------------ (wir) --------------------- (er) ---------------------

5. Wir können nicht gut hören.

(man) ------------------ (ich) --------------------- (er) ---------------------

6. Meine Schwester sieht ihn.

(jemand) ---------------- (ihr) --------------------- (Sie) ---------------------

7. Diese Uhr gehört ihr.

(du) ------------------- (ich) --------------------- (niemand) ----------------

8. Der Lärm gefällt uns nicht.

(sie = they) ------------- (man) --------------------- (ich) -------------------

9. Die Eltern gehen nicht ohne dich.

(wir) ------------------- (ihr) --------------------- (er) ---------------------

10. Mutter hat einen Brief von uns.

(ich) ------------------- (jemand) ----------------- (sie = she) ----------------

E. Complete the answer to each question, using pronouns to refer to the nouns in the questions.

1. Kann man sich auf diesen Wagen verlassen?

Nein, --.

2. Sie haben meinen Bruder in Deutschland kennengelernt, nicht wahr?

Ja, ---.

3. Kommt ihr Bruder mit Frau Schmidt?

Ja, er ---.

4. Kann Robert auf die Frage antworten?

Nein, --.

5. Wollen die Kinder zwischen den Häusern spielen?

Ja, ---.

6. Inge schreibt etwas über die Geschichte, nicht wahr?

Ja, ---.

7. Haben Sie seinen Geburtstag vergessen?

Nein, --.

8. Was gibt's? Hast du jemand gesehen?

Nein, _____.

9. Wer hat das Fenster aufgemacht?

Hans _____.

10. Was liegt auf dem Tisch?

Das Buch _____.

F. Translate into English.

1. Sie gab es ihm. _____

2. Wo ist der Brief? Hier ist er. _____

3. Hier kommt das Mädchen. Haben Sie es kennengelernt? _____

_____

4. Wir wollen ihm helfen. _____

5. Er ruft euch. _____

6. Das kann man nicht tun. _____

7. Jemand hat es gesagt. _____

8. Niemand soll die Menschen hassen. _____

9. Können wir daran glauben? _____

10. Ich werde ihnen alles erklären. _____

11. Sie fragt nach dir. _____

12. Ihr dankt uns dafür. _____

13. Du wirst sie mir zeigen. _____

14. Er erinnert sich an Sie. _____

15. Wir fangen morgen damit an. _____

G. Translate into German.

1. Do you see her? _____

2. Give it to him! _____

3. We know nothing about it. _____

4. Is there any mail for me? _____

5. Yes, we know them. _____

6. They are reading about that. _____

7. She is talking about him. _____

8. Do you like it? (Does it please you?) _____

9. I told it to her. _____

10. We are depending on that. _____

14. RELATIVE AND INTERROGATIVE PRONOUNS

RELATIVE PRONOUNS

A. The relative pronoun joins a subordinate clause to the rest of the sentence. In English, the relative pronouns are the various forms of *who, what, that*. In German, the relative pronouns are the same as the definite articles, except in the genitive case and the dative plural.

DECLENSION OF RELATIVE PRONOUNS

Case	Singular			Plural
NOMINATIVE	der	die	das	die
ACCUSATIVE	den	die	das	die
DATIVE	dem	der	dem	denen
GENITIVE	dessen	deren	dessen	deren

B. The relative pronoun always refers to a noun or pronoun that appears in the sentence. The word that the relative pronoun replaces is its antecedent.

C. The relative pronoun must:

(1) agree in number and gender with its antecedent:

der Mann, **der** mit Franz spricht   the man who is speaking with Frank
<u>antecedent</u>

die Damen, **die** ins Zimmer kommen   the ladies who are coming into the room
<u>antecedent</u>

(2) be in whatever case is needed within its own clause:

Der Film, **den** ich gestern gesehen habe,   The film that I saw yesterday was very
<u>antecedent</u>
    war sehr interessant.   interesting.

The accusative, **den,** is used because it is the direct object of the verb in the relative clause. This is readily seen if the clause itself is reconstructed as a complete sentence: „Ich habe gestern **den** Film gesehen."

D. (1) **Welcher** may sometimes be used as a relative pronoun in place of **der,** but this use is usually considered rather awkward:

der Film, **welchen** ich gesehen habe   the film that I saw

Welcher has the same endings as **der,** except that it has no separate form for the genitive case when it is used as a relative pronoun.

(2) **Welcher** is especially useful to avoid confusing repetitions:

Die, die die Bücher haben, . . .   ⎫
Die, **welche** die Bücher haben, . . .   ⎬   Those who have the books . . .
                                 ⎭

Der, der den Mann kennt, . . .   ⎫
Der, **welcher** den Mann kennt, . . .   ⎬   The one who knows the man . . .
                                 ⎭

E. The relative pronoun (*that, which, whom,* etc.) is often omitted in English but never in German:

> Die Leute, **die** wir kennengelernt haben, waren freundlich.
>
> The people (that, whom) we met were friendly.

F. Relative clauses have the same word order as all other subordinate clauses (see Lesson 23)—the finite verb goes at the end of the clause:

> Der Herr, **dem ich das Buch *gab,*** ist mein Onkel.
>
> The gentleman to whom I gave the book is my uncle.

INTERROGATIVE PRONOUNS

The interrogative pronoun is used to ask a question or when no antecedent appears in the sentence:

> **Wer** hat es getan? Ich weiß nicht, **wer** es getan hat.
>
> Who did it? I don't know who did it.

DECLENSION OF INTERROGATIVE PRONOUNS

Case	Persons	Things
NOMINATIVE	wer	was
ACCUSATIVE	wen	was
DATIVE	wem	—
GENITIVE	wessen	wessen

Note

1. As we have seen, the form of the German relative pronoun is determined by the number and gender of its antecedent. The interrogative pronoun, however, has no antecedent to refer to; hence, it has no distinct forms for singular and plural or for the three genders. The forms of the interrogative pronoun distinguish only between *who?* (**wer?**) and *what?* (**was?**):

> **Wessen** Bücher sind diese?
>
> Whose books are these?

2. **Wer** is always used with a singular verb. **Welches** may be used with either a singular or plural verb to ask *who?* or *which?*

> **Welches ist** das Buch, das Sie gelesen haben?
>
> Which is the book that you read?

> **Welches sind** die Bücher, die Sie gelesen haben?
>
> Which are the books that you read?

> **Welches ist** das Kind, dem Sie das Buch gaben?
>
> Who is the child to whom you gave the book?

> **Welches sind** die Kinder, denen Sie das Buch gaben?
>
> Who are the children to whom you gave the book?

3. **Wer** and **was** are used for the English pronouns *who, which,* and *that* in sentences that are not really questions but do not have specific antecedents:

> Ich weiß nichts, **was** dir helfen kann.
>
> I know nothing *that* (*which*) can help you.

Sie fragt mich, **wer** heute kommt.

She asks me *who* is coming today.

Das ist alles, **was** er kann.

That's all (*that*) he can do.

Der Wagen ist blau, **was** mir gefällt.

The car is blue, *which* pleases me.

Wer keine Karte hat, darf nicht einsteigen.

Whoever (*Anyone who*) does not have a ticket may not get aboard.

4. When a form of **was** is used with a preposition (except **ohne**), **was** is replaced with **wo-**, which is prefixed to the preposition: **womit, wofür,** etc. (This construction is also usually used for the missing dative form of **was.**) If the preposition begins with a vowel, an extra **-r-** is inserted to help pronunciation: **worauf, worin,** etc.

The **wo-** construction is not used in referring to persons:

Worauf warten Sie?

What are you waiting for?

But:

Auf *wen* warten Sie?

For whom are you waiting?

5. In referring to a time expression, **wo** may be used instead of the relative pronoun:

Die Zeit, **wo** es nur wenige Autos gab, ist jetzt vorbei.

The time when there were only a few cars is now past.

6. Bear in mind that in English *who* is used both as a relative pronoun (the man *who* is coming) and as an interrogative pronoun (*Who* is coming?), but German has different words for these two uses. In German, the interrogative pronoun must be used even when a question is not being asked, *if* an antecedent is not expressed in the sentence:

Ich weiß, **wer** kommt.

I know who is coming.

ÜBUNGEN

A. Supply the correct relative pronoun.

1. Die Dame, _____ hier wohnt, ist nicht zu Hause.

2. Der Junge, mit _____ ich spreche, heißt Hans Müller.

3. Die Uhr, _____ ich kaufte, geht nicht richtig.

4. Wo sind die Karten, _____ Sie hatten?

5. Der Kellner, _____ Vater rief, kam an den Tisch.

6. Dort ist der Herr, _____ die Kamera gehört.

7. Das Zimmer, in _____ wir kamen, war sehr klein.

8. Gibt es Zeitungen, _____ wir lesen können?

9. Vater trägt heute eine Krawatte, _____ sehr schön ist.

10. Die Leute, _____ diese Sachen gefallen, sind selten.

11. Das Buch ist auf dem Tisch, _____ in der Ecke steht.

12. Das Café, in _____ wir aßen, war nahe beim Bahnhof.

13. Ich habe viele Bilder gesehen, _____ mir gefallen haben.

14. Hans hat einen Ball, mit _____ wir spielen dürfen.

15. Hier ist das Geschenk, _____ Herr Schmidt mir gab.

B. Supply the correct form of the interrogative pronoun referring to *persons*.

1. _____ haben Sie gesehen?

2. _____ steht an der Tür?

3. _____ gab er das Buch?

4. Ich weiß nicht, _____ kommt.

5. Mit _____ wollen Sie sprechen?

6. Er will wissen, über _____ wir sprechen.

7. _____ Hut ist dies?

8. Wissen Sie, _____ das Haus gehört?

9. _____ hat ihn gerufen?

10. _____ kann die Aufgabe übersetzen?

Supply the interrogative pronoun referring to *things*.

11. _____ haben Sie gesehen?

12. _____ steht vor der Tür?

13. _____ gab er dem Herrn?

14. _____ gibt's?

15. Ich weiß doch, _____ er will.

Combine the preposition in parentheses with the correct form of the interrogative pronoun referring to *things*.

16. (auf) _____ warten Sie denn?

17. (an) Wissen Sie, _____ wir uns erinnern sollen?

18. (für) _____ interessieren sich die Studenten?

19. (nach) _____ fragt die Dame?

20. (um) Ich weiß nicht, _____ er bittet.

C. Supply the correct form of the relative or interrogative pronoun, according to context.

1. Kennen Sie den Jungen, mit _____ ich ins Kino ging?

2. Mit _____ gehen Sie ins Kino?

3. Kennen Sie das Mädchen, _____ singt?

4. Wissen Sie, _____ singt?

5. Ich sehe den Herrn, _____ Sie suchen.

6. Ich weiß schon, _____ Sie suchen.

7. Die Gäste, _____ wir halfen, danken uns.

8. _____ haben wir geholfen?

9. Die Herren, _____ Stimmen wir hören, stehen im nächsten Zimmer.

10. _____ Haus ist da drüben?

11. Ich weiß nicht, _____ Hut dies ist.

12. Er hat nicht gesehen, _____ sie das Buch gab.

13. Wie heißt die Geschichte, _____ er übersetzt hat?

14. Wissen Sie, bei _____ er bleibt?

15. Der Tisch, auf _____ der Brief liegt, steht in der Ecke.

D. Combine the two sentences, using a relative or interrogative pronoun.

EXAMPLES: Ich spreche mit dem Mann. Er ist Amerikaner.
Der Mann, mit dem ich spreche, ist Amerikaner.

Wer hat das Buch? Er weiß nicht.
Er weiß nicht, wer das Buch hat.

1. Wir grüßen die Dame. Die Dame kommt ins Zimmer. _____

_____

2. Wessen Tasse ist dies? Der Kellner fragt uns. _____

_____

3. Die Autos gefallen den Jungen. Die Jungen haben wenig Geld. _____

_____

4. Der Student sitzt in der Bibliothek. Ich kenne ihn. _____

_____

5. Günther hat den Ring gefunden. Ich habe den Ring verloren. _____

_____

6. Wir fahren mit dem Bus. Der Bus fährt nach Bremen. _____

_____

7. Wem gefallen solche Bilder? Der Lehrer wollte wissen. _____

_____

8. Das Orchester spielt. Die Musik ist schön. _____

_____

9. Herr Müller trägt heute eine Krawatte. Die Krawatte ist neu. _____

_____

10. Der Kellner brachte uns Kaffee. Der Kaffee war kalt. _____

_____

E. Replace the noun in italics with each of the nouns in parentheses, making any changes in the sentence that may be required by the substitution.

EXAMPLE: Hier kommt der *Herr*, der mich anruft. (die Damen, ...)
Hier kommen die Damen, die mich anrufen.

1. Der *Schlüssel*, den ich ihm gab, ist neu.

(das Buch) _____

(die Uhr) _____

(die Anzüge)   --

2. Die *Herren*, mit denen er spricht, sind Gäste.

(die Mädchen)   --

(der Junge)   --

(der Bauer)   --

3. Wir gehen ins *Restaurant*, das in der Goethestraße ist.

(das Kino)   --

(der Garten)   --

(die Bibliothek)   --

4. Das *Hotel*, das die Leute suchen, ist nicht weit von hier.

(der Bahnhof)   --

(das Krankenhaus)   --

(der Park)   --

5. Wir fahren durch viele *Dörfer*, die sehr schön sind.

(die Wälder)   --

(die Städte)   --

(die Berge)   --

6. Ich trank die *Milch*, die auf dem Tisch stand.

(der Kaffee)   --

(das Wasser)   --

(der Tee)   --

7. Da drüben ist das *Mädchen*, das ich angerufen habe.

(der Doktor)   --

(die Frau)   --

(der Polizist)   --

8. Die *Handschuhe*, die die Verkäuferin der Dame zeigt, sind rot.

(die Krawatte)   --

(der Mantel)   --

(die Strümpfe)   --

9. Wir wollen der *Dame* helfen, die den Ring verloren hat.

(das Kind)   --

(der Herr)   --

(das Mädchen)   --

10. Wir besuchen die *Familie*, die in diesem Haus wohnt.

(der Bauer)   --

(mein Onkel)   --

(unsere Eltern)   --

F. Translate the English into German.

1. *Whom* haben Sie angerufen? ------------------------

2. Die Gäste, *whom* ich kennengelernt habe, kamen aus München. ------------------------

3. *To whom* gab der Junge die Zeitung? ------------------------

4. Die Dame fragt, *to whom* sie die Karte zeigen soll. ------------------------

5. *On what* kann man sich verlassen? ------------------------

6. *On whom* kann man sich verlassen? ------------------------

7. *On what* setzt sich Hans? ------------------------

8. Wissen Sie, *for what* er sich interessiert? ------------------------

9. Der Tag, *on which* wir nach Hause kamen, war schön. ------------------------

10. Die Tiere, *which* in diesem Wald wohnen, sind wild. ------------------------

11. Hier ist ein Tisch, *on which* er seinen Teller stellen kann. ------------------------

12. Die Dame, *whose* Kind im Krankenhaus ist, bleibt bei uns. ------------------------

13. Die Städte, *which* wir besuchen wollen, sind in Westdeutschland. ------------------------

14. *About what* haben sie gesprochen? ------------------------

15. Die Straße, *over which* die Jungen gelaufen sind, hat viel Verkehr. ------------------------

G. Translate into English.

1. Die Mauer, auf der das Kind sitzt, ist nicht sehr hoch. ------------------------

2. Der Zug, mit dem wir fuhren, ist spät angekommen. ------------------------

3. Ich weiß, wessen Handschuh das ist. ------------------------

4. Worauf warten Sie denn? ------------------------

5. Mit wem spricht ihr Bruder? ------------------------

6. Der Hund, der soviel Lärm macht, gehört nicht mir. ------------------------

7. Das Kind trinkt die Milch, welche die Mutter ihm gibt. ------------------------

8. Der Garten, den wir sahen, hatte viele schöne Blumen. ------------------------

9. Worauf freuen sie sich? ------------------------

10. Die Aufgabe, mit der wir beginnen, ist kurz. ------------------------

11. Welches sind die Kinder, denen der Film gefällt? ------------------------

12. Wo ist das Buch, nach dem das Mädchen fragt? _____

_____

13. Die Dame, deren Kamera er hat, kommt bald zurück. _____

_____

14. Das Frühstück, das der Junge hatte, war sehr gut. _____

_____

15. Ich habe eine Uhr, auf die ich mich verlassen kann. _____

_____

The famous "beetle"—still a familiar sight in traffic the world over—was produced in the *Volkswagen* plant at Wolfburg, West Germany, until 1978. (It is now manufactured in Mexico.)

15. REVIEW OF PART II—NOUNS AND PRONOUNS

WORTSCHATZ

In der Stadt

die **Abteilung, -en,** department
die **Allee, -n,** avenue, boulevard
der **Angestellte, -n,** employee (in an office)
der **Anzug, ⸚e,** suit
der **Arzt, ⸚e,** doctor, physician
der **Ausländer, -,** foreigner
der **Bahnhof, ⸚e,** train station
die **Bank, ⸚e,** bench
der **Beamte, -n,** governmental employee or official
der **Besucher, -,** visitor
die **Brücke, -n,** bridge
der **Brunnen, -,** fountain, well
das **Denkmal, -mäler,** monument
der **Dom, -e,** cathedral
der **Fahrstuhl, ⸚e,** elevator
der **Film, -e,** film, movie
der **Fluß, ⸚sse,** river
der **Fußweg, -e,** footpath
das **Gebäude, -,** building
der **Handschuh, -e,** glove
das **Hotel, -s,** hotel
das **Kino, -s,** movie theater
die **Kirche, -n,** church
der **Kleiderstoff, -e,** dress material
das **Krankenhaus, ⸚er,** hospital

die **Krankenschwester, -n,** nurse
der **Kunde, -n,** customer
der **Marktplatz, ⸚e,** marketplace
das **Museum, -s** (*or* **Museen**), museum
der **Park, -s** (*or* **-e**), park
das **Rathaus, ⸚er,** city hall
der **Ratsherr, -en,** city councilman
der **Ratskeller, -,** restaurant (usually in the basement of a **Rathaus**)
das **Restaurant, -s,** restaurant
die **Rolltreppe, -n,** escalator
das **Schaufenster, -,** shop window, display window
das **Schauspiel, -e,** (stage) play
der **Schauspieler, -,** actor
die **Spielwaren,** toys
die **Stadt, ⸚e,** city
die **Statue, -n,** statue
der **Stock, ⸚e** ⎫ floor, story (of
das **Stockwerk, -e** ⎭ building)
die **Straße, -n,** street
der **Teich, -e,** pond
das **Theater, -,** theater
der **Verkäufer, -,** sales clerk
die **Verkäuferin, -nen,** saleslady
das **Warenhaus, ⸚er,** department store

Note

1. **Angestellte** and **Beamte** are adjectives used as nouns. Thus, they have strong or weak endings in accordance with the rules for the declension of adjectives: **ein junger Angestellt*er*, viele deutsche Beamt*e*.**

2. **Kunde** adds **-n** in every case except the nominative singular: **dem Kunde*n*, die Kunde*n*.**

ÜBUNGEN

A. Write the correct form of the definite article.

1. _____ Rathaus ist neben dem Marktplatz.

2. Wir wollen heute abend _____ neuen Film sehen.

3. _____ Verkäuferin verkauft _____ Herrn ein Paar Schuhe.

4. Ich habe _____ Dom besucht.

5. Die Dame kaufte _____ grauen Anzug.

6. Haben Sie _____ Museum gesehen?

7. _____ Krankenhaus ist nicht weit von hier.

8. Die Kinder wollen sich _____ Spielwaren ansehen.

9. _____ Brücke ist ganz neu.

10. Ich werde _____ Angestellten helfen.

B. Write the correct form of the word in parentheses.

1. (ein)   Er hat _____ Buch gekauft.

2. (kein)   In diesem Park wird der Besucher _____ Bänke finden.

3. (ein)   Jetzt kommt er aus _____ Restaurant heraus.

4. (ein)   Gibt es im Warenhaus _____ Bücherabteilung?

5. (kein)   Im Hotel haben wir _____ Angestellten gesehen.

6. (ein)   Wir wollen _____ gutes Hotel finden.

7. (kein)   Im Ratskeller sieht man heute _____ Ratsherren.

8. (ein)   In dieser Stadt ist _____ großer Dom.

9. (ein)   Der Herr spricht mit _____ Verkäufer.

10. (kein)   Sie hat _____ Ausländern das Denkmal gezeigt.

C. Change each sentence to the plural.

EXAMPLE: Er will sich morgen das neue Schauspiel ansehen.
Sie wollen sich morgen *die neuen Schauspiele* ansehen.

1. Der Ratsherr ißt im Ratskeller. _____

_____

2. Der Brunnen im Park ist sehr schön. _____

_____

3. Der Ausländer sieht die Brücke an. _____

_____

4. Wo ist das Theater? _____

5. Haben Sie das Museum besucht? _____

6. Das Gebäude ist aber groß! _____

7. Es gibt einen Teich im Park. _____

_____

8. Der Kleiderstoff gefällt der Dame. _____

_____

9. Ich möchte den Dom sehen. _____

10. Der Kunde fährt mit dem Fahrstuhl. _____

_____

D. Change the sentences by replacing each italicized expression with a pronoun.

EXAMPLES: Er fährt *mit dem Zug.*
Er fährt *damit.*

Dein Hut ist schön.
Er ist schön.

1. Haben Sie *diesen Film* gesehen? _____

2. Ich habe *meinen Handschuh* verloren. _____

3. Wir können *das nächste Stockwerk* mit der Rolltreppe erreichen. _____

_____

4. Wo haben Sie *den Anzug* gekauft? _____

5. *Die Kunden* wollen *in die Bücherabteilung* gehen. _____

_____

6. Er wartet auf *den Verkäufer.* _____

7. *Die Frau* sitzt *auf einer Bank.* _____

8. Sollen wir uns *das Schauspiel* ansehen? (*Watch word order!*) _____

_____

9. *Die Besucher* fahren *durch die Stadt.* _____

10. *Diese Allee* ist breit und lang. _____

11. Vielleicht kann sie *der Krankenschwester* helfen. _____

_____

12. *Der Kunde* spricht mit *der Verkäuferin.* _____

13. *Hinter dem Museum* ist ein Fluß. _____

14. *Alle Hotels* haben keinen Platz mehr. _____

15. Ich kann nicht *dem Angestellten* antworten. (*Watch word order!*) _____

_____

16. Können Sie *die Schauspieler* hören? _____

17. *Diese Statue* steht *neben dem Brunnen.* _____

18. *Die Ausländer* gehen *auf den Marktplatz.* _____

19. *Das Restaurant* ist *am Bahnhof.* _____

20. *Diese Kirche* ist doch sehr alt. _____

E. Combine the two clauses into a single sentence by using a relative pronoun.

EXAMPLE: Ich habe die Zeitung gelesen. Die Zeitung war auf dem Tisch.
Ich habe die Zeitung gelesen, die auf dem Tisch war.

1. Dort ist der Park. Wir werden durch den Park spazieren. _____

_____

2. Der Fluß fließt unter der Brücke. Der Fluß ist tief. _____

_____

3. Die Verkäuferin zeigte der Dame die Kleiderstoffe. Die Kleiderstoffe gefielen der Dame nicht. _ _
_____

_____

4. Ich habe einen Angestellten kennengelernt. Der Angestellte arbeitet im Hotel. _ _ _ _ _ _ _ _ _ _ _ _
_____

5. Die Ausländer kamen aus Amerika. Sie half den Ausländern. _
_____

6. Die Spielwaren sind teuer. Sie sind im Schaufenster. _
_____

7. Der Angestellte heißt Herr Müller. Ich sprach mit dem Angestellten. _ _ _ _ _ _ _ _ _ _ _ _ _ _ _ _
_____

8. Gestern abend sahen die Gäste einen Film. Der Film war amerikanisch. _ _ _ _ _ _ _ _ _ _ _ _ _ _
_____

9. Die Ausländer werden die Gebäude besuchen. Die Ausländer werden eine Kirche, das Rathaus, und ein Museum besuchen. _
_____

10. Der Verkäufer wollte dem Kunden die Handschuhe verkaufen. Die Handschuhe waren sehr teuer. _
_____

F. Construct questions for which the following might be answers:

1. Man kann einen Anzug in einem Warenhaus kaufen. _
_____

2. Fragen Sie doch den Angestellten! _
_____

3. Das Gebäude hat fünf Stockwerke. _

4. In einem Theater sieht man Schauspiele. _
_____

5. Eine Allee ist oft schöner als eine Straße. _
_____

6. Ich habe mit dem Ausländer gesprochen. _
_____

7. Er will mit dem Fahrstuhl fahren. _

8. Die Spielwarenabteilung gefällt besonders den Kindern. _
_____

9. Er antwortet dem Besucher. _

10. Die Dame will sich die Kleiderstoffe ansehen. --------------------

----

G. Replace the words in italics with the nouns in parentheses, making other changes in the sentence where necessary.

EXAMPLE: Ich sehe *das Haus*. (die Brücke, der Laden, der Fluß)
Ich sehe *die Brücke*. Ich sehe *den Laden*. Ich sehe *den Fluß*.

1. Die Gäste gehen in *das Restaurant*.

(der Ratskeller) --------------------

(die Stadt) --------------------

(das Gebäude) --------------------

2. Wir werden *das Museum* besuchen.

(der Marktplatz) --------------------

(das Theater) --------------------

(der Dom) --------------------

3. Ich helfe *dem Arzt*.

(der Kunde) --------------------

(der Ausländer) --------------------

(die Verkäuferin) --------------------

4. Die Ausländer kommen aus *dem Hotel*.

(der Bahnhof) --------------------

(die Bücherabteilung) --------------------

(der Park) --------------------

5. Wieviele *Hotels* gibt es in dieser Stadt?

(das Gebäude) --------------------

(die Brücke) --------------------

(der Brunnen) --------------------

6. Wo ist *das Hotel*? Es ist da drüben.

(der Brunnen) --------------------

(die Allee) --------------------

(der Fluß) --------------------

7. Fahren wir mit *dem Fahrstuhl*? Ja, wir fahren damit.

(die Rolltreppe) --------------------

(der Bus) --------------------

(das Auto) --------------------

8. Fragt er *den Verkäufer*? Ja, er fragt ihn.

(der Angestellte) --------------------

(der Kunde) _____

(die Ratsherren) _____

9. Haben Sie *die Kirche* gesehen? Ja, ich habe sie gesehen.

(der Teich) _____

(die Statue) _____

(der Film) _____

10. Gibt sie *der Verkäuferin* das Geld? Ja, sie gibt es ihr.

(der Besucher) _____

(die Krankenschwester) _____

(der Schauspieler) _____

H. Translate into English.

1. Die Spielwarenabteilung ist im zweiten Stock. _____

_____

2. In dieser Stadt gibt es eine neue Brücke über dem Fluß. _____

_____

3. Das Denkmal steht im Park zwischen dem Brunnen und dem Teich. _____

_____

4. Im Warenhaus sieht man viele Schaufenster. _____

_____

5. Der Besucher kann viele alte Gebäude in Deutschland sehen. _____

_____

6. Den Ausländern, mit denen wir sprachen, gefiel das Konzert nicht. _____

_____

7. In einer deutschen Stadt sieht man mehrere Hotels, Warenhäuser, Kirchen, und Restaurants.

_____

_____

8. Der Dom, den wir gestern besuchten, war sehr schön. _____

_____

9. Mit wem haben Sie im Restaurant gesprochen? _____

_____

10. Man soll auch das Museum besuchen. _____

_____

11. Auf der Seite des Fußweges, der durch den Park geht, sind Bänke. _____

_____

12. Hier haben wir schon zwei Schauspiele gesehen. _____

_____

13. Der Ratskeller ist ein Restaurant, in dem die Ratsherren oft aßen. _____

_____

14. Man findet in einer deutschen Stadt nicht nur große Gebäude, sondern auch einige Parks._____

_____

15. Welches sind denn die Statuen, die Sie gesehen haben? _____

_____

16. Heute abend wollen sie einen Spaziergang durch den Park machen. _____

_____

17. Wessen Handschuhe hat er in der Hand? _____

_____

18. Wonach fragt der Ausländer? _____

_____

19. Der Angestellte im Hotel hat gar nichts davon gesagt. _____

_____

20. Das Warenhaus, in dem ich den Anzug kaufte, ist da drüben. _____

_____

I. Translate into German.

1. Do you want to take the elevator? _____

_____

2. Which is the theater he was asking about? _____

_____

3. The guests are talking to the clerk. _____

_____

4. The customer did not like the dress materials. _____

_____

5. The nurse has to ask the doctor about that. _____

_____

6. We wanted to eat in the Ratskeller. _____

_____

7. The museum is on the next street. _____

_____

8. The water of the pond is clear and cold. _____

_____

9. I saw the monument which is in the middle of the marketplace. _____

_____

10. There's a lot of traffic on the avenue. _____

_____

11. We went from the cathedral to the station. _____

_____

12. How many churches are there in this city? _____

_____

13. What are you supposed to eat this with? _____

_____

14. The play we saw yesterday evening was very interesting. _____

_____

15. Whose gloves do you have? _____

_____

16. The children are playing with them. _____

_____

17. Which customer is the sales clerk helping now? _____

_____

18. The bench on which they are sitting is not far from here. _____

_____

19. The employee answered the foreigners. _____

_____

20. The buildings in the marketplace are all very old. _____

_____

Part III—Adjectives, Adverbs, and Prepositions

16. ADJECTIVES: STRONG AND WEAK DECLENSIONS

THE STRONG DECLENSION

Any adjective that is followed by a noun has a special ending to show how it is related to that noun. When an adjective follows either an article or a substitute for an article (a limiting word), the adjective has weak endings (see pages 116–117). When the adjective is not preceded by a limiting word, the adjective has strong endings.

STRONG ENDINGS OF ADJECTIVES

Case	SINGULAR			PLURAL
	Class of Nouns			*(all genders)*
	der nouns	**die** nouns	**das** nouns	**die**
NOMINATIVE	**-er**	**-e**	**-es**	**-e**
ACCUSATIVE	**-en**	**-e**	**-es**	**-e**
DATIVE	**-em**	**-er**	**-em**	**-en**
GENITIVE	*-en*	**-er**	*-en*	**-er**

Note

1. The strong endings of the adjective are the same as the declensional endings of the definite article except in the genitive singular, where the masculine and neuter ending **-es** is replaced by **-en.**

2. The endings that are added to the article or adjective indicate how the noun is used. For example, the **-er** on an article or an adjective preceding a **der** noun (**der Kaffee; guter Kaffee**) shows that the noun is the subject of a verb.

USE OF THE STRONG ENDINGS

The strong endings are used on adjectives as follows:

A. When there is no article or limiting word:

| Er trinkt **kaltes** Wasser gern. | He likes to drink cold water. |

B. After **kein**-words when they have no ending:

| Heute ist **ein schöner** Tag. | Today is a beautiful day. |
| In dieser Stadt haben wir **kein gutes** Restaurant. | We do not have a good restaurant in this city. |

C. After numerals:

| Er kauft **drei neue** Bücher. | He's buying three new books. |

D. After indefinite numerical adjectives like **mehrere, einige, ein paar, viele, wenige, andere** (but weak endings are used after **alle**):

Viele alt*e* Wagen sind auf der Straße.   Many old cars are on the street.

Note

1. Predicate adjectives (which follow the noun) have no ending:

Der Mann ist *gut*.

2. The strong endings are never used on an article and an adjective at the same time:

kalt**es** Wasser   cold water

But:

das kalt*e* Wasser   the cold water

3. If one adjective has a strong ending, all other adjectives preceding the noun will also have strong endings: **ein guter, großer, armer Mann.**

WORTSCHATZ

ander-, other
bekannt, well-known
beliebt, popular
besonder, special
einfach, simple

einzig, single, the only
frei, free
furchtbar, terrible
genug (*indecl.*), enough
hungrig, hungry

interessant, interesting
krank, sick
müde, tired
zufrieden, satisfied

Die Farben (*Colors*)

blau, blue
gelb, yellow
grün, green

rosa, rose, pink
rot, red

schwarz, black
weiß, white

Note

The adjective **genug** is indeclinable; that is, it never has any endings.

ÜBUNGEN

A. Add the ending to the adjective where it is required.

1. Die Aufgabe ist ganz einfach_____.

2. Der Herr war nicht damit zufrieden_____.

3. Ich lese jetzt ein interessant_____ Buch.

4. Ein krank_____ Junge soll zu Hause bleiben.

5. Dafür braucht der Student ein besonder_____ Heft.

6. In Köln ist ein bekannt_____ Dom.

7. Ein grün_____ Licht bedeutet frei_____ Fahrt.

8. Im Sommer sieht man weiß_____, rot_____, und gelb_____ Blumen.

9. Hungrig_____ Menschen sind nicht zufrieden_____.

10. Anstatt besonder_____ Freude hat er nur furchtbar_____ Pech.

B. Replace the adjective in each sentence with the adjectives in parentheses.

EXAMPLE: Er hat ein grünes Buch.   (rot)   *Er hat ein rotes Buch.*

1. Das Mädchen sieht müde aus.   (krank, zufrieden)

----

2. Hier ist ein roter Apfel.   (gelb, grün)

----

3. Die Dame kaufte ein Paar schwarze Handschuhe.   (weiß, gelb)

----

4. Wir sprechen von kranken Menschen.   (bekannt, interessant)

----

5. Das Mädchen spielt ein beliebtes Lied.   (besonder, einfach)

C. Write the correct form of the adjective in parentheses.

1. (interessant)   In der Bibliothek sind viele _____ Bücher.

2. (einfach)   Wir haben nur ein paar _____ Aufgaben.

3. (bekannt)   Es gibt mehrere _____ Zeitungen in Deutschland.

4. (besonder)   Ich bringe einige _____ Gäste mit.

5. (furchtbar)   In der Stadt ist der Verkehr _____.

6. (krank)   Ein _____ Herr sitzt im Zimmer.

7. (schwarz)   Immer trägt er _____ Schuhe.

8. (frei)   Eine Republik gefällt _____ Menschen.

9. (hungrig)   Ein _____ Hund läuft ins Haus.

10. (rot)   Mit _____ Gesicht hat er uns gerufen.

THE WEAK DECLENSION

The weak endings are added to adjectives that follow an article or other limiting word, such as **dieser, welcher, jeder, solcher, mancher,** and **alle,** and to those following a **kein**-word when it has an ending.

WEAK ENDINGS OF ADJECTIVES

	SINGULAR			PLURAL
Case	*Class of Nouns*			*(all genders)*
	der nouns	**die** nouns	**das** nouns	**die**
NOMINATIVE	-e	-e	-e	-en
ACCUSATIVE	-en	-e	-e	-en
DATIVE	-en	-en	-en	-en
GENITIVE	-en	-en	-en	-en

Note

When the article or limiting word is used in its primary form (that is, when the article **der** is used with a **der** noun, **die** is used with a **die** noun, or **das** with a **das** noun), the adjectives following the article end in **-e.** In all other cases (including all plurals), the adjectives that follow the limiting word end in **-en.**

Der jung**e Mann** war hier.	The young man was here.

But:

Ich sah **den** jung**en Mann.**	I saw the young man.
Der Name **der** jung**en Dame** ist Weber.	The young lady's name is Weber.
Ich kaufe **das** neu**e Buch.**	I'm buying the new book.

But:

Ich kaufe **die** neu**en Bücher.**	I'm buying the new books.

WORTSCHATZ

alle, all	**hell,** light	**ruhig,** quiet
alt, old	**hoch,** high	**schlecht,** bad
ausgezeichnet, excellent	**jung,** young	**schnell,** fast
billig, cheap	**kalt,** cold	**schön,** beautiful
böse, angry, mean	**klein,** little	**schwer,** heavy
dunkel, dark	**kühl,** cool	**selten,** rare
einige } several, a few	**kurz,** short	**spät,** late
ein paar }	**lang,** long	**teuer,** expensive
falsch, false	**langsam,** slow	**tief,** deep
früh, early	**langweilig,** boring, dull	**viel,** much, a lot (of); *pl.,*
ganz, complete, whole	**laut,** loud	many
gewöhnlich, usual, customary	**mehrere,** several	**warm,** warm
groß, large, tall	**nett,** nice	**wenig,** (a) little; *pl.,* few
gut, good	**neu,** new	**wichtig,** important
halb, half	**recht,** right	**wunderbar,** wonderful
heiß, hot	**richtig,** correct	

Note

1. When **dunkel** is used with an ending, the **e** is dropped:

    eine **dunkle** Nacht   einen **dunklen** Wagen

2. The **c** is dropped from **hoch** whenever an ending is added:

    ein *hoh*es Haus

3. In the singular, **viel** and **wenig** regularly have endings only in the genitive case. In other cases, **viel** and **wenig** for any gender usually have no ending:

Für uns gibt es **wenig** Arbeit mehr.	There is little work for us any more.
Wir haben **viel** Regen in diesem Monat gehabt.	We've had a lot of rain this month.

The outstanding exception is the expression **vielen Dank** (*many thanks*).

ÜBUNGEN

A. Complete the sentence by writing the correct form of the adjective in parentheses.

1. (richtig)   Er hat die _____ Antwort.

2. (ruhig)   Der Gast bestellt ein _____ Zimmer.

3. (bekannt)   Wir singen _____ Lieder.

4. (groß)   Geben Sie dem _____ Jungen das Buch.

5. (dunkel)   In _____ Nacht hörten wir etwas.

6. (schön)   Wir haben jetzt _____ Wetter.

7. (kalt)   Es war ein _____ Tag im Winter.

8. (hungrig)   Ein _____ Kind ist selten ruhig.

9. (teuer)   Sie ist nicht mit den _____ Büchern zufrieden.

10. (halb)   Eine _____ Stunde habe ich schon gewartet.

11. (einzig)   Ich esse in dem _____ Café der Stadt.

12. (laut)   Der _____ Hund muß ruhig werden.

13. (interessant)   Sie haben uns eine _____ Geschichte erzählt.

14. (klein)   Wir haben ein _____ Auto.

15. (kühl)   Im Sommer sucht der Hund eine _____ Ecke.

B. In each sentence, replace the adjective with its opposite.

EXAMPLE: Der Wagen ist alt. Der Wagen ist *neu*.

1. Das Auto ist laut.   _____

2. Die Antwort ist richtig.   _____

3. Die Handschuhe sind teuer.   _____

4. Die Straße ist lang.   _____

5. Das Haus ist groß.   _____

6. Der Name des langsamen Pferdes ist Hugo.   _____

7. Der Anzug ist hell.   _____

8. Das Wetter ist kalt.   _____

9. Der Kaffee ist warm.   _____

10. Die Lehrerin ist jung.   _____

11. Der Kuchen ist ausgezeichnet.   _____

12. Der Bus hat einen lauten Motor.   _____

13. In diesem Monat haben wir manche warme Tage.   _____

14. Er trinkt kaltes Wasser gern.   _____

15. Das Orchester spielt ein Programm alter Musik.   _____

16. Heute gibt es schönes Wetter.   _____

17. Er weiß die richtige Antwort.   _____

18. Über der Stadt liegt hoher Schnee. ------------------------------

19. Ich suche seltene Bücher. ------------------------------

20. Sie hat viele Freunde. ------------------------------

21. Der Unterricht dauert eine halbe Stunde. ------------------------------

22. Er besucht eine große Stadt. ------------------------------

23. Herr Schmidt ist ein netter Mensch. ------------------------------

24. Die Frau kauft billige Kleider. ------------------------------

25. Heute haben wir einen hellen Tag. ------------------------------

C. Replace the adjective in the sentence with the correct form of the adjective in parentheses that is its proper opposite.

EXAMPLE: Die Antwort ist falsch. (richtig, recht) __*richtig*__
Die Antwort ist *richtig*.

1. Er trägt einen alten Anzug. (jung, neu) ------------------------

2. Die Dame hat helle Farben gern. (dunkel, schwer) ------------------------

3. Wir haben wenig Geld. (groß, viel) ------------------------

4. Wo ist der alte Herr? (neu, jung) ------------------------

5. Das Essen ist ausgezeichnet. (böse, schlecht) ------------------------

6. Hier ist ein großer Tisch. (klein, wenig) ------------------------

7. Da ist ein böser Mann. (nett, schön) ------------------------

8. Dieser Wagen ist billig. (hoch, teuer) ------------------------

9. Hat er die richtige Adresse? (schlecht, falsch) ------------------------

10. Die Straße ist lang. (kurz, wenig) ------------------------

D. Complete the answer to the question, placing the adjective *before* the noun it modifies.

EXAMPLE: Ist der Kaffee heiß?

Ja, das ist __*heißer Kaffee*__.

1. Ist Ihr Schlafzimmer klein? Ja, wir schlafen ------------------------.

2. Sind die Bäume im Park groß? Ja, wir haben ------------------------.

3. Ist der Anzug nicht nett? Ja, das ist ------------------------.

4. Ist das Wetter schlecht? Nein, es gibt ------------------------.

5. Ist der Berg hoch? Ja, wir sehen ------------------------.

6. Ist seine Stimme laut genug? Ja, er spricht ------------------------.

7. Ist das Wasser tief? Nein, hier ist kein ------------------------.

8. Ist das Mädchen schön? Ja, das ist ------------------------.

9. Hat er viele Karten? Nein, er hat nur ------------------------.

10. Das Konzert war ausgezeichnet, nicht wahr? Ja, es war ------------------------.

E. Complete the second sentence so as to express the meaning of the first, using a different adjective.

EXAMPLE: Hans hat nie die richtige Antwort.

Er hat _immer eine falsche Antwort_ .

1. Da das Auto so alt ist, kann es nicht schnell fahren.

   Es ist _____.

2. Er kann nicht dafür bezahlen; er hat nicht genug **Geld.**

   Er hat nur _____.

3. Der Preis dieses Wagens ist sehr hoch.

   Der Wagen ist _____.

4. Das Essen in diesem Restaurant ist sehr gut.

   Es ist _____.

5. Der dunkle Anzug gefällt mir nicht.

   Ich trage lieber _____.

6. Das Gebäude sieht so hoch wie der Himmel aus.

   Es ist _____.

7. Solche Hüte sieht man nicht oft.

   Das ist _____.

8. Vater ist nicht mit dem frühen Zug nach Hause gefahren.

   Vater fuhr mit _____.

9. Wenige Menschen schreiben mit der linken Hand.

   Die meisten Leute _____.

10. Er ist kein netter Mensch. Er ist _____ Mensch.

F. Answer each question with a complete German sentence.

1. Wie ist das Wetter heute? _____

2. Warum ißt der Junge so viel? _____

3. Wie ist das Wetter, wenn die Sonne scheint? _____

4. Günther trägt den ganzen Tag schwere Pakete. Wie fühlt er sich jetzt? _____

   _____

5. Wann sind Sie heute aufgestanden? _____

G. Underline the correct adjective in parentheses.

1. Er hat (klein, wenig) Geld.

2. Wie (groß, hoch) ist Ludwig?

3. Fräulein Schmidt ist nicht alt, sondern sie ist (neu, jung).

4. Du hast (recht, richtig).

5. Das Mädchen ist (klein, wenig).

6. Heute ist ein heller Tag; aber gestern war der Himmel (schwer, dunkel).

7. Das Brot ist nicht gut; es ist (böse, schlecht).

8. Das Buch ist nicht teuer; es ist ganz (billig, frei).

9. Die Kirche ist alt, aber das Rathaus ist (jung, neu).

10. In dem alten, dunklen Haus war es (furchtbar, böse).

H. Replace the adjective in each sentence with each of the adjectives in parentheses.

1. Christa kauft einen schönen Hut.   (neu, teuer, groß)

----

2. Heute haben wir kaltes Wetter.   (schön, warm, schlecht)

----

3. Ich lese ein interessantes Buch.   (ausgezeichnet, einfach, gut)

----

4. Wir geben dem jungen Mann das Buch.   (böse, alt, groß)

----

5. Er versteht nichts von schöner Musik.   (neu, selten, gut)

Replace the noun in italics with each of the nouns in parentheses, changing the form of the article or adjective where necessary.

6. Er hilft dem jungen *Studenten*.   (das Mädchen, die Dame, die Männer)

----

7. Franz hat einen blauen *Wagen*.   (das Bild, der Ball, die Augen)

----

8. Wir wollen warme *Brötchen* essen.   (die Kartoffeln, der Kuchen, das Würstchen)

----

9. Das Hotel hat wenige *Gäste*.   (die Zimmer, die Tische, das Wasser)

----

10. Das war ein langes *Jahr*.   (der Tag, die Ferien, die Zeit)

I. Translate into German.

1. In Germany you drive on the right side of the street. ------------------------

----

2. We live in a large, beautiful old house. ------------------------------------

----

3. He sells well-known, fast cars.

4. They work from early in the morning until late in the evening.

5. This is the only hotel in the city.

6. He wrote me a nice letter.

7. The men are carrying the heavy piano.

8. Can you find a free space?

9. We ate an excellent dessert.

10. There's a loud orchestra in the small cafe.

Marx, Freud, and Einstein—three men who helped shape the modern world. The doctrines of *Karl Marx* (left) continue to inspire social revolutions throughout the world. *Sigmund Freud* (center), a Viennese psychiatrist, provided new insights into man's mind and emotions. *Albert Einstein* (right) transformed our understanding of the physical universe.

17. ADJECTIVES: POSSESSIVES AND DEMONSTRATIVES

POSSESSIVE ADJECTIVES

The genitive case of nouns is used to show possession (see Lesson 11, pages 77–79). If the possessor is not expressed by a noun, a possessive adjective or pronoun is used instead. Note that every personal pronoun has a corresponding possessive adjective, as shown in the following table:

	SINGULAR		PLURAL	
Pronoun	*Possessive Adjective*		*Pronoun*	*Possessive Adjective*
ich	**mein,** my		**wir**	**unser,** our
du	**dein,** your (*fam.*)		**ihr**	**euer,** your (*fam.*)
er, es	**sein,** his, its		**sie**	**ihr,** their
sie	**ihr,** her, its		**Sie**	**Ihr,** your

DECLENSION OF POSSESSIVE ADJECTIVES

The possessive adjectives have the same endings as the **kein**-words:

	SINGULAR			PLURAL
Case	*Masc.*	*Fem.*	*Neut.*	*(all genders)*
NOM.	**mein**	**meine**	**mein**	**meine**
ACC.	**meinen**	**meine**	**mein**	**meine**
DAT.	**meinem**	**meiner**	**meinem**	**meinen**
GEN.	**meines**	**meiner**	**meines**	**meiner**

Note

1. The **e** may be dropped from **unser** and **euer** according to the following pattern:

	SINGULAR			PLURAL
Case	*Masc.*	*Fem.*	*Neut.*	*(all genders)*
NOM.	**unser**	**uns(e)re**	**unser**	**uns(e)re**
ACC.	**unser(e)n**	**uns(e)re**	**unser**	**uns(e)re**
DAT.	**unser(e)m**	**uns(e)rer**	**unser(e)m**	**unser(e)n**
GEN.	**uns(e)res**	**uns(e)rer**	**uns(e)res**	**uns(e)rer**

123

2. Possessives usually have strong adjective endings, even when they follow **alle, dieser,** or **jener:**

alle **meine** Freunde	all my friends
diese **unsere** Freunde	these friends of ours

Following the definite article, the possessives have weak endings, but such constructions are rare.

3. *a.* The possessive adjective need not be used if there is no doubt to whom the object belongs:

Er steckt **die** Hand in **die** Tasche.	He sticks his hand in his pocket.

(It would be very strange if he stuck someone else's hand in someone else's pocket!)

Also:

Gestern war ich bei **dem** Vater.	Yesterday I was at my father's.

b. If the reference is not clear—or for emphasis—the possessive adjective is used:

Hans und ich sprachen mit **meinem** Vater.	Hans and I spoke with my father (not Hans's father).

4. The possessive adjectives are also used as possessive pronouns. When the possessive refers to a preceding noun, the strong ending is added to it:

Das ist dein **Heft.** Hier ist **meines.**	That is your notebook. Here is mine.

(**Meines** refers back to **das Heft;** hence, it has the **-es** ending.) However, in general reference, the possessives **mein, dein,** and **sein** have no ending: **Das ist mein.** The other possessives require an ending when they are used in the predicate:

Das Buch ist **ihres.**	That book is hers (theirs).

Preferably this construction should be avoided and the possessive adjective used instead:

Das ist **ihr** Buch.	That is her (their) book. = That book is hers (theirs).

5. For emphasis, the possessive adjective can be followed by **eigen** (*own*), with appropriate endings:

Jeder Schüler soll seinen **eig(e)nen** Bleistift haben.	Each pupil is supposed to have his *own* pencil.

6. The neuter **kein**-words may add **-s** instead of **-es: keins, unsers,** etc.

ÜBUNGEN

A. Add the correct ending.

1. Mein*e*_____ Schwester heißt Hertha.

2. Dürfen wir mit dein_____ Ball spielen?

3. Haben Sie unser*en*_____ Hund gesehen?

4. Er hat alle sein*e*_____ Bücher mitgebracht.

5. Die Dame vergaß ihr*e*_____ Zeitung.

6. Das Schlafzimmer mein*e*_____ Eltern ist oben.

7. Unser_____ Auto fährt nicht.

8. Ihr sollt euer_____ Freunden helfen.

9. Die Herren haben ihr_____ Krawatten verloren.

10. In unser_____ Klasse sind 30 Schüler.

11. Herr Lehrer, Fritz sitzt auf mein_____ Stuhl.

12. Hier ist unser Wagen. Wo ist dein_____?

13. Das Mädchen hat ihr_____ Uhr in der Hand.

14. Alle mein_____ Platten sind alt.

15. Euer_____ Garten ist sehr schön.

B. Write the correct form of the possessive adjective that corresponds to the noun or pronoun given in parentheses.

1. (er)   Ich habe _____ Bruder angerufen.

2. (Frl. Schmidt) Sehen Sie _____ Brief?

3. (wir)   Darf sie _____ Kamera entleihen?

4. (Sie)   Ich habe _____ Tante kennengelernt.

5. (ich)   Haben Sie _____ Ring gefunden?

6. (ihr)   Die Kinder spielen in _____ Keller.

7. (du)   _____ Glas ist auf dem Tisch.

8. (er)   Wo ist _____ Mantel?

9. (wir)   Haben Sie _____ Rathaus gesehen?

10. (der Junge)   Hans kommt mit _____ Rad.

11. (die Leute)   _____ Tänze gefallen uns.

12. (die Dame)   Können Sie _____ Auto sehen?

13. (du)   _____ Plan gefällt mir.

14. (wir)   Wir haben alle _____ Karten mitgebracht.

15. (ich)   Heute bin ich bei _____ Onkel.

C. Write either the definite article or the possessive as needed.

1. Er zieht sich _____ Mantel an.

2. Trotz _____ lauten Stimme, hat Karl mich nicht gehört.

3. Das Mädchen wäscht sich _____ Gesicht.

4. Dieter, kommt _____ Mutter mit?

5. Ich kämme mir _____ Haar.

6. Wir machen uns _____ Frühstück.

7. Unser Haus ist da drüben. Wo ist _____, Herr Braun?

8. Soll ich _____ Hut ablegen?

9. Er hält das Buch in _____ Hand.

10. Mein Bruder und ich suchen _____ Handschuh.

D. Complete the answer to the question, using a possessive pronoun.

1. Wem gehört das Klavier?

   Es ist _____.

2. Wissen Sie meine Adresse?

   Ja, _____.

3. Kinder, habt ihr eure Bücher mit?

   Nein, _____.

4. Haben alle Jungen ein Rad?

   Ja, jeder hat _____.

5. Haben Sie meinen Hund gesehen?

   Leider nicht. Ich _____.

6. Der Herr hat seine Uhr verloren, nicht wahr?

   Ja, er _____.

7. Sind die Kinder in ihrem Schlafzimmer?

   Nur Ilse _____.

8. Wo verbringen wir unsere Ferien?

   Diesen Sommer _____.

9. Gehört dieses Feld dem Bauern?

   Ja, es ist _____.

10. Haben Sie seinen Brief bekommen?

    Nein, _____.

E. Replace the possessive adjective with the possessives in parentheses.

1. Da ist mein Geschenk.

   (dein) _____ (unser) _____ (ihr) _____

2. Ich habe mein Bild.

   (sein) _____ (euer) _____ (ihr) _____

3. Er geht durch seinen Garten.

   (unser) _____ (mein) _____ (dein) _____

4. Ich nehme eure Schuhe mit.

   (sein) _____ (ihr) _____ (unser) _____

5. Sie hat ihren Plattenspieler verkauft.

   (dein) _____ (euer) _____ (mein) _____

6. Er hat alle meine Äpfel gegessen.

   (sein) _____ (unser) _____ (euer) _____

7. Da kommt dein Zug.

   (sein) _____ (Ihr) _____ (mein) _____

8. Die Jungen spielen mit ihrem Fußball.

(unser) _____ (euer) _____ (sein) _____

9. Sie kommen heute abend in unsere Stadt.

(dein) _____ (ihr) _____ (mein) _____

10. Helga zerbrach ihren Teller.

(mein) _____ (euer) _____ (dein) _____

DEMONSTRATIVE ADJECTIVES

The demonstrative adjectives (*this, that,* etc.) generally point out an object or throw special emphasis on it. In German, the definite article itself—**der, die, das**—can be used as a demonstrative:

Das Buch habe ich nie gelesen.   I've never read *that* book.

The other German demonstratives are declined like the definite article:

DECLENSION OF dies-

	SINGULAR			PLURAL
Case	*Masc.*	*Fem.*	*Neut.*	*(all genders)*
NOM.	dies*er*	dies*e*	dies(*es*)	dies*e*
ACC.	dies*en*	dies*e*	dies(*es*)	dies*e*
DAT.	dies*em*	dies*er*	dies*em*	dies*en*
GEN.	dies*es*	dies*er*	dies*es*	dies*er*

Note

Demonstrative adjectives are also used as demonstrative pronouns:

Welchen Hut willst du?   Which hat do you want? This one.
Diesen.

SOME COMMON DEMONSTRATIVES

der, die, das, this, that; the one(s)

dieser, diese, dieses, this

jeder, jede, jedes, each, every

jener, jene, jenes, that

mancher, manche, manches, many a, many

selbst (*indecl.*), -self (*emphatic*); even

solcher, solche, solches, such a, such

Note

1. The demonstratives **dieser, mancher,** and **solcher** may be declined like **kein**-words; that is, they may be used without an ending with the nominative singular of **der** nouns and with the nominative and accusative singular of **das** nouns: *Dies ist mein Bruder.*

2. The demonstratives are regularly followed by adjectives with weak endings, except that **manche** (plural) most often is followed by adjectives with strong endings.

3. If the demonstrative does not have an ending, the adjective following it has a strong ending:

solch**er** nett**e** Mensch

But: such a nice person

solch nett**er** Mensch

4. *a.* If **solch** (without an ending) is not followed by an adjective, the article **ein** may be inserted before the noun:

Solch (ein) Haus ist in der   Such a house is on the next street.
nächsten Straße.

b. **So + ein** is widely used today in the singular in place of the forms of **solcher.** The case of **ein** is determined by its use in its clause:

Ich habe schon **so ein*en***   I have already bought such a car.
Wagen gekauft.

5. *a.* **Selbst** can be used to throw emphasis on a particular noun or pronoun:

Ich sah den Präsidenten **selbst.**   I saw the president himself.

Selbst is usually placed immediately after the word being emphasized.

b. When **selbst** comes at the beginning of the sentence (or before the subject), it usually means *even*:

Selbst ich sah den Präsidenten.   Even I saw the president.

6. The definite article may be used for emphasis in place of the personal pronoun:

Welcher Mann hat das Buch?   Which man has the book?
Der hat es.   *He* has it.

ÜBUNGEN

F. Write the endings for the demonstratives.

1. Jed_____ Mann hat seinen Fehler.

2. Sollen wir in dies_____ Kino gehen?

3. Wo ist der Park? _____ ist hier in der Nähe.

4. Jen_____ Kleid ist zu teuer.

5. Ich habe nicht mit Herrn Müller selbst_____ gesprochen.

6. Manch_____ Lied haben wir gesungen.

7. Können Sie dies_____ sehen?

8. Nie vorher hatten wir solch_____ Musik gehört.

9. Der König selbst_____ hat den Armen besucht.

10. Auf jed_____ Seite steht ein neues Wort.

11. Wir interessieren uns für solch_____ Tänze.

12. Er ist nicht zufrieden mit dies_____ Restaurant.

13. Wegen manch_____ schöner Blumen hat der Garten uns sehr gefallen.

14. Die Dame fragt nach jed_____ Preis.

15. Selbst_____ die Kinder schreiben Geschichten.

G. Translate the English into German.

1. *Such* Bäume wachsen nur in Norddeutschland.   _____

2. Während des Sommers haben wir *each* Kirche besucht.   _____

3. Er wird mit *this* Schiff fahren.   _____

4. *Many a* interessantes Programm habe ich mir angehört.   _____

5. *Even* der Lehrer weiß es nicht.   _____

6. Ich habe mir *that* Film schon angesehen.   _____

7. *Every* Sommer fährt die Familie an die See.   _____

8. Fritz hat das *himself* gemacht.   _____

9. Haben Sie *such a* Tier gesehen?   _____

10. Wir können mit *this* Zug fahren.   _____

H. Replace the word in italics with the correct form of each of the words in parentheses.

1. *Das* Kind kommt spät nach Hause.

(dies) _____   (jedes) _____   (manch) _____

2. Mutter freut sich auf *die* Reise.

(jene) _____   (so eine) _____   (diese) _____

3. Er singt *das* Lied.

(jedes) _____   (solch) _____   (dies) _____

4. *Solch* schönes Wetter ist selten.

(dies) _____   (jenes) _____   (das) _____

5. Eine Zeitung ist auf *dem* Tisch.

(jede) _____   (diese) _____   (jene) _____

Replace the noun in italics with the nouns in parentheses, making any necessary changes in the demonstrative adjective.

6. Jeden *Sommer* fahren wir aufs Land.

(der Winter)   _____

(der Sonntag)   _____

(das Jahr)   _____

7. Oft kaufte er sich solche *Bücher*.

(die Kleider)   _____

(das Pferd)   _____

(der Wagen)   _____

8. Dieses *Klavier* ist sehr schön.

(die Handschuhe) _____

(der Wald) _____

(das Schiff) _____

9. Er wohnt in jener *Straße*.

(das Dorf) _____

(der Staat) _____

(der Stock) _____

10. Manche *Tonbänder* gefallen uns.

(das Programm) _____

(der Plan) _____

(die Farben) _____

I. Translate into English.

1. Heute abend wird er meine Eltern besuchen. _____

2. Der Student versteht nicht jeden Satz der Aufgabe. _____

_____

3. Wollen Sie einen neuen Wagen sehen? Hier ist einer. _____

_____

4. Alle unsere Freunde bleiben heute zu Hause. _____

_____

5. Hier ist das Haus seines Vaters. _____

6. Der Lehrer selbst hat das gesagt. _____

7. Kinder, wo sind eure Hefte? _____

8. Manchem Kind gefällt dieses Buch. _____

9. Jene Krawatte ist schön. _____

10. Ich habe deinen Brief gelesen. _____

J. Translate into German.

1. I'm talking to your father. _____

2. My sister is cooking the meal herself. _____

_____

3. We're reading many a newspaper. _____

4. I know that lady. _____

5. Fritz, here is your present. _____

6. We're staying in this hotel. _____

7. Mr. Schmidt, you forgot your hat. ------------------------------------
----

8. The boy likes to read such books. ----------------------------------

9. I saw the king himself. --

10. Is this my milk? --

The *Kölner Dom*, one of the most beautiful cathedrals of Europe, is an outstanding example of Gothic architecture. The city of Köln, called Cologne in French and English, is widely known for the famous toilet water produced there—"eau de Cologne" or *Kölnisches Wasser*.

18. ADVERBS

Adverbs make clear or more exact the idea introduced by a verb, adjective, another adverb, or even a whole clause. They can express time (*often, later*), place (*there*), attitude and manner (*gladly, hopefully*), or negation (*not*).

In English, adverbs are formed from adjectives usually by adding *-ly*: glad, glad*ly*. (However, some English adjectives end in *-ly*, for example, friendly.) German adjectives may be used as adverbs without any special ending:

Der Wagen ist **schnell.**	The car is fast.
Der Wagen fährt **schnell.**	The car travels rapidly.

Like English, German has a number of words that are regularly adverbs:

GENERAL ADVERBS

also, therefore; well!	**genau,** exactly	**schon,** already
auch, also, too	**gerade,** direct(ly), straight,	**sehr,** very
ein bißchen, a little bit	just (a moment ago)	**ungefähr,** approximately,
eben, even, just (a moment	**leise,** softly	about
ago)	**nicht,** not	**wieder,** again
fast, almost	**noch,** yet, still, even now	**wohl,** indeed; probably
gar (nicht), (not) at all	**nur,** only	

Note

1. **Genau** can also be used as an adjective:

Können Sie mir die **genaue** Zeit sagen?	Can you tell me the exact time?

2. **Immer wieder** means *again and again, over and over again,* or *keeps on (doing something)*:

Er sagt das **immer wieder.**	He says that again and again (over and over again); he keeps on saying that.

3. **Noch nicht** means *not yet*:

Ich habe ihn **noch nicht** gesehen.	I haven't seen him yet.

ADVERBS OF PLACE

da, there	**hinaus,** out of (*moving away from the speaker*)	**rechts,** right-hand side
dort, there	**hinten,** behind	**überall,** everywhere
draußen, outside	**irgendwo,** somewhere	**unten,** below, beneath,
drinnen, inside	**links,** left-hand side	downstairs
drüben, over (there)	**nirgends,** nowhere	**weit,** far (from a place),
fern, distant, far	**oben,** overhead, above,	widely
heraus, out of (*moving toward the speaker*)	upstairs	**zurück,** back
hier, here		**zusammen,** together

Note

1. **Da** and **dort** are interchangeable. They are often used with another adverb:

   da drüben, over there   **dort oben,** up there

2. *There is* and *there are* may be expressed in German in three ways, depending on the meaning:

   a. **Da** or **dort** is used when directing attention or pointing to something seen:

   Da ist das Hotel.   There's the hotel.

   Dort sind deine Freunde.   There are your friends.

   b. **Es gibt** is used when referring to the existence of something or to an unspecified number of things:

   Es gibt einen schönen Park in dieser Stadt.   There is a beautiful park in this city.

   Es gibt mehrere schöne Parks in dieser Stadt.   There are several beautiful parks in this city.

   c. **Es sind** is used to refer to a specific number of things:

   Es sind dreißig Stühle in unserem Klassenzimmer.   There are thirty chairs in our classroom.

3. The prefixes **hin-** and **her-** are used in combination with verbs and adverbs. **Hin-** indicates motion away from the speaker (**hinaus, hinein, wohin**); **her-** indicates motion toward the speaker (**heraus, herkommen, woher**). These prefixes are regularly used to indicate the direction of an action.

   Er kommt aus dem Haus **heraus.**   He's coming out of the house (toward the speaker).

4. *a.* As an adverb, **weit** generally keeps the feeling of its use as an adjective: *wide, spacious*:

   Er ist **weit** (überall) gewandert.   He has hiked far and wide.

   b. **Weit** means *far* when used with place expressions:

   Das Hotel ist nicht *weit* **von hier.**   The hotel is not far from here.

   c. **Fern** always means *far* in the sense of *distant*:

   Wir suchen ihn **fern** und nah.   We're looking for him near and far.

   d. Both **weit** and **fern** are frequently used along with **weg** (*away*):

   Das Schiff ist **fern weg.**   The ship is far away (far off).

ADVERBS OF TIME

bald, soon	**jetzt,** now	**nun,** now
dann, then	**mal,** time(s)	**oft,** often
erst, not until	**manchmal,** sometimes	**selten,** seldom, rarely
(so)gleich, immediately	**nie,** never	**sofort,** immediately
immer, always	**nimmer,** never	

Note

1. The suffix **mal** is added to numbers to indicate the number of times:

ein**mal,** once   drei**mal,** three times

2. **Selten** is also used as an adjective meaning *rare*:

ein **seltener** Film   a rare film

3. Three pairs of these adverbs can be used interchangeably:

jetzt
nun } now   **nie**
nimmer } never   **sogleich**
sofort } immediately

ADVERBS OF ATTITUDE AND MANNER

bitte, please; you're welcome	**gewiß,** certainly	**natürlich,** naturally, surely
danke, thanks	**glücklich,** luckily	**nein,** no
doch, indeed	**hoffentlich,** hopefully, I hope	**sicher,** certainly
fröhlich, happily	**ja,** yes; indeed	**so,** thus, such a way
gern, gladly, to like to	**kaum,** hardly	

Note

1. Context shows whether **bitte** means *please* or *you're welcome*. It is often used with **schön** or **sehr**:

Bitte schön!
Bitte sehr! } You're quite welcome!

2. **Doch** is used as an affirmative reply to a question where a negative answer is expected:

„Sie haben nicht den König gesehen, nicht wahr?"   "You didn't see the king, did you?"

„**Doch!**"   "Indeed I did!"

3. **Fröhlich, glücklich, gewiß, natürlich,** and **sicher** are sometimes used as adjectives:

Fröhliche Weihnachten!   Merry Christmas!

4. *a.* **Gern** may be used with a verb to mean *to like to*:

Sie spielen **gern.**   They like to play.

   b. **Gern haben** means *to like* or *to enjoy*:

Ich habe solche Autos **gern.**   I like cars of that sort.

5. Unlike adjectives, adverbs are not declined.

ÜBUNGEN

A. Underline the adverb in parentheses that may be used to replace the italicized expression.

1. Der Schnee liegt *auf dem Dach*. Der Schnee liegt (oben, drüben, unten).

2. *Jeden Sommer* fahren wir nach Deutschland. Wir fahren (bald, oft, selten) nach Deutschland.

3. *Es macht* mir *Spaß*, Deutsch zu sprechen. Ich spreche Deutsch (kaum, gern, sicher).

4. Das Hotel ist dort, *auf der anderen Seite der Straße*. Das Hotel ist dort (draußen, oben, drüben).

5. Sie spricht *nur wenig* Deutsch. Sie spricht (leise, nicht weit, ein bißchen) Deutsch.

6. Der Hund steht *vor der Tür*. Der Hund steht (draußen, darauf, oben).

7. Der Zug ist *vor einer Minute* angekommen. Der Zug ist (selten, gerade, fast) angekommen.

8. Wir sollen *nicht* mit der Arbeit *warten*. Wir sollen die Arbeit (nimmer, sogleich, rechts) tun.

9. Das ist das *einzige* Gasthaus in diesem Dorf. Dieses Dorf hat (manchmal, selten, nur) ein Gasthaus.

10. *Vielleicht* hat er recht. Er hat (leise, ungefähr, wohl) recht.

    B. Change the adjectives to adverbs.

    EXAMPLE: Der *schnelle* Wagen fährt durch die Stadt.
                 Der Wagen fährt *schnell* durch die Stadt.

1. Er sprach mit lauter Stimme.   Er sprach sehr _____.

2. Er ist mit dem späten Zug nach Hause gefahren.   Er ist _____ nach Hause gekommen.

3. Der Student gibt eine falsche Antwort.   Der Student antwortet _____.

4. Ein heißes Feuer brennt im Ofen.   Das Feuer brennt _____.

5. Man sieht hier seltene Tiere.   Nur _____ sieht man solche Tiere.

    C. Replace the adverb in each sentence with its opposite, which is to be selected from the following list:

dort	**leise**	**rechts**
fern weg	**manchmal**	**überall**
gar nicht	**nie**	**ungefähr**
immer wieder		

1. Er fährt immer mit dem Bus.   _____

2. Das hat er sicher gesagt.   _____

3. Das Haus ist hier.   _____

4. Ich habe das nie gesehen.   _____

5. Wir können nirgends Blumen finden.   _____

6. Er hat laut gesprochen.   _____

7. Sie hat einmal einen Brief geschrieben.   _____

8. Er muß jetzt ganz nahe sein.   _____

9. Hier müssen sie links fahren.   _____

10. Es ist genau 7 Uhr.   _____

    D. Complete the answer to each question, using one of the following adverbial expressions. (Each expression in the list may be used only once in this exercise.)

doch	**jetzt**	**nur wenig**
genau	**links**	**schon**
gern	**manchmal**	**zusammen**
gleich		

1. Lesen Sie jeden Tag die Zeitung?

Nicht jeden Tag, sondern _____.

2. Sie können sehr gut Deutsch, nicht wahr?

Nein, ich _____.

3. Kannst du bald zurückkommen?

Ja, ich _____.

4. Hat das Konzert Ihnen gefällt?

Ja, _____.

5. Wie spät ist es?

Ich habe keine Uhr mit, also kann ich es nicht _____.

6. Haben Sie den Dom besucht?

Ja, _____.

7. Wie kommt man zum Bahnhof, bitte?

Fahren Sie _____.

8. Wann kommt der Bus?

Sehen Sie doch, _____.

9. Wo ist mein Hut?

Ich weiß nicht genau, aber fragen Sie Anna; *sie* _____.

10. Werden Sie allein kommen?

Nein, wir _____.

E. Substitute the adverbs in parentheses for the adverb in each sentence. After each substitution, translate the new sentence into English.

1. Er hat es einmal gesagt.   (viermal, wieder, manchmal)

_____

_____

2. Das tut man immer.   (bald, überall, nicht)

_____

_____

3. Sie sollen leise sprechen.   (wieder, sofort, bald)

_____

_____

4. Das Hotel ist da drüben.   (irgendwo, rechts, fern weg)

_____

_____

5. Ich trinke Milch gern.   (oft, jetzt, manchmal)

----

6. Natürlich haben sie mit ihm gesprochen.   (sicher, hoffentlich, irgendwo)

----

7. Er hat das Buch schon gelesen.   (noch nicht, gleich, immer wieder)

----

8. Sie spricht sogleich.   (fröhlich, gar nicht, ein bißchen)

----

9. Der Bahnhof ist dort drüben.   (nahe dem Hotel, weit von hier, rechts von hier)

----

10. Der Zug ist gerade angekommen.   (sicher, eben, schon)

F. Translate into English.

1. Gibt es irgendwo ein Konzert? --

2. Ungefähr 20 Studenten sitzen im Zimmer. ------------------------------------

----

3. Er hat immer wieder danach gefragt. --

----

4. Ich bin gleich zurück. --

5. Das Schlafzimmer ist oben im ersten Stock. ----------------------------------

----

6. Kommen Sie nicht mit? Doch! ---

7. Der Junge spielt Fußball gern. --

8. Sieh mal her! ---

9. Das kann er wohl nicht tun. ---

----

10. Ich bin überall gewesen. ---

11. Wir sind noch nicht in die Schweiz gefahren. --------------------------------

----

12. Sie kennt fast jeden Studenten. ------------------------------------

13. Der Ring ist nirgends zu finden. ---------------------------------

14. Also, hier kommt der Herr. --

15. Ich weiß nicht genau. --

G. Translate into German.

1. The snow out there is quite deep. ------------------------------------

2. I'll call him immediately. --

3. When are you coming back? ---

4. The students are singing together. --------------------------------

5. I still have to buy a new tie. ------------------------------------

----

6. My watch doesn't keep accurate time (= does not go exactly). -------

----

7. They are probably working today. ----------------------------------

8. I hope the train gets here soon. ----------------------------------

----

9. Do you like to dance? --

10. Please come again soon! ---

Otto von Bismarck (1815–1898), Prime Minister of Prussia, played an essential role in the creation of the German Empire. His aggressive statesmanship made Germany a dominant European power.

19. PREPOSITIONS

A preposition relates a noun or pronoun with another word in a sentence. The noun following the preposition is the object of that preposition. Each preposition is said to govern a certain case; for example, the preposition **trotz** is said to govern the genitive case because its object is always in the genitive. Some German prepositions govern only the genitive case; some govern only the dative case; and others, only the accusative. A few German prepositions govern both the dative and the accusative case.

THE MOST COMMON PREPOSITIONS, GROUPED ACCORDING TO THE CASE THEY GOVERN

Genitive

anstatt (or **statt**), instead of   **während,** during
trotz, in spite of   **wegen,** because of

Dative

aus, out of, from (a place)   **nach,** after, toward; according to
außer, besides, except for   **seit,** since (a certain time)
bei, at, near, at the home of   **von,** of, from (a person), by (a person)
mit, with   **zu,** to

Accusative

bis, until   **gegen,** against, toward
durch, through   **ohne,** without
für, for   **um,** around, about

Dative or Accusative

an, at, on (*vertical*)   **über,** over, above
auf, on (*horizontal*)   **unter,** under, among
hinter, behind   **vor,** before, in front of; ago (*with dative*)
in, in, into   **zwischen,** between
neben, beside, next to

CONTRACTIONS

Some prepositions may be contracted with the article:

an + **dem** = *am*	**in** + **dem** = *im*
an + **das** = *ans*	**in** + **das** = *ins*
auf + **das** = *aufs*	**von** + **dem** = *vom*
bei + **dem** = *beim*	**zu** + **der** = *zur*
für + **das** = *fürs*	**zu** + **dem** = *zum*

Note

1. Both **wegen** and **nach** may sometimes follow their object:

Des schlechten Wetters **wegen,** kann er   Because of the bad weather, he can't come.
nicht kommen.

2. **Nach** is placed after the object only if it means *according to*:

Dem Polizisten **nach,** fährt der Herr zu   According to the policeman, the gentleman is
schnell.   driving too fast.

But:

Er fährt **nach** Berlin.   He is going to Berlin.

3. Prepositions that govern both the dative and the accusative case have their objects in the dative case to show location (answering **wo?**) and in the accusative case to show motion (answering **wohin?**):

Wo ist Franz? Er sitzt **in *dem* Zimmer.**

Wohin geht Franz? Er geht **in *das* Zimmer.**

4. *a.* If the verb shows movement *within* a certain place, the dative is used:

Er fährt **in *der* Schweiz.**   He is traveling in (= inside of) Switzerland.

b. If the verb shows movement *into* a place, the accusative is used:

Er fährt **in *die* Schweiz.**   He is traveling to (= into) Switzerland.

c. Similarly, when **zwischen** means movement *within* a certain area, the dative is used; when **zwischen** indicates movement *into* an area between two places, the accusative is used.

Er wirft den Ball zwischen ***dem* Haus   He throws the ball between (= *within* the area
und *der* Mauer.**   between) the house and the wall.

But:

Er wirft den Ball zwischen ***das* Haus   He throws the ball between (= *into* the area
und *die* Mauer.**   between) the house and the wall.

5. *a.* **Vor** takes the dative when it means *before* (in time) or *ago*:

Vor dem Unterricht muß ich meine   I must correct my exercises before class.
Übungen verbessern.

Vor einer Woche kam ich her.   I came here a week ago.

b. **Vor** takes either the dative or the accusative when it means *in front of*:

Ein Gast steht **vor der Tür.**   A guest is standing in front of the door.

Der Junge wirft den Ball **vor das Haus.**   The boy throws the ball in front of the house.

6. An English preposition may have several German equivalents; hence, it is dangerous to suppose that any English preposition can always be translated by one specific German preposition. For example, "*at* home" becomes „**zu** Hause," but "*at* Mr. Miller's (house)" becomes „**bei** Herrn Müller."

Distinguish the following German equivalents of English prepositions.

from (a person)	von (*von Mutter*)
from (a place)	aus (*aus München*)
on (object is vertical)	an (*an der [die] Wand*)
on (object is horizontal)	auf (*auf dem [den] Tisch*)
on the street (playground)	auf *der Straße (dem Spielplatz)*
on the corner	an *der Ecke*
to (city or country)	nach (*nach Berlin*)
to (persons, buildings, proper names)	zu (*zu meinem Bruder*)
to (into a building or enclosure)	in (*ins Kino, ins Konzert*)
to (up to the edge of)	an (*an die See*)

The following special uses of the prepositions must be learned:

1. Ich fahre **an die See.**
   Ich bleibe **an der See.**

   I'm going to the beach.
   I'm staying at the beach.

2. Ich fahre **aufs Land.**
   Ich bleibe **auf dem Lande.**

   I'm driving into the country.
   I'm staying in the country.

3. Wir essen **im Restaurant.**
   Wir essen **in dem Restaurant.**

   We're going to eat out.
   We're going to eat in that restaurant.

4. Ich gehe **nach Hause.**
   Ich bleibe **zu Hause.**

   I'm going home.
   I'm staying home.

5. Die Autos fahren **auf der Straße.**
   Ich wohne **in der Hauptstraße.**

   The cars are driving in (on) the street.
   I live on Main Street.

6. **Zum Geburtstag (Zu Weihnachten)**
   bekam ich einen neuen Hut.
   Tante Frieda kam **zu Besuch.**

   For my birthday (for Christmas) I got a new hat.
   Aunt Frieda came for a visit.

7. **Vor einer Woche** kam ich her.
   Seit einer Woche bin ich hier.

   I came here a week ago.
   I've been here for a week.

8. Ich fahre **mit dem Zug (Auto, Schiff,** etc.).

   I'm traveling (going) by train (car, ship, etc.).

9. **im Jahre 1950**
   im April
   einmal im Monat

   in (the year) 1950
   in April
   once a month

10. **am ersten April**
    am Montag
    am Abend

    on April first
    on Monday
    in the evening

11. **um 7 Uhr**

    at 7 o'clock

Note

1. *Every preposition has an object.* If a word does not have an object, then it is not a preposition.

2. *a.* English prepositions are often used as parts of compound verbs: to look *for* (= *to seek*), to pick *up* (= *to lift*), to pick *out* (= *to select*), etc. If the English preposition is a part of a compound verb, the preposition will not necessarily be translated separately in German:

He is buying a book *for* his brother.   Er kauft ein Buch **für** seinen Bruder.

 But:

He *looks for* his brother.   Er **sucht** seinen Bruder.
 <u>compound verb</u>

He *pays for* the window.   Er **bezahlt** das Fenster.
 <u>compound verb</u>

b. Compound verbs are also found in German (see Lesson 3):

Er **sieht** sehr müde **aus.**   He looks very tired.

ÜBUNGEN

A. Supply the correct form of the definite article.

1. Der Brief ist für _____ kleine Mädchen.

2. Wir fahren mit _____ Zug.

3. Wir sollen nicht ohne _____ Geschenk kommen.

4. Seit _____ ersten Minute habe ich nichts gehört.

5. Gestern abend waren wir bei _____ Onkel.

6. Während _____ Winters sind wir oft Ski gelaufen.

7. Hier ist eine Karte von _____ Mutter.

8. Die Kinder laufen um _____ Schule.

9. Trotz _____ kalten Wetters werden wir doch schwimmen.

10. Er will durch _____ Land fahren.

11. Wir kommen aus _____ Kirche.

12. Ich muß morgen zu _____ Arzt gehen.

13. Außer _____ alten Wagen sahen wir keinen Verkehr.

14. Nach _____ Essen raucht Vater gern eine Zigarre.

15. Wegen _____ schönen Wetters machen wir einen Spaziergang.

B. Revise the sentence by changing *er steht* to *er geht*.

EXAMPLE: Er steht an der Ecke. Er geht an *die* Ecke.

1. Er steht vor der Schule. _____

2. Er steht an dem Fenster. _____

3. Er steht über dem Fluß. _____

4. Er steht auf dem Schiff. _____

5. Er steht hinter dem Haus. _____

Replace *er geht* with *er steht* in the following:

6. Er geht unter den Baum. _____

7. Er geht ins Kino. --

8. Er geht auf die Straße. --

9. Er geht an die Tür. --

10. Er geht neben das Hotel. --

C. Supply the correct form of the definite article.

1. In ------------ Stadt haben wir viele Autos gesehen.

2. Die Männer stehen vor ------------ Rathaus.

3. Meine Eltern gehen heute abend in ------------ Konzert.

4. Paula sitzt auf ------------ Stuhl.

5. Sie fahren heute in ------------ Stadt.

6. Wir sitzen an ------------ Tisch.

7. Die Kinder spielen auf ------------ Hof.

8. Was haben Sie hinter ------------ Hotel gefunden?

9. Er ist zwischen ------------ beiden Städten gefahren.

10. Wir essen in ------------ Restaurant.

D. Change the phrase in italics by replacing the preposition with each of the prepositions in parentheses.

1. Vater fährt *in die Stadt.*   (über, durch, um)

----

2. Er kommt *mit seinem Bruder.*   (ohne, wegen, zu)

----

3. Das Bild ist *für die Dame.*   (von, neben, vor)

----

4. *Vor den Ferien* wollen wir eine Reise machen.   (nach, während, trotz)

----

5. Die Jungen laufen *an die Mauer.*   (um, gegen, zu)

Change the phrase in italics by using the nouns in parentheses as objects of the preposition.

6. Gestern abend waren sie *bei mir.*   (mein Freund, die Eltern, der Herr)

----

7. *Während der Woche* haben wir Berlin besucht.   (der Monat, das Jahr, der Sommer)

----

8. *Seit dem ersten Mai* bin ich hier.   (die letzte Woche, drei Tage, ein Jahr)

----

9. Die Gäste gehen *ins Restaurant.*   (das Kino, der Keller, das Konzert)

----

10. *Außer diesem Wasser* gibt's nichts zu trinken.   (die Milch, der Kaffee, das Bier)

E. The answers to the following questions appear in parentheses. Answer each question with a complete sentence in German.

1. Wo fährt Frau Schmidt hin?   (to Munich)

----

2. Wo kommen Sie her?   (from Berlin)

----

3. Wie lange sind Sie hier?   (for one month)

----

4. Wann haben wir Ferien?   (during the summer)

----

5. Wo war er gestern abend?   (at his father's)

----

6. Wo ist das Rathaus?   (between the train station and the church)

----

7. Warum bleiben Sie heute zu Hause?   (because of the cold weather)

----

8. Von wem kommt der Brief?   (from my sister)

----

9. Wo ist das Flugzeug jetzt?   (over the city)

----

10. Wo ist Hans?   (in front of the school)

F. Translate the English into German.

1. *In spite of the price* haben wir das Auto gekauft.   -------------------------------------

2. Er ist *against a tree* gefahren.   -------------------------------------

3. Er schrieb *with blue ink*.   -------------------------------------

4. Kommen Sie nicht *without a notebook!*   -------------------------------------

5. Die Kinder spielen *in the cellar*.   -------------------------------------

6. Kinder, kommt *to the table!*   -------------------------------------

7. *Besides breakfast* haben wir heute nichts gegessen.   -------------------------------------

8. Wir haben ein Buch *instead of a newspaper* gelesen.   -------------------------------------

9. Dies haben wir *with great joy* gesehen.   -------------------------------------

10. Schreiben Sie bitte den Satz *on the blackboard!*   -------------------------------------

SOME COMMON VERB-PREPOSITION COMBINATIONS

The preposition that is used with some verbs often has little or nothing to do with the usual meaning of the preposition. The following verb-preposition combinations must be learned separately:

achten auf + *acc.*, to watch out for, to pay attention to (= **beachten**)
antworten auf + *acc.*, to answer (a question) (= **beantworten**)
arbeiten an + *dat.*, to work at (on), be busy with
aufhören mit + *dat.*, to stop (+ *noun*)
beginnen mit (**von**) + *dat.*, to begin with (from)
bitten um + *acc.*, to ask for
bleiben bei + *dat.*, to remain with, to stay at
denken an + *acc.*, to think of, about (*not* in the sense of "to have an opinion of")
einladen in + *acc.*, to invite (someone) to (a place)
einladen zu + *dat.*, to invite (someone) to (an event)
sich erinnern an + *acc.*, to remember
fehlen an + *dat.*, to lack (something), to need
fragen nach + *dat.*, to ask about, inquire
sich freuen an + *dat.*, **über** + *acc.*, to be glad (happy) about
sich freuen auf + *acc.*, to look forward to
gehören zu + *dat.*, to belong to (a group)
glauben an + *acc.*, to believe in, to trust
halten von + *dat.*, to think of (= to have an opinion of)
sich interessieren für + *acc.*, to be interested in
schreiben an + *acc.*, to write to
schreiben von + *dat.*, **über** + *acc.*, to write about
sprechen mit (**zu**) + *dat.*, to speak with (someone)
sprechen von + *dat.*, **über** + *acc.*, to speak of (something)
sterben an + *dat.*, to die of
sich verlassen auf + *acc.*, to depend on, count on
sich vorbereiten auf + *acc.*, to prepare for
warten auf + *acc.*, to wait for
wissen von + *dat.*, to know about (concerning)

Note

1. **Fehlen an** is usually impersonal with a dative object:

    Es **fehlt** mir **an** ein**em** Buch.   I need a book.

2. *a.* The verb **gehören** means *belong to* in the sense of "to be the property of":

    Dies Haus **gehört mir.**   This house belongs to me.

    b. **Gehören zu** means *belong to* in the sense of "to be a part of (something)":

    Dies Haus **gehört zum Bauernhof.**   This house belongs to the farmyard.

3. The meaning of **warten auf** depends on whether the object of **auf** is accusative or dative:

    Ich warte auf **den** Zug.   I'm waiting *for* the train.

    But:

    Ich warte auf *der* Straße.   I'm waiting *on* the street.

ÜBUNGEN

G. Write the correct form of the definite article.

1. Ich schrieb einen Brief an _____ Herrn.

2. Sie müssen auf _____ Verkehr achten.

3. Wir sprachen mit _____ Dame.

4. Ich kann mich nicht auf _____ Auto verlassen.

5. Wieviel wissen Sie von _____ Geschichte?

6. Er erinnert sich an _____ Ferien.

7. Wir freuen uns auf _____ Ausflug.

8. Sie dachte oft an _____ Bruder.

9. Der Kellner bittet die Gäste um _____ Geld.

10. Wir warteten auf _____ Schnellzug, der noch nicht angekommen war.

11. Hören Sie bitte mit _____ Lärm auf!

12. Er interessiert sich für _____ Musik des 18. Jahrhunderts.

13. Sie fragte nach _____ Preis.

14. Ich warte auf _____ Lehrer.

15. Können Sie auf _____ Frage antworten?

H. Write the appropriate preposition.

1. Ich habe mich _____ die Prüfung vorbereitet.

2. Großmutter wird drei Wochen _____ uns bleiben.

3. Haben Sie Fräulein Schmidt _____ Abendessen eingeladen?

4. Hans gehört _____ unserer Klasse.

5. Wir sollen _____ die deutsche Geschichte schreiben.

6. Es fehlt uns _____ Geld.

7. Herr Schmidt hat uns _____ sein Haus eingeladen.

8. Was halten Sie _____ dem Bild?

9. Im letzten Jahr sind viele Tiere _____ einer unbekannten Krankheit gestorben.

10. Sie müssen eine Stunde _____ der Straße warten, bis man das Theater öffnet.

11. Heute abend muß ich _____ der neuen Aufgabe arbeiten.

12. Wir freuen uns sehr _____ das schöne Wetter.

13. _____ wem haben Sie gesprochen?

14. Wir sollen _____ diesem Herrn glauben.

15. Sie wartet _____ die Dame.

I. Translate into English.

1. Anstatt Kaffee habe ich nur Wasser getrunken. ---------------------------------

----

2. Die Familie dachte oft an die Reise nach Deutschland. ---------------------------------

----

3. Meine Freunde sind heute abend bei mir. ---------------------------------

----

4. Die alten Leute erinnern sich an die alten Zeiten. ---------------------------------

----

5. Der Zeitung nach, soll das Wetter besser werden. ---------------------------------

----

6. Gestern abend sind wir ins Kino gegangen. ---------------------------------

----

7. Er freut sich über das neue Radio. ---------------------------------

----

8. Wegen der Bilder habe ich das Buch gekauft. ---------------------------------

----

9. Der Student schreibt von den Sommerferien. ---------------------------------

----

10. Außer dem Lehrer, kenne ich niemanden im Zimmer. ---------------------------------

----

11. Sie standen an der Ecke. ---------------------------------
12. Die Studenten interessieren sich für die Sprache. ---------------------------------

----

13. Die Mädchen sprachen von neuen Kleidern. ---------------------------------

----

14. Er wußte nichts von Kameras. ---------------------------------
15. Mutter saß neben dem Klavier. ---------------------------------

J. Translate into German.

1. The lady asks about a hotel. ---------------------------------

----

2. The gentleman asked for the card. ---------------------------------

----

3. We've been here for three weeks. ---------------------------------

----

4. I like to play, but I don't have the time. --

----

5. The boys are interested in sports. ---

----

6. She lives on Goethe Street. --

7. I arrived a month ago. --

8. He's going to the movies. ---

9. Mother's in the kitchen. --

10. During the summer, we're staying with my uncle. ----------------------------------

----

11. I'm taking a bus to Hamburg. --

12. The boy threw the ball through the window. ---

----

13. Miss Schmidt is staying home today. ---

----

14. I bought a record for my sister for Christmas. --------------------------------------

----

15. They're waiting on the corner. ---

In many German cities, the weeks before Lent are celebrated with parades and merry carnivals similar to Mardi Gras. Typical of these is the *Karneval* in Köln (Cologne), with its masquerade balls and wild costumes.

20. COMPARISON OF ADJECTIVES AND ADVERBS

Both in English and in German, adjectives and adverbs have three degrees of comparison: (1) positive (a *good* man), (2) comparative (a *better* man), and (3) superlative (the *best* man).

COMPARISON OF ADJECTIVES

In German, the comparative is formed by adding **-er** to the adjective, and the superlative is formed by adding **-(e)st-**.

DEGREE	ENGLISH	GERMAN
POSITIVE	fast	schnell
COMPARATIVE	fast*er*	schnell*er*
SUPERLATIVE	fast*est*	schnell*st-*

Note

1. English often uses *more* and *most* to form comparatives; German never does this. All German adjectives form the comparative and superlative degrees in the same way: "more beautiful" = **schöner,** "most beautiful" = **schönst-.**

2. Comparative and superlative adjectives add the regular adjective endings when they are followed by nouns:

CASE	COMPARATIVE		SUPERLATIVE
	the larger car	*a larger car*	*the largest car*
NOM.	der größer*e* Wagen	ein größer*er* Wagen	der größ*te* Wagen
ACC.	den größer*en* Wagen	einen größer*en* Wagen	den größ*ten* Wagen
DAT.	dem größer*en* Wagen	einem größer*en* Wagen	dem größ*ten* Wagen
GEN.	des größer*en* Wagens	eines größer*en* Wagens	des größ*ten* Wagens

3. When no noun follows a comparative-degree adjective, the adjective has no ending:

   Dieser Wagen ist **größer.**   This car is larger.

4. Adjectives ending in **-el, -en,** and **-er** usually drop the **e** in the comparative form (but *not* in the superlative) when an adjective ending is added:

	dunk*el,* ***dunkl*eren**	selt*en,* ***seltn*erer**	teu*er,* ***teur*eres**
But:	den dunk*el*sten	der selt*en*ste	das teu*er*ste

   Dies Kleid ist dunk*el*er als das dort.   This dress is darker than that one.

   Sie will ein ***dunkl*eres** Kleid kaufen.   She wants to buy a darker dress.

   Dies ist das dunk*el*ste Kleid.   This is the darkest dress.

149

5. The superlative always has an ending. If the superlative adjective is followed by a noun, the regular adjective ending is used. If the superlative adjective is *not* followed by a noun, the ending **-en** is added to the adjective and the word **am** is used before it:

Das ist der höchst**e Baum.**   That is the highest tree.

Dieser Baum ist ***am*** höchst**en.**   This tree is the highest.

These two constructions cannot be interchanged.

6. Most one-syllable adjectives take an umlaut (if possible) in both the comparative and superlative forms: **alt, älter, ältest-.** This is not true of adjectives with **au** (**laut, lauter**) or for the adjectives **falsch, wahr, froh,** and **bunt.**

7. An **e** is added before the **-st** in the superlative when necessary for pronunciation (generally with adjectives ending in **-d, -t, -s, -ß, -sch, -z,** or **-eu, -au**):

lau**t,** lau**t**est-   al**t,** äl**t**est-   n**eu,** n**eu**est-

IRREGULAR COMPARATIVE AND SUPERLATIVE FORMS

POSITIVE	COMPARATIVE	SUPERLATIVE
——	——	**erst-,** first, earliest
groß, large	**größer,** larger	**größt-,** largest
gut, good	**besser,** better	**best-,** best
hoch, high	**höher,** higher	**höchst-,** highest
——	——	**letzt-,** latest, last
lieb, dear	**lieber,** dearer	**liebst-,** dearest
nah(e), near	**näher,** nearer	**nächst-,** nearest, next
viel, much, many	**mehr,** more	**meist-,** most

Wir müssen auf einen späteren Zug warten, denn der **erste** ist schon abgefahren.

We must wait for a later train, for the first one has already left.

Hans ist mir sehr **lieb,** aber Franz ist mein **liebster** Freund.

I like Hans very much, but Franz is my best friend.

Das Rathaus ist **näher** als der Bahnhof; es ist in der **nächsten** Straße.

The city hall is nearer than the train station; it is on the next street.

Viele Menschen müssen arbeiten, aber die **meisten** Kinder dürfen spielen.

Many men have to work, but most children may play.

Note

1. The definite article must be used with the adjective **meist-**: *die* **meisten Leute**, *most people.*

2. **Erst** may also be used as an adverb meaning *at the earliest* or *not until*:

Der nächste Zug kommt **erst** morgen an. | The next train arrives tomorrow at the earliest. (The next train will not arrive until tomorrow.)

COMPARISON OF ADVERBS

The comparative degrees of the adverb are generally the same forms as those for the adjective, except that adverbs never have endings. The superlative adverb is always used in the **am . . . -sten** construction.

IRREGULAR COMPARATIVE FORMS OF ADVERBS

POSITIVE	COMPARATIVE	SUPERLATIVE
bald, soon	**eher,** sooner	**am ehesten,** soonest
gern (haben), to like	**lieber (haben),** to like better, to prefer	**am liebsten (haben),** to like most
sehr, very	**mehr,** more	**am meisten,** most
wohl, well	**besser,** better	**am besten,** best

Du bist **bald** gekommen, aber er kam **eher** als du. Franz ist **am ehesten** angekommen. | You came soon but he came earlier than you. Frank arrived earliest.

Er ißt **sehr** viel, Karl ißt **mehr,** aber Hans ißt **am meisten.** | He eats very much, Carl eats more, but Hans eats the most.

Note

1. The comparative and superlative degrees of adjectives and adverbs are sometimes used when only one of the objects of comparison is expressed (the others being implied or understood):

Am besten spielt er Fußball. | He plays soccer best of all.

2. The comparative degree is often used in the sense of "rather" or "quite a":

Vor **längerer** Zeit ist er schon ausgezogen. | He moved out quite a while ago (a rather long time ago).

3. As an adverb, **lieber** often means *to prefer* or *rather*:

Ich gehe **lieber** ins Kino. | I prefer going to the movies. (I would rather go to the movies.)

4. With **gefallen,** the comparative forms **besser** and **am besten** are used:

Die Musik gefällt mir **sehr,** aber das Schauspiel gefällt mir *besser.* Ein guter Film gefällt mir *am besten.*	I like the music, but I like the play more (better). I like a good movie best of all.

EXPRESSIONS OF COMPARISON

A. *Positive Degree*

(eben)so . . . wie, (just) as . . . as

Sie ist **(eben)so** alt **wie** er.	She is (just) as old as he.

nicht so . . . wie, not as . . . as

Sie kennt ihn **nicht so** gut **wie** ich.	She doesn't know him as well as I. (= as well as I know him.)
Ich kenne sie **nicht so** gut **wie** ihn.	I don't know her as well as him. (= as well as I know him.)

Note

The case of the noun or pronoun following **wie** depends on the meaning of the implied clause. In the last German example given (**. . . so gut wie ihn**), the implied meaning is **. . . so gut wie** *ich ihn kenne*; hence, **ihn** is in the accusative case.

B. *Comparative Degree*

als, than

Der Baum ist höher **als** das Haus.	The tree is higher than the house.

je . . . desto, the . . . the

Je größer, **desto** besser.	The bigger, the better.

ÜBUNGEN

A. Change the adjective to the comparative degree.

1. Welcher ist der alte Wagen?   -----------------------------------
2. Er arbeitet mit kleinen Kindern.   -----------------------------------
3. Ich habe ein schönes Konzert gehört.   -----------------------------------
4. Da drüben ist ein tiefes Wasser.   -----------------------------------
5. Er kauft eine teuere Krawatte.   -----------------------------------
6. Sie sitzt an einem großen Tisch.   -----------------------------------
7. Schöne Musik gefällt den Leuten.   -----------------------------------
8. Ich suche ein interessantes Buch.   -----------------------------------
9. Haben Sie einen langen Brief geschrieben?   -----------------------------------
10. Diese Dinge sind gut.   -----------------------------------

B. Change the adjective to the superlative degree.

1. Friedrich ist der kranke Junge.   -----------------------------------

2. Dieses Auto ist neu. -------------------------------------

3. Hier sind unsere warmen Handschuhe. -------------------------------------

4. Berlin ist eine große Stadt in Deutschland. -------------------------------------

5. Wir fangen heute mit der neuen Lektion an. -------------------------------------

6. Der Mantel ist warm. -------------------------------------

7. Der Kölner Dom ist bekannt. -------------------------------------

8. In unserem Garten steht ein hohe Baum. -------------------------------------

9. Ich kaufe mir die neue Medizin. -------------------------------------

10. Das Land ist schön. -------------------------------------

C. Change the adverb to the comparative degree.

1. Wir singen gern. -------------------------------

2. Sie spielt gut Klavier. -------------------------------

3. Zum Abendessen aß er viel. -------------------------------

4. Der Bahnhof ist nahe. -------------------------------

5. Das kann sie billig kaufen. -------------------------------

6. Sie haben uns selten gesehen. -------------------------------

7. Die Studenten müssen viel studieren. -------------------------------

8. Wir sollen oft Deutsch sprechen. -------------------------------

9. Er ruft laut. -------------------------------

10. Die Jungen laufen schnell. -------------------------------

D. Change the adverb to the superlative degree.

1. Die Dame singt schön. -------------------------------------

2. Die Jungen laufen schnell weg. -------------------------------------

3. Ich lese gern Zeitungen. -------------------------------------

4. Gert spielt gut Ball. -------------------------------------

5. Er sprach laut. -------------------------------------

6. Er fuhr weit über das Land. -------------------------------------

7. Sie freut sich sehr darauf. -------------------------------------

8. Das sieht schlecht aus. -------------------------------------

9. Das Feuer brennt hell. -------------------------------------

10. Wer ruft laut? -------------------------------------

E. Replace the comparative or superlative with the corresponding forms of the words in parentheses.

1. Hier ist das letzte Bett. (groß, neu, gut)

----

2. Dieser Brief ist länger.   (interessant, klein, einfach)

----

3. Da drüben ist das Wasser am tiefsten.   (kalt, warm, dunkel)

----

4. Dieses Klavier ist älter als das da.   (neu, billig, laut)

----

5. Frau Schmidt trägt den schönsten Hut.   (dunkel, klein, teuer)

----

6. Wir haben ein böseres Tier gesehen.   (selten, hungrig, furchtbar)

----

7. Ich suche den einfachsten Roman in der Bibliothek.   (bekannt, gut, interessant)

----

8. Das Wetter wird kühler werden.   (warm, schlecht, kalt)

----

9. Er ist ebenso hungrig wie ich.   (groß, müde, zufrieden)

----

10. Je schneller, desto besser.   (langsam ... schlecht, viel ... billig, lang ... langweilig)

F. Complete the answers to the questions.

1. Welcher ist der jüngste Sohn?

   Karl --.

2. Wer von beiden ist älter, Elsbeth oder Günther?

   Günther --.

3. Essen Sie gern Sauerkraut?

   Ja, aber Sauerbraten --.

4. Welche ist die größte Kirche in der Stadt?

   Diese Kirche --.

5. Wer kommt am spätesten?

   Herr Müller --.

6. Ist dieser Wagen so schnell wie der da?

   Nein, dieser --.

7. Kann Helmut gut lesen?

   Ja, aber ich --.

8. Das Buch gefällt ihm sehr, nicht wahr?

Ja, aber dieses _____.

9. Wie wird das Wetter morgen—so kalt wie heute?

Nein, morgen _____.

10. Freuen sich alle Menschen darüber?

Nicht alle, aber _____.

G. Translate into English.

1. Man fährt am schnellsten mit dem Zug. _____

_____

2. Sie singt nicht so schön wie ich. _____

_____

3. Er blieb längere Zeit dort. _____

_____

4. Wann kommt die nächste Post? _____

_____

5. Je hungriger man ist, desto mehr ißt man. _____

_____

6. Herr Müller ist früher angekommen. _____

_____

7. Mein Bruder ist kränker als meine Schwester. _____

_____

8. Dieser Bahnhof ist höher als das Rathaus. _____

_____

9. Hören wir uns lieber ein Symphoniekonzert an! _____

_____

10. Diese Geschichte gefällt den meisten Kindern. _____

_____

H. Translate into German.

1. Hans is luckier than I. _____

2. The garden is very beautiful. _____

3. Most people prefer to go to the movies. _____

_____

4. This is our cheapest paper. _____

5. Have you seen a more beautiful park? _____

_____

6. The sooner we get home, the better. --

----

7. He sang the song most beautifully. --

----

8. This postcard is not as expensive as the other one. --

----

9. The next picture is better than this one. --

----

10. Ursel speaks German the best. --

The *Holstentor*, built in the 15th century, is an historic gateway to the port city of Lübeck.

21. REVIEW OF PART III—ADJECTIVES, ADVERBS, AND PREPOSITIONS

WORTSCHATZ

Zu Hause

der **Abort, -e** ⎫ toilet
die **Toilette, -n** ⎭

das **Bad, ⸚er,** bath
  ein Bad nehmen, to take a bath
das **Badetuch, ⸚er,** bath towel
die **Badewanne, -n,** bath tub
das **Badezimmer, -,** bathroom
der **Balkon, -e (-s),** balcony
das **Bett, -en,** bed
  zu Bett (ins Bett) gehen, to go to bed
der **Boden, -(⸚)** ⎫
die **Bodenkammer, -n** ⎬ attic
der **Bodenraum, -e** ⎭
die **Brause, -n** ⎫ shower
das **Brausebad, ⸚er** ⎭ bath
das **Bücherregal, -e,** bookshelf
das **Dach, ⸚er,** roof
die **Decke, -n,** blanket, bedcover; ceiling
das **Einzelhaus, ⸚er,** individual house (not
  part of a housing complex)
das **Erdgeschoß, -e,** ground floor
der **Fernsehapparat, -e,** television set
das **Fernsehen,** television
der **Flur, -e,** entrance hall (of a house or
  apartment)
der **Fußboden, ⸚,** floor (of a room)
die **Garage, -n,** garage
die **Garderobe, -n,** clothes closet

die **Gardine, -n,** curtain (in a room), drape
das **Handtuch, ⸚er,** (hand) towel
die **Heizung, -en,** heating system, furnace
der **Herd, -e,** kitchen range, stove
das **Klavier, -e,** piano
der **Kleiderständer, -,** hall stand (for hats
  and coats)
die **Küche, -n,** kitchen
die **Lampe, -n,** lamp
die **Mauer, -n,** wall (not part of a house)
das **Möbel, -,** piece of furniture, *pl.,* furniture
der **Nachttisch, -e,** night table
der **Ofen, ⸚,** oven
der **Schrank, ⸚e,** cupboard, closet, bookcase
der **Schreibtisch, -e,** writing table, desk
die **Seife, -n,** soap
der **Sessel, -,** easy chair, upholstered
  armchair
das **Sofa, -s,** sofa, couch
der **Spiegel, -,** mirror
der **Stock, ⸚e (or -werke),** floor, story *(See
  the Note below.)*
die **Stufe, -n,** step (of stairs)
der **Teppich, -e,** carpet, rug
der **Tisch, -e,** table
die **Treppe, -n,** (flight of) stairs, staircase
die **Wand, ⸚e,** wall (of a room)
die **Wohnung, -en,** dwelling, apartment

Note

In German buildings, the first floor (**der erste Stock**) means the first floor *above* ground level
(**das Erdgeschoß**). Thus, **der erste Stock** is the *second* floor in the United States, **der zweite
Stock** is the *third* floor, etc.

ÜBUNGEN

A. Write the correct endings for the adjectives.

1. In unser_____ Wohnzimmer haben wir ein neu_____ Klavier.

2. Im erst_____ Stock habe ich mein_____ Schlafzimmer.

3. Mutter möchte gern einen grün_____ Teppich kaufen.

4. Er setzt sich an den groß_____ Tisch.

5. Die meisten neu_____ Einzelhäuser haben eine Garage.

6. Die Katze sitzt oben auf dem hoh_____ Dach.

7. In der klein_____ Küche ist nicht Platz genug für so ein_____ groß_____ Tisch.

8. Dies_____ alt_____ Kleiderständer gehört mein_____ Vater.

9. Auf sein_____ Nachttisch hat er einige gut_____ Bücher.

10. An der Wand hängt ein groß_____, teuer_____ Spiegel.

11. Wir haben eine klein_____ Badewanne, aber kein_____ Brause.

12. Hell_____ Decken sehen in solch_____ klein_____ Zimmern besser aus.

13. Wir möchten uns einen größer_____ Fernsehapparat kaufen.

14. Auf unser_____ Fußboden haben wir einen grün_____ Teppich.

15. Welch_____ Bett ist dein_____?

16. Wir brauchen einen modern_____ Herd.

17. Mein_____ Schwester interessiert sich für alt_____ Möbel.

18. Ich habe einige mein_____ Freunde in mein_____ Wohnung eingeladen.

19. In welch_____ Schrank werde ich die Handtücher finden?

20. Alle dies_____ schön_____ Teppiche sind zu teuer_____ für mich.

B. Write the correct form of the word in parentheses.

1. (dies)   Auf _____ Herd kann ich nichts kochen.

2. (welch)   In _____ Stock haben die Eltern ihr Schlafzimmer?

3. (solch)   _____ Wohnungen findet man nur selten.

4. (jed-)   Man muß auf _____ Stufe achten.

5. (manch)   _____ Einzelhäuser haben hinten einen kleinen Garten.

6. (welch)   _____ ist der Sessel, den Sie kaufen wollen?

7. (jed-)   In _____ Schlafzimmer gibt es eine Garderobe.

8. (solch)   _____ alten Möbel sind heute sehr teuer.

9. (welch)   _____ Bücherregal gehört dir?

10. (dies)   Ich weiß nichts von _____ Seife.

C. In each sentence, use the comparative form of the modifier in italics.

1. Haben Sie einen *großen* Spiegel?   _____

2. Unser Haus hat ein *neues* Dach.   _____

3. Die Familie will sich einen *guten* Fernsehapparat kaufen.   _____

4. Um den Garten baute Herr Maier eine *hohe* Mauer.   _____

5. Die Kinder setzten sich an den *kleinen* Tisch.   _____

6. Der Flur ist *lang*.   _____

7. Er kauft nur *billige* Möbel.   _____

8. Die Kinder laufen *schnell* die Treppen hinauf.   _____

9. Der Keller ist ein *dunkler* Platz.   _____

10. Unsere Gäste sind *früh* gekommen.   _____

D. Write the sentences of exercise *C*, using the superlative forms of the modifiers in italics.

1. _____

2. _____

3. _____

4. _____

5. _____

6. _____

7. _____

8. _____

9. _____

10. _____

E. Complete each sentence by writing the correct form of the possessive adjective that corresponds to the word in parentheses.

EXAMPLE: (Karl)   Hast du __*sein*__ Buch gesehen?

1. (ich)   _____ Lampe steht auf dem Nachttisch.

2. (Vater)   Die Tür _____ Arbeitszimmers ist geschlossen.

3. (wir)   _____ Haus fehlen neue Möbel.

4. (er)   Vater sitzt an _____ Schreibtisch.

5. (Sie)   _____ Küche ist zu klein.

6. (Herr und Frau Müller)   Herr und Frau Müller fühlen sich sehr wohl in _____ neuen Wohnung.

7. (wir)   Im Sommer sitzen wir oft auf _____ Balkon.

8. (du)   Du sollst _____ Kleider waschen.

9. (Anna)   Anna kann nicht _____ Handtuch finden.

10. (sie = they)   Das Wohnzimmer _____ Hauses hat einen schönen Teppich.

11. (ihr)   Ist _____ Garderobe schon voll?

12. (sie = she)   Die Farben _____ Sofas sind grün und rosa.

13. (Friedrich)   Friedrich kann nicht _____ Handschuhe finden.

14. (ich)   Er hat _____ Eltern geholfen.

15. (sie)   Gestern haben wir _____ Brief bekommen.

F. Write the correct form of the definite article in the blanks.

1. Auf _____ Bücherregal stehen viele Bücher.

2. An Sommerabenden sitzt die Familie oft auf _____ Balkon.

3. Vater sitzt an _____ Schreibtisch.

4. Wieviel hat sie für _____ Lampe bezahlt?

5. Der Junge steigt über _____ Mauer.

6. Mutter kommt jetzt aus _____ Küche.

7. Neben _____ Bett ist _____ Nachttisch.

8. Ich muß _____ Auto in _____ Garage fahren.

9. Unter _____ Erdgeschoß ist der Keller.

10. Die Katze schläft gern hinter _____ Ofen.

11. Das Mädchen steht vor _____ Spiegel.

12. Erinnern Sie sich an _____ Klavier?

13. Seit _____ ersten Oktober wohnen wir nicht mehr in _____ Friedrichstraße.

14. Zum Abendessen sitzen alle Gäste um _____ großen Tisch herum.

15. Ein Kleiderständer steht in _____ Flur.

16. Unter _____ Sofa haben wir den Brief gefunden.

17. Man kann sich nicht auf _____ Heizung verlassen.

18. Nach _____ Abendessen setzte sich Onkel Fritz an _____ Klavier und spielte ein paar Stücke.

19. Mutter freut sich über _____ schönen Gardinen.

20. An _____ Wänden unserer Wohnung haben wir mehrere Bilder.

    G. Write the correct preposition.

1. Hat er _____ die Frage geantwortet?

2. Die Jungen interessieren sich _____ Sport.

3. _____ wen denken Sie?

4. Wie lange hat er schon _____ dich gewartet?

5. Hoffentlich können wir uns _____ sein Auto verlassen.

6. Darf ich Sie _____ ein Glas Wasser bitten?

7. Vater mußte viel Geld _____ die Möbel ausgeben.

8. Heute werden wir _____ der achten Lektion arbeiten.

9. Der alte Herr fragt _____ dem Krankenhaus.

10. Er hat mir _____ das Geschenk gedankt.

11. Wir erinnern uns _____ das Datum.

12. Hör bitte _____ der Katzenmusik auf!

13. Herr Schröder gehört _____ einem bekannten Orchester.

14. Wegen des kalten Winters sind viele Tiere _____ Hunger gestorben.

15. Sie müssen sich _____ die Prüfung vorbereiten.

16. Mutter freut sich _____ dem neuen Sessel.

17. Hoffentlich können Sie ein paar Tage _____ uns bleiben.

18. Man soll _____ den heißen Ofen achten.

19. Er lud mich am Montag _____ dem Abendessen ein.

20. Was halten Sie _____ unserem neuen Einzelhaus?

H. Replace the words in italics with the words in parentheses, making other changes in the sentence where necessary.

    EXAMPLE: Ich *fuhr* in die Stadt.   (kommen, wohnen, bleiben)
              Ich *kam* in die Stadt. Ich *wohnte* in *der* Stadt, etc.

1. Meine Schuhe sind *auf* dem Bett.   (unter, neben, hinter)

---

2. Er *denkt* an seine Mutter.   (schreiben, fragen, warten)

---

3. Die Schüler freuen sich auf *das*   (die Lektion, die Ferien, der Besuch)
    nächste *Programm.*

---

4. Welcher ist der *neueste* Spiegel?   (gut, alt, teuer)

---

5. Der Preis *dieses* Klaviers ist 500 Mark. (jeder, sein, manch)

---

6. Der Kaffee ist *heißer* als der Tee.   (warm, gut, billig)

---

7. Welche Geschichte ist *am bekanntesten.* (kurz, interessant, einfach)

---

8. Die Jungen laufen *an* die Mauer.   (über, um, von … weg)

---

9. Davon habe ich nicht *gefragt.*   (warten, sich erinnern, arbeiten)

---

10. Er setzte sich an *meinen* Tisch.   (ihr, unser, euer)

I. The answers to the following questions appear in parentheses. Answer each question with a complete sentence in German.

1. In welchem Stock findet man den Abort?   (second floor)

---

2. Wo soll ich diese Bücher stellen?   (on the first bookshelf)

---

3. Was machen wir heute abend?   (go to my brother's)

---

4. Was fehlt im Badezimmer noch?   (a good, large mirror)

----

5. Wo legen die Gäste Hut und Mantel ab?   (in the front hall)

----

6. Warum gibt's Wasser auf dem Fußboden?   (we need a new roof)

----

7. Was ist Ihre Adresse?   (our house is on Rhine Street)

----

8. In welchem Stock ist seine Wohnung?   (on the ground floor)

----

9. Was bekommt die Familie zu Weihnachten?   (a new TV set)

----

10. Was für Möbel sieht man im Wohnzimmer?   (a sofa, a couple of easy chairs, a piano)

----

11. Was will Vater um den Hof bauen?   (a wall)

----

12. Wo ist dein Nachttisch?   (beside my bed)

----

13. Warum können wir nicht auf dem Balkon sitzen? (because of the rain)

----

14. Wo haben die Kinder ihr Spielzimmer?   (in the attic)

----

15. Gibt es hier ein Brausebad?   (yes, both tub and shower)

J. Translate into English.

1. Die Heizung unserer Wohnung ist im Keller. --

----

2. Trotz der neuen Badewanne, nehme ich lieber ein Brausebad. --

----

3. Herr und Frau Schmidt kommen heute abend zu uns. _____

_____

4. Sie dürfen Ihren Wagen in unserer neuen Garage lassen. _____

_____

5. Einzelhäuser sind seltener in den Städten als auf dem Land. _____

_____

6. Auf meinem Bett habe ich eine grüne Decke. _____

_____

7. Die Kinder versuchen sich ohne Seife die Hände zu waschen. _____

_____

8. Die Bade- und Handtücher sind in dem Schrank neben der Badezimmertür. _____

_____

9. Am Montag haben wir im Fernsehen das interessanteste Programm gesehen. _____

_____

10. Wegen der neuen Heizung ist das ganze Haus jetzt schön warm. _____

_____

11. Fast jede Wohnung hat ihren eigenen Balkon. _____

_____

12. Bei uns spielt niemand Klavier. _____

_____

13. Auf Vaters Schreibtisch steht eine kleine Arbeitslampe. _____

_____

14. Die Garderobe in ihrem Schlafzimmer ist größer als meine. _____

_____

15. Ein dicker Teppich liegt auf dem Fußboden. _____

_____

K. Translate into German.

1. Most of all, Mother would like new curtains. _____

_____

2. I take a bath every evening. _____

3. In the middle of our living room is a large table at which the whole family sits after dinner. _____

_____

4. Whenever the weather gets warmer, we don't have to use the furnace so much. _____

_____

5. The coat rack in the hall is very old. _____

6. The roofs of the houses in the old city have many colors—red, brown, blue, green. _____

_____

7. The ceilings of the newer houses are not as high as in the older houses. _____

_____

8. My family lived on Lessing Street for many years. _____

_____

9. Their apartment is on the fourth floor of that building over there. _____

_____

10. Even if she has the best kitchen range, my sister still can't cook. _____

_____

Karl der Große, or Charlemagne (742–814), was king of the Franks and laid the foundation for the Holy Roman Empire. Although illiterate himself, he fostered a revival of learning.

Part IV—Sentence Structure

22. WORD ORDER: MAIN CLAUSES

The position of the verb in a German clause does not vary. The finite verb (the verb form that is limited to a specific person and number) is in the second position in the clause. If the finite verb is an auxiliary, the past participle or infinitive that accompanies it is placed at the end of the clause.

BASIC PATTERN OF THE GERMAN SENTENCE

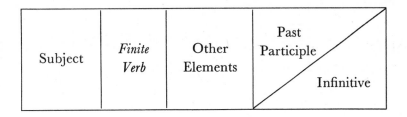

Der Junge *will* **den ganzen Tag mit seinen Freunden spielen.**
subject · finite verb · other elements · infinitive

Der Junge *hat* **den ganzen Tag mit seinen Freunden gespielt.**
subject · finite verb · other elements · past participle

The first slot in the sentence is considered to be the most important. Any element of the sentence —an adverb, object, etc.—may be placed in the first slot for the sake of emphasis. When this is done, the subject comes directly after the finite verb.

Mit seinen Freunden will der
finite verb

Junge den ganzen Tag spielen.
subject · infinitive

The boy wants to play *with his friends* all day.

Den ganzen Tag will der Junge
finite verb · subject

mit seinen Freunden spielen.
infinitive

The boy wants to play with his friends *all day long.*

Gestern hat der Junge den
finite verb · subject

ganzen Tag mit seinen

Freunden gespielt.
past participle

Yesterday the boy played with his friends all day.

An entire clause can be put in the first slot of the sentence (see Lesson 23):

Obgleich der Junge müde war,

hat er Fußball gespielt.
finite verb · subject · past participle

Although the boy was tired, he played soccer.

VARIATIONS OF THE BASIC SENTENCE PATTERN

SUBJECT / Direct Object / Indirect Object / Prepositional Phrase / Adverb / Subordinate Clause	FINITE VERB	SUBJECT	Other Elements — Objects, Adverbs, Prepositional Phrases, etc.	Past Participle	Infinitive
SUBJECT					
Direct Object					
Indirect Object					
Prepositional Phrase					
Adverb					
Subordinate Clause					

Zum letzten Mal haben sie ihn
<u>prepositional phrase</u> <u>finite verb</u> <u>subject</u>

gestern gesehen.
<u>past participle</u>

They saw him for the last time yesterday.

Morgen werden sie ihn kennenlernen.
<u>adverb</u> <u>finite verb</u> <u>subject</u> <u>infinitive</u>

They will meet him tomorrow.

Wenn sie kommt, werde ich mit
<u>subordinate clause</u> <u>finite verb</u> <u>subject</u>

ihr sprechen.
<u>infinitive</u>

When she comes, I will speak with her.

A. Observe the changes that can be made in the sentence **Der Junge gibt dem Herrn das Buch:**

Der Junge	gibt	dem Herrn	das Buch
Dem Herrn	gibt	der Junge	das Buch
Das Buch	gibt	der Junge	dem Herrn

B. The same kinds of changes can be made with **Der Junge hat dem Herrn das Buch gegeben** or with **Der Junge wird dem Herrn das Buch geben:**

Der Junge	hat	dem Herrn	das Buch	gegeben
Dem Herrn	hat	der Junge	das Buch	gegeben
Das Buch	hat	der Junge	dem Herrn	gegeben

Der Junge	wird	dem Herrn	das Buch	geben
Dem Herrn	wird	der Junge	das Buch	geben
Das Buch	wird	der Junge	dem Herrn	geben

Note

Generally speaking, the word receiving the most emphasis in the sentence is placed first. The second most emphatic position is at the end.

GENERAL RULES GOVERNING WORD ORDER

A. Adverbs generally follow the sequence *time/ manner/ place* (**wann/wie/wo**). Thus, expressions of time or of manner come *before* expressions of place, which is the opposite of English:

Er kam **früh nach Hause.**
       time   place

He came home early.

Er kam **schnell nach Hause.**
      manner   place

He came home quickly.

When all three kinds of adverbs appear in the same clause, the time expression is first and the place expression last:

Er kam **heute schnell nach Hause.**
     time manner   place

He came home quickly today.

Generally, however, it is preferable to have time expressions first in the clause: **Heute kam er schnell nach Hause.**

B. When two time expressions are used together, the more general is used first, followed by the more specific:

Wir werden **morgen nach dem Abendessen** ins Konzert gehen.

We will go to the concert after dinner tomorrow.

C. A direct object usually follows adverbs, unless the direct object is shorter than the other elements:

Wir haben **gestern früh**
        adverbs

das Rathaus besucht.
 direct object

We visited the city hall yesterday morning.

But:

Wir haben **es gestern** gesehen.
      direct adverb
      object

We saw it yesterday.

However, if the time element is to be stressed, the adverb would come after the direct object:

Wir haben **das Rathaus**
       direct object

gestern früh gesehen.
 adverbs of time

Yesterday morning we saw the city hall.

D. A prepositional phrase normally follows the word that it modifies:

Er kauft ein **Haus** *mit großen Fenstern.*	He is buying a house with large windows.
Ich **las** *mit großer Freude* Ihren letzten Brief.	I read your latest letter with great joy.

E. (1) When the direct object is a noun, it comes *after* the indirect object:

Er gab <u>mir</u> (Er gab <u>dem Herrn</u>)   He gave me (He gave the gentleman)
    indirect   indirect object   the book.
    object

das Buch.

(2) When the direct object is a pronoun, it comes *before* the indirect object:

Er gab **es** <u>mir</u> (Er gab **es** <u>dem Herrn</u>).   He gave it to me (He gave it to the gentleman).
    indirect   indirect object
    object

F. (1) In regular word order, the reflexive pronoun comes directly after the finite verb:

Er wäscht **sich** jeden Morgen das Gesicht.	He washes his face every morning.

(2) If the subject is not in the first slot:

    a. The reflexive pronoun comes *before* the subject when the subject is a noun.

Jeden Morgen wäscht **sich**   Every morning the boy washes his face.
<u>der Junge</u> das Gesicht.
    subject

    b. The reflexive pronoun comes *after* the subject when the subject is a pronoun.

Jeden Morgen wäscht <u>er</u> **sich**   Every morning he washes his face.
    subject
das Gesicht.

G. (1) **Nicht** usually stands before the part of the sentence that is negated:

Er gab **nicht** *mir* das Geld.	He didn't give *me* the money. (but perhaps to someone else)
Er gab mir **nicht** *das Geld.* Er hat mir **nicht** *das Geld* gegeben.	He didn't give me *the money.*

(2) **Nicht** appears at the end of the clause if the whole clause is negated (but *not* after a past participle or an infinitive):

Er gab mir das Geld **nicht.**

But: He didn't *give me the money.*

Er hat mir das Geld **nicht** *gegeben.*

(3) **Nicht** never stands between the subject and the finite verb when they both occur at the beginning of the clause.

H. Questions and commands are formed by placing the finite verb at the beginning of the sentence, but this change does not affect the order in which the other elements appear in the sentence:

Sie geben **dem Herrn das Buch.**
Geben Sie **dem Herrn das Buch?**
Geben Sie **dem Herrn das Buch!**

Note

When a reflexive verb is used in a question or a command, the reflexive pronoun precedes the subject if the subject is a noun and follows the subject if the subject is a pronoun.

Freuen **sich** die Herren darauf?
<u>subject</u>

Do the gentlemen look forward to it?

Freuen Sie **sich** darauf?
<u>subject</u>

Do you look forward to it?

Sorgen Sie **sich** nicht darum!
<u>subject</u>

Don't worry about that!

These rules apply even when the subject is preceded by an *auxiliary* verb: **Werden** *sich* **die Herren darauf freuen?**

ÜBUNGEN

A. Combine each set of elements in *two* ways to form two declarative sentences.

EXAMPLE: den Zug, wir, haben gesehen, gestern
    a. Wir haben gestern den Zug gesehen.
    b. Gestern haben wir den Zug gesehen.   *Or:* Den Zug haben wir gestern gesehen.

1. einen Hut, kauft, sich, der Herr, im Warenhaus

----

2. morgen, mein Bruder, Geburtstag, hat

----

3. eine neue Sprache, die Studenten, in der Schule, lernen

----

4. ins Kino, am Samstag, sind gegangen, wir

----

5. den Schlüssel, der Dame, zu dem Zimmer, gibt, er

----

6. die Jungen, gern, spielen, auf der Straße, immer

----

7. die Musik, sich, die Gäste, interessieren, für, nur

----

8. angekommen, der Zug, gestern abend, spät, ist

----

9. mir, geben, Mutter, ein Glas Wasser, wird

----

10. im Zimmer, sitzt, dem großen Stuhl, der Junge, auf

B. Reconstruct the sentence so that it begins with the words in italics.

1. Wir sind *heute morgen* früh aufgestanden. -----------------------------------

----

2. Der Herr ißt eine Wurst *am Bahnhof*. -----------------------------------

3. Das Kind nimmt *den Hund* mit in die Schule. -----------------------------

----

4. Es gibt heute *in Berlin* schönes Wetter. -----------------------------------

5. Meine Eltern sind *durch die ganze Welt* gefahren. ------------------------

----

6. Das Mädchen spielt gut *Klavier*. -----------------------------------

7. Die Leute kommen *bald* nach Hause. -----------------------------------

----

8. Ich kaufte mir *neue Handschuhe*. -----------------------------------

9. Sie schrieb einen Brief *an ihren Bruder*. -----------------------------

----

10. Der Kellner brachte *uns* eine Speisekarte. -----------------------------

----

C. Use each sentence to form three new sentences as follows: (*a*) Change the direct object to a pronoun. (*b*) Change the *in*direct object to a pronoun. (*c*) Change both objects to pronouns.

EXAMPLE: Er gab dem Herrn das Buch (*or* ein Buch).

a. Er gab *es* dem Herrn.　*b.* Er gab *ihm* das Buch.　*c.* Er gab *es ihm.*

1. Der Herr zeigt den Gästen den Dom. -----------------------------------

----

2. Ich gab Vater eine Krawatte. ------------------------------------

----

3. Mutter erzählt den Kindern eine Geschichte. ------------------

----

----

4. Können Sie der Dame die Adresse sagen? ----------------------

----

5. Vater verspricht der Familie eine Reise. ----------------------

----

6. Die Verkäuferin verkauft dem Herrn einen Anzug. ------------

----

----

7. Der Lehrer erklärt den Studenten das Wort. --------------------

----

8. Meine Tante schenkt meiner Mutter ein neues Kleid. ----------

----

----

9. Ich möchte meinem Bruder ein Bild schicken. ------------------

----

10. Der Kellner bringt den Gästen das Essen. ----------------------

----

D. Construct a sentence that combines all the expressions in parentheses with the given sentence or sentence fragment.

1. (heute, nach Hause, mit seinem Bruder) Er wird kommen. ----------------

----

2. (in Berlin, am Sonntag) Ich komme an. ----------------------------

----

3. (langsam, ins Kino) Gestern gingen wir. ----------------------------

----

4. (gern, jeden Sommer, auf dem Lande) Wir verbringen unsere Ferien. ------

----

5. (nach Hause, um 7 Uhr) Die Familie kommt an. ----------------------

----

6. (eine Woche, in München) Meine Eltern sind geblieben. --------------

----

7. (hier, seit einer Woche) Ich bin. ----------------------------------

8. (morgen, nach Deutschland, um 9 Uhr) Wir werden abfahren. _____

_____

9. (zu Hause, gestern abend, sicher) Ich war. _____

_____

10. (in acht Tagen, in Köln) Ich werde sein. _____

_____

E. Write each sentence, inserting **nicht** to negate the words in italics.

1. Ich war *zu Hause*. _____

2. Er hat mich *besucht*. _____

3. Der Ring hat *sehr viel* gekostet. _____

4. Mutter kommt *am Montag* an. _____

5. Vater *hilft* mir. _____

6. Sie gibt *ihm* das Geld. _____

7. Hans *hat* das Buch. _____

8. Herr Schmidt ruft *dich*. _____

9. Er hat das Fenster *zerbrochen*. _____

10. Er *bringt* seinen Bruder mit. _____

F. Change the sentence to a question.

1. Er fragt nach dem Preis. _____

2. Ich habe dir nichts gesagt. _____

3. Fräulein Müller freut sich darüber. _____

4. Sie können den Herrn anrufen. _____

5. Sie kämmt sich das Haar. _____

6. Wir sind nach Berlin gefahren. _____

7. Ihr müßt euch beeilen. _____

8. Die Herren setzen sich an den Tisch. _____

9. Ich folgte den Kindern. _____

10. Er hat sich ein neues Auto gekauft. _____

G. Complete the answers to the questions.

1. Was haben Sie sich gekauft?

Einen neuen Mantel _____.

2. Sie werden drei Wochen in Deutschland bleiben, nicht wahr?

Nein, nur zwei Wochen _____.

3. Wen hat er dort kennengelernt?

Meinen Bruder _____.

4. Wie fühlen Sie sich heute?

Heute _____.

5. Bekommt sie am Bahnhof eine Karte?

Ja, eine Karte _____.

6. Gefällt ihm das Hotel?

Nein, ihm _____.

7. Was stellte sich der Junge vor?

Einen warmen Sommertag _____.

8. Kommt Hans morgen wieder nach Hause?

Ja, er _____.

9. Gehen Sie heute abend ins Theater?

Nein, ich _____.

10. Wer hat Ihnen den Schlüssel gegeben?

Die Dame _____.

H. Translate into German.

1. In his pocket is a glove. _____

2. Is Gerhardt interested in sports? _____

3. This letter is not for me. _____

4. Converse in German, children! _____

5. To me he promised a larger room. _____

_____

6. We haven't heard this record. _____

7. Did Mrs. Werner show it to him? _____

8. Are the children getting dressed? _____

9. The guests have been here a month. _____

_____

10. Already the concert is starting in the park. _____

_____

23. WORD ORDER: SUBORDINATE CLAUSES

Every clause has a subject and a verb. An *independent clause* can stand alone as a complete sentence. A *dependent clause*, or *subordinate clause*, can be used only as part of a sentence and does not form a complete sentence by itself.

Conjunctions show the relation between two clauses: coordinating conjunctions (*and, but*, etc.) join two independent clauses; subordinating conjunctions (*although, while*, etc.) connect a dependent clause to an independent clause.

German has five coordinating conjunctions. When these are used, each independent clause has normal word order.

COORDINATING CONJUNCTIONS

> **aber,** but, however
> **denn,** for (= because)
> **oder,** or
> **sondern,** but, on the contrary
> **und,** and

Sie wollen den Film sehen, **aber** sie haben nicht die Zeit dafür.

They want to see the film but they don't have the time.

Note

1. **Sondern** may be used only if the first clause is negative:

Er kommt **nicht** heute, *sondern* er wird morgen kommen.

He is not coming today, but he will come tomorrow.

If these clauses are reversed, then **aber** must be used: **Er wird morgen kommen,** *aber* **heute kommt er nicht.**

2. **Denn** means *for* in the sense of *because*:

Er kommt nicht heute, **denn** er ist krank.

He is not coming today, for (because) he is sick.

Denn must not be confused with **für,** which is always used as a preposition.

COORDINATING CONJUNCTION PAIRS

Several coordinating conjunctions are used in pairs:

> **entweder ... oder,** either ... or
> **je ... desto**
> **je ... um so** } the ... the
> **nicht nur ... sondern auch,** not only ... but also
> **weder ... noch,** neither ... nor, not ... nor

Each term of a conjunction pair may be followed either by a single word or by a clause:

Er kann das Orchester **weder** sehen **noch** hören.

He can neither see nor hear the orchestra.

Weder kann er das Orchester sehen, **noch** kann er die Musik hören.

He can neither see the orchestra nor can he hear the music.

WORD ORDER WITH CONJUNCTION PAIRS

The word order following these conjunction pairs may vary according to the emphasis in the sentence:

A. When the two terms of the conjunction pair are joined in the same clause or simple sentence, the word order is not changed.

Weder mein Bruder **noch** meine Schwester ist hier.

Neither my brother nor my sister is here.

Er ist **entweder** mit dem Zug **oder** mit dem Bus gefahren.

He traveled either by train or bus.

B. If neither clause is emphasized (or if the emphasis is placed on the objects of the verbs), the conjunctions (except **oder**) are treated as adverbs and are followed by the finite verb.

Weder *fährt* Hans mit dem Zug, **noch** *geht* er zu Fuß.

Hans is not going by train, nor is he walking.

Entweder *fährt* Hans mit dem Zug, **oder** er geht zu Fuß.

Hans is either going by train or he is walking.

C. If the subjects are emphasized, they are placed first in each clause.

Entweder *Hans* holt Onkel Fritz ab, **oder** *ich* hole ihn ab.

Either Hans will pick up Uncle Fritz or I'll do it.

D. If the verbs are emphasized, the verb is placed first in each clause.

Entweder *geht* er zur Schule, **oder** *fährt* er.

Either he walks to school or else he drives.

E. **Je** has the finite verb at the end of its clause, and **desto** (or **um so**) has the finite verb in the second slot of its clause.

Je länger ich ihn *kenne,* **desto** (**um so**) lieber *habe* ich ihn.

The longer I know him, the better I like him.

WORK ORDER IN SUBORDINATE CLAUSES

Conjunction	Subject	Other Elements	Past Participle or Infinitive	*Finite Verb*

In a dependent clause, the finite verb appears at the end of the clause:

Obgleich ich ihm oft gern geholfen habe, konnte er noch nicht die Arbeit machen.	Although I often helped him gladly, he still couldn't do the work.

If the subordinate clause comes first in the sentence, it is the first element in the sentence; hence, it is followed by the finite verb of the independent clause:

DEPENDENT CLAUSE			MAIN CLAUSE		
Conj.	*Subject, etc.*	*Verb*	*Finite Verb*	*Subject*	*Other Elements*
Sobald	**der Zug**	**ankommt,**	*läuft*	**der Hund**	**schnell weg.**

Note

1. Separable verbs are not divided in subordinate clauses:

Sobald der Zug **ankommt,** . . .	As soon as the train arrives, . . .

2. The clauses of a German sentence are separated by commas, even though a comma is often not used in English:

Er wußte, daß Vater zu Hause war.	He knew that Father was at home.

SUBORDINATING CONJUNCTIONS

als, when (one time)	**obgleich,** although
bevor, before	**seitdem,** since (a time)
bis, until	**sobald,** as soon as
da, since (= because)	**solange,** as long as
daß, that	**trotzdem,** despite the fact that
ehe, before	**während,** while
nachdem, after	**weil,** because
ob, whether, if	**wenn,** if, when(ever)

Note

1. *When* is expressed in three ways in German:

   a. **Als** refers to a single event in the past.

Als ich nach Hause kam, . . .	When I got home, . . .

   b. **Wann** asks a question.

Wann kommt er?	When is he coming?

   Wann may also be used in indirect discourse:

Vater fragt, **wann** das Konzert beginnt. | Father asks when (at what time) the concert will begin.

    c. **Wenn** is used in all other cases.

       Wenn wir nach Hause kamen, . . . | When(ever) we came (= used to come) home, . . .

2. The conjunctions **bevor** and **ehe** can be used interchangeably.

3. *a.* When *if* means *whether*, it is expressed by **ob**:

       Ich weiß nicht, **ob** er kommt. | I don't know if (= whether) he is coming.

    b. Otherwise, *if* is expressed by **wenn**:

       Wenn er kommt, werden wir ihn sehen. | If he comes, we'll see him.

4. The English conjunction *since* has two distinct meanings: *because* and *ever since (a certain time)*. These meanings are expressed in German as follows:

    a. When *since* = *because*, it is translated by **da** or **weil.**

       Da (**Weil**) ich krank war, ging ich nicht mit. | Since I was sick, I didn't go.

    b. When *since* = *ever since,* it is translated by **seit** or **seitdem.**

       Seit (**Seitdem**) ich krank bin, sehe ich nur wenige Leute. | Since I've been sick, I've seen very few people.

    Note that the present tense, not the present perfect, is used with **seit(dem)** to show that something that began in the past continues into the present.

    c. **Seitdem** is also used as an adverb meaning *since then:*

       Hans ist vor zwei Jahren nach Berlin gezogen. **Seitdem** haben wir nichts mehr von ihm gehört. | Hans moved to Berlin two years ago. *Since then* we've heard nothing more of him.

    d. **Seit** (but never **seitdem**) can also be used as a preposition; that is, it may have a noun object:

       Seit Dienstag bin ich hier. | I've been here since Tuesday.

5. The English conjunction *while* can mean either *during the time that* or *although.* These meanings are expressed in German as follows:

    a. When *while* refers to time, it is translated by **während.**

       Während er den Kaffee trinkt, liest er die Zeitung. | While he drinks his coffee, he reads the newspaper.

    b. When *while* = *although,* it is translated by **obgleich.**

       Obgleich ich nicht spielen kann, kann Hans doch. | While I can't play, Hans can.

6. **Während** has two uses. When it introduces a subordinate clause, it means *while* (see Note 5*a*, above). As a preposition with an object in the genitive case, it means *during*: **während des Sommers,** *during the summer.*

    Be sure not to confuse **weil** (*because*) and "while."

7. Keep in mind: only the five coordinating conjunctions on page 174 are followed by *regular* word order. All other conjunctions require placing the finite verb at the end of the clause.

8. When the main clause contains a verb of *believing, feeling, knowing,* or *saying,* the subordinate clause need not be introduced by **daß.** When **daß** is omitted, such clauses have regular word order:

Er **wußte, daß** Vater zu Hause war.
Er **wußte,** *Vater war zu Hause.*   He knew that Father was at home.

Sie **sagt, daß** er uns besuchen wird.
Sie **sagt,** *er wird uns besuchen.*   She says he will visit us.

Note that the clauses are separated by commas even when **daß** is omitted.

ÜBUNGEN

A. Combine the two clauses, using the conjunction in parentheses.

1. (denn)   Er kommt heute nicht. Er hat keine Zeit.

Er kommt heute nicht, denn er hat keine Zeit.

2. (nachdem)   Wir gehen in die Schule. Wir haben gefrühstückt.

3. (als)   Vater war zu Hause. Ich kam nach Hause.

4. (sondern)   Sie kann nicht Klavier spielen. Sie singt schön.

5. (bis)   Wir warten im Zimmer. Das Wetter wird besser.

6. (während)   Hans hört das Radioprogramm an. Er arbeitet.

7. (bevor)   Ich gehe nach Hause. Ich möchte noch eine Tasse Kaffee trinken.

8. (obgleich)   Der Anzug war nicht sehr gut. Er war teuer.

9. (sobald)   Die Kinder kommen ins Haus. Es regnet.

10. (ob)   Ich weiß nicht. Mutter kommt heute.

B. Reconstruct the sentence, putting the second clause first.

1. Wir fahren nicht, obgleich das Wetter schön ist.

2. Ich muß die Arbeit machen, bevor Vater nach Hause kommt. ---------------------------

----

3. Er ist früh angekommen, trotzdem er langsam gefahren ist.

----

4. Ich werde den Brief lesen, nachdem ich diese Karte geschrieben habe. ------------------

----

5. Wir werden ihn danach fragen, sobald er kommt. --------------------------------

----

6. Die Gäste sitzen im Garten, solange das Wetter schön ist. ---------------------------

----

7. Hans weiß nicht, ob mehr Milch da ist. ------------------------------------

----

8. Sie brachte das Buch mit, als sie ins Zimmer kam. ------------------------------

----

9. Die Leute wollen Kaffee trinken, bevor der nächste Zug kommt. --------------------

----

10. Sie muß zu Hause bleiben, seitdem es kälter wird. ------------------------------

----

C. In the blanks, supply as many conjunctions as possible that make sense in context.

1. -- der Herr auf
sein Essen wartet, liest er ein Buch.

2. Er kann die Musik nicht hören, ------------------------- das Orchester spielt zu leise.

3. --------------------------- ist Mutter in der Küche, ------------------------- sie ist
im Garten.

4. Seit einem Jahr ist Herr Meyer nicht mehr mein Nachbar, ------------------------- er
wohnt jetzt auf dem Lande.

5. --- Anna nach Hause
kam, sah sie das Bild.

6. Man muß die Karte bezahlen, --
----------- man mit der Straßenbahn fährt.

7. --- er in Berlin ankommt, bleibt Hans bei
seinem Freund.

8. ------------------------- schöner der Sommertag ist, ------------------- mehr Leute
sind an der See.

9. --- sie eine Reise
macht, kauft Frau Schmidt neue Kleider.

10. --- wir in die Stadt kommen, müssen wir uns
ein Hotelzimmer suchen.

D. Replace the conjunction in italics with each of the conjunctions in parentheses, making changes in word order where necessary.

1. Das Auto fährt schnell, *aber* es ist alt.   (obgleich, weder . . . noch, trotzdem)

----

2. Ich höre nicht zu, *solange* meine Schwester singt.   (denn, sobald, während)

----

3. *Als* er nach Hause kam, sah er den Herrn nicht.   (bevor, entweder . . . oder, obgleich)

----

4. *Nicht nur* haben wir den Dom gesehen, *sondern auch* sind wir hineingegangen.   (weder . . . noch, nachdem)

----

5. *Nachdem* er hierher gekommen ist, sagte er gar nichts.   (weil, bis, ehe)

Replace the words in italics with each of the incomplete clauses in parentheses, arranging the words in the correct order.

6. Ich komme heute abend, wenn *ich Zeit habe.*   (es regnet nicht, ich bin nicht zu müde, mein Bruder kommt auch mit)

----

7. Ich weiß nicht, ob *dieses Restaurant gut ist.* (meine Schwester ist zu Hause, die Kinder sind im Klassenzimmer, er fährt mit dem Auto)

----

8. Frau Müller sagt, daß *das Buch interessant ist.*   (die Bibliothek ist weit von hier, der Hut ist zu teuer, sie will nach Deutschland fahren)

----

9. Sobald *es regnet,* laufen die Kinder weg.   (der Herr kommt ins Zimmer, Mutter ruft sie, sie hören den Lärm)

----

10. Seitdem *ich in Deutschland bin,* spreche ich oft Deutsch.   (ich studiere Deutsch, Frau Weber ist bei uns, Tante Frieda schreibt mir auf Deutsch)

E. Join the two clauses, using the correct German equivalent of the English word in parentheses.

1. (if)   Er weiß nicht. Er kann heute kommen.

----

2. (when)   Ich werde ihn fragen. Er kommt ins Zimmer.

----

3. (since)   Wir sind in München. Wir haben das Rathaus nicht gesehen.

----

4. (but)   Er kann nicht Deutsch sprechen. Er kann es lesen.

----

5. (that)   Frau Schmidt glaubt. Hans kann die Arbeit machen.

----

6. (before)   Die Kinder waschen sich. Sie frühstücken.

----

7. (for)   Der Lehrer ist heute nicht in der Schule. Er ist krank.

----

8. (after)   Wir kamen aus dem Kino. Wir gingen ins Restaurant.

----

9. (despite the fact that)   Vater fuhr sehr schnell. Er kam zu spät an.

----

10. (until)   Niemand spricht. Hans gibt die Antwort.

F. The answers to the following questions appear in parentheses. Answer each question with a complete sentence in German.

1. Wie fährt man durch Deutschland?   (one either drives a car or rides a train)

----

2. Wie lange sind Sie schon hier?   (since my brother called)

----

3. Wann werden wir abfahren?   (as soon as Mrs. Müller comes)

----

4. Was fragt die Dame?   (if there is a restaurant nearby)

----

5. Warum kauft der Herr den Anzug nicht?   (because he has no money)

----

6. Wann haben Sie meinen Bruder kennengelernt?   (when I was in Hamburg)

----

7. Wie lange darf man in der Bibliothek bleiben?   (as long as he wishes)

----

8. Wann soll man Karten für das Konzert kaufen?   (before the concert begins)

----

9. Wann werden wir den Film sehen?   (after we have paid for the tickets)

----

10. Wie lange müssen wir warten?   (until the waiter comes)

G. Translate into English.

1. Frau Müller sagt, daß sie einen neuen Mantel braucht. ----

----

2. Wir wissen nicht, ob die Bibliothek heute geöffnet ist. ----

----

3. Weder habe ich das Buch gelesen, noch werde ich es lesen. ----

----

4. Als ich ins Restaurant kam, sah ich ihn. _____

_____

5. Der Herr fragt, wann der Zug ankommt. _____

_____

6. Seitdem ich in Deutschland bin, spreche ich nur Deutsch. _____

_____

7. Wir besuchen den Park nicht, denn wir haben nicht genug Zeit. _____

_____

8. Nicht nur kann ich das Tier sehen, sondern auch kann ich es hören. _____

_____

9. Obgleich der Lehrer die Aufgabe erklärt hat, haben die Studenten sie noch nicht verstanden.

_____

_____

10. Nachdem Vater gegessen hat, trinkt er gern eine Tasse Kaffee. _____

_____

H. Translate into German.

1. I'll see him before he leaves. _____

_____

2. Either I left the ticket in my room or I lost it. _____

_____

3. Mother asks if they have seen the picture. _____

_____

4. Despite the fact that we arrived late, we heard the whole program. _____

_____

5. Since the car is old, it does not go very fast. _____

_____

6. If you see Anna, you can ask her about it. _____

_____

7. We listened while he spoke. _____

_____

8. The longer he works, the more tired he gets. _____

_____

9. I want to wait until the mail comes. _____

_____

10. One should pay for the meal as soon as the waiter brings it. _____

_____

42. NUMBERS

Numbers are classified as *cardinal* or *ordinal*. Cardinal numbers are used in counting (one, two, three, etc.); ordinal numbers show the place in a series (first, second, third, etc.).

CARDINAL NUMBERS

0	**null**	11	**elf**	21	**einundzwanzig**
1	**eins**	12	**zwölf**	22	**zweiundzwanzig**
2	**zwei**	13	**dreizehn**	30	**dreißig**
3	**drei**	14	**vierzehn**	40	**vierzig**
4	**vier**	15	**fünfzehn**	50	**fünfzig**
5	**fünf**	16	**sechzehn**	60	**sechzig**
6	**sechs**	17	**siebzehn**	70	**siebzig**
7	**sieben**	18	**achtzehn**	80	**achtzig**
8	**acht**	19	**neunzehn**	90	**neunzig**
9	**neun**	20	**zwanzig**		
10	**zehn**				

100	**hundert**	1 000 000	**eine Million**
101	**hunderteins**	2 000 000	**zwei Millionen**
200	**zweihundert**	1 000 000 000	**eine Milliarde**
1 000	**tausend**	1 000 000 000 000	**eine Billion**

Note

1. The cardinal numbers have no endings: **er hat *zwei* Bücher; sie hat *zweitausend* Bücher.**

2. When they are written out, cardinal numbers are written as single words:

   dreitausendsechshundertzweiundfünfzig = 3,652

3. Usually one does not say **ein hundert** or **ein tausend** unless **ein** is being stressed, but one does say *eine* **Million.**

4. The American *billion* (a thousand millions) is the German **Milliarde;** the American *trillion* (a million millions) is the German **Billion.**

5. *a.* English uses a comma to set off hundreds, thousands, etc. German sets off these groups with spaces:

   1,356,492 (English) = 1 356 492 (German)

   b. A comma is used in German instead of a decimal point:

   1.8 (English) = 1,8 (German)

   The number 1,8 is read **eins komma acht.**

6. Years are written and spoken in the same way as in English: no space comes after the first digit, and the number is read in hundreds:

$$1961 = \textbf{neunzehnhunderteinundsechzig}$$

7. The number of times is indicated by adding **-mal** to the cardinal number:

ein*mal*, *once*; **zwanzig*mal*,** *twenty times*. (However, in multiplication **mal** is written as a separate word.)

8. **Das Mal** is a noun; hence, it is capitalized:

zum letzten **Mal**	for the last time
das erste **Mal**	the first time

ORDINAL NUMBERS

erste, first	**erstens,** first of all
zweite, second	**zweitens,** secondly
dritte, third	**drittens,** thirdly
vierte, fourth	**viertens,** fourthly
vierzigste, fortieth	

Note

1. The ordinal numbers *fourth* through *nineteenth* are formed in German by adding **-te** to the corresponding cardinal numbers:

vier*te*, fünf*te*, sechs*te*, . . . , neunzehn*te*

2. The ordinals *twentieth* and above are formed by adding **-ste:**

zwanzig*ste*, einundzwanzig*ste*, zweiundzwanzig*ste*,

. . . , dreißig*ste*, . . . , vierzig*ste*, . . . , etc.

3. The adverbial form is formed by adding **-ns** to the ordinal number:

dritte**ns,** thirdly	fünfte**ns,** fifthly

4. Since the ordinal numbers are adjectives, they have regular adjective endings:

Hier ist das erst*e* Buch; haben Sie ein zweit*es* Buch gesehen?	Here is the first book; have you seen a second book?

FRACTIONS

halb, half	**ein Zehntel,** one-tenth
anderthalb, one and a half	**drei Viertel,** three-fourths
ein Drittel, one-third	**fünf Achtel,** five-eighths
ein Viertel, one-fourth	

Note

1. Fractions are expressed as follows: the denominators *fourths* to *nineteenths* are formed in German by adding **-tel** (a shortened form of **Teil,** *part*) to the corresponding cardinal numbers:

ein Sechs*tel*, one-sixth   ein Zwölf*tel*, one-twelfth

(*But*: ein Acht*el*, one-eighth)

2. With the exception of **halb,** the denominators of fractions are capitalized and the fraction is written as two words: **drei Fünftel,** *three-fifths*.

EXPRESSIONS USED WITH NUMBERS

im Jahre, in the year	**minus**	} minus, less
das **Jahrhundert,** century	**weniger**	
das **Prozent,** percent	**plus**	} plus
	und	

Wie alt sind Sie?   How old are you?

Ich bin fünfzehn Jahre alt.   I am fifteen years old.

Note

In arithmetic, either **weniger** or **minus** can be used in subtraction, and either **plus** or **und** can be used in addition. For multiplication, **mal** (*times*) is used after the first number. Division can be expressed with **geteilt durch** (*divided by*) or simply **durch.** The symbol used to indicate division is the colon: $12 \div 4$ is written as **12:4.**

$2 + 3 = 5$	**Zwei und (plus) drei ist fünf.**
$5 - 3 = 2$	**Fünf weniger (minus) drei ist zwei.**
$2 \times 3 = 6$	**Zwei mal drei ist sechs.**
$20:5 = 4$	**Zwanzig geteilt durch fünf ist vier.**

INDEFINITE NUMERICAL ADJECTIVES

alle, all (of)	**mehrere,** several
einige, several	**viele,** many
ein paar, a few, several	**wenige,** few

Note

1. **Alle** is followed by adjectives with weak endings:

alle schön*en* Gebäude   all (of) the beautiful buildings

2. The other indefinite numerical adjectives act like cardinal numbers and are followed by strong endings:

mehrere groß*e* Städte   several large cities

ÜBUNGEN

A. Write the following numbers and arithmetic operations in German words:

1. 516 ----- *fünfhundertsechzehn* -----
2. 63 : 9 = 7 ----- *dreiundsechzig geteilt durch neun ist sieben* -----

3. 72 ----- *zweiundsiebzig* -----
4. 21 879 ----- ~~zweitausend~~ *einundzwanzigtausendachthundert* -----

5. 14,3 ----- *~~...~~* -----
6. 3/4 ----- *drei Viertel* -----
7. 87% ----- ~~ist~~ *siebenundachtzig Prozent* -----
8. 4 893 ----- *viertausendachthundertdreiundneunzig* -----
9. 5/8 ----- *fünf geteilt ~~es durch acht ist~~ fünf Achtel* -----
10. 53,8
11. 6 + 5 = 11 ----- *sechs plus fünf* -----
12. 17 − 11 = 6 ----- *siebzehn weniger elf ist sechs* -----
13. 1½ ----- ~~ein~~ *anderthalb* -----
14. 6 × 7 = 42 ----- *sechs mal sieben ist zweiundvierzig* -----
15. 1/8 = 12,5%
16. 186 342 ----- *ein* -----

17. 3 × 15 = 45
18. 168 − 72 = 96

19. 1962
20. 76,3

B. Write the correct ordinal form of the number in parentheses.

1. Er sitzt am (5) ----- *fünfte* ----- Tisch.
2. Ich habe den (1) ----- *erste* ----- Brief gelesen.
3. Nun gibt es ein (3) ----- *dritte* ----- Hotel in diesem Dorf.
4. Am (26) ----- *sechsundzwanzigste* ----- dieses Monats werden wir abfahren.
5. Seit dem (4) ----- *vierte* ----- Tag regnet es nicht mehr.
6. Das war unser (15) ----- *fünfzehnte* ----- Auto.
7. Die Aufgabe steht auf der (216) ----- Seite.

8. Wir fangen heute mit der (22) -- Lektion an.

9. Großvater ist in seinem (83) -- Lebensjahr gestorben.

10. Mein (1) ------------------------- Anzug war blau.

C. Answer each question with a complete sentence in German.

1. Welches Jahr haben wir jetzt? --

----

2. Wieviele Studenten sind in Ihrer Schule? ---------------------------------------

----

3. Wieviele Leute sind in Ihrer Familie? --

----

4. In welchem Schuljahr sind Sie jetzt? --

----

5. Wie alt sind Sie? --

6. Wieviele Stunden bleiben Sie jeden Tag in der Schule? -----------------------

----

7. Wie alt ist Ihre Schule? ---

8. Wieviele Jahre Deutsch gibt es in Ihrer Schule? ----------------------------

----

9. Wieviele Studenten sind in Ihrer Klasse? ------------------------------------

----

10. Wie oft in der Woche geht man ins Laboratorium? ---------------------------

----

11. Wieviele Tage hat das Schuljahr bei Ihnen? -------------------------------

----

12. Wie lange sind Sie schon in dieser Stadt? --------------------------------

----

13. Was ist die Nummer Ihres Hauses? ---

14. Was ist die Nummer Ihres Klassenzimmers? -------------------------------

----

15. In welchem Jahre kamen Sie zum ersten Mal in die Schule? ---------------

----

16. Wie alt sind Ihre Eltern? (Wenn sie es sagen wollen!) --------------------

----

17. Wieviele Geschwister haben Sie? --

----

18. Wie oft ißt man während des Tages? ---

----

19. Wieviele Staaten gibt es in Amerika? ---

----

20. Wie oft haben Sie Deutsch-Unterricht in der Woche? ----------------------------

----

D. Replace the number in each sentence with the corresponding forms of the numbers in parentheses. (Write all numerals in German words.)

1. Er hat das schon viermal versucht.   (2, 12, 7)

----

2. Im Jahre 1946 ist er weggegangen.   (1964, 1829, 1892)

----

3. Am zehnten werden wir ihn suchen.   (5, 27, 18)

----

4. Dies ist sein sechstes Bild.   (3, 8, 1)

----

5. Unsere Schule hat eintausendfünfhundert Studenten. (2 300, 750, 1 800)

----

6. Diese Geschichte kommt aus dem sechzehnten   (12, 17, 8)
Jahrhundert.

----

7. An fünfter Stelle ist Hans.   (2, 1, 17)

----

8. Man soll die Aufgabe zweimal lesen.   (4, 3, 6)

----

9. Drei Viertel unserer Tische sind neu.   (1/8, 4/5, 1/3)

----

10. Heute sind 1,8% der Studenten krank.   (3,6; 8,3; 2,7)

E. Translate the English into German.

1. *On the twenty-ninth* kommt er zurück. --------------------------------------

2. Ich habe den Film schon *five times* gesehen. ----------------------------------

3. Wir kauften *six* Karten. --

4. *Three-quarters* der Studenten sind schon im Zimmer. _____

5. *In nineteen sixty-six* waren wir in Deutschland. _____

_____

6. Morgen fangen wir mit *the fifteenth* Lektion an. _____

7. Dies ist meine *first* Reise nach Deutschland. _____

8. *Nineteen and two-tenths percent* der Leute in dieser Stadt sind über *forty* Jahre alt. _____

_____

9. Ich habe nur *a third* der neuen Wörter gelernt. _____

10. Seit *one and a half* Jahren sind wir hier. _____

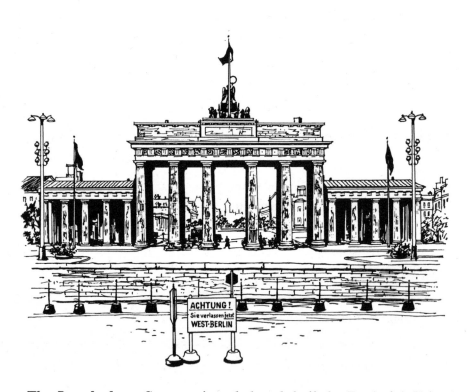

The *Brandenburg Gate*, a triumphal arch built by Frederick II in the 18th century, was a major gateway between East and West Berlin at the end of World War II. It now stands behind the Berlin Wall, which blocks direct access to the Gate from West Berlin. (A portion of the Wall can be seen in the foreground.)

25. THE TIME OF DAY

EXPRESSIONS OF TIME

die Minute, -n, minute
die Sekunde, -n, second
die Stunde, -n, hour (= 60 minutes)
die Uhr, -en, the hour, o'clock

morgens
vormittags } in the morning, A.M.
nachmittags, in the afternoon, P.M.
abends, in the evening, P.M.

nach, after (the hour)
um, at (a certain time)

um wieviel Uhr?, at what time?
um ein Uhr, at one o'clock

vor, before, until (the hour)

Wie spät ist es?
Wieviel Uhr ist es? } What time is it?

Haben Sie die genaue Zeit? | Do you have the correct (exact) time?

Diese Uhr geht vor. | This clock is fast.
Meine Uhr geht nach. | My clock runs slow.
Die Uhr geht richtig. | The clock is right.

Note

1. **Die Stunde** refers to any 60-minute period, for example, 7:25–8:25. **Die Uhr** refers to any of the 24 hours of the day: 8 o'clock, 4 o'clock, etc.

2. *a.* The expressions **morgens, vormittags, nachmittags,** and **abends** refer to usual or repeated times:

   Morgens stehe ich um sieben Uhr auf. | I get up at 7 o'clock in the morning.

   Abends müssen wir unsere Schularbeit machen. | Evenings (In the evening) we have to do our homework.

   b. The expressions **am Morgen, am Abend,** etc., may usually be substituted for **morgens, abends,** etc.

   Am Abend bin ich gewöhnlich zu Hause. | In the evening I am usually at home.

191

3. When referring to a specific morning, evening, etc., the appropriate time expression must be used:

Morgen früh muß ich um sieben Uhr aufstehen.	I have to get up at 7 o'clock in the morning (= tomorrow morning).

TELLING TIME

A. Time can be expressed in terms of minutes before or after the hour:

8:05	**Es ist fünf (Minuten) nach acht.**
8:55	**Es ist fünf (Minuten) vor neun.**
9:00	**Es ist (genau) neun Uhr.**

B. Time may also be expressed in terms of quarter- or half-hours:

8:45	**Es ist (ein) Viertel vor neun.**
9:15	**Es ist (ein) Viertel nach neun.**

C. Unlike English, "half" and "quarter" may be used to show the interval of time that has passed between the last hour and the next hour:

8:30   **Es ist halb neun.** (It is halfway from 8 to 9 o'clock.)

8:15   **Es ist Viertel neun.** (It is a quarter of the way from 8 to 9 o'clock.)

8:45   **Es ist drei Viertel neun.** (It is three-fourths of the way from 8 to 9 o'clock.)

Note

1. In the type of construction shown in C (**Es ist halb neun,** etc.), the prepositions **vor** and **nach** are not used; usually **ein** is also omitted.

2. Since German has no standard abbreviations corresponding to our A.M. and P.M., the context must show which is meant whenever the official, or 24-hour, time system is not used. If there is the possibility of confusion about which time of day is meant, some expression to indicate morning or evening must be used:

Der Unterricht fängt **morgens** um 9 Uhr an.	Class begins at 9 A.M.
Er kommt **abends** um acht Uhr.	He comes at 8 P.M.

3. An actual point in time is indicated with the preposition **um,** an approximate time with **gegen:**

Der Zug fährt **um** 9 Uhr ab.	The train leaves *at* 9 o'clock.
Wir kommen **gegen** 7 Uhr in Berlin an.	We'll arrive in Berlin at *about* 7 o'clock.

4. Note the following use of **genau:**

Es ist **genau** halb sieben.	It is exactly 6:30.

5. The word **ein** never has an ending when it is followed by **Uhr:**

Wir werden um **ein** Uhr abfahren.	We'll leave at one o'clock.

But:

Es ist ein Viertel nach **eins.**	It is a quarter past one.

**Es ist ein Viertel
nach acht.
Es ist Viertel neun.**

**Es ist fünf nach
Viertel neun.**

**Es ist fünf vor
halb neun.**

Es ist halb neun.

**Es ist fünf vor
drei Viertel
neun.**

**Es ist ein Viertel
vor neun.
Es ist drei Viertel
neun.**

TELLING TIME BY THE 24-HOUR SYSTEM

Official and public announcements are made in terms of the 24-hour system. The first twelve hours are from midnight to noon. The afternoon and evening hours—from noon to midnight—are numbered 13 (1:00 P.M.) through 24 (midnight). Thus, to convert official afternoon and evening times to the conventional system, subtract twelve: **15.30 = 3:30 P.M.**

Note

1. The official times are read with **Uhr** following the hour: **15.30** is read **fünfzehn *Uhr* dreißig.** Official times are never read with **vor, nach,** or with quarters and halves. (**15.30** would *not* be read "halb sechzehn"!)

2. In official notation, the hour between midnight and 1 A.M. is written with two zeros before the dot, but it is read as the twenty-fourth hour:

   12:17 A.M. = 00.17 = vierundzwanzig Uhr siebzehn

3. When official times are written with numerals, a period follows the hour: 15.30; 07.17.

4. The official time system is used for public announcements of train, plane, theater, or other official schedules, but is seldom used in conversation.

ÜBUNGEN

A. Write the time in German words, as shown in the following example:

EXAMPLE: 9:15   Es ist Viertel zehn. (*Or:* Es ist ein Viertel nach neun.)

1. 10:35   *Fünfundzwanzig vor zehn*

2. 6:00   *es ist genau sechs*

3. 3:45 _____ *Es ist Viertel vor vier.* _____

4. 11:30 _____ *Es ist halb zwölf.* _____

5. 10:10 _____ *Es ist zehn nach zehn.* _____

6. 1:15 _____ *es ist Viertel nach eins.* _____

7. 4:40 _____ *Es ist zwanzig vor fünf.* _____

8. 7:50 _____ *Es ist zehn vor acht.* _____

9. 8:13 _____ *Es ist dreizehn nach acht.* _____

10. 9:05 _____ *Es ist fünf nach neun.* _____

B. Answer the question **Wann fährt der Zug ab?** by writing the time in German words (*a*) in official form and (*b*) in conventional form.

EXAMPLE: 15.35   *a.* Der Zug fährt *um fünfzehn Uhr fünfunddreißig* ab.

b. Der Zug fährt *nachmittags um fünf (Minuten) nach halb vier* ab.

1. 18.25 *a.* _____ *um achtzehn Uhr fünfundzwanzig ab.* _____

b. _____ *um fünfundzwanzig nach sechs ab.* _____

2. 00.17 *a.* _____ *um vierundzwanzig Uhr siebzehn ab.* _____

b. _____

3. 22.50 *a.* _____

b. _____

4. 16.30 *a.* _____

b. _____

5. 09.15 *a.* _____

b. _____

6. 17.45 *a.* _____

b. _____

7. 05.57 *a.* _____

b. _____

8. 14.40 *a.* _____

b. _____

9. 11.10 *a.* _____

b. _____

10. 12.35 *a.* _____

b. _____

C. Express the following times in a different way.

EXAMPLE: abends um ein Viertel nach acht

abends um Viertel neun or *um zwanzig Uhr fünfzehn*

1. halb elf _____ *Zehn Uhr dreißig* _____

2. drei Viertel sieben --- *fünfzehn vor sieben* ---

3. fünf vor Viertel vier --- *drei Uhr vierzig* ---

4. ein Viertel vor zehn --- *dreiviertel zehn* ---

5. um fünfzehn Uhr fünfzig --- *~~~~ zehn vor vier* ---

6. heute nachmittag um zwanzig nach fünf --- *siebzehn Uhr zwanzig* ---

7. um zwanzig Uhr dreißig --- *um halb neun* ---

8. morgens um zehn vor elf --- *zehn Uhr fünfzig* ---

9. Viertel vier --- ~~dreiviertel~~ *Viertel ~~vor~~ nach ~~drei~~* ---

10. halb eins --- ~~es Uhr~~ *Zwölf Uhr dreißig* ---

11. fünf vor drei Viertel acht --- *sieben Uhr vierzig* ---

12. gestern abend um halb neun --- *gestern, siebzehn Uhr dreißig* ---

13. um zweiundzwanzig Uhr fünfzehn --- *Viertel elf* ---

14. um sieben Uhr fünfunddreißig --- *vormittag fünfundzwanzig vor acht* ---

15. ein Viertel nach zwei --- *Viertel drei* ---

D. (1) Read the original sentence aloud. (2) Read it again, replacing the indicated time with each of the times in parentheses. (3) Write out the times in parentheses in German words.

1. Das Programm beginnt um 17.30.   (18.00, 16.45, 19.00)

2. Die genaue Zeit ist drei Minuten vor elf.   (5:30, 2:26, 9:52)

3. Der Zug fährt um 07.49 ab.   (02.16, 11.38, 01.15)

4. Ich werde Sie um halb zehn anrufen.   (6 Uhr abends, 3:45, 9:15)

5. Die Bibliothek ist morgens um elf Uhr geöffnet.   (1 P.M., 8 A.M., 10:30 A.M.)

E. Answer each question with a complete sentence in German.

1. Was ist jetzt die genaue Zeit? --- *Die genaue Zeit ist ~~elf~~ elf Uhr zweiund dreißig* ---

2. Um wieviel Uhr stehen Sie jeden Morgen auf? *Jeden Morgen stehe ich --- vor neun Uhr auf.*

3. Wann kommen Sie jeden Tag in die Schule? *Ich komme in die Schule --- um zehn Uhr jeden Tag.*

4. Wann fängt der Deutsch-Unterricht an? *Der ~~Deutsch~~ Deutsch-Unterricht fängt um elf Uhr an.*

5. Um wieviel Uhr gehen Sie nach Hause? *Ich gehe nach Hause um zehn Uhr.*

6. Wann gehen Sie gewöhnlich ins Bett? ------------

7. Wann essen Sie zu Mittag? *Ich esse :*

8. Um wieviel Uhr morgens müssen Sie aus dem Hause gehen? ------------

9. Wann erledigen Sie zu Hause die Aufgabe? ------------

10. Um wieviel Uhr kommt Ihr Vater nach Hause? ------------

    F. Translate the English into German.

1. Er wird *at half past ten* herkommen. *halb elf*

2. Ich habe seit *eight o'clock* gewartet. *~~genau~~ acht Uhr*

3. Der Film beginnt *at 13 minutes to 3.* *~~dreizehn~~ dreizehn vor drei*

4. Der Unterricht dauert bis *a quarter of ten.* *Viertel vor zehn*

5. Es ist *exactly three o'clock.* *genau drei Uhr*

6. Wir sind *at 7:30* aufgestanden. *um halb acht*

7. Er muß von *10:15* bis *11 o'clock* im Zimmer sitzen. *elf Uhr*

8. Heute abend werden wir *at a quarter past six* essen. *Viertel nach sechs*

9. Der Zug fährt *at 2:19 this afternoon* ab. *~~zwei~~ vierzehn Uhr neunzehn*

10. Er war *at 4:20* bei mir. *sechzehn Uhr zwanzig*

26. DIVISIONS OF THE YEAR

SEASONS (*die Jahreszeiten*)

der Frühling, spring	**der Herbst,** autumn
der Sommer, summer	**der Winter,** winter

MONTHS (*die Monate*)

der Januar, January	**der Juli,** July
der Februar, February	**der August,** August
der März, March	**der September,** September
der April, April	**der Oktober,** October
der Mai, May	**der November,** November
der Juni, June	**der Dezember,** December

DAYS OF THE WEEK (*die Tage der Woche*)

der Sonntag, Sunday	**der Donnerstag,** Thursday
der Montag, Monday	**der Freitag,** Friday
der Dienstag, Tuesday	**der Sonnabend** } Saturday
der Mittwoch, Wednesday	**der Samstag** }

PARTS OF THE DAY

der Morgen, morning	**der Abend,** evening
der Vormittag, forenoon	**die Nacht,** night
der Mittag, noon	**die Mitternacht,** midnight
der Nachmittag, afternoon	

Note

1. The preposition **im** is used with seasons and months: **im Frühling, im Oktober.** *At night* is **in der Nacht.**

2. The preposition **am** is used with days of the week and parts of the day other than **die Nacht:**

   am Dienstag, on Tuesday   **am Abend,** in the evening

3. Except for **die Nacht** and **die Woche,** the months, days of the week, and divisions of the day are all **der** nouns.

4. In referring to a year, either the number of the year is used alone or the expression **im Jahre** may be used before the number:

> Er fuhr (**im Jahre**) **1948** nach   He went to America in 1948.
>   Amerika.

However, the expression "in 1948" must not be used.

5. The article is regularly used with the names of seasons, months, days of the week, and parts of the day:

> **Der** April macht die Blumen,   April brings forth the flowers for
>   und **der** Mai hat den Dank dafür.   which May receives the praise.

6. The expressions **zu Mittag essen** and **zu Abend essen** mean *to have lunch* and *to have dinner*:

> Ich **esse** im Restaurant **zu Mittag**.   I'm having lunch in the restaurant.

COMMON TIME INTERVALS

heute, today

heute morgen ⎫
heute früh ⎬ this morning

heute abend, this evening

heute nacht, tonight

gestern, yesterday

gestern morgen ⎫ yesterday
gestern früh ⎬ morning

gestern abend, yesterday evening, last night

vorgestern, day before yesterday

morgen, tomorrow

morgen früh, tomorrow morning

morgen abend, tomorrow night

übermorgen, day after tomorrow

heute in acht Tagen, a week from today

(**heute**) **vor acht Tagen,** a week ago (today)

vor einer Woche, a week ago

vor vier Tagen, four days ago

seit vier Tagen, for the past four days, since four days ago

vorige Woche, last week

voriges Jahr, last year

vorigen Dienstag, last Tuesday

nächste Woche, next week

das Datum (*pl.,* **die Daten**), the date

das Jahr, -e, year; **das Schaltjahr,** leap year

der Monat, -e, month

die Woche, -n, week

das Wochenende, -n, weekend

Note

The accusative case is used to indicate *time when*: **vorigen Sommer,** *last summer*.

> **Den wievielten haben wir heute?** ⎫
> **Welches Datum ist heute?** ⎬ What is the date today?
>
> **Welchen Tag haben wir heute?** What day is this?
>
> **Heute haben wir Dienstag.** ⎫
> **Heute ist Dienstag.** ⎬ Today is Tuesday.
>
> **Heute ist der vierte März.** ⎫
> **Heute haben wir den vierten März.** ⎬ Today is March 4.
>
> **Bonn, den 4. März** Bonn, March 4.
>   (*Read:* **den vierten März**)

Note

1. The ending on the numeral in the date (**der vierte März, den vierten März**) is determined according to the rules for weak endings on adjectives.

2. The form **Bonn, den 4. März** is the regular way of heading a letter.

3. When numerals are used, the date comes *before* the month: **20.11.65 = den 20. November 1965.**

ÜBUNGEN

A. Answer each question with a complete sentence in German.

1. In welchem Monat haben wir Weihnachten? *Wir haben Weinachten im Dezember*

2. Welches ist der kürzeste Monat des Jahres? *Der kürzeste Monat des Jahres ist Februar*

3. In welchem Monat beginnt der Unterricht? *Der Unterricht beginnt im September*

4. In welcher Jahreszeit sind der Januar und der Februar? *Der Januar und der Februar sind im Winter*

5. Wann kommen die Blumen heraus? *Die Blumen kommen heraus im der April oder der Mai*

6. In welchem Monat gibt es ein weltbekanntes Fest in München? *Der weltbekanntes Fest in München gibt es in der Oktober*

7. Wann kann man schwimmen? *Man kann schwimmen im Sommer*

8. In welchem Monat ist das Schuljahr zu Ende? *Das Schuljahr ist zu Ende im der Mai*

9. Welchen Tag der Woche haben wir heute? *Wir haben heute Mittwoch*

10. Wann haben Sie Geburtstag? *Ich habe Geburtstag im Dezember*

11. Welches Datum ist heute? *Heute ist 1.8.84*

12. In welcher Jahreszeit gibt es gewöhnlich Schnee?

13. Wann stehen wir auf?

14. An welchem Tag gehen die meisten Leute in die Kirche?

15. Welches sind die Schultage?

16. Wann geht man ins Bett?

17. An welchen Tagen gibt es keinen Unterricht? ------------------------------------

----

18. Wann frühstückt man? --

----

19. Wann essen Sie das größte Essen des Tages? ---------------------------------------

----

20. Welcher Tag ist Ihnen am liebsten? ---

21. Wo essen Sie gewöhnlich zu Mittag? ---

----

22. An welchem Tag gibt es Fußballspiel? --

23. Mit welchem Tag beginnt das neue Jahr? --

----

24. Welches ist der erste Tag der Woche? --

----

25. Welches ist der längste Tag des Jahres? ---

B. If today is Wednesday, October 15, write the day of the week and the date indicated by each time expression.

EXAMPLE: heute   *Mittwoch, der 15. Oktober*

1. vorgestern   *Montag, des 13. Oktober*

2. morgen   *Donnerstag, des 16. Oktober*

3. gestern   *Dienstag, der 14. Oktober*

4. übermorgen   *Freitag, des 17. Oktober*

5. vor acht Tagen   --

C. Assume that today is Monday, March 21. Write a time expression that corresponds to each of the following days or dates:

1. vorigen Samstag   --

2. nächsten Mittwoch   --

3. der 28. März   --

4. der 20. März   --

5. der 14. März   --

D. Write the italicized dates in German words.

1. Heute ist der *5.* August. ---

2. Berlin, *10.6.57* ---

3. Heute haben wir den *16.* Mai. ---

4. München, den *23.* Juli ---

5. Morgen ist der *18.* Februar. ------------------------------------

6. Hamburg, *27.10.64* --

7. Gestern hatten wir den *12.* Januar. ----------------------------

8. Heute ist der *2.* Dezember. -------------------------------------

9. Köln, *8.11.48* ---

10. Bonn, den *25.* Juli ---

E. Translate the English into German.

1. Wir sind *a week ago* in Berlin
   angekommen. *Vorige Woche*

2. *The day before yesterday* hatte mein Bruder
   Geburtstag.

3. *Tomorrow morning* werden wir früh
   aufstehen.

4. Ich werde ihn *this evening* besuchen.

5. Schon *one week from today* werden wir in
   Deutschland sein.

6. *On Monday* fängt der Unterricht wieder
   an.

7. *Last Summer* haben wir unsere Ferien auf
   dem Lande verbracht. ~~Vorige Somn~~

8. Ich muß *on December 12* nach Hause
   fahren.

9. *Yesterday* habe ich einen Brief geschrieben. ~~Gestern~~

10. Heute haben wir *March 16.*

11. *This weekend* werden wir abfahren.

12. Vater kommt *the day after tomorrow*
    zurück.

13. Er hat den Brief *on May 19* geschickt. *am 19. Mai*

14. *At night* hörte ich etwas. *~~Am~~ Im der Nacht*

15. Meine Eltern sind *the whole summer* an der
    See geblieben.

16. Ich habe Herrn Müller *three days ago*
    gesehen.

17. *Next week* fangen wir mit der neuen
    Aufgabe an. *nächte Woche*

18. Er ist schon *for four months* hier. *für vier Monaten*

19. *Tomorrow evening* gehen wir ins Konzert. *Morgen abend*

20. *Last month* kaufte sie einen neuen Wagen. *Letzte Monat*

F. Translate into English.

1. Gestern früh sind wir abgefahren. --

2. Sie wird übermorgen mit dem Schiff fahren. ------------------------------------

----

3. Seit zwei Wochen bin ich hier. --

4. Der Unterricht fängt im Herbst wieder an. ----------------------------------

5. Im Frühling wird das Wetter wieder warm. ----------------------------------

----

6. Am Sonnabend werden wir tanzen. --

7. Im Oktober hast du Geburtstag, nicht wahr? -----------------------------

----

8. Wir haben viel Schnee im Winter. --

9. Ich muß am Freitag arbeiten. --

10. Dieses Wochenende werden wir die Großmutter besuchen. ----------------

----

Konrad Adenauer was the first Chancellor of the Federal Republic. His strong leadership played a major role in the reconstruction of his devastated country after World War II. When he left office in 1963, West Germany had become one of the most prosperous countries in Europe.

27. REVIEW OF PART IV—SENTENCE STRUCTURE

WORTSCHATZ

DIE FREIZEIT

die **Barren,** parallel bars
bergsteigen, ist berggestiegen, to go mountain-climbing
bergsteigen gehen, ging bergsteigen, ist bergsteigen gegangen, to go mountain-climbing
die **Blindekuh,** blindman's buff
boxen, boxte, geboxt, to box
das **Camping,** camping
Drachen steigen lassen, to fly a kite
sich **erholen, erholte, erholt,** to rest, relax, recuperate
die **Erholung,** rest, relaxation
fechten, focht, gefochten, to fence
die **Freizeit, -en,** spare time
der **Fußball, ̈e,** soccer (ball)
die **Achterbahn, -en** ⎫
die **Gebirgsbahn, -en** ⎬ roller coaster
die **Jugendherberge, -n,** youth hostel
das **Karussell** (*pl.,* **-s** or **-e**), merry-go-round
kegeln, kegelte, gekegelt, to bowl
das **Lachkabinett, -e,** fun house
malen, malte, gemalt, to paint (pictures)
die **Mannschaft, -en,** team
~~**Murmel spielen,** to shoot marbles~~
musizieren, musizierte, musiziert, to make music
die **Party,** party
das **Pferd, -e,** horse (animal), horse (gymnastics)
das **Reck, -e,** horizontal bar
die **Reise, -n,** journey
reisen, reiste, ist gereist, to travel
reiten, ritt, ist geritten, to ride (on horseback)
das **Riesenrad, ̈er,** ferris wheel
der **Ring, -e,** ring(s) (gymnastics)
~~der **Ringelreihen,** ring-around-the-rosy, circle dance~~
ringen, rang, gerungen, to wrestle
der **Rollschuh, -e,** roller skate
rollschuhlaufen, lief Rollschuh, ist rollschuhgelaufen, to roller-skate
rudern, ruderte, ist gerudert, to row, paddle
der **Rummelplatz, ̈e,** fairgrounds, amusement park

~~das **Sackhüpfen,** sack race~~
das **Schach,** chess
die **Schaukel, -n,** swing
(sich) **schaukeln, schaukelte, geschaukelt,** to swing
der **Schlager, -,** popular song
der **Schlitten, -,** sled
schlittenfahren, fuhr Schlitten, ist schlittengefahren, to go sledding
der **Schlittschuh, -e,** ice skate
schlittschuhlaufen, lief Schlittschuh, ist schlittschuhgelaufen, to ice-skate
das **Schwimmbad, ̈er,** swimming pool
schwimmen, schwamm, ist geschwommen, to swim
das **Segelboot, -e,** sailboat
das **Segelflugzeug, -e,** glider, sailplane
segeln, segelte, ist gesegelt, to sail
~~**seilhüpfen, hüpfte Seil, ist seilgehüpft**~~ ⎫
~~**seilspringen, sprang Seil, ist seilgesprungen**~~ ⎬ ~~to skip rope~~
Ski laufen, lief Ski, ist Ski gelaufen, to ski
die **Sommerferien** (*pl.*), summer vacation
das **Steckenpferd, -e,** hobby
turnen, turnte, geturnt, to do gymnastics
die **Turnhalle, -n,** gymnasium
der **Turnverein, -e,** gymnastics club, sports club
übernachten, übernachtete, übernachtet, to spend the night
das **Versteckten,** hide-and-seek
sich **verstecken,** to hide; play hide-and-seek
der **Wanderer, -,** hiker
wandern, wanderte, ist gewandert, to hike, roam (on foot)
die **Wanderung, -en,** hiking trip
die **Wippe, -n,** seesaw
wippen, wippte, gewippt, to seesaw

Note

1. "To ride on" the amusement rides is **fahren** *auf* + *dative case*. (The expression **fahren mit** is used when speaking of a means of transportation.)

> Martha will **auf** dem Riesenrad **fahren.**　　Martha wants to ride the ferris wheel.

2. The verbs **rudern, schwimmen,** and **segeln** may have the auxiliary **haben** when referring to the motion as an activity and not as a means of reaching a destination:

> Ich **bin** über den See **gesegelt.**　　I sailed across the lake.
>
> *But*:
>
> Ich *habe* den ganzen Tag **gesegelt.**　　I went sailing all day long.

3. **Ski laufen** is usually written as two words, but **bergsteigen** (with a small *b*), which usually appears only as an infinitive or past participle, is written as one word.

> Diesen Sommer wollen wir **bergsteigen.**　　This summer we want to go mountain-climbing.
>
> Vor zwei Jahren sind wir **berggestiegen.**　　Two years ago we went mountain-climbing.

Although **bergsteigen** may be used alone, it is usually used in conjunction with **gehen**:

> Mein Bruder **geht** heute **bergsteigen.**　　My brother is going mountain-climbing today.

ÜBUNGEN

A. Reconstruct the sentence so that it begins with the expression in italics.

1. Man turnt *gewöhnlich* in einer Turnhalle. --- *Gewöhnlich turnt man* _____

_____

2. Das Lachkabinett gefällt *den Kindern.* _____

_____

3. Wanderer musizieren gern *am Abend* in der Jugendherberge. _____

_____

4. Viele Menschen *in Deutschland* spielen Schach. _____

_____

5. Die Familie will *nächsten Sommer* an die See fahren. _____

_____

6. Manche Leute laufen *während des Winters* Ski. _____

_____

7. Man kann *in Süddeutschland* bergsteigen. _____

_____

8. Die Kinder spielen *auf dem Spielplatz.* _____

_____

9. Klaus bekommt Schlittschuhe *zu Weihnachten.* ------------------------------

----

10. Die kinder verstecken sich *im Garten.* ---------------------------------

----

B. Combine the elements into sentences.

1. auf dem Riesenrad/ die Kinder/ letzte Woche/ fuhren ------------------

----

2. geschwommen/ über den Fluß/ sind/ die Jungen --------------------

----

3. Schwimmbad/ in dieser Stadt/ kein/ es gibt ----------------------

----

4. brauchen/ auf dem Spielplatz/ wir/ eine Wippe --------------------

----

5. in Süddeutschland/ während des Winters/ viel Schlittenfahren/ gibt es ----------

----

6. Schach/ möchte/ mit Ihnen/ spielen/ er/ ? ----------------------

----

7. Mädchen/ seilspringen/ kleine/ gern ----------------------------

----

8. viele Jungen/ gegangen/ auf die Wanderung/ sind/ jedes Jahr --------------

----

9. kleine Kinder/ auf dem Spielplatz/ gern/ schaukeln --------------------

----

10. Barren/ ein Reck/ findet/ in jeder deutschen Turnhalle/ man/ und ----------

----

11. malen/ in ihrer Freizeit/ schöne Bilder/ viele Leute ------------------

----

12. reitet/ durch den Wald/ langsam/ der Herr ----------------------

----

13. am Mittwoch/ möchte/ kegeln/ sie -----------------------------

----

14. gewöhnlich/ einen Turnverein/ man/ in der Stadt/ findet ---------------

----

15. besuchen/ das Lachkabinett/ die Kinder/ werden/ auf dem Rummelplatz ----------

----

C. Change the following statements to questions:

1. Heute werden wir rollschuhlaufen. _____

2. Er ist schon weit gereist. _____

3. Peter läßt seinen Drachen steigen. _____

4. Die Gebirgsbahn sieht gefährlich aus. _____

5. Auf dem Rummelplatz sind viele Karusselle. _____

6. In den Ferien übernachten viele Deutsche auf Campingplätzen. _____
_____

7. Die Kinder schaukeln im Park. _____

8. Es gibt eine Jugendherberge in dem nächsten Dorf. _____
_____

9. Jeden Sonntag sind einige Mannschaften über den See gerudert. _____
_____

10. Am Nachmittag haben die Kinder Blindekuh gespielt. _____
_____

D. Use the conjunction in parentheses to combine the two clauses into a single sentence.

1. (sobald) Das Wetter wird warm. Viele junge Leute sind auf der Wanderung. _____
_____
_____

2. (wenn) Man will schlittenfahren. Man muß Schnee haben. _____
_____

3. (entweder ... oder) Die Studenten lernen fechten. Sie lernen ringen. _____
_____

4. (da) Ich habe so viel gearbeitet. Ich möchte eine Erholungsreise machen. _____
_____
_____

5. (nachdem) Die Wanderer haben in der Jugendherberge zu Abend gegessen. Sie singen und
tanzen. _____
_____

6. (nicht nur ... sondern auch) Mein Bruder ist auf dem Karussell gefahren. Er ist durch das
Lachkabinett gegangen. _____
_____
_____

7. (wenn) Man will turnen. Man braucht Barren, Ringe, ein Reck, und ein Pferd. _____
_____

8. (solange) Das Wetter war sehr warm. Wir haben gern geschwommen. ------------

----

9. (je ... desto) Der Wind wurde stärker. Wir segelten schneller. ------------

----

10. (seitdem) Ich habe mich zwei Wochen erholt. Ich fühle mich viel besser. ------------

----

11. (weder ... noch) Ich kann kegeln. Ich kann rollschuhlaufen. ------------

----

12. (obgleich) Er fliegt mit dem Segelflugzeug gern. Er kann es nicht, weil er wenig Zeit hat. ---

----

----

13. (daß) Sie haben nicht gewußt. Es gibt ein Riesenrad auf dem Rummelplatz. ------------

----

14. (ob) Die Kinder wußten nicht. Sie dürfen auf dem Hof Blindekuh spielen. ------------

----

15. (sondern) Er hat nicht gerudert. Er hat gesegelt. ------------

----

E. Reconstruct the sentence so that the second clause comes first.

1. Er kann noch nicht rollschuhlaufen, obgleich er zum Geburtstag Rollschuhe bekommen hat. --

----

----

2. Die Wanderer werden musizieren, nachdem sie gegessen haben. ------------

----

3. Wir wollen uns erholen, da wir so müde sind. ------------

----

4. Jeden Tag haben wir gesegelt, solange wir an der See waren. ------------

----

5. Wir werden auf der Gebirgsbahn wieder fahren, nachdem wir das Lachkabinett besucht

haben. ------------

----

6. Sie waren schon auf einer Reise, als ich das hörte. ------------

----

7. Die Kinder wollen auf dem Karussell fahren, sobald sie auf den Rummelplatz angekommen

sind. ------------

----

8. Wir können immer noch Ski laufen, obgleich das Wetter wärmer geworden ist. _____

_____

_____

9. Sie kann erst malen, wenn das Licht besser wird. _____

_____

10. Wir werden Fußball spielen, wenn die andere Mannschaft ankommt. _____

_____

F. Answer the following questions in complete German sentences, using the replies in parentheses:

1. Was kann man in Süddeutschland machen? (go skiing and mountain-climbing) _____

_____

2. Was finden wir auf dem Spielplatz? (swings and a seesaw) _____

_____

3. Was machen viele junge Deutsche während des Sommers? (they go hiking) _____

_____

4. Wo sieht man ein Karussell, ein Riesenrad, und eine Gebirgsbahn? (at the fairgrounds) _____

_____

_____

5. Was machen die Kinder auf dem Spielplatz? (they fly kites and shoot marbles) _____

_____

6. Worauf reitet der Herr? (on a horse) _____

_____

7. Was machen die Wanderer am Abend in der Jugendherberge? (they play music and dance)

_____

8. Warum können wir heute nicht segeln? (because there is no wind) _____

_____

9. Wann sind Sie bergsteigen gegangen? (when we were in Bavaria [**Bayern**]) _____

_____

10. Kann Gretchen seilspringen? (I don't know) _____

_____

G. Write the sentence, replacing the italicized expressions with the expressions in parentheses.

1. Auf dem Spielplatz *spielen* die Kinder. (schaukeln, Drachen steigen lassen, wippen) _____

_____

2. Heinrich will weder *schwimmen* noch *segeln*. (boxen . . . ringen, bergsteigen . . . schlittenfahren, malen . . . musizieren) _____

_____

3. Während *wir auf der Wanderung waren*, besuchten wir viele Städte. (er erholte sich auf dem Land, Sie segelten über den See, wir wanderten durch Deutschland) `-----------------`

`----------------------------------------------------------------`

`----------------------------------------------------------------`

4. Entweder *haben* die Jungen *geturnt*, oder sie *haben gekegelt.* (sind geritten . . . sind gewandert, haben gerungen . . . haben geschwommen, sind Ski gelaufen . . . sind schlittengefahren) `-----`

`----------------------------------------------------------------`

`----------------------------------------------------------------`

5. Da der Tag so warm war, *haben* die Jungen nicht *gefochten.* (haben geschaukelt, sind geritten, sind rollschuhgelaufen) `---------------`

`----------------------------------------------------------------`

6. Bei der Party haben alle Gäste *getanzt.* (musiziert, Schach gespielt, Schlager gesungen) `------`

`----------------------------------------------------------------`

7. Er wußte nicht, ob *er turnen konnte.* (er sollte seilspringen, wir durften Murmel spielen, er konnte einen Drachen steigen lassen) `-----------------------`

`----------------------------------------------------------------`

8. In jedem Dorf haben wir entweder *eine Jugendherberge* oder *ein Hotel* gefunden. (ein Schwimmbad . . . einen See, einen Rummelplatz . . . eine Turnhalle, ein Karussell . . . ein Riesenrad) `-----`

`----------------------------------------------------------------`

`----------------------------------------------------------------`

9. In seiner Freizeit interessiert er sich für *das Bergsteigen.* (sein Steckenpferd, Camping, Turnen)

`----------------------------------------------------------------`

10. Sobald *er auf den Rummelplatz ankam*, wollte er auf der Achterbahn fahren. (er sah den Rummelplatz, wir hatten ihm etwas davon gesagt, er kaufte sich eine Karte) `---------------------`

`----------------------------------------------------------------`

`----------------------------------------------------------------`

H. Translate into English.

1. In Süddeutschland kann man mit einem Segelflugzeug fliegen. `---------------`

`----------------------------------------------------------------`

2. Wenn es genug Wind gibt, können wir heute Drachen steigen lassen. `------------`

`----------------------------------------------------------------`

3. Er kann sowohl Schlager als Volkslieder singen. `---------------------`

`----------------------------------------------------------------`

4. Obgleich ich gern wandere, reite ich noch lieber. `----------------------`

`----------------------------------------------------------------`

5. Mit seinem Steckenpferd verbringt man gern seine Freizeit. _____

_____

6. Solange die Wanderer auf einer Wanderung sind, brauchen sie nur wenig Geld. _____

_____

7. Der Junge will auf der Gebirgsbahn und auf dem Riesenrad fahren. _____

_____

8. Wenn das Wetter nicht etwas wärmer wird, können wir weder schwimmen noch segeln. _____

_____

9. Entweder kegeln wir am Samstag, oder wir gehen ins Kino._____

_____

10. Mein Bruder kann nicht nur boxen, sondern er kann auch gut ringen. _____

_____

I. Translate into German.

1. The girl wants either to swing or to seesaw. _____

_____

2. We went to the beach last summer. _____

_____

3. My sister can neither sing nor dance. _____

_____

4. During the winter they like to ice-skate. _____

_____

5. Whenever we saw a ferris wheel or a merry-go-round, we always wanted to ride on it. _____

_____

6. The children were flying kites at the playground last week. _____

_____

7. My mother paints as a hobby (= for pleasure). _____

_____

8. Ever since he learned to sail, he wants to spend every summer on the sea. _____

_____

9. We must rest up before we return to school. _____

_____

10. The more often he rode the ferris wheel, the less he enjoyed it. _____

_____

Part V—Idioms and Proverbs

28. IDIOMS

A. *Greetings and Departures*

Guten Morgen!	Good Morning!
Guten Tag!	Hello! Good afternoon!
Guten Abend!	Good evening!
Gute Nacht!	Good night!
Grüß Gott! (*South Germany*)	Hello. Greetings!
Auf Wiedersehen!	Good-bye.
Kommen Sie gut nach Hause!	Get home safely.

B. *Polite Requests and Replies*

Bitte!	Please!
Danke schön! / **Vielen Dank!**	Thanks! Thank you!
Bitte schön!	You're welcome.
Einen Augenblick, bitte!	One moment, please.
Entschuldigen Sie, bitte!	Excuse me, please.
Verzeihung!	Pardon me.
Ist das Ihnen recht?	Is that all right with you?
Haben Sie viel zu tun?	Are you busy?
Wie geht's? / **Wie geht es Ihnen?**	How are you?
Danke, es geht mir gut.	I'm fine, thanks.
Danke, gut, und Ihnen?	Fine, thanks. And you?

C. *Sympathy and Joy*

Das tut mir leid. / **Das tut mir weh.**	I'm sorry about that.
Das ist schade! / **Wie schade!** / **Leider!**	That's too bad!
Was ist denn los?	What's the matter?
Gute Besserung!	Get well soon.
Prima! / **Großartig!** / **Wunderbar!**	That's wonderful! Excellent! Great!

Das freut mich.   } I'm happy about that.
Das laß ich mir gefallen!

Das macht Spaß!   That's fun.

Das ist fabelhaft!   That's fabulous!

D. *New Persons and Places*

Wie heißen Sie?   What's your name?

Ich heiße (Karl Schmidt).   My name is (Charles Smith).

Darf ich vorstellen? Herr Schmidt.   }
Darf ich bekannt machen? Herr   May I introduce Mr. Schmidt.
   Schmidt.

Guten Tag!   How do you do?

Ich bin fremd hier.   I'm a stranger here.

Wissen Sie hier Bescheid?   Do you know your way around here?

Ich werde Ihnen Bescheid sagen.   I'll tell you how to get where you want to go.

E. *On a Visit*

Bitte legen Sie ab!   Please take off your things.

Bitte nehmen Sie Platz!   Please have a seat.

Machen Sie sich's bequem!   Make yourself comfortable.

Fühlen Sie sich wie zu Hause!   Make yourself at home.

Bitte bedienen Sie sich!   Please help yourself.

F. *Interjections*

Ach so!   Oh, I see.

Ach, du meine Güte!   Good grief!

Hoppla!   Oops! Oh oh!

Nanu!   That's certainly a surprise.

Na, wenn schon!   So what! What of it?

Gott sei Dank!   Thank heavens.

G. *Agreement and Disagreement*

Gewiß!   }
Freilich!   Certainly! Of course!
Ja, sicher!

Das stimmt!   That's for sure!

Das läßt sich hören!   That's good to hear.

Das macht mir nichts aus.   }
Das ist mir gleich.   That makes no difference to me.
Das ist mir egal.

Sie haben recht.   You're right.

Und ob!   And how!

Na, na!	Uh, uh!
Nein, durchaus nicht.	Definitely not. By no means.
Nichts zu machen!	Nothing doing!
So **siehst du aus!**	That's what you think!

H. *Acceptance and Encouragement*

Da ist nichts zu machen. **Das läßt sich nicht ändern.** **Daran läßt sich nichts ändern.**	That can't be helped.
Das macht nichts.	That doesn't matter.
Das schadet nichts.	That does no harm.
Das ist ja gar nicht so schlimm.	That's not so bad.
Drücken Sie den Daumen!	Keep your fingers crossed.
Hals- und Beinbruch!	Lots of luck!
Hoffentlich!	I hope so.
Man muß zufrieden sein.	I can't complain.
Unberufen! Toi-toi-toi!	Knock on wood!
Viel Vergnügen!	Have fun!

I. *Exasperation*

Auch *das* **noch!** **Ausgerechnet!**	Oh no, not that!
Da schlägt's dreizehn! **Das ist doch die Höhe!**	That's the last straw.
Das ist eine schöne Bescherung.	That's a fine mess!
Das ist ja unglaublich!	That's unbelievable.
Das ist verheerend!	That's terrible.

J. *Miscellaneous*

Da geht mir ein Licht auf.	*Now* I understand.
Das tut man nicht.	One doesn't do that. (It's not done.)
Das wird sich finden.	We'll see about that.
Gib nicht so an!	Don't make such a fuss. Don't brag.
Ich kann ja nichts dafür.	There's nothing I can do about that.
Nur die Ruhe!	Take it easy.
Passen Sie auf!	Be careful! Pay attention!
Scherz beiseite.	All kidding aside.
Seien Sie mir nicht böse!	Don't be angry with me.
Vorsicht!	Caution!
Was soll (darf) es sein?	What will you have?

ÜBUNGEN

A. Circle the letter of the most appropriate response to each statement.

1. Darf ich vorstellen? Ursula Weber.

   (a) Das tut mir weh.   (b) Gib nicht so an!   (c) Guten Tag!

2. Bitte bedienen Sie sich!

   (a) Danke, es geht mir gut.   (b) Danke schön!   (c) Man muß zufrieden sein.

3. Der Bus kommt heute nicht. Wir müssen also zu Fuß gehen.

   (a) Das macht Spaß!   (b) Das ist eine schöne Bescherung.   (c) Hals- und Beinbruch!

4. Wie geht es Ihnen?

   (a) Das ist mir egal.   (b) Danke, gut, und Ihnen?   (c) Freilich!

5. Willst du mit dem Ball spielen?

   (a) Ja, sicher!   (b) Das wird sich finden.   (c) Das ist ja unglaublich.

6. Heute kommt unser Lehrer wieder zur Schule.

   (a) Nanu! Gestern war er noch im Krankenhaus.   (b) Ich bin fremd hier.   (c) Verzeihung!

7. Heute brachte Karl weder Heft noch Buch mit.

   (a) Das läßt sich hören!   (b) Auch *das* noch!   (c) Was darf es sein?

8. Seit vier Tagen bin ich krank.

   (a) Seien Sie mir nicht böse.   (b) Das macht Spaß!   (c) Gute Besserung!

9. Der Plan gefällt dem Herrn nicht.

   (a) Was ist denn los?   (b) Machen Sie sich's bequem!   (c) Viel Vergnügen!

10. Sie sind fremd hier, nicht wahr?

    (a) Drücken Sie den Daumen!   (b) Das läßt sich nicht ändern.   (c) Ich werde Ihnen Bescheid sagen.

11. Sie möchten das beste Papier, nicht wahr?

    (a) Nanu!   (b) Gewiß!   (c) Ich kann ja nichts dafür.

12. Nächsten Sommer werden wir eine Reise nach Deutschland machen.

    (a) Das macht Spaß!   (b) Da schlägt's dreizehn!   (c) Nur die Ruhe!

13. Heute abend gibt's keine Schularbeit.

    (a) Das ist ja unglaublich!   (b) Bitte nehmen Sie Platz!   (c) Das tut man nicht.

14. Meine Großeltern kommen morgen zu Besuch.

    (a) Fühlen Sie sich wie zu Hause!   (b) Das tut man nicht.   (c) Wunderbar!

15. Der Lehrer ist mir böse, weil ich einen Ball durch das Fenster ins Klassenzimmer warf.

    (a) Wie schade!   (b) Kommen Sie gut nach Hause!   (c) Ist das Ihnen recht?

16. Welchen Wagen fahren Sie lieber—diesen hier oder den da drüben?

    (a) Da geht mir ein Licht auf.   (b) Das macht mir nichts aus.   (c) Haben Sie viel zu tun?

17. Ihre Uhr geht nicht richtig.

(*a*) Ach, du meine Güte! (*b*) Das laß ich mir gefallen! (*c*) Bitte bedienen Sie sich!

18. Können wir um 7 Uhr abfahren?

(*a*) Scherz beiseite! (*b*) Entschuldigen Sie, bitte! (*c*) Hoffentlich!

19. Vater kauft unserer Familie heute ein schönes, neues Auto.

(*a*) Das ist ja gar nicht so schlimm. (*b*) Vorsicht! (*c*) Das ist fabelhaft!

20. Ohne Geld kann man nicht weit reisen.

(*a*) Gott sei Dank! (*b*) Das stimmt! (*c*) Ausgerechnet!

B. Circle the letter of the most appropriate response.

What might you say if . . .?

1. Someone offered to help you wash the dishes.

(*a*) Nein, durchaus nicht. (*b*) Das laß ich mir gefallen. (*c*) Das tut man nicht.

2. A guest has just arrived in your home.

(*a*) Machen Sie sich's bequem! (*b*) Gute Besserung! (*c*) Verzeihung!

3. Someone told you that there are 72,963 anteaters in South America.

(*a*) Hoppla! (*b*) Das läßt sich hören! (*c*) Na, wenn schon!

4. You want to ask someone's advice, but you're afraid he may not have the time to talk with you.

(*a*) Viel Vergnügen! (*b*) Haben Sie viel zu tun? (*c*) Scherz beiseite.

5. You are about to tell your girl friend that she has bad breath.

(*a*) Das ist verheerend! (*b*) Gib nicht so an! (*c*) Sei mir nicht böse!

6. After failing two tests during the day, you are told when you get home that you can't use the car that night.

(*a*) Grüß Gott! (*b*) Da schlägt's dreizehn! (*c*) Hoppla!

7. The coach tells the student body that the team is all set to win the big game.

(*a*) Das läßt sich hören! (*b*) Auch *das* noch! (*c*) Da ist nichts zu machen!

8. You are telling someone that you have been lucky enough to have escaped having the flu this winter, and you hope your luck holds out.

(*a*) Das macht mir nichts aus. (*b*) Unberufen! Toi-toi-toi! (*c*) Ist das Ihnen recht?

9. You are saying good-bye to a visitor as he leaves for home.

(*a*) Kommen Sie gut nach Hause! (*b*) Das läßt sich hören! (*c*) Fühlen Sie sich wie zu Hause!

10. Someone has just thanked you for rescuing his pet cat from a tree.

(*a*) Das ist doch die Höhe! (*b*) Nur die Ruhe! (*c*) Bitte schön!

11. Someone told you that you had just won a thousand-dollar prize in a contest.

(*a*) Das ist fabelhaft! (*b*) Das ist eine schöne Bescherung! (*c*) Auch *das* noch!

12. You are ending your visit to a sick friend.

(*a*) Was ist denn los? (*b*) Gute Besserung! (*c*) *So* siehst du aus!

13. You just spilled a whole pot of soup.

    (*a*) Grüß Gott! (*b*) Ach, du meine Güte! (*c*) Nanu!

14. Your teacher is preparing to take his driver's license test—for the second time!

    (*a*) Drücken Sie den Daumen! (*b*) Wissen Sie hier Bescheid? (*c*) Das läßt sich nicht ändern.

15. You disagree with a friend from a rival school who says his school's team will win the next game against your team.

    (*a*) Da ist nichts zu machen. (*b*) Hoffentlich. (*c*) Das wird sich finden.

16. What might a weatherman reply if someone complained to him that it had rained every day for two weeks?

    (*a*) Passen Sie auf! (*b*) Ich werde Ihnen Bescheid sagen. (*c*) Ich kann ja nichts dafür.

17. What does the teacher say when Fritz reads $8 + 12 = 13$?

    (*a*) Wissen Sie hier Bescheid? (*b*) Nein, durchaus nicht! (*c*) Das schadet nichts.

18. What did the man at the city hall say when citizens complained about a bridge that had been washed out?

    (*a*) Man muß zufrieden sein. (*b*) Wie schade! (*c*) Hals- und Beinbruch!

19. What might a child say if invited to go to a circus?

    (*a*) Nur die Ruhe! (*b*) Gute Besserung! (*c*) Großartig!

20. What sign would you expect to find in a dynamite factory?

    (*a*) Verzeihung! (*b*) Vorsicht! (*c*) Viel Vergnügen!

C. (*Idiom and Listening-Comprehension Drill*) The teacher will read a statement or question in German. Circle the letter of the appropriate response to each.

1. (*a*) Das tut mir leid. (*b*) Prima! (*c*) Gott sei Dank!

2. (*a*) Das macht spaß! (*b*) Man muß zufrieden sein. (*c*) Das ist ja gar nicht so schlimm.

3. (*a*) Drücken Sie den Daumen! (*b*) Gewiß! (*c*) Nichts zu machen!

4. (*a*) Das läßt sich hören! (*b*) Sie haben recht. (*c*) Kommen Sie gut nach Hause!

5. (*a*) Daran läßt sich nichts ändern. (*b*) Scherz beiseite. (*c*) Ja, da geht mir ein Licht auf!

6. (*a*) Fühlen Sie sich wie zu Hause! (*b*) Viel Vergnügen! (*c*) Machen Sie sich's bequem!

7. (*a*) Das wird sich finden. (*b*) Das ist doch die Höhe! (*c*) Das stimmt!

8. (*a*) Leider nicht. (*b*) Daran läßt sich nichts ändern. (*c*) Unberufen! Toi-toi-toi!

9. (*a*) Das tut mir leid. (*b*) Da schlägt's dreizehn! (*c*) Hoffentlich.

10. (*a*) Das schadet nichts. (*b*) Und ob! (*c*) Das ist verheerend!

11. (*a*) Was ist denn los? (*b*) Bitte bedienen Sie sich! (*c*) Das ist doch die Höhe!

12. (*a*) Ausgerechnet! (*b*) Da geht mir ein Licht auf. (*c*) Na, wenn schon!

13. (*a*) Das läßt sich hören! (*b*) Prima! (*c*) Gib nicht so an!

14. (*a*) Ach so! (*b*) Das freut mich! (*c*) Hoppla!

15. (*a*) Ach, du meine Güte! (*b*) Nanu! (*c*) Das laß ich mir gefallen!

16. (*a*) Das wird sich finden. (*b*) Da schlägt's dreizehn! (*c*) Drücken Sie den Daumen!

17. (*a*) Das stimmt!   (*b*) Nur die Ruhe!   (*c*) Ausgerechnet!

18. (*a*) Daran läßt sich nichts ändern.   (*b*) Sie haben recht.   (*c*) Das ist mir gleich.

19. (*a*) Vorsicht!   (*b*) Und ob!   (*c*) *So* siehst du aus!

20. (*a*) Haben Sie viel zu tun?   (*b*) Man muß zufrieden sein.   (*c*) Nichts zu machen!

Jugendherberge, or youth hostels, are found throughout West Germany. They provide shelter for the many thousands of young tourists—German and foreign—who love to wander about Europe on foot or by bicycle.

29. PROVERBS

A. To the left of each German proverb in column *A*, write the letter of the equivalent English proverb in column *B*.

	A		*B*
K	1. Wände haben Ohren.	a.	Practice makes perfect.
d	2. Eine Hand wäscht die andere.	b.	To err is human.
g	3. Reden ist Silber, Schweigen ist Gold.	c.	April showers bring May flowers.
l	4. Es ist nicht alles Gold, was glänzt.	d.	One hand washes the other.
j	5. Eine Schwalbe macht noch keinen Sommer.	e.	When the cat's away, the mice will play.
i	6. Aus den Augen, aus dem Sinn.	f.	By their fruits shall ye know them.
m	7. Ein gebranntes Kind scheut das Feuer.	g.	Speech is silver, but silence is golden.
n	8. Ein Sperling in der Hand ist besser als eine Taube auf dem Dache.	h.	Rome was not built in a day.
o	9. Wer zuletzt lacht, lacht am besten.	i.	Out of sight, out of mind.
a	10. Übung macht den Meister.	j.	One swallow does not make a summer.
b	11. Irren ist menschlich.	k.	The walls have ears.
h	12. Rom war nicht an einem Tag erbaut.	l.	All that glitters is not gold.
e	13. Wenn die Katze außer dem Haus ist, tanzen die Mäuse.	m.	Once burned, twice shy.
f	14. Den Baum erkennt man an den Früchten.	n.	A bird in the hand is worth two in the bush.
c	15. Der April macht die Blumen, und der Mai hat den Dank dafür.	o.	He who laughs last, laughs best.

B. To the left of each German proverb in column *A*, write the letter of its English equivalent in column *B*.

	A		*B*
c	1. Kinder und Narren reden die Wahrheit.	a.	Too many cooks spoil the broth.
i	2. Viele Hände machen bald ein Ende.	b.	It is better to suffer injustice than to commit injustice.
j	3. Aus nichts wird nichts.	c.	Children and fools speak the truth.
e	4. Hochmut kommt vor dem Fall.	d.	Don't look a gift horse in the mouth.
h	5. Wer zuerst kommt, mahlt zuerst.	e.	Pride goes before a fall.
b	6. Besser Unrecht leiden als Unrecht tun.	f.	It's easier to forgive than to forget.
a	7. Viele Köche verderben den Brei.	g.	One shouldn't buy a pig in a poke.
g	8. Man muß die Katze nicht im Sack kaufen.	h.	First come, first served.
f	9. Vergeben ist leichter als vergessen.	i.	Many hands make light work.
d	10. Einem geschenkten Gaul sieht man nicht ins Maul.	j.	Nothing ventured, nothing gained.

C. Write the letter of the English expression in column *B* that best captures the meaning of each German proverb in column *A*.

_f_ **1.** Wer *A* sagt, muß auch *B* sagen.

_i_ **2.** Jeder ist seines Glückes Schmied.

_g_ **3.** Dem Reinen ist alles rein.

_k_ **4.** Was Hänschen nicht lernt, lernt Hans nimmermehr.

_o_ **5.** Lügen haben kurze Beine.

_c_ **6.** Was man wünscht, glaubt man gern.

_m_ **7.** Gleich und gleich gesellt sich gern.

_j_ **8.** Liebe und Verstand gehen selten Hand in Hand.

_e_ **9.** Die Kunst ist lang, das Leben kurz.

_n_ **10.** Das Glück suchen wir, das Unglück sucht uns.

_a_ **11.** Du kannst alles was du willst, wenn du nur willst was du kannst.

_l_ **12.** Was man nicht im Kopf hat, muß man in den Beinen haben.

_d_ **13.** Die Lügen sind gleich den Schneebällen: je weiter man sie fortwälzt, desto größer werden sie.

_h_ **14.** Wie du mir, so ich dir.

_b_ **15.** Ein Narr kann mehr fragen als sieben Weise sagen.

a. You can do what you will, if you will do what you can.

b. A fool can ask more questions than seven wise men can answer.

c. We believe what we wish to believe.

d. Lies are like snowballs—the farther they roll, the greater they grow.

e. Life is short, art is long.

f. You must finish what you start.

g. All things are pure to the pure in heart.

h. Tit for tat.

i. Man forges his own destiny.

j. Love and understanding are rarely found together.

k. What the child does not learn, the man will never learn. (As the twig is bent, so grows the tree.) Old dog new tricks

l. One should use his head to save his back.

m. Birds of a feather flock together. (Water seeks its own level.)

n. We seek good fortune, misfortune seeks us.

o. Lying will get you nowhere.

Part VI—Civilization

30. GEOGRAPHY OF GERMANY

WHERE GERMAN IS SPOKEN

German is the language of Germany, Austria, and most of Switzerland, and is spoken by about 120,000,000 people.

THE TWO GERMANYS

In 1945, after its defeat in World War II, Germany was divided by its conquerors into four zones of occupation (see Lesson 31, page 233). Under the control of the occupying powers, these zones developed into two separate republics: the *Federal Republic of Germany* (**die Bundesrepublik Deutschland**) in the west, and the *German Democratic Republic* (**die Deutsche Demokratische Republik,** or **D.D.R**) in the Soviet sector. The Soviet sponsorship of the D.D.R. as a "sovereign republic" was considered to be a violation of the Potsdam agreement (1945), which called for the unification of Germany with frontiers to be determined by a final peace treaty. ~~For that reason,~~ the United States, the Federal Republic, and other countries do ~~not~~ recognize the East German regime.

THE POLITICAL DIVISIONS OF THE FEDERAL REPUBLIC

The **Bundesrepublik,** with its capital at Bonn, became fully independent in May 1955, after the United States, Britain, and France ended all controls over the country. It consists of 8 **Länder,** or states: Baden-Württemberg, Bayern (Bavaria), Hessen, Niedersachsen, Nordrhein-Westfalen, Rheinland-Pfalz, Schleswig-Holstein, Saarland; and 3 **Freistädte,** or city states: Bremen, Hamburg, and Berlin (West).

(The **D.D.R.,** with its capital in East Berlin, was proclaimed by the German Communists in 1949.) *May 23, 1949*

Note. In these pages, we will sometimes refer to the two German republics as "Germany" where it is appropriate to consider the two regions as a unity.

LOCATION, SIZE, AND POPULATION

Germany is situated in north-central Europe. The area of West Germany (including West Berlin) is 96,000 square miles, or about that of Oregon. East Germany is about two-fifths the size of *Tennessee* the Bundesrepublik. The population of West Germany is 60,165,000—almost four times that of the D.D.R. *16, million*

BOUNDARIES

West Germany. In the north, the Bundesrepublik is bounded by the North Sea (**die Nordsee**) and Denmark (**Dänemark**). On the west, it borders the Netherlands (**die Niederlande**), Belgium (**Belgien**), Luxemburg, and France (**Frankreich**). To the south, West Germany is bounded by Switzerland (**die Schweiz**) and Austria (**Österreich**); to the east, by Czechoslovakia (**die Tschechoslowakei**) and East Germany.

East Germany. The D.D.R. is bounded on the north by the Baltic Sea (**die Ostsee**); on the west, by West Germany; and to the east, by Poland (**Polen**). It also shares a common frontier with Czechoslovakia.

CLIMATE

Although Germany's southern border is at the same latitude as Quebec or Seattle, the whole country enjoys a moderate climate because prevailing westerly winds bring warmth from the Atlantic

Gulf Stream. Temperatures rarely fall below 30°F in winter or rise above 75°F in summer. The sheltered river valleys of western Germany have the warmest temperatures in the country—an important factor in the cultivation of the grape in the wine country.

TERRAIN

Germany rises from sea level in the north to an average elevation of 1800 to 2000 feet in the south. The country can be divided into three regions:

1. *The North German Plain.* The northern quarter of Germany is a region of flat lowlands called **Tiefland.**

2. *The Central Highlands.* The north-central part of Germany is a country of rolling hills and low mountain ranges. The south-central part is a region of high plateaus dotted with outcroppings of jagged rocks and low mountain peaks.

3. *The Foothills of the Alps.* This hilly region in southern Bavaria is called the **Alpenvorland.**

Mountain Ranges (**Gebirge**)

1. The **Harz** mountains are situated in the center of Germany. The line dividing West Germany from East Germany cuts directly through this range.

2. The **Eifel** and **Hunsrück** ranges, west of the Rhine, are separated by the Mosel river. East of the Rhine and north of the Main river are the **Taunus, Vogelsberg,** and **Rhön** groups.

3. The **Schwäbische Alb,** an area of white cliffs and picturesque mountain pastures, runs along the Danube river and borders the Bavarian plateau.

4. The **Fichtelgebirge** and **Erzgebirge** are found along the southeastern borders of Germany next to Czechoslovakia.

5. The **Bayrische Alpen** (Bavarian Alps), on the southern border with Austria, have the highest peaks in Germany. The tallest mountain in this range is the **Zugspitze,** which is 9,721 feet high.

   2,900 m

Rivers

Except for the Danube, the major rivers of Germany flow from the Alps in the south to the North Sea or to the Baltic in the north.

1. The *Rhine* river (**der Rhein**) is the longest in Germany and the most important river in the Bundesrepublik. It flows for 537 miles from Lake Constance (**der Bodensee**) on the Swiss border to the North Sea coast of Holland.

2. The *Oder* (**die Oder**) flows from Czechoslovakia to the Baltic. Along with the **Neiße,** the Oder marks the boundary between East Germany and Poland.

3. The *Elbe* (**die Elbe**) cuts diagonally across East Germany for most of its length, crossing the northern part of West Germany as it flows toward the North Sea.

4. The *Danube* (**die Donau**) rises in the Black Forest and flows eastward to the Black Sea.

Canals

1. The **Nord-Ostsee Kanal** (Kiel Canal) joins the North Sea and the Baltic, opening the way to Lübeck and providing access to ports along the Baltic coast.

2. The **Mittelland Kanal** forms a continuous waterway that runs for 200 miles across northern Germany from the Ems river to the Elbe. The canal passes through East Germany and is one of the "access corridors" to West Berlin; hence, it is an important passageway between that city and the rest of the world.

Forests

About one-fourth of Germany is covered with forests.

The famous Black Forest (**der Schwarzwald**) is situated in the southwest corner of West Germany, bounded on one side by the Rhine. Other extensive forests are the **Teutoburger Wald,** bordered by the Mittelland Kanal and the Weser river, the **Thüringer Wald** in the southwest corner of the D.D.R., and the **Böhmer Wald** north of the Danube along the West German-Czechoslovakian frontier.

THE ECONOMY

INDUSTRY

West Germany is one of the world's most advanced industrial nations.

1. *Manufacturing.* The most important products are chemicals, steel, machinery, automobiles, textiles, and beer.

   The Ruhr valley, in the west, contains the chief industrial cities: Dortmund, Essen, and Düsseldorf. West Berlin is a major production center of electronic components.

2. *Mining.* The chief mineral resource is coal. Large coal deposits are mined in the Saarland and in the low mountain ranges near the Ruhr valley. (This accounts for the development of the great industrial plants of the Ruhr, which depend on coal for their operation.) Iron ore is mined extensively in the Harz mountains and the Erzgebirge.

AGRICULTURE

West German farms do not supply enough food for the needs of the country; hence, the Bundesrepublik must import almost half of its food from abroad.

1. *Chief Agricultural Products.* Wheat, rye, sugar beets, potatoes, barley, oats, hops, malt, corn, and various common fruits are grown.

2. *Wine and Beer Production.* The extensive vineyards of West Germany are situated in the Rhine and Mosel valleys. The most famous German beers are brewed in Bavaria from the excellent hops for which that region is noted.

FISHERIES

The important fishing industry is based in the port cities along the northern seacoast.

CITIES

1. **West Berlin,** the largest city in the Bundesrepublik, is located deep within East Germany and has more than two million inhabitants. It is separated from East Berlin by the Berlin Wall (**die Mauer**), which was built by the East German regime in 1961 to block the mass emigration of East Germans to the Federal Republic. Much of Berlin was destroyed during World War II, but the western half has been almost completely rebuilt.

PLACES OF INTEREST (**Sehenswürdigkeiten**)

The **Kurfürstendamm** is a famous boulevard in West Berlin. The street is lined with elegant shops and theaters.

The **Kaiser Wilhelm Gedächtniskirche** (Memorial Church), at the east end of the Kurfürstendamm, was left standing after the war. Its bombed-out tower remains as a grim reminder of the cost of war. A new modern structure has been built around it.

The **Tiergarten** is a huge park northeast of the Kurfürstendamm.

The **Straße des 17. Juni** is a wide boulevard that passes through the Tiergarten. It received its name from the unsuccessful revolt of East Berliners against the Communist regime on June 17, 1953.

Holland

The **Dahlem Museum** is noted for its gallery of classical paintings by Rembrandt, *Holland* Bruegel, Holbein, and other renowned artists of northern Europe. The **Egyptian Museum** displays the world-famous sculptured head, made 3000 years ago, of Queen Nefertiti of Egypt.

2. **East Berlin** is open to West Germans under restricted conditions. The most popular crossing point between West and East Berlin was formerly the **Brandenburg Gate (das Brandenburger Tor),** which had stood at the center of Berlin before the city was partitioned. This access is now completely blocked by the Berlin Wall. However, visitors may cross into East Berlin at a point a few blocks from the Brandenburg Gate.

Much of East Berlin still has not been rebuilt. However, the Soviets and the East German government did rebuild the area surrounding the Brandenburg Gate as a showplace to the West.

Only a few blocks into East Berlin is **Alexanderplatz,** a major business center that has been rebuilt. Also nearby is the **Staatsoper,** the State Opera House, which was not destroyed in the war. **Humboldt University,** established in 1810, is in East Berlin. When the university came under Communist domination after World War II, German students established the Free University (**die Freie Universität**) in West Berlin.

3. **Hamburg,** the second largest city in Germany, is the largest port and shipping center in the Federal Republic. It is situated at the mouth of the Elbe.

4. **Bremen** is the second largest seaport in the Bundesrepublik, although it is located on the Weser river about 40 miles from the North Sea.

5. **Hannover,** situated on the Mittelland Kanal between the Weser and the Elbe, is a railway center and an important commercial and industrial city.

6. Along the Rhine are found **Bonn,** the present capital of the Bundesrepublik, and **Köln** (Cologne), noted for its Gothic cathedral (**der Kölner Dom**). On the upper Rhine, the cities of **Speyer** and **Worms** date back to Roman times.

7. **Frankfurt am Main** has always been an important commercial center because of its central location in Germany. A famous historical landmark is the **Wachtturm,** a tower standing in the middle of a busy Frankfurt street, which once formed part of an outer wall —a reminder of the days when Frankfurt was a fortified town.

8. **Heidelberg,** on the Neckar, is best known for its ancient university.

9. **München** (Munich), in the middle of Bavaria, is renowned for its beer and **Oktoberfest** (October Festival).

10. Along the Elbe in East Germany are the cities of **Dresden,** famed for its porcelain, and **Wittenberg,** where Martin Luther posted his ninety-five theses.

TRANSPORTATION

1. The *rivers and canals* of Germany have always provided a major means of transportation. The Rhine is navigable for most of its length, and about one-third of the goods that enter or leave West Berlin is carried on the Mittelland Kanal.

2. *Public transportation* is operated by the government. Buses and trains will take the traveler almost anywhere he wishes to go. Among the several classes of trains that operate in Germany, the most streamlined is the TEE (Trans-Europ-Express).

3. *Autobahnen,* which rival America's turnpikes and freeways, join all parts of the Bundesrepublik.

4. Besides automobiles, there are motorcycles and various kinds of motorbikes (*Mopeds*) and bicycles that are used by adults and young people. In 1965 there were almost 2,000,000 motorcycles and motorbikes on West German streets, and more than 3,000,000 cars. But there were over 17,000,000 bicycles!

ÜBUNGEN

A. Referring to Map I on the next page, indicate by letter (A to J) the location of each of the following countries:

___F___ **1.** Czechoslovakia   ___C___ **6.** France

___A___ **2.** Netherlands   ___I___ **7.** Sweden

___G___ **3.** Poland   ___D___ **8.** Switzerland

___E___ **4.** Austria   ___H___ **9.** Denmark

___J___ **5.** German Democratic Republic   ___B___ **10.** Belgium

B. Referring to Map I, indicate by letter (K to U) the location of each of the following *Länder* and *Freistädte*:

___T___ **1.** Bayern (Bavaria)   ___P___ **7.** Hessen

___K___ **2.** Schleswig-Holstein   ___M___ **8.** Niedersachsen (Lower Saxony)

___N___ **3.** Bremen   ___Q___ **9.** Rheinland-Pfalz

___R___ **4.** Saarland   ___U___ **10.** Berlin-West

___L___ **5.** Hamburg   ___O___ **11.** Nordrhein-Westfalen (North Rhine-Westphalia)

___S___ **6.** Baden-Württemberg

C. Referring to Map I, indicate by number the location of each of the following forests and mountain ranges:

___1___ **1.** Schwarzwald   ___2___ **6.** Schwäbische Alb

___5___ **2.** Böhmerwald (Bohemian Forest)   ___9___ **7.** Thüringerwald

___7___ **3.** Harz Gebirge   ___4___ **8.** Alpenvorland

___3___ **4.** Bayrische Alpen   ___10___ **9.** Fichtelgebirge

___8___ **5.** Teutoburgerwald   ___6___ **10.** Erzgebirge

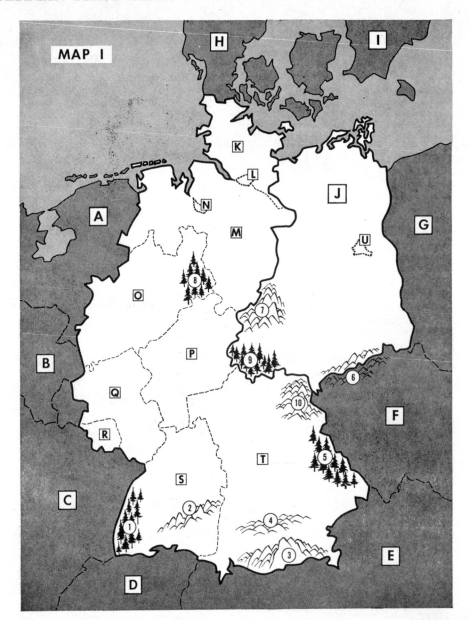

D. Referring to Map II on the next page, indicate by letter (A to J) the location of each of the following rivers and waterways:

__D__ **1.** Mittelland Kanal   __B__ **5.** Elbe   __A__ **8.** Nord-Ostsee Kanal

__F__ **2.** Rhein   __I__ **6.** Donau (Danube)   __J__ **9.** Oder

__G__ **3.** Mosel   __H__ **7.** Main   __K__ **10.** Neiße

__C__ **4.** Weser

E. (Refer to Map II.) In **I** and **II**, indicate by number the location of each city.

I

__17__ **1.** Wien (Vienna)   __5__ **5.** Berlin   __14__ **8.** München (Munich)

__16__ **2.** Zürich   __8__ **6.** Hamburg   __10__ **9.** Köln (Cologne)

__20__ **3.** Salzburg   __3__ **7.** Bremen   __4__ **10.** Hannover

__11__ **4.** Bonn

II

_____1___ **1.** Kiel   _____14_ **5.** Frankfurt am Main   ____7__ **8.** Leipzig

_____9_ **2.** Düsseldorf   _____13_ **6.** Stuttgart   ____8_ **9.** Weimar

___15_ **3.** Saarbrücken   ___18__ **7.** Nürnberg   ____6_ **10.** Dresden

____12_ **4.** Heidelberg

F. Identify each of the following as: (_a_) river, (_b_) mountain range, (_c_) forest, or (_d_) city.

___c__ **1.** Böhmer Wald   ___d_d **6.** Essen   ___b_ **11.** Harz Gebirge

___b__ **2.** die Alpen   ___c__ **7.** Teutoburger Wald   __a__ **12.** die Elbe

___d__ **3.** Wittenberg   __d_ **8.** Hamburg   __d_ **13.** Bremen

___a__ **4.** die Oder   ___a_ **9.** die Weser   __b_ **14.** Taunus

__b__ **5.** Erzgebirge   ___d__ **10.** Frankfurt am Main   __a__ **15.** der Rhein

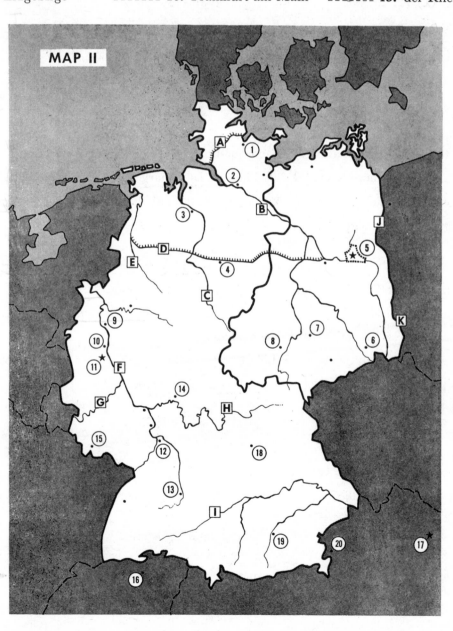

G. To the left of each name in column *A*, write the letter of the phrase in column *B* that identifies it.

	COLUMN A		COLUMN B
d	**1.** Bonn	*a.*	seaport on the Weser
i	**2.** der Nord-Ostsee Kanal	*b.*	largest seaport in the Federal Republic
g	**3.** der Mittelland Kanal	*c.*	important industrial area
b	**4.** Hamburg	*d.*	capital of the Federal Republic
c	**5.** Dortmund, Essen, Düsseldorf	*e.*	forest in the southwestern part of West Germany
j	**6.** der Bodensee	*f.*	mountain ranges in central Germany
a	**7.** Bremen	*g.*	waterway connecting the Ems and the Elbe
e	**8.** der Schwarzwald	*h.*	large city on the Mittelland Canal
h	**9.** Hannover	*i.*	joins the North Sea and the Baltic Sea
f	**10.** Harz, Eifel, Taunus	*j.*	Alpine lake between Germany and Switzerland

H. Underline the correct answer to each question.

1. Welches Land liegt nördlich von Deutschland? (Dänemark, Österreich, die Tschechoslowakei)

2. Wieviele Länder und Freistädte findet man in Westdeutschland? (3, 5, 11)

3. Welch großes Land liegt an der westlichen Grenze Westdeutschlands? (die Schweiz, Luxemburg, Frankreich)

4. In welchem Teil Deutschlands liegt Bayern? (im Süden, im Westen, in der D.D.R.)

5. Welcher ist der größte Fluß Deutschlands? (die Elbe, die Weser, der Rhein)

6. Welcher Bruchteil (fraction) Deutschlands ist Tiefland? (ein Drittel, ein Viertel, die Hälfte)

7. Welcher ist der wichtigste westdeutsche Seehafen? (Berlin, München, Hamburg)

8. Was ist die Hauptstadt der Bundesrepublik? (Bonn, Frankfurt am Main, Heidelberg)

9. Wo liegt Polen? (westlich, nördlich, östlich von Deutschland)

10. An welchem Fluß liegt Hamburg? (an der Weser, an der Elbe, am Rhein)

11. Welcher Fluß fließt durch Bayern nach Österreich? (die Donau, der Bodensee, der Rhein)

12. Welche zwei Täler (valleys) sind für ihren Wein bekannt? (der Donau und der Neckar, des Rheins und der Mosel, der Oder und der Neiße)

13. Wie kommt ein Drittel aller Waren in Berlin-West an? (auf dem Wasserweg, mit dem Flugzeug, mit Mopeds und Fahrrädern)

14. Welche Länder liegen südlich von Westdeutschland? (Österreich und die Schweiz, Frankreich und Belgien, Polen und die Tschechoslowakei)

15. Aus welchem Land kommen die Elbe und die Oder? (aus Polen, aus der Tschechoslowakei, aus Österreich)

I. If the statement is true, write *richtig*; if false, write *falsch*.

1. Im Winter ist das Wetter im Alpenvorland bitterkalt. _richtig_

2. Düsseldorf ist eine Industriestadt. _richtig_ ~~falsch~~

3. Die Weser ist der bekannteste Fluß in Deutschland. _falsch_

4. Die Mosel fließt aus Frankreich in den Rhein. _richtig_ ~~falsch~~

5. Berlin ist der größte Seehafen Deutschlands. _falsch_

6. Die Oder ist eine Grenze zwischen Deutschland und Polen. _richtig_ ~~falsch~~

7. Bayern ist ein Land der D.D.R. _falsch_

8. Der Bodensee liegt zwischen Westdeutschland und der Schweiz. _richtig_

9. Der Rhein fließt aus den Alpen durch Deutschland. _richtig_

10. Das Brandenburger Tor findet sich heute in Berlin-Ost. _richtig_

11. Es gibt kein Gebirge im Süden. _falsch_

12. München ist im südlichen Teil der Bundesrepublik. _richtig_

13. Westdeutschland ist nur halb so groß wie der Staat Oregon. _falsch_

14. Berlin-West hat über zwei Millionen Einwohner (inhabitants). _richtig_

15. Aus dem Rheintal (Rhine Valley) kommt guter Wein. _richtig_

The large emblem (center) is the coat of arms of the Federal Republic of Germany. On the left are the coats of arms of Prussia (top) and Rhineland-Palatinate (bottom); on the right, those of Schleswig-Holstein (top) and Hamburg (bottom).

31. HISTORY OF GERMANY

ORIGINS OF THE GERMAN STATE

EARLIEST INHABITANTS

In the centuries before the Christian era, several Germanic tribes roamed the forests of northern Europe. When Greek and Roman civilizations were flourishing, these tribes were still living in thatch-roofed huts and moving frequently from place to place. The diversity of tribal backgrounds that divided the ancient Germans may help explain why Germany has seldom been united.

THE GERMANIC INVASIONS AND THE FALL OF ROME

During the early centuries of the Christian era, German tribes continually raided the borders of the Roman Empire. As Roman power declined, the Germans invaded and occupied various parts of the Empire. These invasions ultimately destroyed the Empire in the west. By the 7th century, eight Germanic kingdoms had arisen in the former Roman provinces. Christianity became the dominant religion of these kingdoms.

MEDIEVAL TIMES

Karl der Große (or *Charlemagne*) organized an empire that included what is now France, Germany, the northern lowlands, and the northern half of Italy. Karl's empire was dedicated to Christian ideals. In 800 A.D., the Pope crowned him emperor of the Romans. After Karl's death in 814, his empire broke up into three kingdoms. In the next century, the western kingdom became the kingdom of France, and the rest of Karl's empire became the foundation of the Holy Roman Empire.

Otto I was crowned king of Saxony in 936 at the palace of Karl der Große in Aachen. Otto sought and received the support of the Pope for his claim to the title of Emperor. In 962, Otto became the first emperor of the Holy Roman Empire (**das Heilige Römische Reich Deutscher Nation**). The Empire continued to exist at least in name until 1806.

Feudalism became firmly established in the Empire, which was an assortment of domains ruled by petty kings and nobles. The Emperor usually had little real power. His authority depended on the support of feudal lords who paid him homage but retained their independence. These lords, in turn, derived their power from the support of lesser nobles.

Friedrich I Barbarossa, crowned Emperor in 1152, attempted to wrest from the feudal lords the power that formally belonged to the Emperor. Barbarossa personified the ideals of chivalry. Both at home and abroad, he was the Christian knight defending the faith. Together with the French king and Richard the Lion Hearted, King of England, Barbarossa in 1189 led the Third Crusade to the Holy Land. After his death on the way to the Holy Land, Barbarossa became a legendary figure to the German people.

The Hanseatic League (**die Hanse**), established in the 12th century, was a group of fifty cities in northern Germany, Holland, Denmark, and Sweden that were organized for mutual commercial benefit. The Hanse operated its own fleet of ships and had its own flag. Its members became virtually independent of the countries in which the cities were situated.

THE REFORMATION

A dramatic event marked the beginning of the Protestant break with the Church of Rome. In 1517, **Martin Luther,** a German monk and professor of theology, tacked his Ninety-Five Theses to the door of All Saints' Church at Wittenberg. The Theses expressed Luther's opposition to some of the doctrines and practices of the Roman Church at that time.

A **Peasant Revolt,** provoked by the cruelty of the nobles and inspired by Luther's ideas, broke out in 1524–1525. Luther denounced the revolt and sided with the nobles. The nobles crushed the uprising savagely, killing more than 100,000 peasants.

The northern German states formed a **Protestant Union** in 1608. In reaction, the southern states established the **Catholic Liga** in 1609. In the ensuing conflict between German Protestants and Catholics, neighboring European powers allied themselves with one side or the other.

The **Thirty Years War** was a series of battles fought between Protestant and Catholic forces in the interval from 1618 to 1648. Germany was the major battleground for this war. The war was so destructive that the German population was reduced from more than 18 million to less than 7 million persons. As a result of the war, the Hanse was dissolved and the local lords became more powerful than ever.

The Rise of Prussia and the Struggle for German Unity

Prussia (**Preußen**) emerged in the 18th century as the most powerful and influential of the many German states. Beginning with Friedrich I in 1701, Prussia built up a powerful army and an efficient, disciplined government bureaucracy.

Friedrich II, called **Friedrich der Große,** became the Prussian king in 1740. He was the model of an "enlightened despot." Although he ruled as an absolute monarch, he was keenly interested in the arts and humanities and surrounded himself with outstanding scholars and artists from all parts of Europe.

The armies of **Napoleon,** Emperor of France, overran Germany at the beginning of the 19th century. He put an end to the Holy Roman Empire in 1806, and weakened Prussia's power and influence. Following Napoleon's defeat at Waterloo in 1815, the French Empire was dissolved and the number of German states was reduced from more than 100 to 38.

After 1815, there was increasing pressure for unification of the German states under some form of republican government. In 1848, delegates from the various German states met in Frankfurt am Main to establish a democratic government for a unified Germany, but nothing came of their efforts. During the same year, revolutions broke out in Berlin and Vienna in attempts to achieve the same objectives—democracy and German unity—but they were quickly suppressed.

THE FORMATION OF THE MODERN GERMAN REICH

World War I

The **Franco-Prussian War** (1870–71), which ended with the defeat of France, served to consolidate the German states under the Prussian leadership of Kaiser (Emperor) Wilhelm I and Reichskanzler (Prime Minister) **Otto von Bismarck.** Often called the "Iron Chancellor," Bismarck was a strong-willed, authoritarian leader. He managed to unify and stabilize Germany politically, so that it gained a position as a respected European power.

Kaiser Wilhelm II succeeded Wilhelm I in 1888. Wilhelm II desired to play an active personal role in world affairs—a policy that Bismarck bitterly opposed. In 1890, Bismarck was removed from office. Eager to make Germany a major world power, Wilhelm II seized the opportunity in 1914 to go to war against France and her allies, thus precipitating the outbreak of the first World War. In this conflict, Germany, Austria-Hungary, Bulgaria, and Turkey fought against France, Belgium, Great Britain, Russia, and Serbia. In 1917, the United States entered the war to support the French and their allies.

Germany surrendered to the Allies with the signing of an armistice on November 11, 1918. The Treaty of Versailles, which ended the war, allowed Germany only a small army and forbade her to manufacture armaments. The treaty also required Germany to make reparations to the Allies to pay for the war.

The Weimar Republic

A democratic republic with its capital in Weimar (**die Weimarer Republik**) was established in Germany in 1919. The new republic was weakened by many problems.

Economic chaos was aggravated by the burden of reparation payments. A weak constitution gave the Chancellor little real control of the government. The republic was further undermined by the militant opposition of radical political organizations determined to destroy it. To make matters worse, many Germans believed that the German army had not been defeated in the field, but had been "stabbed in the back" by the wartime civilian authorities. Hence, the Weimar Republic was seen as a symbol of defeat by treachery.

The inflation that reached its peak at the end of 1923 was devastating. The German Mark had been valued at 4 Marks to the American dollar; by the end of 1922, it had fallen to 6,000 Marks to the dollar. Before the inflation ended in November 1923, the rate had gone to four billion Marks to the dollar!

Adolf Hitler, who had taken control of the insignificant German Workers Party, made an unsuccessful attempt to seize control of the Bavarian government. In his famous **Putsch,** he marched on the Munich *Rathaus* on November 9, 1923—only a few days before the inflation came to an end. After serving a short prison term for this action, Hitler reorganized his party with the aim of gaining political power legally. He changed its name to the **National Socialist (Nazi) party.**

The great depression, which struck the United States in 1929, was also felt in Germany. It brought unemployment and impoverishment to millions of Germans. Increasing hostility toward the Weimar Republic, which was unable to cope effectively with the economic crisis, and fear of the growing strength of the communists and socialists enabled the Nazi party to become influential enough to demand that Hitler be named Chancellor.

The Third Reich

Hitler was installed as Chancellor in January, 1933. Within two months, he had been granted complete dictatorial powers. The Nazis, who called their brutal regime **das Dritte Reich,** ruled with absolute power for the next twelve years. In rapid succession all political parties other than the Nazis were outlawed, the labor movement was brought under Nazi control, Nazis were placed in all principal positions of government, and the systematic harassment of the Jews—which later developed into a program of genocide, or mass murder of a whole population—was begun.

World War II

In defiance of the Treaty of Versailles, German troops reentered the Rhineland unopposed in 1936. Austria and Czechoslovakia were added to the Third Reich in 1938. On September 1, 1939, the Germans invaded Poland. England and France responded by declaring war on Germany. World War II had begun.

The German **Blitzkrieg** (lightning war), with its use of massive air power and rapid mechanized ground forces, destroyed the Polish army in a few weeks. The Germans also attacked in the west. Nine months after the invasion of Poland, the German armies had taken Warsaw, Denmark, Norway, Holland, Belgium, and Paris. A Nazi invasion of England seemed imminent.

In June 1941, the German armies invaded the U.S.S.R. and rapidly advanced as far as Stalingrad, where the Russian stand and the bitter winter cost the Germans 300,000 troops.

Germany's allies in the war were fascist Italy and Japan. On December 7, 1941, the Japanese air force attacked the U.S. fleet at Pearl Harbor, in Hawaii, and Hitler declared war on the United States.

After 1941, the Nazi armies were slowly pushed back in Russia, Africa, and Italy. Armies of the western Allies landed in France in June 1944. Soviet troops entered Berlin early in May 1945. Hitler committed suicide in Berlin, and Germany surrendered unconditionally on May 8, 1945.

POST-WAR GERMANY

THE OCCUPATION

After the war, Germany was divided into four occupation zones (**Besatzungszonen**). Each zone was controlled by one of the four major Allied powers: the United States, Great Britain, France, and the Soviet Union. Some eastern German territories were absorbed by Poland and Russia, and their German populations were expelled.

Although Berlin was located deep within the Soviet occupation zone, it was placed under four-power control. Access routes from the West to Berlin were guaranteed by the U.S.S.R.

The **Black Market** (the illegal selling of scarce or rationed items, usually at very high prices) became active in Germany in the first years of the occupation. Since the war had destroyed the German economy and left the country in ruins, many necessities of life were available only on the Black Market. The Reichsmark no longer had any real value; the "hard currency" of that time was the cigarette.

THE CHANGING MAP OF GERMANY

Holy Roman Empire 1648

German Empire 1871–1914

Weimar Republic 1919–1933

Germany Today

THE RECONSTRUCTION

The reconstruction (**Wiederaufbau**) of West Germany began with the currency reform (**Währungsreform**) of June 1948. The reform made it compulsory to exchange the Nazi Reichsmark for the **Deutsche Mark** (**DM**), the new official currency, at the ratio of ten to one. This step put an end to the Black Market, eliminated the danger of inflation, and stabilized the price structure of the economy. On June 20, the West German government issued 40 DM to each man, woman, and child in West Germany and West Berlin. As a result of the economic progress achieved during the years following the Währungsreform, the Deutsche Mark eventually became the most stable currency in Europe.

The "economic miracle" (**Wirtschaftswunder**) accomplished in the decades following 1948 was spurred by United States aid for West German industry, provided through the Marshall Plan (1948–1952). Because of the great expansion of German industry, unemployment was unknown in West Germany in the 1950's and 1960's. In fact, it became necessary to import more than a million workers from other European countries to relieve labor shortages. West German workers today are among the best paid in Europe, and their living standard ranks with the highest on the continent.

THE FEDERAL REPUBLIC

The Federal Republic (**Bundesrepublik**) was formally established in 1949 by joining the three western occupation zones. It consists of 8 **Länder,** or states, and 3 **Freistädte,** or city states (see Lesson 30, page 220). The capital of the Bundesrepublik is Bonn.

The Federal Republic is governed by a parliament composed of two houses: the **Bundesrat,** or upper house, and the **Bundestag,** or lower house. The Bundesrat, whose members are appointed by the state governments for indefinite terms, has 3 to 5 delegates from each state. The Bundestag has 518 representatives chosen by popular election for four-year terms. In both houses, the Berlin representatives have only advisory functions and do not vote.

POLITICS

In the years following World War II, two major political parties emerged in West Germany: the Christian Democrats (**die Christlich-Demokratische Union,** or **CDU**) and the Social Democrats (**die Sozialdemokratische Partei Deutschlands,** or **SPD**). One of the original differences between the two parties was that the CDU favored strong ties with the West, especially with the United States, whereas the SPD advocated a more neutral policy for West Germany. In 1969, the leaders of the two parties agreed that West Germany should develop friendlier relations with East Germany and the U.S.S.R.

The **Bundeskanzler** (Chancellor or Prime Minister) is selected by the Bundestag. In the first elections in the Bundesrepublik, the CDU had the controlling majority in the Bundestag. Its leader, **Konrad Adenauer,** became the first Bundeskanzler, a post that he held till he was replaced by Ludwig Erhard in 1963. In 1969, **Willy Brandt,** former mayor of Berlin, became the first member of the SPD to be elected Bundeskanzler. When Brandt resigned his position in 1974, the Bundestag chose **Helmut Schmidt** to replace him. Schmidt was reelected Bundeskanzler in 1976 and 1980.

BERLIN

Berlin has played a key role in the Cold War between East and West ever since its occupation in 1945. The Soviet army seized the city in May 1945. American, British, and French troops formally entered Berlin on July 1, 1945. The city's location made it a peephole in the otherwise impenetrable Iron Curtain (**der Eiserne Vorhang**).

The Berlin Blockade (**die Blockade**) was the occasion of the first open break between the United States and the Soviet Union following World War II. In June 1948, the Soviets tried to force the western powers to leave Berlin by stopping all water and land travel to the city. Since only about 1% of the goods entering and leaving Berlin is normally shipped by air, the blockade was a severe blow.

The United States immediately established an airlift (**die Luftbrücke**) to carry into Berlin food, coal, raw materials for industry, and all other goods needed to sustain life in the city. The airlift was so effective that it defeated the attempt to starve Berlin, and the Russians lifted the blockade eleven months later, in May 1949.

East Berlin workers revolted against the Communist regime on June 17, 1953. Soviet tanks were called in, and the uprising was crushed. Between 1949 and 1961, about 1,800,000 refugees (**Flüchtlinge**) fled East Germany by passing through the Brandenburg Gate into West Berlin. From there, most were flown into West Germany, about 190,000 remaining to work in West Berlin. The East German government halted this flow of emigrants to the West by erecting the infamous Berlin Wall in August 1961. In the following years, the Wall (**die Mauer**) effectively sealed off East Germany from the Federal Republic.

East Germany

In 1949, at the time the Bundesrepublik was established, the Soviet Occupation Zone was converted into the German Democratic Republic (**die Deutsche Demokratische Republik,** or **D.D.R.**) under the leadership of **Walter Ulbricht.** In the Communist D.D.R., however, there was no Soviet equivalent of the Marshall Plan. In fact, the Russians carried back to the Soviet Union almost all German machinery (including complete factories) that had not been destroyed in the war.

In the years following the construction of the Wall, East Germany underwent a change much like the Wirtschaftswunder of West Germany. There was a marked rise in industrial production and living standards. East Germany became the second largest manufacturing center in the Communist bloc, second only to the U.S.S.R. itself.

In 1971, Ulbricht resigned his position and **Erich Honecker** became the new leader of the East German government. In 1979, Honecker's government enacted a currency law designed to stop the widespread use of West German marks in the D.D.R. to buy Western goods on the black market.

WORTSCHATZ

die **Besatzung,** the military occupation

die **Blockade,** Soviet stoppage of surface transportation between West Germany and Berlin

der **Bund, -e,** union, confederation

der **Bundesrat,** one of the two houses of parliament of the Bundesrepublik, consisting of members selected by the government of each *Land*, or state, of the republic.

die **Bundesrepublik,** German Federal Republic, formally established in 1949, which was originally intended as a temporary governing organization for West Germany until reunification of West with East Germany; Bonn is the capital of the Federal Republic

der **Bundestag,** one of the two houses of parliament of the Bundesrepublik, consisting of representatives elected by the people for four-year terms

die **Burg, -en,** castle fortification

die **Demokratie, -n,** democracy

die **Deutsche Demokratische Republik,** the German People's Republic (DDR), the Communist-controlled government of East Germany

der **Eiserne Vorhang,** the Iron Curtain

der **Flüchtling, -e,** refugee (especially one who fled from East to West Germany)

der **Führer, -,** leader; the title adopted by Adolf Hitler

die **Geschichte,** history

die **Hauptstadt, ⸚e,** capital city

der **Kaiser, -,** emperor (from Latin *Caesar*); title assumed by Wilhelm I and Wilhelm II

der **Kampf, ⸚e,** battle, struggle

der **Kanzler,** chancellor

der **König, -e,** king

der **Kreuzzug, ⸚e,** Crusade (to the Holy Land)

der **Krieg, -e,** war (**der Weltkrieg** = World War)

das **Land, ⁒er,** political subdivision within the Bundesrepublik, corresponding to a state within the United States

die **Luftbrücke,** the Airlift, which brought all goods into Berlin during the Soviet blockade of 1948–1949

die **Mauer,** the Wall dividing East and West Berlin

das **Mittelalter,** Middle Ages

die **Partei, -en,** (political) party

die **Politik,** politics

der **Präsident, -en,** president

das **Reich, -e,** empire, dominion, state (Adolf Hitler referred to his regime as *das Dritte Reich.*)

der **Reichskanzler,** Chancellor (of the Reich)

die **Religion, -en,** religion

die **Republik, -en,** republic

der **Schwarze Markt** (**der Schwarzhandel**), the Black Market

der **Staat, -en,** state, country

der **Staatsmann, ⁒er,** politician, statesman

die **Stadt, ⁒e,** city

die **Vergangenheit,** the past

die **Verwaltung, -en,** supervision, administration

die **Waffe, -n,** weapon, arm

der **Waffenstillstand,** the Armistice

die **Währungsreform,** currency reform

die **Wiederaufbau,** reconstruction

das **Wirtschaftswunder,** the "economic miracle" in West Germany after 1947

ÜBUNGEN

A. To the left of each item in column *A*, write the letter of the corresponding item in column *B*.

COLUMN A	COLUMN B
_____ **1.** Martin Luther	*a.* the East German government
_____ **2.** Walter Ulbricht	*b.* the Wall dividing Berlin
_____ **3.** die Bundesrepublik	*c.* post-war source of illegal goods
_____ **4.** Otto von Bismarck	*d.* enlightened despot
_____ **5.** the Black Market	*e.* transportation of goods into Berlin during the Blockade
_____ **6.** die Luftbrücke	*f.* first head of the D.D.R.
_____ **7.** die Währungsreform	*g.* the first Bundeskanzler
_____ **8.** der Bundesrat	*h.* the "economic miracle" in West Germany
_____ **9.** Konrad Adenauer	*i.* founder of Protestantism
_____ **10.** Otto I	*j.* West German currency reform
_____ **11.** die Flüchtlinge	*k.* government of West Germany
_____ **12.** die D.D.R.	*l.* first Emperor of the Holy Roman Empire
_____ **13.** die Mauer	*m.* upper house of the West German parliament
_____ **14.** das Wirtschaftswunder	*n.* refugees from East to West Germany
_____ **15.** Friedrich der Große	*o.* the "Iron Chancellor"

B. Match the dates in column *B* with the persons or events in column *A*.

COLUMN A	COLUMN B
_____ 1. coronation of *Karl der Große*	*a.* June 1948
_____ 2. beginning of Berlin Blockade	*b.* 1806
_____ 3. Thirty Years War	*c.* January 1933
_____ 4. East Berlin workers' revolt	*d.* 800
_____ 5. year of the inflation and Hitler's *Putsch*	*e.* August 1961
_____ 6. *das Heilige Römische Reich* comes to an end	*f.* 1618–1648
_____ 7. *die Hanse* established	*g.* 1517
_____ 8. Hitler becomes Chancellor	*h.* June 17, 1953
_____ 9. Berlin Wall is built	*i.* 1923
_____ 10. Luther's Theses	*j.* twelfth century

C. Underline the answer in parentheses that correctly completes each statement.

1. Karl der Große wurde im Jahre (800, 1740, 1888) Kaiser.

2. Die meisten Kaiser des Heiligen Römischen Reiches Deutscher Nation hatten (viel, nur wenig, ziemlich große) Macht.

3. Das Heilige Römische Reich dauerte (zwölf, zwei hundert, fast ein tausend) Jahre.

4. (Karl der Große, Otto I, Friedrich I Barbarossa) war der Kaiser, der auf einem Kreuzzug ins Heilige Land gestorben ist.

5. Der Bund von nordeuropäischen Städten im dreizehnten Jahrhundert hieß (das Heilige Römische Reich, die Hanse, die Bundesrepublik).

6. (Friedrich I Barbarossa, Martin Luther, Friedrich der Große) schlug 1517 die fünfundneunzig Thesen an die Tür einer Kirche zu Wittenberg an.

7. Im achtzehnten Jahrhundert wurde (Frankreich, die Hanse, Preußen) der größte deutsche Staat.

8. Otto von Bismarck war Reichskanzler unter (Friedrich den Großen, Wilhelm I, Adolf Hitler).

9. Nach dem ersten Weltkrieg wurde (Berlin, Bonn, Weimar) die Hauptstadt der Republik.

10. Adolf Hitler wurde (1923, 1933, 1945) Reichskanzler.

11. Nach dem zweiten Weltkrieg gab es in Deutschland (zwei, drei, vier) Besatzungszonen.

12. Gerade nach dem Kriege kaufte man allerlei (auf dem Schwarzen Markt, von Freunden, in den Laden).

13. Die (Wiederaufbau, Währungsreform, Blockade) fand mit Hilfe des Marshall-Plans statt. (*stattfinden* = to take place)

14. Während der Blockade kamen Güter (goods) durch (die Eisenbahn, Wagen, die Luftbrücke) in Berlin an.

15. Seit dem Jahre 1949 gibt es in Westdeutschland die (Weimarer Republik, Deutsche Demokratische Republik, Bundesrepublik).

16. In der Bundesrepublik sind (drei, acht, elf) Länder und Freistädte.

17. (Berlin, Bonn, Weimar) ist die Hauptstadt der Bundesrepublik.

18. In (Berlin, Wien, München) steht die Mauer.

19. In der Bundesrepublik gibt es (sehr wenig, ziemlich viel, große) Arbeitslosigkeit (unemployment).

20. Die Regierung (government) in Ost-Deutschland heißt (das Dritte Reich, die Deutsche Demokratische Republik, die Sozialistische-Partei Deutschlands).

The *Kongreßhalle*, in West Berlin, is a convention hall
notable for its striking and highly original architecture.

32. GERMAN CUSTOMS

PERSONAL LIFE

PRIVACY

Germans greatly value personal privacy. This feeling is shown in many ways:

1. The man who works in an office is more apt to keep his office door closed than is his American counterpart.

2. Most German city-dwellers live in apartments. These apartments often have balconies, but each balcony is built so that it cannot be seen from the other apartments in the building.

3. Those who live in a private house (**Einzelhaus**) usually have an effective fence around the yard.

4. In apartments as well as private houses, the residents customarily keep their drapes drawn in the evening.

FORMAL AND INFORMAL ADDRESS

1. The emphasis on privacy is also reflected in the social relations between individuals. The formal **Sie** along with the appropriate title—**Herr, Frau, Herr Doktor,** etc.—is used for all adults except those few who are members of the family or intimate friends.

2. Adults who are on cordial terms with one another are **Bekannte,** but they continue to address each other as **Sie.**

3. The term **Freund,** used with **du** and the first name, is reserved for those intimate friends who become a part of one's private life.

SOCIAL CUSTOMS

1. Germans usually shake hands both when greeting one another and when parting, even after a brief chat.

2. On a date (**zum Date**), a young couple may go to a dance, a movie or opera, to the theater, or for a walk in a nearby park.

3. When a guest is invited to someone's home, he is expected to arrive on time. In Germany, it is bad taste to arrive "stylishly late."

RESTAURANTS

Public eating places go by several names:

1. **Das Restaurant** has a varied menu of hot foods, including perhaps a **Spezialität.**

2. **Der Ratskeller** is a restaurant located in the city hall (**das Rathaus**).

3. **Die Gaststätte,** found especially in smaller villages, is similar to our cafés and is frequently a source of authentic cooking.

4. **Das Café** is essentially a coffee house that usually has pastries available and occasionally other snacks.

5. **Die Konditorei** is a pastry shop, often connected with a **Café.** Here the patron may slowly

sip a cup of coffee with **Schlagsahne** (whipped cream) while he nibbles at a piece of exotic pastry.

6. Especially in the smaller towns and neighborhood **Gaststätten,** there is usually a table marked **Stammtisch.** This table is reserved for the group of regular patrons who spend a part of every evening around the table discussing the day's events or arguing politics or playing cards. The **Stammtisch** is also a part of the German private life. Thus, a newcomer sits at this table only when he is invited to join the **Stammgäste.**

SCHOOLS

CLASS SCHEDULES

1. Schools in Germany generally do not meet as long each day as American schools. Students have no lunch hour at school, but go home around one o'clock. However, classes are held six days each week.

2. Many subjects are not studied each day in the week, as they are in American schools. The student in a German high school may have as many as eight or nine different subjects at a time, some of which he may study only two or three days each week.

TEACHERS AND STUDENTS

1. Even today, the relationship between teachers and students at the high school level is much more formal than it is in the United States. The casual, friendly atmosphere that one usually finds in an American high school classroom is almost unknown in Germany.

2. In the classroom, the teacher is treated with deference and respect by his students, and he usually remains somewhat aloof. As a sign of respect for the teacher's position, students all rise when he enters the room. A student stands beside his desk when he recites in class.

SOCIAL LIFE

1. The schools play no role in the student's social life. Although schools do have a physical education program, extracurricular activities (sports, clubs, dances, etc.), which are so much a part of the American high school program, are unknown in German schools.

2. The individual student pursues such interests as individual or team sports and various hobbies by joining a local **Verein** devoted to his particular interest.

RELIGION

1. Northern Germany is predominantly Protestant (especially **evangelisch,** that is, Lutheran). Southern Germany is mostly Roman Catholic.

2. Unlike schools in the United States, West German schools offer religious instruction as a regular part of the curriculum. A church tax is also collected by local governments for support of the predominant church.

FESTIVALS AND HOLIDAYS

RELIGIOUS CELEBRATIONS

The two major religious celebrations are Christmas and Easter.

1. The Christmas season extends for a full month.
   Sankt Nikolaus (St. Nicholas), who has a long beard and a bishop's miter and staff, comes in a sled drawn by a donkey on the evening of December 6, bringing sweets to those children who have been good.
   Christmas presents are exchanged on Christmas eve.
   As with other major religious holidays, both the festival day and the day following are legal holidays. Thus, both December 25 and 26 are celebrated as Christmas (**die Weihnachten**). The season officially ends on January 6, the day of the three kings (**der drei Königstag**).

2. Easter (**Ostern**) is celebrated with colored eggs and candies, Easter egg hunts, rides, firewheels, and in some places with bonfires. Good Friday (**Karfreitag**) and the Monday following Easter are legal holidays.

OTHER FESTIVALS

1. *Wine festivals* are held in Koblenz, Mainz, Trier, Bingen, and most of the smaller towns in the wine country. The **Wurstmarkt,** which dates back to 1442, is actually a wine festival held annually toward the end of September at Bad Dürkheim in the Pfalz.

2. The **Oktoberfest** in München dates back a little more than 150 years. This beer festival begins in September and continues into October.

3. **Karneval,** with a history that goes back into pre-Christian times, actually begins in November and continues until Lent. Some carnival activities are scheduled in January and early February, but the real celebration takes place during the last two weeks before Lent.
   Köln (Cologne), Mainz, and München (Munich) are the three big *Karneval* cities, each with its own style of celebration. The term *Karneval* actually applies only to the festival in Köln. In Mainz, the *Karneval* goes by the name **Fastnacht;** in München, it is **Fasching.** All of the celebrations have a Mardi Gras character, complete with parades, masquerade balls, wild costumes, and much merrymaking.
   In Schwabenland, the *Karneval* takes the form of **Fasnet,** which has many traces of ancient German cults.

LEISURE TIME

CLUBS

Special interest groups (**Vereine**) give individuals the opportunity to meet others with similar interests, whether it be singing, stamp collecting, or gymnastics.

SPORTS

1. *Team sports* are not so popular in Germany as in the United States. Soccer (**Fußball**) is the most popular team sport.

2. Even fairly small villages will have several public tennis courts and a public swimming pool (**Schwimmbad**). Usually there is also a tennis club and swimming club in connection with these.

3. Gymnastics (**Turnen**) is much more widely practiced in Germany than in the United States. Gymnastics tournaments, as well as track and field competitions, attract many individuals.

4. In the highlands of southern Germany, both skiing and mountain climbing are popular. Wherever there are lakes and rivers—and especially in the northern sections—sailing and rowing are popular activities.

5. Especially in southern and central Germany, where the hills and mountains provide suitable thermal currents, many people build and fly glider planes.

CAMPING AND HIKING

The love of nature (**die Naturliebe**) is deeply ingrained in the German heritage. Thus, outdoor activities are always popular, whether it be only a stroll through a park or a cross-country summer hike (**eine Wanderung**).

1. Since World War II, camping has become increasingly popular in Germany. Unlike campers in many parts of the United States, however, the German family usually camps only overnight and then moves on.

2. Youth hostels (**Jugendherbergen**) are spotted throughout the country. Students, either hiking or on bicycles, can stay in a *Jugendherberge* for much less than one dollar per night. During the school year, whole classes sometimes use the *Herbergen* while on nature-study field trips.

ÜBUNGEN

A. Underline the answer that best completes each statement.

1. Man gebraucht *du*, wenn man mit einem (Freund, Bekannten, Fremden) spricht.

2. Die meisten Leute in der Stadt wohnen in (Wohnungen, Einzelhäusern, Hotels).

3. In Gaststätten auf dem Lande findet man oft (eine Konditorei, Schlagsahne, einen Stammtisch).

4. Deutsche Schüler gehen (sechs Tage in der Woche, fünf Tage in der Woche, jeden Tag) zur Schule.

5. Wenn der Lehrer ins Klassenzimmer kommt, (stehen alle Schüler auf, setzen sich alle Schüler, rufen die Schüler „Hallo!" mit lauter Stimme).

6. Religion ist ein Teil des Unterrichts in (privaten Schulen, den Universitäten, allen öffentlichen Schulen).

7. Sankt Nikolaus kommt am (sechsten Dezember, Weihnachtsabend, sechsten Januar).

8. Beim Oktoberfest trinkt man (Wein, Bier, Milch).

9. Der beliebteste Sport in Deutschland ist (Turnen, Ski laufen, Fußball).

10. Beim Wandern können Jungen ganz billig in (einem Hotel, einer Jugendherberge, dem Wald) übernachten.

B. If the statement is true, write *richtig*; if false, write *falsch*.

1. Deutsche Wohnungen haben oft ein Balkon. ___R___

2. Wenn man mit einem Bekannten spricht, gebraucht man *Sie*. ___R___

3. Zum Date sitzen junge Leute immer zu Hause. ___F___

4. Wenn man zum Abendessen eingeladen ist, soll man eine halbe Stunde später kommen. _F_

5. Jede Stadt hat mehrere Ratskeller. _IWN_

6. Nur Stammgäste sitzen am Stammtisch. _R_

7. Samstags gehen viele deutsche Schüler zur Schule. _R_

8. Deutsche Lehrer und Schüler sind oft gute Freunde. _F_

9. Wenn der Lehrer ins Klassenzimmer kommt, stehen die Schüler auf. _R_

10. Der Sport ist ein Teil des Unterrichts in deutschen Schulen. _FR_

11. Die Länder in Süddeutschland sind meistens evangelisch. _F_

12. Religion ist ein Teil des Unterrichts in allen deutschen Schulen. _R_

13. Die Weihnachtszeit beginnt am 24. Dezember. _R_

14. Sankt Nikolaus bringt den deutschen Kindern am 24. Dezember Weihnachtsgeschenke. _R_

15. Das Oktoberfest feiert man nur in Norddeutschland. (*feiern* = to celebrate) _F_

16. *Karneval* findet während des Sommers statt. (*stattfinden* = to take place) _F_

17. Niemand in Deutschland interessiert sich für Fußball. _F_

18. Da das Wetter so kühl ist, kann man nur selten in Deutschland schwimmen. _RM_ _R_

19. Die Naturliebe ist den Deutschen sehr wichtig. _R_

20. Wanderer können in einer Jugendherberge ganz billig übernachten. _R_

C. To the left of each item in column *A*, write the letter of the corresponding item in column *B*.

COLUMN A	COLUMN B
_e_ 1. Karneval	a. youth hostel
_f_ 2. Café	b. gymnastics
_a_ 3. Jugendherberge	c. Munich version of *Karneval*
_g_ 4. Ratskeller	d. beer festival in München
_i_ 5. Stammtisch	e. pre-Lenten festival in Köln
_c_ 6. Fasching	f. coffee shop
_j_ 7. Konditorei	g. restaurant in the basement of the city hall
_h_ 8. Gaststätte	h. small restaurant
_d_ 9. Oktoberfest	i. table reserved for regular guests
_b_ 10. Turnen	j. pastry shop

33. PHILOSOPHY AND SCIENCE

PHILOSOPHY

1. **Immanuel Kant** (1724–1804) is one of the greatest philosophers in the history of Europe. In *Die Kritik der reinen Vernunft (Critique of Pure Reason)*, he identified the limits of human knowledge. Kant argued that the mind contains inherent concepts and thought processes with which it organizes sense impressions. Thus, the mind in effect creates experience, and from this experience comes human knowledge. In *Die Kritik der praktischen Vernunft (Critique of Practical Reason)*, he expounded his moral philosophy. Kant argued that the laws of morality should be obeyed for their own sake, regardless of the personal consequences, since the proper aim of life is not to be happy but to do one's duty.

2. **Arthur Schopenhauer** (1788–1860) was a pessimist who saw life as a tragic drama of endless strife and frustration. In his major work, *Die Welt als Wille und Vorstellung (The World as Will and Idea)*, he held that the driving force of the universe is blind will, which in man is the root of all our desires and the cause of all our suffering. Schopenhauer believed that relief from the pain of being human could be found in contemplation of the arts and music, and that freedom from suffering could be found by renouncing desire and rejecting concern for the self, that is, by negating the will.

3. **Georg Friedrich Hegel** (1770–1831) was a philosopher with a special interest in history. Hegel saw history as a reflection of God's will, which revealed itself in human affairs as a progression of social and political changes resulting from conflict between opposing forces in society. In each conflict, an initial force, called the *thesis*, clashes with an emerging counterforce, the *antithesis*, to create a new stage in social evolution called the *synthesis*.

4. **Karl Marx** (1818–1883) applied Hegel's concept of history to economics and concluded that communism is the "synthesis" that would emerge from the conflict between management and labor in a capitalistic society. His major work, *Das Kapital*, is a critical analysis of capitalism.

5. The thought of **Friedrich Nietzsche** (1844–1900) had a marked influence on the work of many major European philosophers, psychologists, novelists, and poets of the 20th century. In writings such as *Also sprach Zarathustra (Thus Spake Zarathustra)* and *Jenseits von Gut und Böse (Beyond Good and Evil)*, Nietzsche attacked Christianity as decadent. He argued that it repressed the creative spirit by forcing men into molds of virtuous mediocrity. Nietzsche believed that the source of all creativity was a "will to power," and that the hope of mankind lay in the rise of a higher type of man, the *Übermensch* (superman), a person of superior intellect and passionate creativity whose genius was untrammeled by the restraints of Christian morality.

SCIENCE

1. **Johannes Gutenberg** (1397–1468) invented movable type and the printing press. At Mainz, around 1450, he printed the Latin Bible.

2. **Nicolaus Copernicus** (1473–1543) shook the foundations of medieval thought by proposing that the earth was not the center of the universe, but that it and the other planets moved around the sun.

3. **Johannes Kepler** (1571–1630) further developed the ideas introduced by Copernicus. He prepared tables of the motions of the planets and formulated three mathematical laws of planetary motion.

4. **Adolf von Baeyer** (1835–1917) made important discoveries in the chemistry of organic substances while working on the synthesis of an indigo dye. His researches contributed

greatly to the development of the German chemical industry. He received the Nobel Prize in Chemistry in 1905.

5. **Robert Koch** (1843–1910) did important research in bacteriology. He isolated and identified the tuberculosis bacillus and developed the tuberculin test. He also developed a technique for staining bacteria on microscope slides so that they could be observed with greater clarity. He received the Nobel Prize in Medicine in 1905.

6. **Wilhelm Röntgen** (1845–1923) discovered the penetrating qualities of X rays (*Röntgenstrahlen*) almost by chance in 1895. He received the Nobel Prize for Physics in 1901.

7. **Sigmund Freud** (1856–1939), a Viennese physician, set the stage for the development of psychology and psychiatry in the 20th century. He introduced many important concepts in clinical psychology—psychoneurosis, the Oedipus Complex, the unconscious, id, ego, and superego. He was also the founder of *psychoanalysis*, a method for treating certain psychological disorders by uncovering the unconscious sources of the patient's distress.

8. **Heinrich Rudolph Hertz** (1857–1894) discovered the existence of electromagnetic waves and thereby laid the foundations for the development of radio, television, and radar.

9. **Max Planck** (1858–1947) introduced the *quantum theory* in 1900. The theory dealt with the ways in which light and other forms of radiant energy are absorbed and emitted by matter and was of major importance in the development of nuclear physics. He received the Nobel Prize in Physics in 1918. Today there are 39 Max Planck Institutes in West Germany for all branches of science.

10. **Albert Einstein** (1879–1955) strongly influenced the course of modern physics and our understanding of the universe. His *theory of relativity* created new concepts of space, time, mass, motion, and gravitation. He established the convertibility of matter and energy, which provided the theoretical basis for the development of atomic energy. In 1921, he received the Nobel Prize for Physics. Einstein left Germany in 1933 and spent the rest of his life in the United States.

ÜBUNGEN

A. Write the letter of the item in column *B* that is associated with the name in column *A*.

COLUMN A	COLUMN B
_____ 1. Adolf von Baeyer	*a.* printing press
_____ 2. Immanuel Kant	*b.* psychoanalysis
_____ 3. Albert Einstein	*c.* tuberculosis bacillus
_____ 4. Wilhelm Röntgen	*d.* three laws of planetary motion
_____ 5. Johannes Gutenberg	*e.* quantum theory
_____ 6. Robert Koch	*f.* held that happiness was not the primary aim of life
_____ 7. Johannes Kepler	
_____ 8. Max Planck	*g.* theory of relativity
_____ 9. Georg Friedrich Hegel	*h.* discoveries in organic chemistry
_____ 10. Sigmund Freud	*i.* X rays
	j. philosophy of history

B. Circle the letter of the answer that best completes each statement.

1. (*a*) Nicolaus Copernicus   (*b*) Immanuel Kant   (*c*) Arthur Schopenhauer   believed that desire was the root cause of human suffering.

2. Many concepts of modern psychiatry were introduced by   (*a*) Max Planck   (*b*) Sigmund Freud   (*c*) G. F. Hegel.

3. The title of Karl Marx's major work is   (*a*) *Röntgenstrahlen*   (*b*) *Das Kapital*   (*c*) *Also sprach Zarathustra*.

4. (*a*) Friedrich Nietzsche   (*b*) Robert Koch   (*c*) Sigmund Freud   asserted that the source of human creativity was the will to power.

5. A philosopher noted for his theories of knowledge and morality was   (*a*) Immanuel Kant   (*b*) Robert Koch   (*c*) Nicolaus Copernicus.

6. Karl Marx took his notion of conflict between economic forces from an idea introduced by   (*a*) Johannes Kepler   (*b*) Immanuel Kant   (*c*) G. F. Hegel.

7. Christianity is attacked as a decadent religion in   (*a*) *Die Welt als Wille und Vorstellung*   (*b*) *Die Kritik der reinen Vernunft*   (*c*) *Jenseits von Gut und Böse*.

8. The first book printed by Gutenberg was   (*a*) *Kritik der reinen Vernunft*   (*b*) the Bible   (*c*) *Das Kapital*.

9. (*a*) Nicolaus Copernicus   (*b*) Robert Koch   (*c*) Albert Einstein   was the medieval thinker who held that the earth goes around the sun.

10. One of Albert Einstein's major contributions to modern physics was   (*a*) the discovery of electromagnetic waves   (*b*) the quantum theory   (*c*) a new concept of the relation between matter and energy.

11. Kepler's discoveries owed a great deal to the work of   (*a*) Adolf von Baeyer   (*b*) Nicolaus Copernicus   (*c*) Max Planck.

12. The Nazis, who ruled Germany from 1933 to 1945, believed that the Germans were a "master race" and could impose their will upon "inferior races" without moral restraints, since power alone determined what was right or wrong. Some Nazis claimed they found support for this doctrine in the writings of   (*a*) Immanuel Kant   (*b*) Karl Marx   (*c*) Friedrich Nietzsche.

13. The quantum theory is concerned with   (*a*) gravitation   (*b*) radiant energy   (*c*) social conflict.

14. The development of radio and television is historically linked to the discoveries of   (*a*) Max Planck   (*b*) Heinrich R. Hertz   (*c*) Adolf von Baeyer.

15. The   (*a*) *Übermensch*   (*b*) *reine Vernunft*   (*c*) Oedipus Complex   is an important concept of Freudian psychology.

34. THE ARTS

LITERATURE

EARLY PERIOD

1. **Old High German** (800–1050 A.D.) was used mostly for church literature. Heroic sagas, such as *Das Nibelungenlied* (*Song of the Nibelungs*) and *Das Gudrunlied*, originated during this time but were not written down until later. The Anglo-Saxon epic *Beowulf*, which appeared in England in the 8th century, and the *Song of Roland*, which appeared in France in the 11th century, were Germanic in origin.

2. The **Middle High German** period (1050–1300) saw the appearance in written form of the *Nibelungenlied* and the *Gudrunlied*. During this period, the ideals of chivalry and courtly love that had been introduced into the culture were reflected in such tales as **Gottfried von Strassburg's** *Tristan und Isolde* and **Wolfram von Eschenbach's** *Parzifal*. The themes of these two epics and of the *Nibelungenlied* were presented in operatic form by Richard Wagner in the 19th century.

3. The 12th and 13th centuries were also the age of the popular *Minnesänger*, wandering German minstrels who, like the French troubadours, composed lyric poems and love songs and sang them in the courts of the nobility. The best-known lyric poet of the period is **Walther von der Vogelweide** (1170–1230).

LATE MEDIEVAL PERIOD

4. The beginning of the **New** (Modern) **High German** era is marked by the growing influence of the cities. Literature turned away from the courtly lyric and chivalric epic and became *bürgerlich* (middle class) in character.

5. German mysticism was represented in the writings of **Meister Eckhart** (1260–1327) and **Thomas à Kempis** (1380–1471).

6. **Fables** patterned after those of Aesop became very popular. One of the best-known characters, *Reineke Fuchs*, appeared in the 15th century.

7. **Sebastian Brant's** *Das Narrenschiff* (*The Ship of Fools*) appeared in 1494. This book provided the inspiration for Katherine Anne Porter's novel *Ship of Fools* in the 20th century.

8. In reaction to the growing influence of the cities, a series of rustic tales circulated in the 16th century. These were comical satires centered around *Till Eulenspiegel*, the peasant who consistently outwitted the sophisticated city-dwellers, and the *Schildbürger*, a group of incredibly dull-witted townspeople.

9. **Martin Luther** (1483–1546) standardized modern High German with his translation of the Bible (1522–1534). He also published religious treatises, a proposal for a general system of education, and a violent denunciation of the peasants who had revolted in 1524–1525. He composed many hymns, of which the best known is "Ein' feste Burg ist unser Gott" ("A Mighty Fortress is our God").

10. In the 15th century, some artisans and tradesmen began to form guilds for the cultivation of poetry and music. Members of such guilds were called "master singers." The most renowned *Meistersinger* of his time was **Hans Sachs** of Nürnberg (1494–1576). Wagner made him a central character in his opera *Die Meistersinger von Nürnberg*.

11. In 1587 *Die Historia von Dr. Johann Faustus* appeared anonymously. It was anti-intellectual in spirit, showing the perils of seeking to know too much. But it provided the theme from which Goethe created his *Faust*.

BEGINNING OF MODERN LITERATURE

12. Modern German literature begins with *die Aufklärung* (the Enlightenment) in the late 18th century. Typical of the *Aufklärung* was an unlimited faith in man's capacity to know and, through knowledge, master the universe. The writers of the Enlightenment advocated religious tolerance and greater religious freedom. In the 19th century this developed into literary romanticism and, later, into realism. The poet and novelist **Christoph Martin Wieland** (1733–1813) was one of the first authors to set the new trend for the *Aufklärung*.

13. Three writers—Lessing, Goethe, and Schiller—composed the bulk of the "classics" of German literature. Although many authors were active in Germany at this time, these three men are best remembered.

   a. **Gotthold Ephraim Lessing** (1729–1781) was both a critic and dramatist. One of his best-known works is the play *Nathan der Weise* (1779), which is an impassioned appeal for religious tolerance and the brotherhood of all men.

   b. **Johann Wolfgang von Goethe** (1749–1832) is generally considered the greatest figure in German literature. He strove to be a universal man on the order of Leonardo da Vinci. A statesman by profession, Goethe was interested in the natural sciences and performed some scientific experiments, in addition to writing novels, poetry, and drama. He first achieved fame with a romantic novel, *Die Leiden des jungen Werthers* (*The Sorrows of Young Werther*). During his long life, Goethe initiated or participated in several phases of German literature. His first drama, *Götz von Berlichingen*, was loosely based on a 16th-century figure. Goethe's interest in classical Greece is typified by his play *Iphigenie auf Taurus*. His *Wilhelm Meisters Lehrjahre*, showing character development through fiction, is considered the first modern German novel. Although Goethe wrote much lyric poetry and many plays, his greatest fame comes from *Faust*, a poetic drama that he finished only a short time before his death.

   c. **Friedrich von Schiller** (1759–1805) was a lyric poet, dramatist, and historian. His first play was *Die Räuber* (*The Robbers*). Many of his plays had historical themes: *Die Jungfrau von Orleans* (*The Maid of Orleans*) was a romanticized treatment of Joan of Arc, *Maria Stuart* stemmed from English history, and his *Wallenstein* trilogy had the Thirty Years War as its background. His *Wilhelm Tell*, dealing with the Swiss fight for freedom, is widely known through its operatic treatment by Rossini. Schiller's *Ode an die Freude* (*Ode to Joy*) was the text for Beethoven's *Ninth* ("Choral") *Symphony*.

14. The Brothers **Grimm** (**Jakob**, 1785–1863; **Wilhelm**, 1786–1859) published *Kinder- und Hausmärchen*, a collection of German folk tales, in 1812 and 1815. They found that certain traditional folk tales and legends, called *Märchen*, were common to several different cultures. Their study of *Märchen* led to the foundation of comparative linguistics.

15. **Heinrich Heine** (1797–1856) is one of the world's great lyric poets. Many of his poems were set to music by later composers. Among his best-known poems are "Du bist wie eine Blume" and "Die Lorelei," which has become a folk song.

16. The *Novelle*—something between a long short-story and a short novel—was developed to a high degree by several 19th-century German authors. This literary form, patterned after the earlier tales of Boccaccio and Chaucer, was introduced into German literature by Goethe. **Heinrich von Kleist** (1777–1811) perfected the classical form of the *Novelle*, which dealt in a simple way with a single event. The form was adapted to the different styles of **E. T. A. Hoffmann** (1776–1822) and **Theodor Storm** (1817–1888). Hoffmann's tales are filled with mysterious and occult qualities. The form of the *Novelle* has been further developed by several 20th-century authors: Thomas Mann, Hermann Hesse, Franz Kafka, and Wolfgang Borchert.

The 20th century produced a number of German authors who are as well known elsewhere as in Germany. Especially following World War I, a wealth of important German novels appeared. During the years 1933–45, however, the Nazi insistence on conformity to party philosophy brought this literary production to a halt, and many writers were forced to flee from their country.

17. **Gerhart Hauptmann** (1862–1946) is remembered for such dramas as *Die Weber* (*The Weavers*), which was concerned with the exploitation of weavers in Silesia. He received the Nobel Prize in Literature in 1912.

18. **Thomas Mann** (1875–1955) was an outstanding novelist and short-story writer. His novels often have several levels of meaning. Two major themes of Mann's fiction are the relation between creativity and neurosis and the conflict between instinct and intellect. His most notable novels include *Der Zauberberg* (*The Magic Mountain*), *Buddenbrooks, Der Tod in Venedig* (*Death in Venice*), and *Doktor Faustus*. He received the Nobel Prize in Literature in 1929. An opponent of the Hitler regime, Mann fled to the United States in 1938. After World War II he returned to Switzerland, where he died at the age of 80.

19. **Hermann Hesse** (1877–1962) wrote novels about the loneliness of sensitive and artistic young men who withdraw from society to find inner peace. In recent years, his fiction has achieved great popularity in the United States. Four of his novels—*Siddhartha, Demian, Der Steppenwolf,* and *Narziss und Goldmund*—are now widely sold in paperback translations, although they were all written more than 40 years ago. Hesse received the Nobel Prize for Literature in 1946.

20. The stories of **Franz Kafka** (1883–1924) often have a strange, dreamlike quality, although his prose style is remarkably clear and precise. His symbolic novels *Der Prozess* (*The Trial*), *Das Schloss* (*The Castle*), and *Die Verwandlung* (*Metamorphosis*) depict modern man as oppressed by isolation, guilt, and anxiety in his futile efforts to placate the dark social forces that block his quest for personal salvation.

21. **Franz Werfel** (1890–1945) numbered among his works the novels *Die vierzig Tage des Musa Dagh* (*The Forty Days of Musa Dagh*), *Das Lied von Bernadette* (*The Song of Bernadette*, which became an American movie), and the play *Jakobowsky und der Oberst* (*Jakobowsky and the Colonel*).

22. **Bertolt Brecht** (1898–1956) was a powerful playwright noted for his radical innovations in the theater arts. In 1928 he collaborated with **Kurt Weill,** a composer, to write *Die Dreigroschenoper* (*The Three-Penny Opera*). Brecht's major theme was the oppression of the poor by capitalist society. A fervent Communist, he settled in East Berlin in 1948 and served the East German government as director of a state-controlled theater group.

23. **Erich Maria Remarque** (1898–1970) achieved international renown with his first novel, *Im Westen nichts Neues* (*All Quiet on the Western Front*), which depicts the horrors of modern warfare as experienced by German soldiers in the trenches of World War I. The novel was converted into an equally successful American film. Other novels by Remarque that were made into American films are *Der Triumphbogen* (*The Arch of Triumph*), set against the fall of Paris in 1942, which deals with the plight of refugees from Nazi Germany; and *Zeit zu leben, Zeit zu sterben* (*Time to Live, Time to Die*), which is set in the Germany of World War II. Some of his other novels are *Drei Kameraden*, which depicts Germany during the early Hitler era, and *Der schwarze Obelisk*, a vivid account of German life during the 1923 inflation.

24. **Erich Kästner** (1899–1974) was best known for *Emil und die Detektive,* a humorous novel that has become familiar reading to American students of German. He wrote modern adaptations of the Baron von Münchhausen tales and numerous short stories.

After World War II, significant work by new authors did not emerge for several years, unlike the literary ferment that followed the first World War. The Nazi era had produced a literary vacuum, since the Nazis had suppressed all "non-Aryan" literature (that is, works that did not conform to Nazi ideals) during the 12 years of Hitler's rule. Many outstanding writers had fled from Germany. Thus, after the war the Germans had to renew their acquaintance with the bulk of Western literature. Even today in German theaters Shakespearean plays are the most popular, with the German classics of Schiller in second place.

25. **Wolfgang Borchert, Heinrich Böll,** and a few other new authors received recognition in Germany within the first decade following the collapse of the Nazi regime. **Günter Grass** won international recognition with his novels *Die Blechtrommel* (*The Tin Drum*), *Katz und Maus* (*Cat and Mouse*), and *Hundejahre* (*The Dog Years*).

26. The Swiss playwright **Friedrich Dürrenmatt** has had a great impact on the theater throughout Western countries. His *Der Besuch der alten Dame* appeared on Broadway as *The Visit* and was later converted to a film. *Die Physiker* (*The Physicists*) played throughout Europe and the United States. He has also written numerous *Hörspiele* (radio plays) and television dramas.

27. **Rolf Hochhuth** stirred up international turmoil with his play *Der Stellvertreter* (*The Deputy*), in which Pope Pius XII is accused of refusing to use his authority and influence to oppose the Nazi extermination of the Jews. The dramatist **Peter Weiss** is best known in recent years for *Marat/Sade* and *Die Ermittlung* (*The Investigation*).

MOVIES AND TELEVISION

1. During the silent-film era, some German directors were experimental and creative and had notable success. One of the first "talkies" was *Die Dreigroschenoper*, a film version of Brecht's *Three-Penny Opera*. Shortly after sound was added to films, *Der blaue Engel* (*The Blue Angel*), with Marlene Dietrich, and *M*, with Peter Lorre, brought these performers to the attention of Hollywood and launched them on long, successful careers.

2. The propaganda potential of films was well understood by the Nazis. Hitler spared no expense for the filming of the 1934 Nürnberg *Parteitag* (political rally). The resulting film, *Triumph des Willen* (*Triumph of the Will*), was considered so effective that even today it is available for showings in the United States only at academic institutions and a few other carefully chosen locations.

3. After World War II, the German movie industry slowly revived. Only four films were made in 1946. In the late 1940's, German film makers were using the same techniques and plots that Hollywood had abandoned in the 1930's. Apart from an occasional film of genuine merit, such as *Die letzte Brücke* (*The Last Bridge*) or *Der Rest ist Schweigen* (*The Rest is Silence*), German film producers have devoted their attention to pictures intended to appeal to a mass audience.

4. In radio and television, both operated by the state, programming has developed very well. German TV stations carry a number of popular American series as well as programs developed by the German studios. East German television is still poor and consists primarily of propaganda broadcasts. Whenever possible, East Germans prefer to tune in to West German TV stations and Radio Free Europe.

MUSIC

1. **Johann Sebastian Bach** (1685–1750) is one of the great innovators in Western music. He was a member of a famous musical family that produced several generations of composers and performers. His compositions for harpsichord and for organ are still frequently

performed. Although he also wrote many secular pieces, Bach's sacred music—such as "Jesu, Joy of Man's Desiring"—is best known today.

2. **Georg Friedrich Händel** (1685–1759) spent much of his life in England and is buried in Westminster Abbey. He wrote a variety of compositions, but he is probably best known today for his oratorio *The Messiah*, with its rousing "Hallelujah Chorus."

3. **Franz Josef Haydn** (1732–1809) established the form of the symphony and wrote a great many himself. The melody from a shorter work, *The Emperor Quartet*, became the tune for both the German and Austrian national anthems.

4. **Wolfgang Amadeus Mozart** (1756–1791) was both a child prodigy and a musical genius. One of his operas was performed when he was only ten, and at the age of fourteen he directed the premiere of another of his operas. Although he died—penniless—at the age of thirty-five, he left an enormous number of concertos, works for small ensembles, symphonies, and operas. Among his operas that are still popular today are *Figaros Hochzeit* (*The Marriage of Figaro*), *Don Giovanni*, and *Die Zauberflöte* (*The Magic Flute*).

5. **Ludwig van Beethoven** (1770–1827) is one of the greatest composers in the history of symphonic music. In addition to his opera *Fidelio*, nine symphonies, and many works for small ensembles, Beethoven perfected the sonata form. Among his many works for piano is the familiar *Mondscheinsonate* (*Moonlight Sonata*). By the age of thirty-one, Beethoven realized that he was losing his hearing. Although he was totally deaf by the age of fifty, he continued to compose. Long after he had become completely deaf, he wrote the *Ninth Symphony*, which concludes with Schiller's *Ode an die Freude* as the choral text.

6. **Franz Schubert** (1797–1828) is best remembered as a composer of *Lieder*. He set the verses of many German poets to music. Every piano student is familiar with his *Serenade*. Probably the best known of his orchestral works is his *Symphony No. 7*, the "Unfinished Symphony."

7. **Felix Mendelssohn-Bartholdy** (1809–1847) wrote incidental music to Shakespeare's *Midsummer Night's Dream*. (Included in this music is the well-known "Wedding March.") His *Violin Concerto* is a standard audition piece for aspiring young violinists.

8. **Robert Schumann** (1810–1856) set to music the verses of many German lyric poets. In addition to his popular *Lieder*, he composed chamber music, symphonies, and a number of pieces for piano. His "Träumerei" is a standard piano selection.

9. **Richard Wagner** (1813–1883) was an unconventional composer whose music was widely criticized in his time. It is mostly due to Wagner that so many of the Germanic epics (*Heldensagen*) and Teutonic myths are familiar to us today. He was an innovator in opera, always striving to fit the music to the action of the drama. Some of his operas are *Tannhäuser, Tristan und Isolde, Parzifal, Lohengrin, Der fliegende Holländer* (*The Flying Dutchman*)*, Der Ring der Nibelungen* (a group of four operas), and *Die Meistersinger von Nürnberg*. Because of Wagner's glorification of the Teutonic past, his music was greatly admired by Hitler.

10. **Johann Strauss** the Younger (1825–1899), like his father, composed many of the waltzes we associate with *Alt' Wien* ("Old Vienna"). He earned the title "Waltz King" with such standard waltzes as *An der schönen blauen Donau* (*The Blue Danube*) and *Geschichten aus dem Wiener Wald* (*Tales from the Vienna Woods*). He also wrote the comic operas *Die Fledermaus* (*The Bat*) and *Der Zigeunerbaron* (*The Gypsy Baron*).

11. **Johannes Brahms** (1833–1897) brought the symphony to a new level and wrote *Lieder* as well. His "Lullaby" is very familiar. Brahms incorporated several well-known folk songs in a symphonic setting for his "Academic Festival Overture."

12. **Richard Strauss** (1864–1949) wrote tone poems based on figures from Germany's past, such as *Till Eulenspiegel* and *Also sprach Zarathustra* (the title of a book by Nietzsche). He also composed the operas *Salome* and *Der Rosenkavalier*.

13. **Arnold Schönberg** (1874–1951) composed music in a twelve-tone scale. After the Nazis classified his art as "degenerate," he left the Prussian Academy of Arts in 1933. From 1936 until his death, he taught at the University of Southern California.

14. **Paul Hindemith** (1895–1963) is probably best known for the opera *Mathis der Maler* (*Matthias the Painter*). He left Germany in 1938, and in 1942 he became head of the music department at Yale University. However, he returned to Europe in 1953 and taught at Zürich.

PAINTING AND ARCHITECTURE

1. **Albrecht Dürer** (1471–1528), a painter and engraver, is best known for his woodcuts. Among his famous engravings are *The Four Horsemen of the Apocalypse; Knight, Death, and the Devil;* and *Praying Hands.*

2. **Matthias Grünewald** (1480–1528) painted religious subjects. His masterpiece, the *Isenheimer Altar* (*Isenheim Altarpiece*), is a group of paintings on three folding panels.

3. **Lucas Cranach** (1472–1553) painted several portraits of Martin Luther and other leaders of the Reformation. He also painted anachronistic scenes from Greek mythology: for example, in *The Judgment of Paris*, Cranach depicted the landscape and costumes of 16th-century Germany rather than those of ancient Greece.

4. **Hans Holbein** the Younger (1497–1543) was a celebrated portrait painter. He was born in Germany but lived most of his life in Switzerland and England. Among his best-known portraits are those of Erasmus of Rotterdam and Henry VIII of England.

5. Typical of the classical influence on German art during the Enlightenment was the *Brandenburg Gate*, built in Berlin in 1788–91, which **Karl Langhans** modeled after the marble gateway of the ancient Athenian Acropolis.

6. **Die Brücke** was a community of Expressionist painters who gathered in Dresden in 1905. Among the members of this group were **Emil Nolde** (1867–1956) and **Max Beckmann** (1884–1950). Beckmann's paintings *The Dream* (1921) and *Departure* (1932–35) now seem prophetic of the coming of the Nazis, from whom Beckmann fled to the United States.

7. **Der Blaue Reiter** was a group of artists who gathered in Munich before World War I. One of its most notable members was Russian-born **Wassily Kandinsky** (1866–1944), whose abstract paintings were done with brilliant colors. **Paul Klee** (1879–1940), a Swiss painter, was also associated with this group after he came to Munich in 1906. Klee's drawings are noted for their fine, detailed lines and delicate figures.

8. **Georg Grosz** (1893–1959) painted bitter satires of German society after World War I. His *Germany, a Winter's Tale* is a chaotic display of the various sinister forces that helped mold the German citizen.

9. **Walter Gropius** (1883–1969), a German architect, designed the *Bauhaus* at Dessau, an art school of which he was the director. His "functional" architecture, based on the principle that "form follows function," has greatly influenced modern styles of structural design. He used powerful steel frameworks as building supports, which enabled him to design buildings with walls that were an almost continuous surface of glass. An excellent example of this structural concept is the United Nations building in New York.

WORTSCHATZ

die **Ausstellung, -en,** exhibition
der **Dichter, -,** poet, dramatist, writer
das **Drama, Dramen,** drama
der **Dramatiker, -,** dramatist
der **Film, -e,** film, movie
der **Filmstar, -s,** movie star
die **Galerie, -n,** gallery
das **Gedicht, -e,** poem
das **Gemälde, -,** picture, painting
der **Holzschnitt,** woodcut
das **Hörspiel, -e,** radio play
der **Humor,** wit, humor
die **Kapelle, -n,** band
die **Komödie, -n,** comedy
der **Komponist, -en,** composer

das **Konzert, -e,** concert
die **Kunst, ⸚e,** art, skill
der **Künstler, -,** artist, craftsman, skilled
performer
der **Maler, -,** painter
die **Musik,** music
der **Musiker, -,** musician
die **Oper, -n,** opera
das **Orchester, -,** orchestra
der **Roman, -e,** novel
das **Schauspiel, -e,** stage play
der **Schriftsteller, -,** writer, author
die **Symphonie, -n,** symphony
die **Tragödie, -n,** tragedy
der **Verfasser, -,** author, writer, composer

ÜBUNGEN

A. Circle the letter of the word or expression that correctly completes the sentence.

1. Im zwölften Jahrhundert sangen die _ _ _ _ _ Liebeslieder.

    (*a*) Minnesänger   (*b*) Meistersinger   (*c*) Nibelungen

2. Martin Luther übersetzte die Bibel im _ _ _ _ _ Jahrhundert.

    (*a*) vierzehnten   (*b*) fünfzehnten   (*c*) sechzehnten

3. Die Aufklärung begann im _ _ _ _ _ Jahrhundert.

    (*a*) siebzehnten   (*b*) achzehnten   (*c*) zwanzigsten

4. _ _ _ _ _ schrieb das Drama *Faust.*

    (*a*) Von Eschenbach   (*b*) Schiller   (*c*) Goethe

5. Die Brüder Grimm interessierten sich für _ _ _ _ _.

    (*a*) Märchen   (*b*) Liebeslieder   (*c*) Opern

6. Im neunzehnten Jahrhundert schrieben Kleist, Hoffmann, und Storm _ _ _ _ _.

    (*a*) Novellen   (*b*) Märchen   (*c*) Lieder

7. Thomas Mann bekam im Jahre _ _ _ _ _ den Nobelpreis für Literatur.

    (*a*) 1587   (*b*) 1912   (*c*) 1929

8. Bertolt Brecht und Kurt Weill schrieben _ _ _ _ _.

    (*a*) "Die Lorelei"   (*b*) *Die Dreigroschenoper*   (*c*) *Das Lied von Bernadette*

9. Albrecht Dürer ist besonders für seine _ _ _ _ _ bekannt.

    (*a*) Holzschnitte   (*b*) Gebäude   (*c*) Symphonien

10. _ _ _ _ _ sind zwei Romane Remarques, die amerikanische Filme geworden sind.

    (*a*) *Drei Kameraden* und *Jakobowsky und der Oberst*

    (*b*) *Im Westen nichts Neues* und *Der Triumphbogen*

    (*c*) *Im Westen nichts Neues* und *Das Lied von Bernadette*

11. Der beliebteste Dramatiker heute in Westdeutschland ist _____.

(*a*) Dürrenmatt   (*b*) Weiß   (*c*) Shakespeare

12. _____ schrieb *Die Blechtrommel*.

(*a*) Rolf Hochhuth   (*b*) Erich Kästner   (*c*) Günter Grass

13. _____ hat über die Probleme der Jugend geschrieben.

(*a*) Peter Lorre   (*b*) Hermann Hesse   (*c*) Richard Wagner

14. _____ hat einige Bilder von Martin Luther gemalt.

(*a*) Lucas Cranach   (*b*) Karl Langhans   (*c*) Paul Klee

15. _____ hat mehrere Hörspiele geschrieben.

(*a*) Friedrich Dürrenmatt   (*b*) Rolf Hochhuth   (*c*) Peter Weiß

16. _____ sind zwei amerikanische Filmstars, die in deutschen Filmen angefangen haben.

(*a*) Bertolt Brecht und Kurt Weill   (*b*) Marlene Dietrich und Peter Lorre   (*c*) Marlene Dietrich und Peter Weiß

17. _____ war einige Maler, die 1905 in Dresden arbeiteten.

(*a*) Die Brücke   (*b*) Der Blaue Reiter   (*c*) Das Bauhaus

18. Händel verbrachte in _____ einen größeren Teil seines Lebens.

(*a*) England   (*b*) der Schweiz   (*c*) den Vereinigten Staaten

19. Ein bekanntes Klavierstück Beethovens heißt _____.

(*a*) *Die Mondscheinsonate*   (*b*) "Die Lorelei"   (*c*) *Die Fledermaus*

20. Mozart war _____ Jahre alt als er starb.

(*a*) vierzehn   (*b*) fünfunddreißig   (*c*) achtzig

21. Paul Klee gehörte zur Gruppe, die _____ hieß.

(*a*) Isenheimer Altar   (*b*) die Brücke   (*c*) den Blauen Reiter

22. Beethoven schrieb _____ Symphonien.

(*a*) sieben   (*b*) neun   (*c*) zehn

23. _____ sind zwei Komponisten, die besonders für Lieder bekannt sind.

(*a*) Franz Schubert und Robert Schumann

(*b*) Felix Mendelssohn und Johann Strauß

(*c*) Franz Schubert und Arnold Schönberg

24. _____ hat Opern über deutsche Heldensagen geschrieben.

(*a*) Richard Wagner   (*b*) Gottfried von Straßburg   (*c*) Johannes Brahms

25. Walter Gropius hat Gebäude _____ gebaut.

(*a*) ohne Fenster   (*b*) ohne Wände   (*c*) mit Wänden mit vielen großen Fenstern

B. Identify each of the following as (*a*) author, (*b*) composer, (*c*) artist, or (*d*) fictional character:

_____ **1.** Jakob und Wilhelm Grimm   _____ **4.** Thomas à Kempis

_____ **2.** Don Giovanni   _____ **5.** Wassily Kandinsky

_____ **3.** Robert Schumann   _____ **6.** Arnold Schönberg

------- 7. Johann Sebastian Bach   ------- 24. Heinrich von Kleist

------- 8. G. E. Lessing   ------- 25. Richard Wagner

------- 9. Emil   ------- 26. Hermann Hesse

------- 10. Johann Strauß   ------- 27. Reineke Fuchs

------- 11. G. F. Händel   ------- 28. Matthias Grünewald

------- 12. Albrecht Dürer   ------- 29. Paul Hindemith

------- 13. die Schildbürger   ------- 30. Bertolt Brecht

------- 14. Thomas Mann   ------- 31. Tannhäuser

------- 15. Wolfgang Amadeus Mozart   ------- 32. Max Beckmann

------- 16. Mathis der Maler   ------- 33. Friedrich von Schiller

------- 17. J. W. von Goethe   ------- 34. Lohengrin

------- 18. Felix Mendelssohn-Bartholdy   ------- 35. Iphigenie

------- 19. Georg Grosz   ------- 36. Kurt Weill

------- 20. Till Eulenspiegel   ------- 37. Ludwig van Beethoven

------- 21. Rolf Hochhuth   ------- 38. Erich Kästner

------- 22. Günter Grass   ------- 39. Dr. Johann Faustus

------- 23. Tristan   ------- 40. Steppenwolf

C. In **I** and **II**: To the left of each item in column *A*, write the letter of the item in column *B* that is associated with it.

I

COLUMN A	COLUMN B
------- 1. *Wilhelm Tell*	*a.* the twelve-tone scale
------- 2. Meister Eckhart	*b.* an author of the Enlightenment
------- 3. *Das Nibelungenlied*	*c.* *Der Rosenkavalier*
------- 4. *die Aufklärung*	*d.* medieval mystic
------- 5. Hans Sachs	*e.* play by Schiller
------- 6. Martin Luther	*f.* wandering poet-singers
------- 7. *Nathan der Weise*	*g.* the Enlightenment
------- 8. Heinrich Heine	*h.* renowned *Meistersinger*
------- 9. *Minnesänger*	*i.* German Bible
------- 10. *Novelle*	*j.* play by Lessing
------- 11. Friedrich Dürrenmatt	*k.* lyric poet
------- 12. E. M. Remarque	*l.* short novel
------- 13. C. M. Wieland	*m.* Swiss playwright
------- 14. Richard Strauß	*n.* *Im Westen nichts Neues*
------- 15. Arnold Schönberg	*o.* *Heldensage* converted into an opera by Wagner

II

COLUMN A	COLUMN B
_____ 1. Ludwig van Beethoven	a. Brandenburg Gate
_____ 2. *Isenheimer Altar*	b. portrait of Luther and scenes from Greek mythology
_____ 3. Johann Strauß	c. the "Waltz King"
_____ 4. Hans Holbein	d. group of artists in Munich around 1905
_____ 5. *Triumph des Willen*	e. portraits of Erasmus and Henry VIII
_____ 6. Johann Sebastian Bach	f. Matthias Grünewald
_____ 7. der Blaue Reiter	g. *Figaros Hochzeit*
_____ 8. Wolfgang Amadeus Mozart	h. music for organ and harpsichord
_____ 9. Karl Langhans	i. Nazi propaganda film
_____ 10. Lucas Cranach	j. perfected the sonata form

Willy Brandt, former mayor of West Berlin, became the first member of the Social Democratic party to be elected Chancellor of the Bundesrepublik. He served from 1969 until 1974, when he resigned as a result of a scandal within his administration. Because of his efforts in 1970 to improve East-West relations, he was awarded the Nobel Peace Prize in 1971.

PART VII—Exercises in Auditory and Reading Comprehension

35. AUDITORY COMPREHENSION

To the Teacher: For the 25 questions or statements that comprise this exercise, please see the Answer Key to *German First Year.*

Directions to the Student: The teacher will read aloud a question or statement in German, and will repeat it. After the *second* reading, circle the letter of the most appropriate response to the question or statement from among the four alternatives given below.

1. *a.* Es regnet.
   c. Es ist ein schöner Tag.
   b. Heute ist Mittwoch.
   d. Heute gehen wir zur Schule.

2. *a.* Das macht Spaß.
   c. Er war krank.
   b. Er wohnt in Köln.
   d. Die ganze Familie ist aufs Land gefahren.

3. *a.* Gern. Ich möchte ein paar Bücher entleihen.
   c. Mein Bruder liest Romane gern.
   b. Das Wetter war sehr schlecht.
   d. Es gibt zuviel Lärm drinnen.

4. *a.* Ja, darum habe ich so wenig dafür bezahlt.
   c. Nein, das Warenhaus war nicht weit von hier.
   b. Ja, daher konnte ich ihn nicht kaufen.
   d. Nein, der blaue Anzug gefällt mir am besten.

5. *a.* Wir werden eine neue Aufgabe anfangen.
   c. Ich habe meine Schularbeit korrigiert.
   b. Ich komme jeden Morgen um neun Uhr in die Schule herein.
   d. Wir gehen nicht morgen in die Schule.

6. *a.* Da drüben ist ein gutes Restaurant.
   c. Um halb eins.
   b. Ich möchte eine Tasse Kaffee.
   d. Das tut man nicht.

7. *a.* Darf ich mitkommen?
   c. Warum müssen Sie immer zu Hause bleiben?
   b. Können Sie nicht etwas weiter fahren?
   d. Morgen werden Sie ihn wiedersehen.

8. *a.* Ja, heute können wir schwimmen.
   c. Man braucht heute einen Mantel.
   b. Ja, es ist ein schöner Sommertag.
   d. Nein, heute ist Donnerstag.

9. *a.* Das ist ein Volkswagen.
   c. Wir fahren mit dem Bus nach Frankfurt.
   b. Das ist ein neues Fahrrad.
   d. Das ist mein Vaters Auto.

10. *a.* Sie ist jetzt zehn Jahre alt.
    c. Im Jahre 1962.
    b. Ich habe ihr ein schönes Kleid zum Geburtstag gegeben.
    d. Am 27. November.

11. *a.* Ich bin seit sechs Monaten hier.
    c. Ich besuche meinen Bruder in Düsseldorf.
    b. Ich komme aus Amerika.
    d. Ich fahre morgen nach München.

12. *a.* Gehen wir in die Bücherei!   *b.* Haben Sie es gestern gelesen?

     c. Hoffentlich wird es Ihnen gefallen.   *d.* Das kostet zuviel.

13. *a.* Sie müssen den ganzen Tag zu Hause bleiben.   *b.* Sobald es dunkel wird.

     c. Ihre Eltern sind noch nicht angekommen.   *d.* Heute kommt Ihr Bruder zu Besuch.

14. *a.* Der Zug fährt um 7 Uhr ab.   *b.* Nein, ich habe den Film schon gesehen.

     c. Das Auto fährt zu schnell.   *d.* Gestern abend habe ich den Dom besucht.

15. *a.* Das Fenster ist auf.   *b.* Da draußen scheint die Sonne.

     c. Aber ich habe ein Buch mitgebracht.   *d.* Sie ist aber doch schon geschlossen.

16. *a.* Jeden Tag.   *b.* Um neun Uhr morgens.

     c. In der Schule.   *d.* Ich muß meine Schularbeit erledigen.

17. *a.* Ja, ich freue mich darauf.   *b.* Na, wenn schon!

     c. Ja, ich hatte es sehr gern.   *d.* Mir auch; hoffentlich können wir uns morgen wiedersehen.

18. *a.* Es ist nicht weit von hier.   *b.* In dieser Stadt gibt es nicht so eines.

     c. Viel Glück!   *d.* Müssen Sie nach Hause?

19. *a.* Ich habe einen Bruder und zwei Schwestern.   *b.* Meine Eltern sind gestorben.

     c. Zwei Söhne und eine Tochter.   *d.* Mein Onkel ist jetzt bei uns.

20. *a.* Ich habe ein Stück Kreide in der Tasche.   *b.* Leider habe ich meinen Bleistift verloren.

     c. Haben Sie einen Kugelschreiber? Ich habe meinen vergessen.   *d.* Ich kann nicht die Tafel sehen.

21. *a.* Wir fahren aufs Land.   *b.* Ich bringe meine Eltern mit.

     c. Damit kann man über den See segeln.   *d.* Vom Ende Juni bis den 15. August.

22. *a.* Ich bin sehr müde.   *b.* Meine erste Stunde ist um acht Uhr.

     c. Es ist schon 7 Uhr.   *d.* Ich möchte gern schlafen.

23. *a.* Es war eine Symphonie von Mozart.   *b.* Sie spielt gut Klavier.

     c. Das war ein altes Volkslied.   *d.* Sie singt mit schöner Stimme.

24. *a.* Schön. Ich bleibe den ganzen Tag zu Hause.   *b.* Rufen Sie bitte mit lauter Stimme!

     c. Es ist ein schöner Tag.   *d.* Haben Sie den Brief geschrieben?

25. *a.* Mein Auto geht nicht mehr.   *b.* Der Zug ist spät angekommen.

     c. Nein, der Bus ist schon weg.   *d.* Mir gefällt der Zug.

36. PASSAGES FOR READING COMPREHENSION

Each of the following passages ends with a set of questions. After reading the passage, choose the best answer to each question.

1. Auf einer Reise kam einmal ein Deutscher nach Paris. Als er durch die Stadt wanderte, merkte er, daß jede Haustür ein kleines Guckloch (peephole) hatte. Er wußte nicht, wie das Guckloch heißen sollte. Er zeigte auf das Löchelchen und fragte einen französischen (French) Herrn: „Können Sie mir sagen, was das ist?" Der Herr verstand die Frage nicht, denn er sprach kein Wort Deutsch. Der Deutsche wiederholte die Frage: „Was ist das?" Selbst der französische Herr wußte nicht, wie das Guckloch heißen sollte, und er antwortete also: „C'est ça." (Das bedeutet: „Das ist es.")

Während des Tages stellte der Deutsche immer wieder dieselbe Frage: „Was ist das?" Immer wieder bekam er dieselbe Antwort: „C'est ça." In Paris nennt man bis heute das kleine Guckloch in der Tür „un vasistas," und man glaubt, daß es ein französisches Wort ist.

(1) Wer kam nach Paris?

    a. ein französischer Herr   *b.* ein Löchelchen   *c.* ein Deutscher

(2) Was bemerkte der Besucher, als er durch die Stadt wanderte?

    a. Die Häuser hatten viele Türen.

    b. Die Tür jedes Hauses hatte ein Löchelchen.

    c. Fast alle französischen Herren konnten Deutsch.

(3) Was wollte der Besucher wissen?

    a. wie das Guckloch auf französisch hieß

    b. warum niemand in Paris kein Wort Deutsch konnte

    c. warum der französische Herr auf das Guckloch zeigte

(4) Was war die Meinung der Antwort, die der Deutsche von jedem bekommen hat?

    a. Ich kann wenig Deutsch.

    b. Ich weiß nicht, wie das heißt.

    c. Das ist es.

(5) Wie heißt das Guckloch heute in Paris?

    a. c'est ça   *b.* un vasistas   *c.* das ist es

2. Es kam einmal ein deutscher Handwerksbursche (craftsman) nach Amsterdam. Er interessierte sich für alles, was da zu sehen war: große Gebäude, schöne Häuser, viele Schiffe. Ein besonderes Haus interessierte ihn am meisten. Er fragte einen Herrn, der eigentlich kein Wort Deutsch verstand: „Guter Freund, sagen Sie mir, bitte, wem gehört dieses schöne Haus." Der Holländer verstand die Frage nicht und antwortete: „Kannitverstan." Das ist ein holländisches Wort, das auf Deutsch bedeutet: „Ich kann nicht verstehen."

Der Deutsche meinte aber, einem Herrn Kannitverstan gehörte das Haus. Als der Deutsche sich später andere Gebäude ansah, fragte er wieder jemanden: „Wem gehören diese Gebäude?" Wieder bekam er dieselbe Antwort: „Kannitverstan." „Das ist doch wunderbar," dachte der Deutsche bei sich. „Der Herr Kannitverstan muß ein reicher Mann sein."

Als er um eine Ecke kam, sah der Besucher einen Leichenzug (funeral procession) kommen. Genau so wie die anderen Leute, stand der Deutsche still, und hielt den Hut in der Hand. Nachdem

der Leichenzug vorbei war, fragte der Deutsche seinen Nachbarn: „Wer ist gestorben?" „Kannitverstan" kam die Antwort. Der Deutsche wurde traurig (sad): „Armer Kannitverstan," dachte er,
„was helfen dir jetzt dein schönes Haus und deine großen Gebäude? Nun hast du nichts als ein
enges Grab."

(1) Wofür interessierte sich der Deutsche, als er nach Amsterdam kam?

    a. besondere Häuser   *b.* Schiffe   *c.* alles, was zu sehen war

(2) Welche Frage stellte der Deutsche?

    a. wem die schönen Gebäude gehörten

    b. warum der Holländer „Kannitverstan" hieß

    c. wie man auf holländisch „Ich verstehe nicht" sagte

(3) Welche Antwort gab der Holländer auf die Frage?

    a. Ich verstehe Sie nicht.

    b. Kannitverstan.

    c. Das ist ein holländisches Wort.

(4) Was machte der Deutsche, als er den Leichenzug sah?

    a. Er kam um eine Ecke.   *b.* Er nahm den Hut ab.   *c.* Er setzte sich.

(5) Warum wurde der Deutsche traurig?

    a. Sein Nachbar ist gestorben.

    b. Die Holländer wollten nicht auf seine Frage antworten.

    c. Der reiche „Kannitverstan" konnte sich nicht mehr an seine schönen Gebäude freuen.

3. Eine Amerikanerin machte mit dem Zug eine Reise durch Deutschland. Als der Zug in den
Bahnhof einer Großstadt einfuhr,[1] suchte die Dame einen Gepäckträger (porter), denn sie hatte
viel Gepäck (baggage) bei sich. In einem Englisch-Deutschen Wörterbuch schlug sie „engaged"
nach, da sie einen freien Gepäckträger finden wollte. Als sie einen Gepäckträger sah, rief sie: „ Herr
Gepäckträger, sind Sie verlobt?"[2]

Der Gepäckträger verstand nicht, was die Dame meinte. Er sagte nichts. Die Amerikanerin
stellte ihre Frage noch einmal: „Ich suche einen Mann. Kann ich Sie haben?"

„Es tut mir leid, gnädige Frau," antwortete der Gepäckträger. „Ich habe schon eine Frau und
fünf Kinder zu Hause."

---

[1] *einfahren, fuhr ein, ist eingefahren*, to arrive (in a station)
[2] *sich verloben* = to be engaged (*as fiancés*)

(1) Wer machte in Deutschland eine Reise?

    a. ein Amerikaner   *b.* ein Gepäckträger   *c.* eine Amerikanerin

(2) Wen suchte die Dame?

    a. ihren Mann   *b.* einen Gepäckträger   *c.* den Bahnhof

(3) Warum wollte die Dame einen Gepäckträger?

    a. Sie hatte viel Gepäck.

    b. Sie war nicht verlobt.

    c. Sie wollte in den Zug einsteigen.

(4) Was wollte die Dame fragen?

    a. „Sind Sie verlobt?"

    b. „Können Sie mir helfen?"

    c. „Wann fährt der Zug ein?"

(5) Welches war die Frage, die die Dame wirklich stellte?

    a. „Sind Sie frei?"

    b. „Wieviele Kinder haben Sie zu Hause?"

    c. „Werden Sie bald eine Frau haben?"

4. „Mutter," rief die kleine Anna, „der Magen (stomach) tut mir weh!" Ihre Mutter antwortete: „Der ist doch ganz leer. Wir wollen etwas hineintun (put something in it), dann wird alles wieder gut werden." Sobald das Mädchen etwas aß, fühlte es sich besser.

Am Abend, als der Vater nach Hause kam, hatte er Kopfschmerzen (headache). Die kleine Anna sagte zu ihm: „Der Kopf tut dir weh, weil er leer ist. Du sollst etwas hineintun, dann wirst du dich wieder wohl fühlen."

(1) Was war mit dem Mädchen los?

    a. Es konnte nicht essen.   *b.* Der Magen tat ihm Weh.   *c.* Es war krank.

(2) Welchen Vorschlag machte die Mutter?

    a. Anna sollte etwas essen.

    b. Man fühlt sich besser, wenn der Magen leer ist.

    c. Anna sollte nichts in den Magen hineintun.

(3) Warum fühlte sich der Vater nicht gut?

    a. Sein Kopf war leer.   *b.* Er hatte Kopfschmerzen.   *c.* Seine Tochter tat ihm weh.

(4) Dem Mädchen nach, was war das Problem?

    a. Der Vaters Kopf war leer.   *b.* Ihr Vater hatte nichts gegessen.   *c.* Ihr Vater hatte Hunger.

(5) Was sollte der Vater tun?

    a. etwas in den Kopf hineintun   *b.* sich setzen   *c.* etwas essen

5. Ein bekannter Arzt erzählte diese Geschichte aus seiner Jugend:

Als ich noch Schüler war, stand jeden Morgen vor unserer Schule ein Milchwagen mit einem kleinen Esel. Die anderen Schüler ärgerten (teased) das arme Tierchen jeden Tag. Oft hatte der Milchmann mit dem Direktor darüber gesprochen, und der Direktor und die Lehrer verboten es den Schülern. Aber es half alles nichts.

Eines Morgens ärgerten die Schüler den Esel wieder. Er rief laut: „I ... A!" Der Milchmann kam sehr schnell, aber die anderen Jungen liefen schneller weg.[1] Ich blieb stehen, denn ich hatte nichts getan. Der Milchmann war so böse, daß er kein Wort sprechen konnte. Er wollte nicht glauben, daß ich nichts getan hatte. Daher schlug er mich sehr.

Ich schrie und lief ins Schulgebäude. Ich wollte dem Direktor sagen, was der Milchmann getan hatte. Als ich schnell durch die Tür des Gebäudes ging, rannte[2] ich gegen Doktor Wegener, meinen Klassenlehrer. Er trug viele Bücher und Hefte auf dem Arm, die alle auf den Boden fielen. Er schlug mich auch, und ich schrie noch lauter. Der Direktor hörte den Lärm und kam aus dem Zimmer. Er fragte mich: „Was fehlt dir denn?"

„Der Herr Dr. Wegener hat mich geschlagen," erklärte ich, „und ich habe dem Esel gar nichts getan."

Da sagte der Direktor, daß ich den Lehrer nicht einen Esel nennen sollte, und auch er schlug mich. So bekam ich dreimal Schläge und hatte doch gar nichts getan.

[1] *weglaufen, lief weg, ist weggelaufen,* to run away
[2] *rennen, rannte, ist gerannt,* to run (fast)

(1) Was stand vor der Schule?

    a. ein Milchwagen *b.* der Direktor *c.* ein bekannter Arzt

(2) Was taten die Schüler, als der Milchmann kam?

    a. Sie riefen: „I … A!" *b.* Sie sprachen mit ihm. *c.* Sie ärgerten seinen Esel.

(3) Warum schlug der Milchmann den Schüler, der nicht weglief?

    a. Der Schüler hatte den Esel geärgert.

    b. Der Schüler hatte nichts getan.

    c. Er wollte nicht glauben, daß der Schüler seinem Tier gar nichts getan hatte.

(4) Gegen wen rannte der Schüler, als er ins Schulgebäude lief?

    a. gegen den Esel *b.* gegen den Direktor *c.* gegen seinen Lehrer

(5) Was sagte der Schüler zum Direktor?

    a. „Was fehlt dir denn?"

    b. „Ich habe dem Esel gar nichts getan."

    c. „Warum schlagen Sie mich?"

6. Einmal kam der Schulinspektor (school inspector) zu Besuch in eine Schule auf dem Lande. Der Besucher wollte herausfinden, wieviel die Schüler lernten. Er fragte einen Jungen, der auf der ersten Bank saß: „Nun, kleiner Mann, nenne mir eine Zahl!"

„Vierundzwanzig," antwortete der Junge.

Der Inspektor schrieb die Zahl an die Tafel, aber verkehrt (backwards): 42. Da der Schüler nichts dagegen sagte, fragte der Inspektor: „Sag' mir noch eine Zahl!"

Der Schüler antwortete: „Sechsundsiebzig."

Der Inspektor schrieb auch diese Zahl an die Tafel, aber wieder verkehrt: 67. Und wieder sagte der Schüler nichts.

Der Inspektor versuchte noch einmal: „Gib mir noch eine Zahl!"

Der Junge war nicht zufrieden mit diesem Spiel. „Vierundvierzig," sagte er schnell. „Nun, schreiben Sie *das* mal verkehrt, Herr Schulinspektor!"

(1) Was fragte der Schulinspektor den kleinen Jungen?

    a. wieviel die Schüler gelernt hatten

    b. wer sich auf die erste Bank setzte

    c. ihm eine Zahl zu nennen

(2) Wie hat der Inspektor jede Zahl geschrieben?

    a. richtig *b.* verkehrt *c.* mit Bleistift

(3) Was sagte der Junge, als der Inspektor die Zahlen falsch schrieb?

    a. „Gib mir noch eine Zahl!" *b.* gar nichts *c.* „Sechsundsiebzig."

(4) Als der Junge „sechsundsiebzig" sagte, welche Zahl hat der Inspektor geschrieben?

    a. siebenundsechzig *b.* sechsundsiebzig *c.* zweiundvierzig

(5) Welche Zahl konnte der Inspektor nicht verkehrt schreiben?

    a. vierundvierzig *b.* vierundzwanzig *c.* sechsundsiebzig

    7. Der Lehrer merkte einmal, daß jemand sein Buch weggenommen hatte. Er fragte die Schüler in der Klasse: „Wer hat das Buch?" Niemand antwortete.

    „Also," sagte der Lehrer. „Ich werde Detektiv spielen. Ich werde bald den Dieb finden." Dann sagte der Lehrer, daß alle Schüler den Kopf auf den Tisch legen sollten. Alle taten, was der Lehrer sagte. „Habt ihr alle den Kopf auf dem Tisch?" fragte der Lehrer.

    „Ja," antworteten alle Schüler.

    „Der Dieb auch?" fragte der Lehrer.

    „Ja," antwortete einer mit heller Stimme.

(1) Was hat der Lehrer bemerkt?

    a. Sein Buch war nicht zu finden.

    b. Niemand hatte sein Buch weggenommen.

    c. Ein Schüler wollte eine Frage stellen.

(2) Was hat der Lehrer geglaubt?

    a. Die Schüler hatten nicht ihre Bücher mitgebracht.

    b. Jemand hatte sein Buch genommen.

    c. Er hatte sein Buch vergessen.

(3) Was wollte der Lehrer spielen?

    a. Dieb *b.* Schüler *c.* Detektiv

(4) Was sagte der Lehrer, daß alle Schüler tun sollten?

    a. das Buch suchen *b.* den Kopf auf den Tisch legen *c.* auf seine Frage antworten

(5) Wie hat der Lehrer den Dieb gefunden?

    a. Alle Schüler taten, was der Lehrer sagte.

    b. Niemand hat den Kopf auf den Tisch gelegt.

    c. Der Junge hat auf die letzte Frage auch geantwortet.

8. Einmal verlor ein reicher Mann seine Tasche mit 800 Mark. Er versprach dem Finder 100 Mark. Ein guter Mann fand die Tasche und brachte sie dem reichen Mann zurück. Dieser wollte nicht die 100 Mark bezahlen. Der reiche Mann sagte also: „Ich habe 900 Mark verloren. In der Tasche sind jetzt 800 Mark. Sie haben sich Ihre 100 Mark schon genommen. Das ist gerade recht. Ich danke Ihnen herzlich."

Der Finder sagte: „Ich habe kein Geld aus der Tasche genommen. Ich habe sie Ihnen gegeben, genau wie ich sie gefunden habe."

Endlich kamen die zwei Herren vor den Richter (judge). Der reiche Mann sagte immer wieder, daß er 900 Mark verloren hätte. Der andere Mann wiederholte, daß er nur 800 Mark gefunden hätte.

Der Richter verstand, was der reiche Mann tun wollte. Der Richter sagte zu dem reichen Mann: „Sie haben eine Tasche mit 900 Mark verloren, aber diese Tasche hatte nur 800 Mark. Es steht fest (it is established), dieser Mann hat nicht Ihr Geld gefunden."

Zu dem Mann, der die Tasche gefunden hatte, sagte der Richter: „Sie behalten (keep) die 800 Mark, bis jemand kommt, der genau 800 Mark verloren hat." Zu dem reichen Mann sagte der Richter: „Und sie müssen warten, bis jemand Ihre Tasche mit 900 Mark findet."

(1) Wieviel Geld hat der reiche Mann verloren?

    a. 100 Mark   *b.* 800 Mark   *c.* 900 Mark

(2) Was verspricht der reiche Mann?

    a. Ein guter Mann wird das Geld finden.

    b. Der Finder wird 100 Mark bekommen.

    c. Er wird dem Finder 800 Mark geben.

(3) Warum sagte dem Finder der reiche Mann, daß er 900 Mark verloren hätte?

    a. Er will dem Finder nichts bezahlen.

    b. Der Finder hat sich seine 100 Mark schon genommen.

    c. Der Finder hat ihm 900 Mark gegeben.

(4) Wem gab der Richter die 800 Mark?

    a. dem reichen Mann   *b.* dem Finder   *c.* niemandem

(5) Worauf mußte der reiche Mann warten?

    a. bis der Richter sein Geld findet

    b. bis jemand kommt, der 800 Mark verloren hat

    c. bis jemand seine Tasche mit 900 Mark findet

9. Ein Bauer und sein Sohn gingen einmal mit einem Esel in die Stadt. Der Bauer ritt auf dem Esel, und der Junge ging zu Fuß. Es kam jemand vorbei, der sagte: „Das ist nicht recht. Der Vater ist stärker als der Junge. Der Vater soll zu Fuß gehen, nicht der Sohn." Der Bauer setzte seinen Sohn auf den Esel, und er ging zu Fuß.

Bald darauf kam ein anderer Mann. Dieser sagte: „Der Vater ist älter als der Sohn. Der Vater soll nicht zu Fuß gehen." Die beiden setzten sich auf den kleinen Esel.

Da kam ein dritter Mann, und er rief: „Die beiden sitzen zur gleichen Zeit auf dem armen Tier. Das ist furchtbar!" Dann gingen der Bauer und sein Sohn beide zu Fuß.

Ein anderer Mann kam und fragte: „Warum reitet niemand den Esel? Das ist aber dumm!"

Der Sohn sagte zu dem Vater: „Niemand ist zufrieden. Vielleicht sollen wir lieber den Esel tragen."
Der Bauer und sein Sohn trugen den Esel in die Stadt.

Das sahen die Leute und sie riefen: „Da sind zwei Esel—und sie tragen den dritten nach Hause."

(1) Warum sollte der Vater zu Fuß gehen?

    a. Der Esel war müde.

    b. Ein Bauer wollte auf dem Esel reiten.

    c. Er war stärker als sein Sohn.

(2) Was taten Vater und Sohn, nachdem der zweite Mann mit ihnen sprach?

    a. Die beiden ritten zur gleichen Zeit auf dem Esel.

    b. Die beiden gingen zu Fuß.

    c. Der Vater setzte sich auf den Esel und der Junge ging zu Fuß.

(3) Warum sollten die beiden nicht zur gleichen Zeit auf dem Esel sitzen?

    a. Der dritte Mann war ihnen sehr böse.

    b. Es war dem Esel zu schwer, die beiden zu tragen.

    c. Es gefiel dem Esel nicht.

(4) Welchen Vorschlag machte der Sohn?

    a. Der Vater sollte zu Fuß gehen.

    b. Der Vater sollte sich auf den Esel setzen.

    c. Die beiden sollten das Tier tragen.

(5) Was dachten die Leute, als sie den Bauer und seinen Sohn sahen?

    a. Ein dritter Mann sollte ihnen helfen, das Tier zu tragen.

    b. Der Bauer und sein Sohn hatten einen dritten Esel zu Hause.

    c. Die zwei Menschen waren so dumm wie ihr Esel.

    10. Eines Tages kam ein Dieb auf einen Bauernhof, als der Bauer nicht zu Hause war. Der Dieb nahm das beste Pferd und ritt in die Stadt. Als der Bauer wieder nach Hause kam, wurde er traurig (sad), weil sein bestes Pferd weg war. Einige Tage später kam der Bauer auch in die Stadt. Da sah er sein Pferd, das der Dieb verkaufen wollte. Der Bauer sagte zu dem Dieb: „Das ist mein Pferd. Woher haben Sie es bekommen?"

„Nein, mein Herr," antwortete der Dieb, „das ist falsch. Ich habe dieses Tier schon seit einem Jahr. Dieses Pferd gehört mir."

Der Bauer machte soviel Lärm, daß viele andere Bauern zuhörten. Der Bauer nahm seinen Mantel ab und warf ihn über den Kopf des Pferdes. „Wenn Sie das Pferd schon seit einem Jahr haben, dann können Sie mir auch sagen, auf welchem Auge es blind ist."

Der Dieb wußte eigentlich nicht, was für eine Antwort er geben sollte. *Eine* Antwort mußte er aber geben. „Gewiß," sagte der Dieb, „auf dem linken Auge ist es blind."

„Falsch, ganz falsch!" rief der Bauer. Bevor er noch etwas sagen konnte, sagte der Dieb: „Sie haben recht. Jetzt erinnere ich mich daran. Das Pferd ist auf dem rechten Auge blind."

„Wieder falsch!" rief der Bauer, als er seinen Mantel von dem Kopf des Pferdes nahm. Mit lauter Stimme sagte der Bauer: „*Mein* Pferd ist auf keinem Auge blind, weder auf dem linken noch auf dem rechten. Dieser Mann ist ein Dieb!" Jetzt war es ganz klar, daß das Pferd dem Bauern gehörte. Die anderen Bauern nahmen den Dieb in ihre Mitte, und riefen den Polizisten.

(1) Wer nahm das Pferd vom Bauernhof weg?

    a. ein Bauer   *b.* ein Dieb   *c.* der Mann, dem das Tier gehörte

(2) Wo sah der Bauer sein Pferd wieder?

    a. eines Tages   *b.* der Dieb   *c.* in der Stadt

(3) Was sagte der Dieb, als der Bauer ihn nach dem Pferde fragte?

    a. Er wollte das Pferd verkaufen.   *b.* Das Pferd war seines.   *c.* Dem Bauern gehörte das Pferd.

(4) Warum konnte der Dieb die Frage des Bauern nicht richtig beantworten?

    a. Das Pferd hatte ihm eigentlich nie gehört.

    b. Er war auf einem Auge blind.

    c. Er hatte die richtige Antwort vergessen.

(5) Auf welchem Auge war das Pferd blind?

    a. dem linken   *b.* dem rechten   *c.* keinem

11. Friedrich II. baute in der Nähe der Stadt Potsdam ein Schloß, welches er Sans-Souci nannte. Hier verbrachte er die letzten Jahre seines Lebens, da er den Lärm der Großstadt vermeiden wollte.

Neben dem königlichen Park lag eine Mühle. Oft wollte Friedrich schlafen oder lesen, aber wegen des Lärmes der Mühle konnte er es nicht. Friedrich rief den Müller zu sich und fragte ihn: „Ich möchte die Mühle kaufen. Wieviel kostet sie?"

Der Müller antwortete: „Ich verkaufe sie nicht." Friedrich versprach, viel Geld für die Mühle zu bezahlen. Der Müller aber wiederholte, daß er die Mühle nicht verkaufen wollte. „Diese Mühle," sagte er, „gehörte meinem Vater und meinem Großvater. Wenn ich sterbe, soll sie meinen Kindern gehören."

Friedrich war mit dieser Antwort gar nicht zufrieden, und er wurde böse. „Vergessen Sie nicht," sagte Friedrich, „daß ich der König bin!"

„Ja," antwortete der Müller, „aber in Berlin gibt es Richter (judges)." Diese Antwort des Müllers gefiel dem König, und er ließ dem Müller seine Mühle.

(1) Was war Sans-Souci?

    a. ein Schloß   *b.* eine Stadt   *c.* der König

(2) Wo lag die Mühle?

    a. in Potsdam   *b.* neben dem Schloß   *c.* im königlichen Park

(3) Warum hat Friedrich II. das Schloß gebaut?

    a. Er wollte nicht in der Stadt wohnen.

    b. Er wollte die Mühle kaufen.

    c. Er wollte die letzten Jahre seines Lebens in einer Großstadt verbringen.

(4) Warum wollte der Müller nicht die Mühle verkaufen?

    a. Der König wollte nicht viel Geld dafür bezahlen.

    b. Sie gehörte ihm nicht.

    c. Er wollte sie seinen Kindern geben.

(5) Hat Friedrich die Mühle endlich bekommen?

    a. Ja.   *b*. Nein.   *c*. Die Geschichte erzählt es uns nicht.

12. Oft war der Philosoph Moses Mendelssohn (der Großvater des Komponisten Felix Mendelssohn) ein Tischgast Friedrichs des Großen. Einmal waren alle anderen Gäste schon bei Tisch—nur Mendelssohn fehlte noch. Niemand wußte, wo der Philosoph war. Einer der Gäste sagte: „So sind diese Philosophen; wenn sie hinter ihren Büchern sitzen, vergessen sie alles." Friedrich schrieb auf ein Stück Papier:

MENDELSSOHN IST EIN ESEL.
FRIEDRICH II.

Dies Briefchen legte ein Diener unter Mendelssohns Teller. Bald darauf kam der Philosoph ins Zimmer, ging an seinen Platz, las die Worte, und steckte das Papier, ohne ein Wort zu sagen, in die Tasche. Sobald Mendelssohn sich setzte, rief der König mit lauter Stimme: „Was für ein Briefchen liest der Philosoph? Will er uns nicht davon erzählen?" Mendelssohn stand auf und antwortete: „Ja, ich lese es gerne vor."

Er nahm das Stück Papier aus der Tasche und las: „„Mendelssohn ist *ein* Esel, Friedrich der *zweite*."" Friedrich und die Gäste mußten lachen.

(1) Wer war Moses Mendelssohn?

    a. ein Komponisten   *b*. ein Philosoph   *c*. der Königs Großvater

(2) Was wußten Friedrich und die Gäste nicht?

    a. warum Mendelssohn noch nicht angekommen war

    b. warum die Philosophen hinter ihren Büchern sitzen

    c. daß Mendelssohn fehlte

(3) Wer hat aufs Stück Papier geschrieben?

    a. der König   *b*. ein Gast   *c*. ein Diener

(4) Als Mendelssohn hereinkam, was tat er mit dem Briefchen?

    a. Er legte es unter einen Teller.   *b*. Er steckte es in die Tasche.   *c*. Er gab es dem König.

(5) Wovon wollte der König, daß Mendelssohn erzählen sollte?

    a. warum er so spät gekommen war

    b. warum er das Stück Papier in die Tasche gesteckt hatte

    c. was im Briefchen steht

For passages 13–15, answer the questions in *English*.

13. Baron von Münchhausen lebte im siebzehnten Jahrhundert. Während seines Lebens hat er viele Reisen durch alle Länder der Welt gemacht. Nachdem er wieder nach Hause kam, erzählte er von seinen wunderbaren Reisen.

Als er einmal in Rußland war, machte er eine Reise mit der Post. Tiefer Schnee lag auf dem Boden, und das Wetter war bitterkalt. Als der Baron mit den anderen Leuten auf einem engen Weg durch die Berge fuhr, bat Baron von Münchhausen, daß man mit dem Horn eine laute Warnung (warning) geben sollte. Der Fahrer (driver) versuchte, aber er konnte es nicht. Immer wieder setzte der Mann das Horn an den Mund, aber nichts war zu hören.

Am Abend kamen alle in ein Dorf und fanden im Wirtshaus (inn) Platz. Das Horn stellte man neben den Ofen. Als das Horn wärmer wurde, kam die schönste Musik heraus. Jetzt konnte man verstehen: während des Tages war das Wetter so kalt, daß die Töne (notes) im Horn eingefroren waren (had frozen). Im warmen Zimmer kamen die Lieder hell und klar heraus, und die Gäste konnten sich ein schönes Konzert anhören.

(1) Who was Baron von Münchhausen? --

----

(2) How was the weather during the Baron's trip in Russia? ------------------------------

----

(3) What did Baron von Münchhausen tell the driver to do? --------------------------------

----

(4) What happened when the driver tried to blow the horn? --------------------------------

----

(5) What happened that evening in the inn? ---

----

14. Vor vielen Jahren gab es irgendwo in Deutschland ein Dorf, das Schilda hieß. Die Leute, die in diesem Dorf wohnten, nannte man die Schildbürger. Und die Schildbürger waren wegen ihrer Dummheit weltbekannt. Sie sollten die dümmsten Menschen der ganzen Welt gewesen sein. Man erzählt dieses Beispiel:

Eines Tages merkte der Bürgermeister, daß auf der Mauer eines Hauses, das vor vielen Jahren zur Erde gefallen war, schönes grünes Gras wuchs. Im Rathaus erklärte der Bürgermeister den anderen Ratsherren: „Es ist schade—Gras wächst auf der Mauer, und niemand kann es gebrauchen." Da die Mauer ziemlich hoch und ganz alt war, wollte keiner hinaufsteigen,[1] um das Gras zu bekommen. Jemand schlug vor, man sollte eine Kuh auf die Mauer stellen, und dann könnte die Kuh selbst das Gras fressen (eat).

Am nächsten Morgen führte der Bürgermeister seine eigene Kuh zur Mauer. Die Mauer war aber so hoch, daß die Kuh nicht hinaufsteigen konnte. Alle versuchten, die Kuh auf die Mauer zu schieben (push). Es half alles nichts.

Endlich holte man ein langes Seil (rope). Das eine Ende band (tied) man um den Hals der Kuh, das andere warf man über die Mauer. Dann zogen daran alle Bürger und versuchten, die Kuh auf die Mauer zu bringen. Der Plan hatte wenig Erfolg (success), und das arme Tier hing (hung) in der Luft. Nach kurzer Zeit starb die Kuh. Die Schildbürger wußten nicht, was sie mit der Kuh machen sollten. Der beste Vorschlag war, ein Fest zu feiern. Es gab Fleisch genug dazu.

Der Bürgermeister war sehr traurig (sad). „Hätte (had) ich nicht das Gras auf der Mauer gesehen, dann lebte noch meine arme Kuh. Ich bin noch nicht dumm genug."

[1] *hinaufsteigen, stieg hinauf, ist hinaufgestiegen,* to climb up

(1) For what were the Schildbürger known? ---

----

(2) What problem did the Bürgermeister present to the town council? ----------------------

----

(3) How did the members of the council propose to solve this problem? --------------------

----

(4) What happened when the townspeople tried to get the cow onto the wall? _____

_____

(5) Why was the Bürgermeister sad? _____

_____

15. Im vierzehnten Jahrhundert lebte ein junger Bauer mit Namen Till, der sich Eulenspiegel nannte. Er wanderte durch das ganze Land, von Dorf zu Dorf und Stadt zu Stadt. Immer wieder machte er dumme Streiche (pranks). Hier folgt ein Beispiel:

Einmal kam Eulenspiegel nach Nürnberg. Dort nannte er sich einen großen und wunderbaren Arzt. Der Direktor des Krankenhauses versprach ihm zwei hundert Taler, wenn Till die kranken Leute aus dem Krankenhaus bringen könnte. Till sagte, das könnte er.

Sehr leise unterhielt sich Till mit jedem kranken Menschen. Zu jedem sagte Till dieselben Worte: „Ich will euch allen helfen. Ich kann eine wunderbare Medizin machen. Aber, um diese Medizin zu machen, muß ich einen von euch zu Pulver (powder) verbrennen. Ich habe mir auch schon überlegt, wen von euch ich zu Pulver verbrennen werde: den kränksten Menschen im Krankenhaus. In einer halben Stunde werde ich mit dem Direktor an der Tür stehen. Mit lauter Stimme werde ich rufen: ‚Wer von euch nicht krank ist, soll herauskommen!‘ Wer nicht aus dem Krankenhaus herauskommt, *den* werde ich zu Pulver verbrennen. Vergiß es nicht, mein Lieber!"

Nachdem Till mit jedem gesprochen hatte, stand er mit dem Direktor an der Tür des Krankenhauses. Mit lauter Stimme rief er: „Wer von euch nicht krank ist, soll herauskommen!" In drei Minuten war das Krankenhaus leer! Alle liefen schnell aus dem Krankenhaus hinaus. Einige waren seit zehn Jahren nicht aus dem Bett gekommen. Selbst diese liefen schnell hinaus.

Der Direktor freute sich sehr. Er sagte zu Till: „Sie sind der beste Arzt der Welt!" Gerne gab der Direktor Till das Geld, welches er versprochen hatte. Sogleich nahm Till das Geld und fuhr aus der Stadt hinaus. Am nächsten Tage kamen alle kranken Leute ins Krankenhaus zurück. Sie erzählten dem Direktor, was Till ihnen gesagt hatte. „Ich bin ein Esel," sagte der Direktor. „Dem Schalk (scoundrel) habe ich zwei hundert Taler bezahlt, und noch habe ich ein volles Krankenhaus."

(1) Who was Till Eulenspiegel? _____

_____

(2) What did the hospital director want Till to do? _____

_____

(3) What did Till tell each patient? _____

_____

(4) What happened when Till called out from the door? _____

_____

(5) Who came to the hospital on the next day? _____

_____

PASSAGES IN GOTHIC TYPE

Today almost all printing in Germany is done in roman type—that is, the same typeface we use in the United States. Until some years ago, however, the typeface commonly used in Germany was *Fraktur*, or Gothic, which closely resembles "Old English" print. Perhaps you have learned the Gothic alphabet in class. Since you may have occasion, some day, to use German publications printed in *Fraktur*, it may be useful to develop some skill in reading that typeface. The following passages are Gothic reprints of passages 2, 4, and 10 on pages 259–260, 261, and 265. Try to read these passages without referring back to those pages.

1. Es kam einmal ein deutscher Handwerksbursche nach Amsterdam. Er interessierte sich für alles, was da zu sehen war: große Gebäude, schöne Häuser, viele Schiffe. Ein besonderes Haus interessierte ihn am meisten. Er fragte einen Herrn, der eigentlich kein Wort Deutsch verstand: „Guter Freund, sagen Sie mir, bitte, wem gehört dieses schöne Haus." Der Holländer verstand die Frage nicht und antwortete: „Kannitverstan." Das ist ein holländisches Wort, das auf Deutsch bedeutet: „Ich kann nicht verstehen."

Der Deutsche meinte aber, einem Herrn Kannitverstan gehörte das Haus. Als der Deutsche sich später andere Gebäude ansah, fragte er wieder jemanden: „Wem gehören diese Gebäude?" Wieder bekam er dieselbe Antwort: „Kannitverstan." „Das ist doch wunderbar," dachte der Deutsche bei sich. „Der Herr Kannitverstan muß ein reicher Mann sein."

Als er um eine Ecke kam, sah der Besucher einen Leichenzug kommen. Genau so wie die anderen Leute, stand der Deutsche still, und hielt den Hut in der Hand. Nachdem der Leichenzug vorbei war, fragte der Deutsche seinen Nachbarn: „Wer ist gestorben?" „Kannitverstan" kam die Antwort. Der Deutsche wurde traurig: „Armer Kannitverstan," dachte er, „was helfen dir jetzt dein schönes Haus und deine großen Gebäude? Nun hast du nichts als ein enges Grab."

2. „Mutter," rief die kleine Anna, „der Magen tut mir weh!" Ihre Mutter antwortete: „Der ist doch ganz leer. Wir wollen etwas hineintun, dann wird alles wieder gut werden." Sobald das Mädchen etwas aß, fühlte es sich besser.

Am Abend, als der Vater nach Hause kam, hatte er Kopfschmerzen. Die kleine Anna sagte zu ihm: „Der Kopf tut dir weh, weil er leer ist. Du sollst etwas hineintun, dann wirst du dich wieder wohl fühlen."

3. Eines Tages kam ein Dieb auf einen Bauernhof, als der Bauer nicht zu Hause war. Der Dieb nahm das beste Pferd und fuhr damit in die Stadt. Als der Bauer wieder nach Hause kam, wurde er traurig, weil sein bestes Pferd weg war. Einige Tage später kam der Bauer auch in die Stadt. Da sah er sein Pferd, das der Dieb verkaufen wollte. Der Bauer sagte zu dem Dieb: „Das ist mein Pferd. Woher haben Sie es bekommen?"

„Nein, mein Herr," antwortete der Dieb, „das ist falsch. Ich habe dieses Tier schon seit einem Jahr. Dieses Pferd gehört mir."

Der Bauer machte soviel Lärm, daß viele andere Bauern herumstanden. Der Bauer nahm seinen Mantel ab und warf ihn über den Kopf des Pferdes. „Wenn Sie das Pferd schon seit einem Jahr haben, dann können Sie mir auch sagen, auf welchem Auge es blind ist."

Der Dieb wußte eigentlich nicht, was für eine Antwort er geben sollte. Eine Antwort mußte er aber geben. „Gewiß," sagte der Dieb, „auf dem linken Auge ist es blind."

„Falsch, ganz falsch!" rief der Bauer. Bevor er noch etwas sagen konnte, sagte der Dieb: „Sie haben recht. Jetzt erinnere ich mich daran. Das Pferd ist auf dem rechten Auge blind."

„Wieder falsch!" rief der Bauer, als er seinen Mantel von dem Kopf des Pferdes nahm. Mit lauter Stimme sagte der Bauer: „Mein Pferd ist auf keinem Auge blind, weder auf dem linken noch auf dem rechten. Dieser Mann ist ein Dieb!" Jetzt war es ganz klar, daß das Pferd dem Bauern gehörte. Die anderen Bauern nahmen den Dieb in ihre Mitte, und riefen den Polizisten.

PART VIII—Principal Parts of Irregular Verbs

Note

1. The indicative forms of the present and past tenses are given in the third person singular.
2. The present-tense form is given only if it is irregular.
3. The past participle is preceded by **ist** if the auxiliary verb used in forming the perfect tenses is **sein.**
4. The verbs **fahren, rennen,** and **schwimmen** require the auxiliary **haben** in certain usages.

Infinitive	Present	Past	Past Participle
beginnen *to begin*		begann	begonnen
bitten *to ask for*		bat	gebeten
bleiben *to stay*		blieb	ist geblieben
brechen *to break*	bricht	brach	gebrochen
brennen *to burn*		brannte	gebrannt
bringen *to bring*		brachte	gebracht
denken *to think*		dachte	gedacht
dürfen *to be allowed*	darf	durfte	gedurft
einladen *to invite*	lädt ein	lud ein	eingeladen
entleihen *to borrow*		entlieh	entliehen
essen *to eat*	ißt	aß	gegessen
fahren *to drive, travel*	fährt	fuhr	ist gefahren
fallen *to fall*	fällt	fiel	ist gefallen
fangen *to catch*	fängt	fing	gefangen
finden *to find*		fand	gefunden
fliegen *to fly*		flog	ist geflogen
fließen *to flow*		floß	ist geflossen
geben *to give*	gibt	gab	gegeben
gehen *to go*		ging	ist gegangen

geschehen *to happen*	geschieht	geschah	ist geschehen
haben *to have*	hat	hatte	gehabt
halten *to hold*	hält	hielt	gehalten
hängen *to hang*		hing	gehangen
heißen *to be named, called*		hieß	geheißen
helfen *to help*	hilft	half	geholfen
kennen *to know*		kannte	gekannt
kommen *to come*		kam	ist gekommen
können *to be able, can*	kann	konnte	gekonnt
lassen *to let*	läßt	ließ	gelassen
laufen *to run*	läuft	lief	ist gelaufen
lesen *to read*	liest	las	gelesen
liegen *to lie*		lag	gelegen
mögen *to desire, like*	mag	mochte	gemocht
müssen *to have to, must*	muß	mußte	gemußt
nehmen *to take*	nimmt	nahm	genommen
nennen *to name*		nannte	genannt
reiten *to ride (horseback)*		ritt	ist geritten
rennen *to run*		rannte	ist gerannt
ringen *to ring*		rang	gerungen
rufen *to call*		rief	gerufen
schlafen *to sleep*	schläft	schlief	geschlafen
schlagen *to strike, hit*	schlägt	schlug	geschlagen
schließen *to close*		schloß	geschlossen
schneiden *to cut*		schnitt	geschnitten
schreiben *to write*		schrieb	geschrieben
schreien *to scream*		schrie	geschrien

schwimmen *to swim*		schwamm	ist geschwommen
sehen *to see*	sieht	sah	gesehen
sein *to be*	ist	war	ist gewesen
singen *to sing*		sang	gesungen
sitzen *to sit*		saß	gesessen
sollen *should,* *ought to*	soll	sollte	gesollt
sprechen *to speak*	spricht	sprach	gesprochen
stehen *to stand*		stand	gestanden
steigen *to climb*		stieg	ist gestiegen
sterben *to die*	stirbt	starb	ist gestorben
tragen *to carry*	trägt	trug	getragen
treffen *to meet*	trifft	traf	getroffen
trinken *to drink*		trank	getrunken
tun *to do*		tat	getan
vergessen *to forget*	vergißt	vergaß	vergessen
verlieren *to lose*		verlor	verloren
vermeiden *to avoid*		vermied	vermieden
wachsen *to grow*	wächst	wuchs	ist gewachsen
waschen *to wash*	wäscht	wusch	gewaschen
werden *to become*	wird	wurde	ist geworden
werfen *to throw*	wirft	warf	geworfen
wissen *to know*	weiß	wußte	gewußt
wollen *to want*	will	wollte	gewollt
ziehen *to pull*		zog	gezogen

Part IX—German-English Vocabulary

Symbols Used in the Vocabulary

1. An apostrophe (') following a prefix indicates that the prefix is separable: **ab'fahren.**

2. Nouns are shown only in the nominative singular and plural forms. When the genitive singular is unusual, it is indicated in parentheses as follows: **das Herz (-ens), -en.**

3. The following abbreviations indicate the case that normally follows a given verb or preposition:

(A) accusative	(D/A) dative or accusative
(D) dative	(G) genitive

4. The third-person-singular forms of irregular verbs appear in parentheses as follows: (1) *present indicative*, (2) *imperfect*, (3) *present perfect*.

EXAMPLE: **brechen (er bricht, brach, hat gebrochen)**

---

der **Abend, -e,** evening; **abends (am Abend),** in the evening, P.M.; **zu Abend essen,** to have dinner

das **Abendessen, -,** dinner

aber, but

ab'fahren (er fährt ab, fuhr ab, ist abgefahren), to leave, depart

ab'holen, to pick up (someone), call for

ab'legen, to take off (clothing)

der **Abort, -e,** toilet

ab'setzen, to let out (at a place), drop off (someone)

die **Abteilung, -en,** department

ab'wischen, to erase, wipe off

achten auf (A), to watch out for, pay attention to

die **Achterbahn, -en,** roller coaster

die **Adresse, -n,** address

alle, all (of); **alle guten Schüler,** all (of) the good pupils

die **Allee, -n,** avenue, boulevard

allerlei, all kinds (sorts) of; **allerlei Menschen,** all kinds of people

als, as, when (*with past tense only*), than; **mehr (weniger) als,** more (less) than

also, therefore, thus

alt, old; **älter,** older; **am ältesten,** oldest

das **Altertum,** antiquity

Amerika, America

an (D/A), at, on; **an der See,** at the beach; **an die See,** to the beach; **am Abend,** in the evening; **am Montag,** on Monday

ander-, other

anderthalb, one and a half

an'fangen (er fängt an, fing an, hat angefangen), to begin

der **Angestellte (-n), -n,** employee (in an office)

sich **an'hören,** to listen to; **ich höre mir das Konzert an,** I'm listening to the concert

an'kommen (er kommt an, kam an, ist angekommen), to arrive; **ankommen auf** (A), to depend on, matter

an'machen: das Licht anmachen, to turn on the light

an'nehmen (er nimmt an, nahm an, hat angenommen), to receive, accept

an'rufen (er ruft an, rief an, hat angerufen), to call to, call on the phone

sich **an'sehen (er sieht sich an, sah sich an, hat sich angesehen),** to look at

anstatt (G), instead of

die **Antwort, -en,** answer

antworten (D), to answer (a person); **auf eine Frage antworten,** to answer a question

an'zeigen, to report (to authorities), advertise, indicate

sich **an'ziehen (er zieht sich an, zog sich an, hat sich angezogen),** to dress oneself, get dressed

der **Anzug, ̈-e,** suit (clothing)

der **Apfel, ̈-,** apple

der **April,** April; **im April,** in April; **am zweiten April,** on April 2

die **Arbeit, -e,** work, job, task

arbeiten, to work; **arbeiten an** (D), to work on (at), be busy with

arm, poor

der **Arm, -e,** arm

der **Arzt, ̈-e,** doctor, physician

auch, also, too; **auch das noch!,** Oh no, not that!

auf (D/A), on, onto (*something horizontal*); **auf dem Land,** in the country; **aufs Land,** to the country; **auf der Straße,** on the street; **wie sagt man das auf deutsch?,** how does one say that in German?

die **Aufgabe, -n,** assignment

auf'halten (er hält auf, hielt auf, hat aufgehalten), to hold up, detain; **sich aufhalten,** to stop, delay, sustain; **sich aufhalten bei** (D), to stay at (someone's house)

auf'hören (mit), to stop (doing something)

auf'machen, to open

auf'passen, to pay attention, watch out, be careful

auf'stehen (er steht auf, stand auf, ist aufgestanden), to stand up, get up

das **Auge, -n,** eye

der **August,** August; **im August,** in August

aus (D), out of, from (a place)

der **Ausflug, ̈-e,** excursion, short trip, outing

aus'geben (er gibt aus, gab aus, hat ausgegeben), to spend; **(Geld) ausgeben für,** to spend (money) for

aus'gehen (er geht aus, ging aus, ist ausgegangen), to go out

ausgezeichnet, excellent, distinguished

der **Ausländer, -,** foreigner

aus'machen: das Licht ausmachen, to turn off the light

aus'radieren, to erase (on paper)

aus'sehen (er sieht aus, sah aus, hat ausgesehen), to appear, look (a certain way), to seem

außer (D), besides, except for; outside

aus'steigen (er steigt aus, stieg aus, ist ausgestiegen), to get off (a vehicle), disembark

aus'tauschen: Blätter austauschen, to exchange papers

auswendig lernen, to memorize, learn by heart

aus'werfen (*see* werfen), to throw out

aus'ziehen (er zieht aus, zog aus, ist ausgezogen), to move out; **sich ausziehen,** to undress oneself

das **Auto, -s,** car, automobile

der **Autobus, -se,** bus

das **Bad, ̈-er,** bath

das **Badezimmer, -,** bathroom

der **Bahnhof, ̈-e,** railway station

bald, soon

der **Ball, ̈-e,** ball

die **Bank, ̈-e,** bench

die **Bank, -en,** bank

bauen, to build

der **Bauer (-n), -n,** farmer

der **Baum, ̈-e,** tree

beachten, to notice, pay attention to

der **Beamte (-n), -n,** government employee, official

beantworten: eine Frage beantworten, to answer a question bedeuten, to mean

sich **beeilen,** to hurry

beginnen (er beginnt, begann, hat begonnen), to begin

behandeln, to deal with, handle (something)

bei (D), at, near, at the home of; **bei mir,** at my house

das **Bein, -e,** leg

das **Beispiel, -e,** example

bekannt, well known

der **Bekannte (-n), -n,** acquaintance

bekommen (er bekommt, bekam, hat bekommen), to get, receive

beliebt, popular, well liked

der **Berg, -e,** mountain

der **Bericht, -e,** report

besonder-, special

besser, better

best-, best

bestehen (er besteht, bestand, hat bestanden), to pass (a test)

bestellen, to order

der **Besuch, -e,** visit; **zu Besuch,** for a visit

besuchen, to visit

der **Besucher, -,** visitor

das **Bett, -en,** bed; **zu (ins) Bett gehen,** to go to bed

bevor, before *(conj.)*

bezahlen, to pay (for)

die **Bibliothek, -en,** library

das **Bild, -er,** picture

billig, cheap, inexpensive

bis (A), until

bißchen: ein bißchen, a little bit (of), a little

bitte, please; you're welcome

bitten (um) (er bittet, bat, hat gebeten), to ask (for), request; **sie bittet um das Geld,** she asks for the money

das **Blatt, ̈er,** sheet (of paper)

blau, blue

bleiben (er bleibt, blieb, ist geblieben), to stay, remain; **er bleibt bei uns,** he's staying with us (at our house)

der **Bleistift, -e,** pencil

die **Blume, -n,** flower

der **Boden, ̈,** floor, ground, attic

böse, mean, angry, nasty

brechen (er bricht, brach, hat gebrochen), to break (something)

breit, broad, wide

brennen (er brennt, brannte, hat gebrannt), to burn (= to be on fire)

der **Brief, -e,** letter

bringen (er bringt, brachte, hat gebracht), to bring

das **Brot, -e,** (loaf of) bread

das **Brötchen, -,** (bread) roll

die **Brücke, -n,** bridge

der **Bruder, ̈,** brother

das **Buch, ̈er,** book

die **Bücherei, -en,** library

die **Burg, -en,** castle, fortification

der **Bürgermeister,** mayor

das **Büro, -s,** office

der **Bus, -se,** bus

die **Butter,** butter

das **Café, -s,** cafe, coffee house

da, there; *(conj.)* since, because

das **Dach, ̈er,** roof

daher, therefore, for that reason

die **Dame, -n,** lady, woman

der **Dank,** thanks; **vielen Dank!,** thanks very much!

danken (D) **(für),** to thank (for); **danke,** thanks!

dann, then

darum, therefore, for that reason

daß, that *(conj.)*

das **Datum** *(pl.,* **Daten),** (calendar) date; **welches Datum ist heute?,** what is the date today?

dauern, to last, continue

die **Decke, -n,** blanket, bedcover; ceiling

dein, your *(fam. sing.)*

denken (er denkt, dachte, hat gedacht), to think; **denken an** (A), to think about

denn, *(conj.)* for, because; *(particle)* then, well, etc. *(often not translatable)*; **was ist denn los?,** (well,) what's the matter?; **wo ist er denn?,** where can he be?

deutsch, German; **sag' es auf deutsch!,** say it in German

der **Deutsche (-n), -n,** German

Deutschland, Germany

der **Dezember,** December

der **Dichter, -,** poet, dramatist, writer *(of fiction)*

der **Dieb, -e,** thief

der **Diener, -,** servant

der **Dienstag,** Tuesday

dieser, this

das **Ding, -e,** thing

der **Direktor, -en (die Direktorin, -nen),** principal

doch, indeed, but, however

der **Doktor, -en,** doctor

der **Dom, -e,** cathedral

der **Donnerstag,** Thursday

das **Dorf, ̈er,** village

dort, there

das **Drama** *(pl.,* **Dramen),** drama

draußen, outside

drinnen, inside

drüben, over there

dumm, stupid; **die Dummheit, -en,** stupidity; **der Dummkopf,** dumbbell

dunkel (dunkl-), dark

durch (A), through

durch'fallen (er fällt durch, fiel durch, ist durchgefallen), to fail, flunk; **ich bin in der Prüfung durchgefallen,** I flunked the exam

dürfen (er darf, durfte, hat gedurft), may, to be allowed (to); **darf ich rauchen?,** may I smoke?

eben, even, yet, just; **ebenso ... wie,** (just) as ... as; **er ist eben hereingekommen** he just came in

die **Ecke, -n,** corner; **an der Ecke,** on the corner

ehe, before *(conj.)*

eigen (eign-), own; **er brachte sein eig(e)nes Buch,** he brought his own book

der **Eimer, -,** pail

einfach, simple

einige, some, a few

ein'kaufen, to buy, shop for

ein'laden (er lädt ein, lud ein, hat eingeladen), to invite; **einladen in** (A), to invite to (a place); **einladen zu** (D), to invite to (an event)

einmal, once; **einmal im Monat,** once a month; **noch einmal,** once more

ein paar, several, a few

ein'steigen (er steigt ein, stieg ein, ist eingestiegen), to get aboard, get into (a vehicle)

einzig, single, only *(adj.)*

die **Eisenbahn, -en,** railroad

die **Eltern** *(pl.),* parents

das **Ende, -n,** end

eng, narrow

entleihen (er entleiht, entlieh, hat entliehen), to borrow; **er hat mir das Geld entliehen,** he borrowed the money from me

entschuldigen, to excuse

entweder ... oder, either ... or

die **Erde,** earth

sich **erholen,** to rest, relax, recover, recuperate

erinnern: sich erinnern an (A), to remember

erklären, to explain, clarify

erledigen, to finish, complete

erreichen, to reach (a place)

erst, first; at the earliest, not until; **er kommt erst morgen an,** he's not coming until tomorrow

erwarten, to expect, await

erzählen, to tell

der **Esel, -,** donkey

essen (er ißt, aß, hat gegessen), to eat *(used with human subjects only)*

der **Eßsaal, -säle,** dining hall

etwas, something

euer (eur-), your *(fam. pl.)*

das **Examen,** exam

fahren (er fährt, fuhr, ist gefahren), to drive, go, travel, ride *(in a vehicle)*; **ich fahre mit dem Zug,** I'm going by train

das **Fahrrad, ̈er,** bicycle

der **Fahrstuhl, ̈e,** elevator

fallen (er fällt, fiel, ist gefallen), to fall

falsch, false, wrong, incorrect

die **Familie, -n,** family

fangen (er fängt, fing, hat gefangen), to catch

die **Farbe, -n,** color

fast, almost

der **Februar,** February

die **Feder, -n,** feather, pen

fehlen, to be missing, to lack, be absent; **es fehlt mir an einem Bleistift,** I need a pencil

der **Fehler, -,** mistake, error

der **Feiertag, -e,** holiday

das **Feld, -er,** field

das **Fenster, -,** window

die **Ferien** *(pl.),* vacation

fern, distant, far

der **Fernsehapparat, -e,** television set

fertig, finished, ready

fertig'machen, to prepare, get ready

das **Fest, -e,** celebration, festival, holiday

das **Feuer,** fire

der **Film, -e,** film, movie

finden (er findet, fand, hat gefunden), to find

das **Fleisch,** meat

fließen (es fließt, floß, ist geflossen), to flow

das **Flugzeug, -e,** airplane

der **Fluß, ̈sse,** river

folgen (D), *(aux.* **sein)** to follow; *(aux.* **haben)** to obey

die **Frage, -n,** question; **eine Frage stellen,** to ask a question

fragen, to ask; **fragen nach** (D), to ask about

die **Frau, -en,** woman, wife, Mrs.

das **Fräulein, -,** young lady, Miss

frei, free, unlimited

der **Freitag,** Friday

die **Freizeit, -en,** spare time

fremd, strange, foreign; **ich bin hier fremd,** I'm a stranger here

die **Freude, -n,** joy

freuen, to please, make happy; **sich freuen,** to be pleased, be glad; **sich freuen an (D)** or **über (A)**, to be glad (happy) about; **sich freuen auf (A)**, to look forward to

der **Freund, -e,** friend; **die Freundin, -,** (girl) friend

fröhlich, happy; **fröhliche Weihnachten!,** merry Christmas!

früh, early; **morgen früh,** tomorrow morning; **heute früh,** this morning; **gestern früh,** yesterday morning

der **Frühling,** spring(time)

das **Frühstück, -e,** breakfast

frühstücken, to have breakfast

fühlen, to feel; **sich fühlen** to feel (a certain way)

der **Füllfederhalter, -,** fountain pen

für (A), for; **für sich lesen,** to read silently

furchtbar, terrible, frightful

der **Fürst, -en,** prince

der **Fuß, "e,** foot

der **Fußball, "e,** soccer, soccer-ball

der **Fußboden, ",** floor (of a room)

der **Fußweg, -e,** footpath

der **Gang, "e,** motion, path, pace

ganz, quite, complete, whole

gar, at all; **gar nicht,** not at all; **gar kein,** none at all

die **Garage, -n,** garage

die **Garderobe, -n,** clothes closet, cloakroom

die **Gardine, -n,** curtain, drape

der **Garten, ",** garden, yard

der **Gast, "e,** guest

die **Gaststätte, -n,** restaurant

das **Gebäude, -,** building

geben (er gibt, gab, hat gegeben), to give; **es gibt (A),** there is, there are

gebrauchen, to use

der **Geburtstag, -e,** birthday; **zum Geburtstag,** for my (your, his, her, etc.) birthday

das **Gedicht, -e,** poem

gefährlich, dangerous

gefallen (D) (es gefällt, gefiel, hat gefallen), to please; **es gafällt mir,** I like it

gegen (A), against, towards

die **Gegenwart,** present (time)

gehen (er geht, ging, ist gegangen), to go; **zu Fuß gehen,** to go on foot (to walk); **zu (ins) Bett gehen,** to go to bed; **wie geht's?,** how are you?

gehören (D), to belong to (a person), be the property of; **gehören zu,** to belong to (an organization, group, etc.), be a member of, be part of

gelb, yellow

das **Geld,** money

das **Gemälde, -,** painting

genau, exact(ly)

genug, enough

gerade, straight, direct; exactly, just (a moment ago)

gern, gladly; verb + **gern,** to like to (do something); **gern haben,** to like (something); **ich schwimme gern,** I like to swim; **ich habe es sehr gern,** I like it very much

das **Geschäft, -e,** business

geschehen (es geschieht, geschah, ist geschehen), to happen

das **Geschenk, -e,** gift, present

die **Geschichte, -n,** story, history

die **Geschwister,** brother(s) and sister(s)

das **Gesicht, -er,** face, appearance

gestern, yesterday; **gestern abend,** last night; **gestern früh,** yesterday morning

gewiß, certainly

gewöhnlich, usual(ly)

das **Glas, "er,** glass

glauben (D), to believe (a person); (with (A)): to believe (a story, statement, etc.)

gleich, same, alike; immediately

das **Glück,** good luck

glücklich, happy, lucky

gnädig, gracious; **Gnädige Frau,** dear madam, my dear lady

der **Gott, "er,** God (pl., gods)

das **Grab, "er,** grave

die **Grenze, -n,** boundary, limit

groß, large, big, tall, great

die **Großmutter, ",** grandmother; **der Großvater, ",** grandfather

grün, green

der **Gruß, "e,** greeting

grüßen, to greet

der **Gummi, -s,** (pencil) eraser

gut, good

haben (er hat, hatte, hat gehabt), to have; **gern haben,** to like; **recht haben,** to be right; **Hunger haben,** to be hungry

der **Hafen, ",** port, harbor

halb, half; **um halb eins,** at half past twelve; **die Hälfte, -n,** a half

der **Hals, "e,** neck

halten (er hält, hielt, hat gehalten), to hold, stop; **was halten Sie von meinem neuen Hut?,** what do you think of my new hat?

die **Hand, "e,** hand; **die Hand geben,** to shake hands

der **Handschuh, -e,** glove

das **Handtuch, "er,** (hand) towel

hängen (er hängt, hing, hat gehangen), to hang

hassen, to hate

die **Hauptstadt, "e,** capital city

das **Haus, "er,** house; **nach Hause gehen,** to go home; **zu Hause,** at home

das **Heft, -e,** notebook

heiß, hot

heißen (er heißt, hieß, hat geheißen), to be named, be called; **wie heißen Sie?,** what is your name?; **ich heiße,** my name is

helfen (D) (er hilft, half, hat geholfen), to help

hell, light, bright

heraus, out of (moving toward the speaker)

der **Herbst,** autumn, fall; **im kommenden Herbst,** next fall

der **Herd, -e,** kitchen range, stove

her'kommen (er kommt her, kam her, ist hergekommen), to come here; **wo kommen Sie her?,** where do you come from?

der **Herr (-n), -en,** gentleman, Mr., sir, lord

das **Herz (-ens), -en,** heart

heute, today; **heute abend,** this evening; **heute früh,** this morning; **heute in 8 Tagen,** a week from today; **heute vor 8 Tagen,** a week ago today

hier, here

die **Hilfe,** help

der **Himmel,** heaven, sky

hinaus, out of (moving away from the speaker)

hinaus'fahren (er fährt hinaus, fuhr hinaus, ist hinausgefahren), to go (ride) out of

hin'fahren (er fährt hin, fuhr hin, ist hingefahren), to go (ride) away, depart

hin'gehen (er geht hin, ging hin, ist hingegangen), to go there

hinter (D/A), behind, back of

hoch, high, tall; **höher,** higher; **höchst-,** highest

der **Hof, "e,** courtyard, yard

hoffen, to hope; **hoffentlich,** hopefully, I hope

holen, to get, fetch, bring

das **Holz, "er,** wood

hören, to hear, listen; **hören auf (A),** to obey

das **Hotel, -s,** hotel

der **Hund, -e,** dog

hungrig, hungry

der **Hut, "e,** hat

die **Hütte, -n,** cabin

ihr, you (fam. pl.); her, their; **Ihr,** your

immer, always; **immer wieder,** again and again

in (D/A), in, into

interessant, interesting

interessieren, to interest; **sich interessieren (für),** to be interested (in)

irgendwo, somewhere

ja, yes, indeed

das **Jahr, -e,** year; **vor einem Jahr,** a year ago; **im nächsten Jahr,** next year

das **Jahrhundert, -e,** century

der **Januar,** January

je . . . desto (je . . . um so), the . . . the; **je mehr, desto besser,** the more the merrier

jeder, each, every; **jeden Tag,** every day

jemand, someone

jener, that, that one

jetzt, now

die **Jugend,** youth, young people

die **Jugendherberge, -n,** youth hostel

der **Juli,** July

jung, young; **jünger,** younger; **jüngst-,** youngest

der **Junge (-n), -n,** boy

der **Juni,** June

der **Kaffee,** coffee

kalt, cold; **kälter,** colder; **kältest-,** coldest

die **Kamera, -s,** camera

sich kämmen, to comb one's hair

die **Karte, -n,** card, ticket

die **Kartoffel, -n,** potato

kaufen, to buy

kaum, hardly

kein, no (adj.), not any; **keiner,** nobody, none

der **Keller, -,** cellar

der **Kellner, -,** waiter

kennen (er kennt, kannte, hat gekannt), to know, be acquainted with (a person)

kennen'lernen (er lernt kennen, lernte kennen, hat kennengelernt), to meet, get to know, make the acquaintance of

das **Kind, -er,** child

das **Kino, -s,** movie theater

die **Kirche, -n,** church

die **Klasse, -n,** class, grade level (in school)

das **Klassenzimmer, -,** classroom

das **Klavier, -e,** piano

das **Kleid, -er,** dress; pl., clothes

klein, small, little

kochen, to cook, boil

kommen (er kommt, kam, ist gekommen), to come

die **Konditorei, -en,** pastry shop

der **König, -e,** king

können (er kann, konnte, hat gekonnt), can, be able to, know how to; **können Sie Deutsch?,** do you know (can you speak) German?

das **Konzert, -e,** concert

der **Kopf, ̈e,** head

korrigieren, to correct

kosten, to cost

krank, sick

das **Krankenhaus, ̈er,** hospital; **die Krankenschwester, -n,** nurse

die **Krawatte, -n,** necktie

die **Kreide,** chalk

der **Krieg, -e,** war

die **Küche, -n,** kitchen

der **Kuchen, -,** cake

der **Kugelschreiber, -,** ballpoint pen

kühl, cool

der **Kunde (-n), -n,** customer

die **Kunst, ̈e,** art, skill

kurz, short, brief; **kürzer,** shorter; **kürzest-,** shortest

lachen, to laugh

der **Laden, ̈ (or -),** shop, store

die **Lampe, -n,** lamp

das **Land, ̈er,** country, land; **auf dem Lande,** in the country; **aufs Land,** to the country

die **Landkarte, -n,** map

lang, long

lange, for a long time; **wie lange sind Sie schon hier?,** how long have you been here?

langsam, slow(ly)

langweilig, boring, dull

der **Lärm,** noise

lassen (er läßt, ließ, hat gelassen), to leave (a thing), to let

laufen (er läuft, lief, ist gelaufen), to run

laut, loud(ly); **laut vorlesen,** to read aloud

leben, to live

leer, empty, hollow, vacant

legen, to lay, set down, place; **sich legen,** to lie down

der **Lehrer, -,** (man) teacher; **die Lehrerin, -nen,** (woman) teacher

leider, unfortunately

leise, softly

die **Lektion, -en,** lesson

lernen, to learn, study

lesen (er liest, las, hat gelesen), to read; **für sich lesen,** to read to oneself

letzt-, last, latest

die **Leute** (pl.), people

lieb, dear

lieben, to love, like

lieber, rather (= preferably); **ich bleibe lieber zu Hause,** I'd rather stay home

das **Lied, -er,** song

liegen (er liegt, lag, hat gelegen), to lie, recline, be situated; **liegen an** (D), to depend on

die **Limonade,** lemonade

links, to the left

das **Loch, ̈er,** hole; **das Löchelchen,** little hole

die **Luft,** air

machen, to make, do; **eine Reise machen,** to take a trip

das **Mädchen, -,** girl

der **Mai,** May

mal, (adv.) ever, just, etc. (often not translatable); **sag' mal,** just tell me; **warte mal!,** wait a minute!; (noun) times; **sechs mal zwei,** 6×2; **einmal, zweimal, . . .,** once, twice, etc.

das **Mal, -e,** time (= occurrence); **zum ersten Mal,** for the first time

man (indef. pron.), one, you, people, etc.; **wie macht man das?,** how is that done?; **wie sagt man das auf deutsch?,** how does one (do you) say that in German?

mancher, many (a)

manchmal, sometimes

der **Mann, ̈er,** man, husband

der **Mantel, ̈,** coat

die **Mark, -,** Mark (unit of German money)

der **Marktplatz, ̈e,** market place

der **März,** March

die **Mathematik,** mathematics

die **Mauer, -n,** (outside) wall

die **Medizin, -en,** medicine, medication

das **Meer, -e,** sea, ocean

mehr, more; **mehr als,** more than; **nicht mehr,** no longer

mehrere, several

mein, my

meinen, to think, believe, mean

meist-, most; **die meisten Leute,** most people; **meistens,** mostly, usually

der **Meister, -,** master

sich **melden,** to announce oneself, report

der **Mensch (-en), -en,** human being, person, man

sich **merken,** to notice, keep in mind

die **Milch,** milk

die **Minute, -n,** minute

mit (D), with, by; **er fährt mit der Eisenbahn,** he's going by train

mit'bringen (er bringt mit, brachte mit, hat mitgebracht), to bring along

mit'kommen (er kommt mit, kam mit, ist mitgekommen), to accompany, come with

mit'nehmen (er nimmt mit, nahm mit, hat mitgenommen), to take along

der **Mittag, -e,** noon; **zu Mittag,** at noon; **zu Mittag essen,** to have lunch

die **Mitternacht,** midnight

der **Mittwoch,** Wednesday

das **Möbel, -,** piece of furniture; pl., furniture

möchte(n), would like

mögen (er mag, mochte, hat gemocht), to like; **ich mag es nicht,** I don't like it

der **Monat, -e,** month; **einmal im Monat,** once a month

der **Mond,** moon

der **Montag, -e,** Monday; **am Montag,** on Monday

der **Morgen, -,** morning; **guten Morgen!,** good morning!

morgen, tomorrow; **heute morgen,** this morning; **morgen abend,** tomorrow night; **morgen früh,** tomorrow morning; **morgens,** in the morning, A.M.

müde, tired

die **Mühle, -n,** mill; **der Mühler,** miller

der **Mund, -e,** mouth

das **Museum, -een** (or -s), museum

die **Musik,** music

müssen (er muß, mußte, hat gemußt), must, to have to

die **Mutter, ̈,** mother

nach (D), after, towards, according to; **nach Hause gehen (kommen),** to go (come) home; **ich fahre nach Berlin,** I'm going to Berlin; **dem Lehrer nach,** according to the teacher

der **Nachbar (-n), -n,** neighbor

nachdem, after (conj.), afterwards

der **Nachmittag,** afternoon; **nachmittags (am Nachmittag),** in the afternoon, P.M.

nach'schlagen (er schlägt nach, schlug nach, hat nachgeschlagen), to look up (in a book), check on

nach'sehen (er sieht nach, sah nach, hat nachgesehen), to look after, attend to, check on

nächst-, nearest, next; **nächste Woche,** next week

die **Nacht, ̈e,** night; **nachts,** at night

der **Nachtisch, -e,** dessert

nah(e), near; **näher,** nearer

die **Nähe,** vicinity, neighborhood

der **Name (-ns), -n,** name

nämlich, namely, that is, as you (may) know; **er war nämlich krank,** he was sick, you see (know)

natürlich, natural(ly)

neben (D/A), beside, next to

nehmen (er nimmt, nahm, hat genommen), to take

nein, no

nennen (er nennt, nannte, hat genannt), to name, call

nett, nice, kind

neu, new

nicht, not; **gar nicht,** not at all; **nicht mehr,** no longer; **nicht nur . . . sondern auch,** not only . . . but also; **nicht wahr?,** isn't it true?; **noch nicht,** not yet

nichts, nothing; **gar nichts,** nothing at all

nie, never

niemals, never

niemand, no one

nimmer, never

nirgends, nowhere

noch, still, yet; **noch einmal,** once more; **noch nicht,** not yet

der **Norden,** north; **nördlich,** northern, to the north

die **Note, -n,** grade, mark (on a test or report card)

der **November,** November

nun, now

nur, only

ob, whether, if (= whether); **ich weiß nicht, ob er kommt,** I don't know if (whether) he's coming

oben, at the top, above, upstairs; **dort oben,** up there

obgleich, although

das **Obst, -arten,** fruit

oder, or

der **Ofen, ̈,** oven, stove

öffnen, to open

oft, often

ohne (A), without

das **Ohr, -en,** ear

der **Oktober,** October

der **Onkel, -,** uncle

das **Orchester, -,** orchestra

der **Osten,** east; **östlich,** eastern, to the east

paar: ein paar, some, a few

das **Paar, -e,** pair, a couple

das **Paket, -e,** package

das **Papier,** paper

der **Papierkorb, ̈e,** wastebasket

der **Park, -e** (*or* **-s**), park
passen (D), to suit, be suitable; **der Mantel paßt mir nicht,** the coat doesn't suit me
das **Pech,** trouble, hard luck
der **Pfennig, -e,** penny
das **Pferd, -e,** horse
der **Philosoph (-en), -en,** philosopher
der **Plan, ̈e,** plan
die **Platte, -n,** (phonograph) record, disc
der **Plattenspieler, -,** record player
der **Platz, ̈e,** place, seat; (city) square; **bitte, nehmen Sie Platz!,** please have (take) a seat!
die **Polizei,** police
der **Polizist (-en), -en,** policeman
die **Post,** mail
der **Preis, -e,** price, prize
Prima!, great!
probieren, to test, try, taste
das **Programm, -e,** program
die **Prüfung, -en,** examination, quiz, test; **eine Prüfung bestehen,** to pass a test; **in einer Prüfung durchfallen,** to fail (flunk) a test
das **Pult, -e,** (student) desk
der **Punkt, -e,** point, period; **Punkt drei Uhr,** three o'clock sharp

das **Rad, ̈er,** wheel, bicycle
das **Radio, -s,** radio
sich **rasieren,** to shave
das **Rathaus, ̈er,** courthouse, town hall
der **Ratskeller, -,** restaurant (*usually in the basement of the Rathaus*)
die **Rechnung, -en,** account, bill, check (*to be paid*)
recht, right, just; **die rechte Hand,** right hand; **du hast recht,** you're right; **zur rechten Zeit,** just in time; **rechts,** on (to) the right
rechtzeitig, punctual(ly), on time
reden, to talk, speak
der **Regen,** rain
regnen, to rain
reich, rich, wealthy
die **Reise, -n,** trip, journey; **eine Reise machen,** to take a trip; **glückliche Reise!,** have a pleasant trip!
reisen (*aux.* **sein**), to travel
reiten (er reitet, ritt, ist geritten), to ride (*on horseback*)
rennen (er rennt, rannte, ist gerannt), to run
das **Restaurant, -s,** restaurant
richtig, right, correct

der **Ring, -e,** ring
der **Roman, -e,** novel
rosa, pink
die **Rose, -n,** rose
rot, red
der **Rücken, -,** back
rudern (*aux.* **sein**), to row, paddle
rufen (er ruft, rief, hat gerufen), to call, shout
ruhig, quiet, peaceful; **ruhe!,** quiet!
der **Rummelplatz, ̈e,** fairgrounds, amusement park

die **Sache, -n,** thing, matter, affair
sagen, to say, tell
der **Samstag,** Saturday
der **Satz, ̈e,** sentence
schade: das ist schade, that's too bad (a shame)
die **Schallplatte, -n,** phonograph record
schauen (nach), to look (at)
das **Schaufenster, -,** display (shop) window
das **Schauspiel, -e,** (stage) play; **der Schauspieler, -,** actor
schenken, to give (*a gift*)
schicken, to send
das **Schiff, -e,** ship
schlafen (er schläft, schlief, hat geschlafen), to sleep
das **Schlafzimmer, -,** bedroom
schlagen (er schlägt, schlug, hat geschlagen), to strike, hit, beat
schlecht, bad
schließen (er schließt, schloß, hat geschlossen), to close, shut
das **Schloß** (*gen. sing.,* **Schlosses;** *pl.,* **Schlösser),** castle, palace; lock
der **Schlüssel, -,** key
der **Schnee,** snow
schneiden (er schneidet, schnitt, hat geschnitten), to cut
schnell, quick(ly), fast, rapid(ly)
schon, already; **schon gut!,** all right
schön, beautiful, pretty, fine, nice; **bitte schön!,** you're welcome
der **Schrank, ̈e,** cupboard, closet, bookcase
schreiben (er schreibt, schrieb, hat geschrieben), to write; **schreiben** (D) *or* **schreiben an** (A), to write to (someone); **schreiben von** (D) *or* **über** (A), to write about
der **Schreibtisch, -e,** writing table, desk
schreien (er schreit, schrie,

hat geschrien), to scream, shout, yell
der **Schuh, -e,** shoe
die **Schularbeit,** homework
die **Schule, -n,** school; **in die Schule,** to school
der **Schüler, -,** pupil
die **Schülerin, -nen,** (girl) pupil
schwarz, black
das **Schwein, -e,** hog
schwer, heavy, hard, difficult
die **Schwester, -n,** sister
schwimmen (er schwimmt, schwamm, ist geschwommen), to swim
der **See, -n,** lake
die **See, -n,** sea, ocean; **an die See,** to the beach (seashore); **an der See,** at the beach (seashore)
sehen (er sieht, sah, hat gesehen), to see; **sehen auf** (A), to look at
sehr, very (much); **sehr wenig,** very little; **danke sehr!,** thanks very much
die **Seife, -n,** soap
sein (er ist, war, ist gewesen), to be
sein, his, its
seit (D), since (a certain time); **ich bin seit einer Woche hier,** I've been here for a week
seitdem, (*conj.*) since (that time)
die **Seite, -n,** page, side
selbst, myself, yourself, etc.; even; **der Direktor selbst besuchte die Klasse,** the principal himself visited the class; **selbst Hans ist mitgekommen,** even Hans came along
selten, rare, seldom
der **September,** September
der **Sessel, -,** easy chair, upholstered armchair
setzen, to place, set; **sich setzen,** to sit down
sicher, certain(ly), sure(ly); **ja, sicher!,** yes, of course!
sie, she, her, it, they, them
Sie, you (polite)
singen (er singt, sang, hat gesungen), to sing
sitzen (er sitzt, saß, hat gesessen), to sit; **sitzen auf** (D), to sit on; **sitzen an** (D), to sit at
so, so, thus, therefore; as; well!; **soviel wie,** as much as; **so einen Hund habe ich nie gesehen,** I've never seen such a dog
sobald, as soon as
das **Sofa, -s,** sofa, couch
sofort, immediately
der **Sohn, ̈e,** son
solange, (*conj.*) as long as
solcher, such (a)

sollen (er soll, sollte, hat gesollt), ought, to be supposed (expected) to; **was soll ich tun?,** what shall I do?; **er soll heute zu Hause bleiben,** he is to stay home today; **der Film soll sehr gut sein,** the movie is supposed to be very good
der **Sommer, -,** summer
die **Sommerferien** (*pl.*), summer vacation
sondern, but (on the contrary)
der **Sonnabend,** Saturday
die **Sonne,** sun
der **Sonntag,** Sunday
sonst, else, otherwise
sorgfältig, careful(ly)
der **Spaß,** fun
spät, late; **wie spät ist es?,** what time is it?
spazieren'gehen (er geht spazieren, ging spazieren, ist spazierengegangen), to take a stroll, go for a walk
der **Spaziergang, ̈e,** stroll, walk; **einen Spaziergang machen,** to take a walk
die **Speisekarte, -n,** menu
der **Spiegel, -,** mirror
das **Spiel, -e,** play, game
spielen, to play
spitzen, to sharpen (a pencil)
der **Sport, -s,** sports
die **Sprache, -n,** language, speech
sprechen (er spricht, sprach, hat gesprochen), to speak, talk; **sprechen mit (zu)** (D), to speak to (someone)
der **Staat, -en,** state
die **Stadt, ̈e,** city; **in die Stadt,** to the city, downtown; **in der Stadt,** in the city
stark, strong; **stärker,** stronger; **stärkst-,** strongest
statt'finden (es findet statt, fand statt, hat stattgefunden), to take place, occur
stehen (er steht, stand, hat gestanden), to stand; (D) to be suitable, look good: **der Anzug steht dir gut,** the suit looks good on you; **stehen auf** (D), to be located (*on a page or shelf*)
steigen (er steigt, stieg, ist gestiegen), to climb, rise
der **Stein, -e,** stone, rock
die **Stelle, -n,** place, spot
stellen, to place, put; **eine Frage stellen,** to ask a question
sterben (er stirbt, starb, ist gestorben), to die; **sterben an** (D), to die of
still, still, quiet, unmoving
die **Stimme, -n,** voice

der **Stock,** ¨e, stick, floor (story) of a building

die **Straße, -n,** street; **auf der Straße,** on the street

die **Straßenbahn, -en,** streetcar; **mit der Straßenbahn,** by streetcar

der **Strumpf,** ¨e, stocking, sock; *pl.*, hosiery

das **Stück, -e,** piece, play *(theater)*, musical selection

der **Student (-en), -en,** college student

die **Studentin, -nen,** (girl) college student, coed

studieren, to study *(at a college)*

der **Stuhl,** ¨e, chair

die **Stunde, -n,** hour, class period; **eine halbe Stunde,** half an hour

suchen, to seek, look for; **suchen nach** (D), to search for

der **Süden,** south; **südlich,** southern, to the south

die **Symphonie, -n,** symphony

die **Tafel, -n,** blackboard, chart

der **Tag, -e,** day; **am Tage,** during the day; **eines Tages,** one day; **den ganzen Tag,** all day long; **guten Tag!,** hello!

das **Tal,** ¨er, valley

die **Tante, -n,** aunt

der **Tanz,** ¨e, dance

tanzen, to dance

die **Tasche, -n,** pocket purse, handbag

die **Tasse, -n,** cup

der **Tee,** tea

der **Teil, -e,** part, section, share

das **Telefon, -e,** telephone

telefonieren, to telephone

der **Teller, -,** plate

das **Teppich, -e,** carpet, rug

teuer (teur-), dear, expensive

das **Theater, -,** theater; **ins Theater,** to the theater

tief, deep

das **Tier, -e,** animal

die **Tinte, -n,** ink

der **Tisch, -e,** table, teacher's desk

die **Tochter,** ¨, daughter

die **Toilette, -n,** toilet

tragen (er trägt, trug, hat getragen), to carry, wear

treffen (er trifft, traf, hat getroffen), to meet

die **Treppe, -n,** stairs, staircase

treu, faithful, loyal

trinken (er trinkt, trank, hat getrunken), to drink

trotz (G), in spite of; **trotzdem,** in spite of (that), nevertheless

tun (er tut, tat, hat getan), to do, make, put; **es tut mir leid,** I'm sorry

die **Tür, -en,** door

über (D/A), over, across, above, about (concerning); **über die Straße (den Platz) gehen,** to cross the street (square); **sich freuen über** (A), to be glad (happy) about

überall, everywhere, all over

sich **überlegen,** to think over, consider; **ich werde es mir überlegen,** I'll think about it

übermorgen, day after tomorrow

übernachten, to spend the night, stay overnight

überraschen, to surprise

übersetzen (in (A)**),** to translate (into); **übersetzen Sie ins Deutsche!,** translate into German

die **Übung, -en,** exercise

die **Uhr, -en,** clock, watch, o'clock; **wieveil Uhr ist es?,** what time is it?; **es ist vier Uhr,** it is four o'clock

um (A), around, about; at *(clock time)*; **um die Ecke,** around the corner; **um neun Uhr,** at nine o'clock

und, and

ungefähr, about, approximately

uns, us, to us

unser (unsr-), our

unten, below, downstairs

unter (D/A), under, below; among; **unter ihnen** among them

sich **unterhalten (er unterhält sich, unterhielt sich, hat sich unterhalten),** to converse

unternehmen (er unternimmt, unternahm, hat unternommen), to undertake

der **Unterricht,** instruction, teaching, class session

unterrichten, to teach, instruct

unterscheiden (er unterscheidet, unterschied, hat unterschieden), to distinguish, tell apart; **der Unterschied, -e,** difference

usw., *abbrev. of* **und so weiter,** and so forth, "etc."

der **Vater,** ¨, father

verbessern, to correct

verbrennen (er verbrennt, verbrannte, hat verbrannt), to burn (= set on fire)

verbringen (er verbringt, verbrachte, hat verbracht), to spend *(time)*

verdienen, to earn

vergessen (er vergißt, vergaß, hat vergessen), to forget

das **Vergnügen, -,** pleasure, enjoyment; **viel Vergnügen!,** have fun!

verkaufen, to sell

der **Verkäufer, -,** salesman; **die Verkäuferin, -nen,** saleslady

der **Verkehr,** traffic

verlassen (er verläßt, verließ, hat verlassen), to leave; **sich verlassen auf** (A), to depend (rely) on

verlieren (er verliert, verlor, hat verloren), to lose

vermeiden (er vermeidet, vermied, hat vermieden), to avoid

versprechen (er verspricht, versprach, hat versprochen), to promise

verstehen (er versteht, verstand, hat verstanden), to understand

versuchen, to try, attempt

verwalten, to manage, supervise

die **Verzeihung,** pardon

der **Vetter, -n,** (male) cousin

viel, much, a lot (of); **viele,** many; **vielen Dank!,** thanks very much!

von (D), from, of, about, by

vor (D/A), in front of; (D) ago; **vor der Tür,** in front of the door; **es ist Viertel vor eins,** it's a quarter to one; **vor einer Woche,** a week ago

vorbei'kommen (er kommt vorbei, kam vorbei, ist vorbeigekommen), to pass by, stop in

vor'bereiten (auf (A)**),** to prepare (for)

vorgestern, day before yesterday

vor'haben (er hat vor, hatte vor, hat vorgehabt), to plan, intend, have in mind; **was hast du morgen vor?,** what are you going to do tomorrow?

vorig-, previous, last; **voriges Jahr,** last year

vor'lesen (er liest vor, las vor, hat vorgelesen), to read aloud

der **Vormittag,** forenoon; **vormittags,** in the morning, A.M.

vor'schlagen (er schlägt vor, schlug vor, hat vorgeschlagen), to suggest; (D) *to someone*

die **Vorsicht,** caution

vor'stellen, to introduce; **er stellte mich seinem Freund vor,** he introduced me to his friend; **sich vorstellen,** to imagine

wachsen (er wächst, wuchs, ist gewachsen), to grow

der **Wagen, -,** car, automobile

wahr, true; **nicht wahr?,** isn't it so?, doesn't he?, haven't you?, etc.

während (G), during; *(conj.)* while

der **Wald,** ¨er, woods, forest

die **Wand,** ¨e, wall

wandern *(aux. sein)*, to hike, roam, wander; **der Wanderer, -,** hiker; **die Wanderung, -en,** hiking trip

wann?, when?

das **Warenhaus,** ¨er, department store

warm, warm

warten (auf (A)**),** to wait (for)

warum?, why?

was?, what?; **was für ein?,** what sort of?

waschen (er wäscht, wusch, hat gewaschen), to wash; **ich wasche mir die Hände,** I'm washing my hands

das **Wasser,** water

weder . . . noch, neither . . . nor

der **Weg, -e,** road, way; **auf dem Weg,** on the way

wegen (G), on account of, because of

das **Weh,** trouble, grief, pain

die **Weihnachten** *(pl.),* Christmas; **zu Weihnachten,** for Christmas

weil, because

weiß, white

weit, far

welcher, which (one)

die **Welt,** world

wem?, to whom?

wenig, (a) little; *pl.*, few

wenn, if, when(ever)

wer, who?, he who

werden (er wird, wurde, ist geworden), to become, get (+ *adj.*); *(as aux. in fut. tense)* shall, will; **es wird kalt,** it's getting cold; **ich werde bleiben,** I shall (I'm going to) stay; **werden aus** (D), to come from; **werden zu** (D), to change into

werfen (er wirft, warf, hat geworfen), to throw

der **Westen,** west; **westlich,** western, to the west

das **Wetter,** weather

wichtig, important

wie, how, as; **wie geht's?,** how are you?; **wie heißen Sie?,** what's your name?; **wie lange?,** how long?; **so viel wie,** as much as

wieder, again; **immer**

wieder, over and over again

wiederholen, to repeat

wiedersehen, to see again; **auf Wiedersehen!,** goodbye

wieviel?, how much?; **wieviele?,** how many?; **wieviel Uhr ist es?,** what time is it?

der **Wind, -e,** wind

der **Winter,** winter

wissen (er weiß, wußte, hat gewußt), to know

wo?, where?; **woher?,** from where?; **wohin?,** to where?; **wo kommen Sie her?,** where do you come from?; **wo gehen Sie hin?,** where are you going?

die **Woche, -n,** week;

zweimal die Woche, twice a week; **das Wochenende, -n,** weekend

wohl, well, indeed, probably

wohnen, to live, dwell

die **Wohnung, -en,** apartment, dwelling

wollen (er will, wollte, hat gewollt), to will, want to

das **Wort,** word; *pl.,* **Wörter** *(single words)* and **Worte** *(connected words, e.g., the words of a poem or speech)*

der **Wortschatz, ̈e,** vocabulary

wunderbar, wonderful

wünschen, to wish

die **Wurst, ̈e,** sausage

die **Zahl, -en,** number

zahlen, to pay

zählen, to count

zeigen, to show, point out; **zeigen auf** (A), to point to

die **Zeit, -en,** time

die **Zeitung, -en,** newspaper

zerbrechen (er zerbricht, zerbrach, hat zerbrochen), to break, shatter

das **Zeugnis, -se,** report card

ziehen (er zieht, zog, hat gezogen), to pull, drag

ziemlich, rather, quite

die **Zigarette, -n,** cigarette

das **Zimmer, -,** room

zu (D), to, on, at, for, too; **zu Besuch,** for a visit; **zu Fuß,** on foot; **zum Geburtstag,** for the birthday; **zu Hause,** at home; **zu Mittag,** at noon; **zu viel,**

too much; **zu Weihnachten,** for Christmas

zuerst, (at) first

zufrieden, satisfied

der **Zug, ̈e,** train

zu'hören, to listen, pay attention (to)

zu'machen, to close

zurück, back *(adv.)*

zurück'kommen (er kommt zurück, kam zurück, ist zurückgekommen), to come back, return

zusammen, together

zu'schauen (D), to watch

zuviel, too much

zweimal, twice; **zweimal die Woche,** twice a week

zwischen (D/A), between

able: to be able to, können (er kann, konnte, hat gekonnt)

about, *(approximately)* ungefähr; *(concerning)* über (A), von (D); *(around)* um (A); **about four o'clock,** gegen vier Uhr

above, *(adv.)* oben; *(prep.)* über (D/A)

absent: to be absent, fehlen

accept, an'nehmen (er nimmt an, nahm an, hat angenommen)

accompany, mit'kommen (er kommt mit, kam mit, ist mitgekommen)

according to, nach (D); **according to the teacher,** dem Lehrer nach

acquaintance, der Bekannte (-n), -n

acquainted: to be acquainted with, kennen (er kennt, kannte, hat gekannt); **to become acquainted with,** kennen'lernen (er lernt kennen, lernte kennen, hat kennengelernt)

acquire, bekommen (er bekommt, bekam, hat bekommen)

across, über (D/A)

actor, der Schauspieler, -; **actress,** die Schauspielerin, -nen

address, die Adresse, -n

advertise, an'zeigen

after, *(prep.)* nach (D); *(conj.)* nachdem; **after school,** nach dem Unterricht

afternoon, der Nachmittag; **in the afternoon,** nachmittags (am Nachmittag); **this afternoon,** heute nachmittag; **tomorrow afternoon,** morgen nachmittag

afterwards, später, nachher, nachdem

again, wieder; **again and again,** immer wieder

against, gegen (A)

ago, vor (D); **many years ago,** vor vielen Jahren

air, die Luft

airplane, das Flugzeug, -e

all, alle, alles, ganz; **all day,** den ganzen Tag; **not at all,** gar nicht

almost, fast

alone, allein

along: to bring along, mitbringen; **to come along,** mitkommen

aloud: to read aloud, (laut) vor'lesen (er liest vor, las vor, hat vorgelesen)

already, schon

also, auch

although, obgleich

always, immer

A.M., morgens, vormittags

America, Amerika; **to America,** nach Amerika

among, unter (D); **among them,** unter ihnen

and, und

angry, böse

animal, das Tier, -e

announce, an'zeigen; **to announce oneself** (= *to report*), sich melden

another, *(different)* ein and(e)rer; *(one more)* noch ein

answer, die Antwort, -en; **to answer,** *(a person)* antworten (D); *(a question)* antworten auf (A), beantworten (A)

any: not . . . any, kein

anything, etwas; **not . . . anything,** nichts

anyway, jedenfalls

apartment, die Wohnung, -en

appear (= to look + *adj.*), aus'sehen (er sieht aus, sah aus, hat ausgesehen)

appearance, das Gesicht, -er

apple, der Apfel, ¨

approximately, ungefähr

April, der April; **in April,** im April; **on April 2,** am zweiten April

around, *(prep.)* um (A); **around the table,** um den Tisch (herum); **around 7 o'clock,** gegen 7 Uhr

arrive, an'kommen (er kommt an, kam an, ist angekommen)

as, wie, so; **as big as,** so groß wie; **as long as,** *(conj.),* solange; **as soon as,** so bald

ask, fragen; **to ask a question,** eine Frage stellen; **to ask about,** fragen nach (D); **to ask for,** bitten um (A) (er bittet, bat, hat gebeten)

assignment, die Aufgabe, -n

at, an (D/A); **at all,** gar; **at home,** zu Hause; **at the home of,** bei (D); **at six o'clock,** um sechs Uhr; **at night,** nachts; **at school,** in der Schule; **at college,**

auf der Universität; **at the station,** auf dem Bahnhof

attempt, versuchen

attention: to pay attention to, zu'hören, auf'passen, achten auf (A), beachten

August, der August

aunt, die Tante, -n

author, der Verfasser, -

automobile, das Auto, -s; der Wagen, -

autumn, der Herbst; **next autumn,** im kommenden Herbst

avenue, die Allee, -n

avoid, vermeiden (er vermeidet, vermied, hat vermieden)

await, warten auf (A); erwarten

away, weg

back, der Rücken, -; *(adv.)* zurück; **to come back,** zurück'kommen

bad, schlecht; **that's too bad,** das ist schade

ball, der Ball, ¨e

ballpoint pen, der Kugelschreiber, -

bank, die Bank, -en; **to the bank,** zur Bank

bath, das Bad, ¨er; **to take a bath,** ein Bad nehmen

bathroom, das Badezimmer; *(toilet)* die Toilette, -n, der Abort, -e

be, sein (er ist, war, ist gewesen); *(health)* gehen; **how are you?,** wie geht es Ihnen?; **I am well (better),** es geht mir gut (besser); *(present progressive: does not exist in German)* **I am working,** ich arbeite, **he is going,** er geht, etc.

beach, der Strand; **to the beach,** an die See; **at the beach,** an der See

beat, schlagen (er schlägt, schlug, hat geschlagen)

beautiful, schön

because, da, weil; **because of,** wegen (G)

become, werden (er wird, wurde, ist geworden)

bed, das Bett, -en; **to go to bed,** ins (zu) Bett gehen

bedroom, das Schlafzimmer, -

before, *(conj.)* bevor, ehe; *(prep.)* vor (D/A)

begin, an'fangen (er fängt an, fing an, hat angefangen), beginnen (er beginnt, begann, hat begonnen)

behind, hinter (D/A)

believe, glauben (D/A), meinen; **he believes her,** er glaubt ihr; **he believes it,** er glaubt es

belong to, *(be the property of)* gehören (D); *(be a part or a member of)* gehören zu (D); **it belongs to me,** es gehört mir

below, *(prep.)* unter (D/A); *(adv.)* unten

bench, die Bank, ¨e

beneath, *(prep.)* unter (D/A)

beside, neben (D/A)

besides, außer (D)

best, *(adj.)* best-; *(adv.)* am besten

better, besser

between, zwischen (D/A)

bicycle, das (Fahr)rad, ¨er

big (bigger, biggest), groß (größer, größt-)

bill, die Rechnung, -en

birthday, der Geburtstag, -e; **for my (his, her, etc.) birthday,** zum Geburtstag

bit: a little bit, ein bißchen

black, schwarz

blackboard, die (Wand)tafel, -n

blanket, die Decke, -n

blue, blau

board: to board (a vehicle), ein'steigen (in)

book, das Buch, ¨er; **bookcase,** der Schrank, ¨e; **bookshelf,** das Bücherregal, -e

boring, langweilig

borrow, entleihen (D) (er entleiht, entlieh, hat entliehen); **he borrows the book from me,** er entleiht mir das Buch

both, beide; **both my brothers,** meine beiden Brüder; **both . . . and,** sowohl . . . als (auch)

boy, der Junge (-n), -n

bread, das Brot, -e

break *(something),* brechen (er bricht, brach, hat gebrochen); **to break to pieces,** zerbrechen

breakfast, das Frühstück, -e; **to have (eat) breakfast,** frühstücken

bridge, die Brücke, -n

brief, kurz

bright, hell

bring, bringen (er bringt, brachte, hat gebracht); holen; **to bring along,** mit'bringen

brother, der Bruder, ¨

brown, braun

build, bauen

building, das Gebäude, -

burn, *(to be on fire)* brennen (es brennt, brannte, hat gebrannt); *(to set on fire)* verbrennen

bus, der (Auto)bus, -se

business, das Geschäft, -e

busy, beschäftigt; **to be busy with,** arbeiten an (D)

but, aber; *(after a negative clause)* sondern

butter, die Butter

buy, kaufen; **to buy a ticket,** eine Fahrkarte lösen

by, *(authorship)* von (D); *(vehicle)* mit (D); **by Goethe,** von Goethe; **he's going by bus,** er fährt mit dem Autobus

cake, der Kuchen, -

call, rufen (er ruft, rief, hat gerufen); *(to name)* nennen (er nennt, nannte, hat genannt); **to call up (on the phone),** an'rufen; **to call for (someone),** ab'holen; **to be called,** heißen (er heißt, hieß, hat geheißen)

camera, die Kamera, -s

can können (er kann, konnte, hat gekonnt); (= **may**) dürfen (er darf, durfte, hat gedurft)

car, das Auto, -s, der Wagen, -

card, die Karte, -n

care: to take care of, sorgen für (A)

careful (= **cautious**), vorsichtig; **to be careful,** auf'passen; **carefully,** sorgfältig

carry, tragen (er trägt, trug, hat getragen)

castle, das Schloß *(gen.* Schlosses; *pl.* Schlösser)

catch, fangen (er fängt, fing, hat gefangen); **to catch cold,** sich erkälten

cathedral, der Dom, -e

caution, die Vorsicht

ceiling, die Decke, -n

celebrate, feiern; **celebration,** das Fest, -e

cellar, der Keller, -

certain, sicher; **certainly,** gewiß

chair, der Stuhl, ⸚e; **easy chair,** der Sessel, -

chalk, die Kreide

chalkboard, die (Wand)-tafel, -n

change, ändern

chart, die Tafel, -n

cheap, billig

check *(restaurant bill),* die Rechnung, -en; **to check (up) on,** nach'schlagen, nach'sehen

child, das Kind , -er

Christmas, die Weihnachten *(pl.);* **for Christmas,** zu Weihnachten

church, die Kirche, -n

cigarette, die Zigarette, -n

city, die Stadt, ⸚e; **city hall,** das Rathaus, ⸚er

class, die Klasse, -n; *(= lesson)* der Unterricht, -; *(= class hour)* die Stunde, -n

classroom, das Klassenzimmer, -

climb, steigen (er steigt, stieg, ist gestiegen)

clock, die Uhr, -en

close, schließen (er schließt, schloß, hat geschlossen), zu'machen

closet, *(for clothes)* der Kleiderschrank, ⸚e

clothes, die Kleider *(pl.);* **clothing,** die Bekleidung

coat, der Mantel, ⸚

coed, die Studentin, -nen

coffee, der Kaffee

cold (colder, coldest), kalt (kälter, kältest-); **I am cold,** mir ist kalt; **to have a bad cold,** stark erkältet sein

color, die Farbe, -n

comb, sich kämmen

come, kommen (er kommt, kam, ist gekommen); **to come along,** mit'kommen (er kommt mit, kam mit, ist mitgekommen); **to come back,** zurück'kommen; **to come from,** (her)kommen aus; **to come here,** her'kommen; **to come home,** nach Hause kommen; **he's not coming,** er kommt nicht

complete, ganz; **to complete,** erledigen

concert, das Konzert, -e

converse (with), sich unterhalten (mit) (er unterhält sich, unterhielt sich, hat sich unterhalten)

cook (= to boil), kochen

cool, kühl

corner, die Ecke, -n; **on the corner,** an der Ecke

correct, richtig; **my watch is correct,** meine Uhr geht richtig; **to correct,** korrigieren, verbessern

cost, kosten

couch, das Sofa, -s

could, *(was able to)* konnte

country, das Land, ⸚er; **in the country,** auf dem Land; **to go to the country,** aufs Land fahren

course: of course, gewiß

cousin, *(male)* der Vetter, -; *(female)* die Kusine, -n

cup, die Tasse, -n; **a cup of tea,** eine Tasse Tee

customer, der Kunde (-n), -n

cut, schneiden (er schneidet, schnitt, hat geschnitten)

dance, der Tanz, ⸚e; **to dance,** tanzen

dark, dunkel (dunkl-)

date *(calendar),* das Datum *(pl.* Daten)

daughter, die Tochter, ⸚

day, der Tag, -e; **every day,** jeden Tag; **all day,** den ganzen Tag; **three days ago,** vor drei Tagen

deal: a great deal (of), viel

dear, lieb; *(= expensive)* teuer (teur-)

December, der Dezember

deep, tief

delay, sich auf'halten (er hält sich auf, hielt sich auf, hat sich aufgehalten)

depart, ab'fahren (er fährt ab, fuhr ab, ist abgefahren)

department store, das Warenhaus, ⸚er

depend: to depend on, sich verlassen auf (A) (er verläßt sich, verließ sich, hat sich verlassen); **it all depends,** es kommt darauf an

desk, *(teacher's)* der Tisch, -e; *(pupil's)* das Pult, -e

detain, auf'halten (er hält auf, hielt auf, hat aufgehalten)

dessert, der Nachtisch, -e

did *(as aux.:* **did you have?, did they go?,** etc.), *use the present perfect tense:* hast du gehabt?, sind sie gegangen?, etc.

die, sterben (er stirbt, starb, ist gestorben)

difficult, schwer

dinner, das Abendessen; **to have (eat) dinner,** zu Abend essen

do, machen, tun (er tut, tat, hat getan); *as aux.* (**do you have?, does he go?,** etc.), *use the present tense:* haben Sie?, geht er?, *etc.*

doctor, der Arzt, ⸚e, der Doktor, -en

dog, der Hund, -e

donkey, der Esel, -

door, die Tür, -en

downstairs, unten

downtown: to go downtown, in die Stadt gehen (fahren)

dress, das Kleid, -er; **to dress oneself, get dressed,** sich an'ziehen (er zieht sich an, zog sich an, hat sich angezogen)

drink, trinken (er trinkt, trank, hat getrunken)

drive, fahren (er fährt, fuhr, ist gefahren)

drop off (at a place), ab'setzen

dull (= **boring**), langweilig

during, während (G)

dwell, wohnen; **dwelling,** die Wohnung, -en

each, jeder; **each other,** einander *(or use reflex. pron.)*; **they speak to each other,** sie sprechen miteinander; **they love each other,** sie lieben sich

early, früh; **(at the) earliest,** erst-

earn, verdienen

earth, die Erde

east, der Osten; **East Germany,** Ostdeutschland; **eastern,** östlich

Easter, die Ostern

easy, leicht

eat, *(for human subjects)* essen (er ißt, aß, hat gegessen); *(animals)* fressen (er frißt, fraß, hat gefressen)

either . . . or, entweder . . . oder

elevator, der Fahrstuhl, ⸚e

employee, *(office)* der Angestellte (-n), -n; *(government)* der Beamte (-n), -n

end, das Ende, -n; **at (in) the end,** am Ende; **at the end of April,** Ende April

English: do you speak English?, sprechen Sie Englisch?

enjoy: to enjoy oneself, sich amüsieren, sich vergnügen (er vergnügt sich, vergnügte sich, hat sich vergnügt)

enough, genug

enter, ein'treten (er tritt ein, trat ein, ist eingetreten), herein'kommen (er kommt herein, kam herein, ist hereingekommen)

erase, *(blackboard)* ab'wischen; *(on paper)* aus'radieren

eraser, *(pencil)* der (Radier)-gummi, -s; *(blackboard)* der Wischer, -

error, der Fehler, -

etc., usw. (= und so weiter)

even, *(adv.)* eben, selbst; **even Hans came,** selbst Hans ist gekommen; **even if he comes,** wenn er auch kommt

evening, der Abend, -e; **in the evening,** am Abend, abends; **Monday evening,** Montag abend; **this evening,** heute abend; **yesterday evening,** gestern abend

every, jeder; **every day,** jeden Tag, alle Tage

everybody, jeder(mann)

everything, alles

everywhere, überall

exact, genau

examination, das Examen, -, die Prüfung, -en; **to take an examination,** eine Prüfung ab'legen

excellent, ausgezeichnet

except (for), außer (D)

excursion, der Ausflug, ∸e;
to go on an excursion,
einen Ausflug machen
excuse, die Ausflucht, ∸e; **to
excuse,** entschuldigen
exercise, die Übung, -en
expect, erwarten
expensive, teuer (teur-)
explain, erklären
eye, das Auge, -n

face, das Gesicht, -er
fail, durch'fallen (er fällt
durch, fiel durch, ist durchgefallen); **to fail an examination,** in einer Prüfung durchfallen
fall, der Herbst; **to fall,**
fallen (er fällt, fiel, ist
gefallen); **to fall asleep,**
ein'schlafen (er schläft ein,
schlief ein, ist eingeschlafen)
false, falsch
family, die Familie, -n
famous, berühmt
far, fern, weit
·farm, der Bauernhof, ∸e;
(American) die Farm, -en
farmer, der Bauer (-n), -n
fast, schnell; **my watch is
fast,** meine Uhr geht vor
fat, dick
father, der Vater, ∸
February, der Februar
feel, (sich) fühlen; **I don't
feel well,** ich fühle mich
nicht wohl; **I feel cold,** mir
ist kalt
fetch, holen
few, wenige *(pl.);* **a few,**
einige, ein paar
field, das Feld, -er
fifty, fünfzig
film, der Film, -e
find, finden (er findet, fand,
hat gefunden)
fine, schön, herrlich; **I'm fine,**
es geht mir gut
finish, erledigen, fertig'machen; **finished,** fertig
fire, das Feuer
first, erst, zuerst; **the first
time,** das erste Mal
five, fünf
floor, der Boden, ∸; **on the
second floor,** im ersten
Stock
flower, die Blume, -n
flunk, durch'fallen (er fällt
durch, fiel durch, ist durchgefallen)
follow, folgen (D); **I followed him,** ich bin ihm
gefolgt
foot, der Fuß, ∸e
for, für (A); *(= because)*
denn; **for dinner,** zum
Abendessen; **for the first
time,** zum ersten Mal; **I've
been here for a week,** ich
bin schon seit einer Woche
hier; **he lived in Berlin for**

two years, er wohnte zwei
Jahre in Berlin; **to ask for,**
bitten um (A)
foreign, fremd; **foreign language,** die Fremdsprache,
-n
foreigner, der Ausländer, -
forenoon, der Vormittag
forest, der Wald, ∸er
forget, vergessen (er vergißt,
vergaß, hat vergessen)
forty, vierzig
fountain pen, die Füllfeder,
-n
four, vier
free, frei
Friday, der Freitag; **on
Friday,** am Freitag
friend, *(m.)* der Freund, -e;
(f.) die Freundin, -nen
from, von (D), aus (D); **a
letter from home,** ein
Brief von zu Hause; **where
do you come from?,** woher
kommen Sie? (wo kommen
Sie her?); **I come from the
United States,** ich komme
aus den Vereinigten Staaten
front: in front of, vor (D/A)
fruit, das Obst, -arten
fun, der Spaß, das Vergnügen; **have fun!,** viel Spaß!,
viel Vergnügen!
furniture, das Möbel, -

garage, die Garage, -n
garden, der Garten, ∸
generally, im allgemeinen,
gewöhnlich
gentleman, der Herr (-n),
-en
German, *(adj.)* deutsch;
(language) das Deutsch;
(person) m., der Deutsche
(-n), -n (ein Deutscher); f.,
die Deutsche, -n; **German
class,** der Deutschunterricht, -; **in German,** auf
deutsch; **to translate into
German,** ins Deutsche
übersetzen; **you speak
German well,** Sie sprechen
gut Deutsch
Germany, Deutschland;
East Germany, Ost-
deutschland
get, *(receive)* bekommen (er
bekommt, bekam, hat be-
kommen); *(fetch)* holen;
(become) werden (er wird,
wurde, ist geworden); **to
get dressed,** sich an'zieh-
en (er zieht sich an, zog
sich an, hat sich angezogen);
to get into (a vehicle),
ein'steigen (er steigt ein,
stieg ein, ist eingestiegen);
to get married, sich
verheiraten; **to get off,**
aus'steigen; **to get ready,**
sich fertig'machen; **to get
to know,** kennen'lernen;

to get up, auf'stehen (er
steht auf, stand auf, ist
aufgestanden); **it's getting
cold,** es wird kalt
gift, das Geschenk, -e
girl, das Mädchen, -; **girl
friend,** die Freundin, -nen
give, geben (er gibt, gab, hat
gegeben); *(make a gift of)*
schenken
glad: to be glad, sich freuen;
I'm glad about that, Das
freut mich
gladly, gern
glass, das Glas, ∸er
glove, der Handschuh, -e
go, gehen (er geht, ging, ist
gegangen); *(in a vehicle)*
fahren (er fährt, fuhr, ist
gefahren); **to go away,**
hin'fahren, weg'fahren; **to
go home,** nach Hause
gehen; **to go out,** hinaus'-
fahren, aus'gehen; **to go
there,** hin'gehen; **to go by
train (bus),** mit dem Zug
(Autobus) fahren; **to go to
the movies,** ins Kino gehen;
I'm going, ich gehe, ich
fahre; **going to** (= shall
or will), werden; **I'm going
to see him,** ich werde ihn
sehen
God, der Gott; **the gods,** die
Götter
good, gut; **good morning,**
guten Morgen; **goodbye,**
auf Wiedersehen
grade, *(year in school)* die
Klasse, -n, die Stufe, -n;
(mark on test or report card)
die Note, -n, die Zensur,
-en
grandfather, der Großvater, ∸; **grandmother,** die
Großmutter, ∸
great, groß; **great!,** prima!;
a great deal, viel, vieles
green, grün
greet, grüßen; **greeting,**
der Gruß, ∸e
grow, wachsen (er wächst,
wuchs, ist gewachsen)
guest, der Gast, ∸e

hair, das Haar, -e
half, halb, die Hälfte; **at half
past twelve,** um halb eins;
half an hour, eine halbe
Stunde; **half of . . . ,** die
Hälfte von (D) . . .
hall, der Korridor, -e
hand, die Hand, ∸e; **to
shake hands,** (sich) die
Hand geben; **to hand**
(something to someone),
reichen; **to hand in,**
ein'reichen
hang, hängen (es hängt, hing,
hat gehungen)
happen, geschehen (es ge-
schiet, geschah, ist gesche-

hen), passieren (ist passiert)
happy, fröhlich, glücklich; **to
be happy (about),** sich
freuen (an (D) *or* über (A))
hard (= *difficult*), schwer; **to
work hard,** schwer arbei-
ten; **to study hard,** fleißig
studieren
hardly, kaum
hat, der Hut, ∸e
hate, hassen
have, haben (er hat, hatte,
hat gehabt); **do you have
. . .?,** haben Sie . . .?; **to
have to,** müssen (er muß,
mußte, hat gemußt); **I have
to go,** ich muß gehen
he, er
head, der Kopf, ∸e
**headache: to have a head-
ache,** Kopfschmerzen haben
healthy, gesund
hear, hören
heart, das Herz (-ens), -en
heavy, schwer
help, helfen (D) (er hilft, half,
hat geholfen)
her, (D) ihr; (A) sie; *(pos-
sess. adj.)* ihr; **her book,** ihr
Buch
here, hier; **to come here,**
her'kommen (er kommt her,
kam her, ist hergekommen)
high (higher, highest), hoch
(höher, höchst-)
highway, die Autobahn, -en
hike, wandern (ist gewandert);
hiker, der Wanderer, -;
hiking trip, die Wanderung, -en; **to hitchhike,**
per Anhalter fahren
him, (D) ihm; (A) ihn
his, sein
history, die Geschichte, -n
hit, schlagen (er schlägt,
schlug, hat geschlagen)
hog, das Schwein, -e
hold, halten (er hält, hielt,
hat gehalten); **to hold up**
(= *delay*), auf'halten
holiday, der Feiertag, -e, das
Fest, -e
home: at home, zu Hause;
at the home of, bei (D);
to go home, nach Hause
gehen
homework, die Schularbeit,
-en; **to do homework,**
die Schularbeit machen
hope, hoffen; **I hope he
comes soon,** hoffentlich
kommt er bald
horse, das Pferd, -e
hospital, das Krankenhaus,
∸er
hostel, die Jugendherberge,
-n
hot, heiß; **I'm hot,** mir ist
heiß
hotel, das Hotel, -s
hour, die Stunde, -n
house das Haus ∸er

how, wie; **how are you?,** wie geht's?, wie geht es Ihnen?; **how long?,** wie lange?; **how many?,** wie viele?; **how much?,** wieviel?

however, aber, doch

human being, der Mensch (-en), -en

hundred: a hundred, hundert; **two hundred,** zweihundert

hungry, hungrig; **I am hungry,** ich habe Hunger, ich bin hungrig

hurry, sich beeilen

husband, der Mann, ⸚er

if, wenn; *(= whether)* ob: **I don't know if he's coming,** ich weiß nicht, ob er kommt

ill, krank

imagine, sich vor'stellen

immediately, gleich, sofort

important, wichtig

in, in (D/A); **in front of,** vor (D/A); **in spite of,** trotz (G), trotzdem *(conj.)*; **in May,** im Mai; **in school,** in der Schule; **into,** in (A)

incorrect, falsch

inexpensive, billig

ink, die Tinte, -n

inside, drinnen

instead of, (an)statt (G)

intend, vor'haben (er hat vor, hatte vor, hat vorgehabt)

interest, interessieren; **to be interested in,** sich interessieren für (A); **interesting,** interessant

introduce, vor'stellen; **she introduces me to the guests,** sie stellt mich den Gästen vor

invite, ein'laden (er lädt ein, lud ein, hat eingeladen); *(to an event)* einladen zu (D); *(to a place)* einladen in (A)

it, es, er, sie

its, sein, ihr

January, der Januar

job, die Arbeit, -en; *(office position)* die Stellung, -en

journey, die Reise, -n

joy, die Freude, -n

July, der Juli; **in July,** im Juli

jump, springen (er springt, sprang, ist gesprungen)

June, der Juni

just, eben, gerade, recht; *(= only)* nur; **he has just come in,** er ist eben hereingekommen; **just right,** gerade richtig; **just in time,** zur rechten Zeit, rechtzeitig

key, der Schlüssel, -

kind: what kind of, was für · (ein); **all kinds of,** allerlei

king, der König, -e

kitchen, die Küche, -n

know, *(a fact)* wissen (er weiß, wußte, hat gewußt); *(a person or place)* kennen (er kennt, kannte, hat gekannt); *(a language)* können (er kann, konnte, hat gekonnt); **to know about,** wissen von (D)

lady, die Dame, -n; **young lady,** das Fräulein, -

lake, der See, -n

lamp, die Lampe, -n

language, die Sprache, -n

large (larger, largest), groß (größer, größt-)

last, letzt-; **at last,** endlich; **last night,** gestern abend; **last summer,** vorigen Sommer; **last week,** vorige Woche; **to last,** dauern

late, spät; *(=tardy)* zu spät; **latest,** letzt-

laugh, lachen

lay *(= to put, place)*, legen

lazy, faul

leader, der Führer, -

learn, lernen; **to learn by heart,** auswendig lernen

leave, lassen (er läßt, ließ, hat gelassen); *(a person or place)* verlassen; *(= depart)* ab'fahren (er fährt ab, fuhr ab, ist abgefahren)

left: to the left, links

leg, das Bein, -e

lend, leihen (er leiht, lieh, hat geliehen); **he lends me his book,** er leiht mir sein Buch

lesson, die Lektion, -en, die Aufgabe, -n

let, lassen (er läßt, ließ, hat gelassen); **let's go!,** gehen wir!

letter, der Brief, -e

library, die Bibliothek, -en, die Bücherei, -en

lie *(= be situated)*, liegen (er liegt, lag, hat gelegen); **to lie down,** sich legen

life, das Leben, -

light, *(color)* hell; *(= not heavy)* leicht

like, *(adv.)* wie; **to like,** gern haben, mögen (er mag, mochte, hat gemocht); *(= be pleased with)* gefallen (D) (es gefällt, gefiel, hat gefallen); **to like (to do something),** gern + *verb*; **would like,** möchte(n) (gern); **I like it,** ich habe es gern, es gefällt mir; **I don't like him,** ich mag ihn nicht; **I like to swim,** ich schwimme gern; **I would**

like to go, ich möchte (gern) gehen

listen, zu'hören (D), sich an'hören (A); **they are listening to the concert,** sie hören sich das Konzert an

little, *(= small)* klein; *(quantity)* wenig; **a little (bit),** ein bißchen, ein wenig

live, leben; *(= to reside)* wohnen

located: to be located, liegen (er liegt, lag, hat gelegen); *(on a page or shelf)* stehen auf (D)

long (longer, longest), lang (länger, längst-); **a long time,** lange

look, *(= appear)* aus'sehen (er sieht aus, sah aus, hat ausgesehen); **to look at,** an'sehen; **to look for,** suchen; **to look forward to,** sich freuen auf (A); **to look up** (words in a dictionary, etc.), nach'schlagen (er schlägt nach, schlug nach, hat nachgeschlagen); **look out!,** passen Sie auf!; **the dress looks good on you,** das Kleid steht dir gut

lose, verlieren (er verliert, verlor, hat verloren)

lot: a lot of, viel(es)

loud, laut

love, lieben

luck: good luck, das Glück; **lucky,** glücklich; **bad luck,** das Pech

lunch, das Mittagessen; **to have (eat) lunch,** zu Mittag essen

mail, die Post; **to mail a letter,** einen Brief auf die Post bringen

make, machen

man, der Mann, ⸚er; *(= mankind)* der Mensch (-en), -en

many, viele; **many a,** mancher (manch ein)

map, die Landkarte, -n

March, der März; **in March,** im März

mark, *(German money)* die Mark; *(= grade)* die Zensur, -en

market, der Markt, ⸚e; **to the market,** auf den Markt; **marketplace,** der Marktplatz, ⸚e

mathematics, die Mathematik

matter: what's the matter?, was ist los?; **it doesn't matter,** es macht nichts

may, dürfen (er darf, durfte, hat gedurft); **may I come?,** darf ich kommen?

May, der Mai

me, (D) mir; (A) mich

mean, *(adj.)* böse; **to mean,** bedeuten, meinen

meat, das Fleisch

medicine, die Medizin, -en

meet, treffen (er trifft, traf, hat getroffen); *(= to make someone's acquaintance)* kennen'lernen; **let's meet at the movies,** treffen wir uns beim Kino; **he met her (made her acquaintance) yesterday,** er lernte sie gestern kennen (*or* er hat sie gestern kennengelernt)

member, das Mitglied, -er; **to be a member of,** gehören zu (D)

menu, die Speisekarte, -n

middle: in the middle of, in der Mitte + *gen.*

midnight, die Mitternacht

milk, die Milch

minute, die Minute, -n

mirror, der Spiegel, -

Miss, das Fräulein, -

miss, *(a class)* schwänzen; *(a train)* verpassen; **to be missing,** fehlen

mistake, der Fehler, -

Monday, der Montag; **on Monday,** am Montag

money, das Geld

month, der Monat, -e

moon, der Mond

more, mehr; **more than,** mehr als; **once more,** noch einmal

morning, der Morgen, -; **all morning,** den ganzen Morgen; **in the morning,** morgens; **this morning,** heute morgen (früh); **yesterday morning,** gestern früh; **tomorrow morning,** morgen früh

most, meist-; **most people,** die meisten Leute

mother, die Mutter, ⸚

mountain, der Berg, -e

move, ziehen (er zieht, zog, ist gezogen); **to move out,** aus'ziehen

movie, der Film, -e; **movie theater,** das Kino, -s; **to go to the movies,** ins Kino gehen

Mr., Herr; **Mr. Smith's hat,** Herrn Schmidts Hut

Mrs., Frau

much, viel; **how much?,** wieviel?

music, die Musik

must, müssen (er muß, mußte, hat gemußt)

my, mein

name, der Name (-ns), -n; **to name,** nennen (er nennt, nannte, hat genannt); **can you name the days of the week?,** kannst du die Wochentage nennen?; **to**

be named, heißen (er heißt, hieß, hat geheißen); **what's your name?,** wie heißen Sie?; **my name is Charles,** ich heiße Karl

natural(ly), natürlich

nasty, böse

near, nahe (D), bei (D)

necktie, die Krawatte, -n

need, brauchen

neighbor, *(m.)* der Nachbar (-n), -n, *(f.)* die Nachbarin, -nen; **neighborhood,** die Nähe, die Gegend

neither . . . nor, weder . . . noch

never, nie, nimmer

new, neu

newspaper, die Zeitung, -en

next, nächst-; **next month,** nächsten Monat; **next to,** neben (D/A)

nice, nett, schön

night, die Nacht, ⸚e; **last night,** gestern abend; **to spend the night,** übernachten

nine, neun

no, nein; *(= not any)* kein; **I have no time,** ich habe keine Zeit

nobody (no one), niemand

noise, der Lärm

noon: at noon, mittags

north, der Norden; **northern,** nördlich

not, nicht; **not . . . any,** kein; **not at all,** gar nicht; **not only . . . but also,** nicht nur . . . sondern auch; **not yet,** noch nicht; **not until,** erst; **he's not coming until tomorrow,** er kommt erst morgen an

notebook, das Heft, -e

nothing, nichts

notice, beachten, sich merken auf (A)

novel, der Roman, -e

November, der November

now, jetzt, nun

nowhere, nirgends

number, die Zahl, -en

nurse, die Krankenschwester, -n

obey, folgen (D), hören auf (A)

occur, *(= to happen)* geschehen (es geschieht, geschah, ist geschehen); *(= to take place)* statt'finden (es findet statt, fand statt, hat stattgefunden)

ocean, das Meer, -e, die See, -n

o'clock: at 7 o'clock in the evening, um 7 Uhr abends

October, der Oktober

of, von (D); **a glass of water,** ein Glas Wasser

office, das Büro, -s

official, *(government)* der Beamte (-n), -n

often, oft

old (older, oldest), alt (älter, ältest-)

on, *(vertical surface)* an (D/A); *(horizontal surface)* auf (D/A); **on Monday,** am Montag; **on April 4,** am vierten April

once, einmal; **once more,** noch einmal

one, ein; *(counting)* eins; **one day,** eines Tages; **which one?,** welcher?; **this one,** dieser; *(indef. pron.)* man

one and a half, anderthalb

only, *(adv.)* nur; *(adj.)* einzig-; **his only son,** sein einziger Sohn; **it's only 3 o'clock,** es ist erst 3 Uhr

open, *(adj.)* offen; **to open,** auf'machen, öffnen

or, oder

orchestra, das Orchester, -

order, *(in a restaurant, etc.)* bestellen

other, ander-

ought, sollen (er soll, sollte, hat gesollt); **I ought to go,** ich sollte gehen

our, unser (unsr-)

out (of), aus (D); *(toward the speaker)* heraus; *(away from the speaker)* hinaus; **he came out of the house,** er kam aus dem Haus heraus

outside, draußen

oven, der Ofen, ⸚

over, über (D/A); **over there,** (da) drüben; **overhead,** oben; **class is over,** der Unterricht ist aus; **he's over thirty,** er ist über dreißig Jahre alt

own, eigen (eign-); **bring your own pencil,** bringe deinen eig(e)nen Bleistift!

package, das Paket, -e

page, die Seite, -n; **on page 20,** auf Seite 20

pain, das Weh, der Schmerz, -en

paint, *(pictures)* malen; *(a house)* an'streichen; **painting,** das Gemälde, -

pair, das Paar, -e; **a pair of shoes,** ein Paar Schuhe

palace, das Schloß *(pl.* Schlösser)

paper, das Papier; **sheet of paper,** das Blatt, ⸚er

pardon, die Verzeihung; **pardon me,** Verzeihung, bitte

parents, die Eltern *(pl.)*

park, der Park, -e *(or* -s)

part, der Teil, -e; **be part of,** gehören zu (D)

party, die Party; **political party,** die Partei, -en

pass: to pass by, vorbei'kommen (er kommt vorbei, kam vorbei, ist vorbeigekommen); **to pass a test,** eine Prüfung bestehen

past, die Vergangenheit; **half past six,** halb sieben

pay: to pay for, bezahlen; **to pay attention (to),** auf'passen, beachten

pen, die Feder, -n; **fountain pen,** die Füllfeder, -n; **ballpoint pen,** der Kugelschreiber, -

pencil, der Bleistift, -e

penny, der Pfennig, -e

people, die Leute *(pl.)*

percent, das Prozent

period, *(in school)* die Stunde, -n

phone, das Telefon, -e; **to phone,** an'rufen (er ruft an, rief an, hat angerufen)

physician, der Arzt, ⸚e

piano, das Klavier, -e

pick up (someone), ab'holen

picture, das Bild, -er; **to take pictures,** Aufnahmen machen

piece, das Stück, -e

pink, rosa

place, der Platz, ⸚e, die Stelle, -n; **marketplace,** der Marktplatz, ⸚e; **to place,** legen, setzen, stellen

plan, der Plan, ⸚e; **what do you plan to do tomorrow?,** was haben Sie morgen vor?

plate, der Teller, -

play, *(theater)* das Stück, -e, das Schauspiel, -e; **to play,** spielen

please, *(adv.)* bitte; **to please,** freuen, gefallen (D) (es gefällt, gefiel, hat gefallen)

P.M., nachmittags, abends

pocket, die Tasche, -n

poem, das Gedicht, -e

poet, der Dichter, -

point to, zeigen auf (A)

policeman, der Polizist (-en), -en

polite, höflich

politics, die Politik

pool: swimming pool, das Schwimmbad, ⸚er

poor, arm

popular, beliebt; **popular song,** der Schlager, -

possible, möglich

post office, das Postamt, ⸚er

potato, die Kartoffel, -n

prefer, lieber + *verb*; **I prefer milk,** ich trinke lieber Milch; **I prefer to stay home,** ich bleibe lieber zu Hause

prepare, vor'bereiten, fertig'machen; **to prepare for,** vor'bereiten auf (A)

present, *(= gift)* das Geschenk, -e; *(time)* die Gegenwart; **at present,** augenblicklich

president, der Präsident (-en) -en

pretty, hübsch, schön

price, der Preis, -e

principal, *(m).* der Direktor, -en; *(f).* die Direktorin, -nen

prize, der Preis, -e

probably, wohl, wahrscheinlich; **he'll probably come,** er wird wohl noch kommen

program, das Programm, -e

promise, versprechen (er verspricht, versprach, hat versprochen)

pull, ziehen (er zieht, zog, hat gezogen)

pupil, *(m.)* der Schüler, -; *(f.)* die Schülerin, -nen

purse, die Tasche, -n

put, stellen, legen

question, die Frage, -n; **to ask a question,** eine Frage stellen

quick, schnell

quiet, ruhig, still; **be quiet!,** Ruhe!

quite, ganz

quiz, die Prüfung, -en

radio, das Radio, -s

railroad, die Eisenbahn, -en; **railroad station,** der Bahnhof, ⸚e

rain, der Regen; **to rain,** regnen; **it's raining,** es regnet

rapid(ly), schnell

rare, selten

rather, lieber + *verb*; *(= somewhat)* ziemlich; **I'd rather stay home,** ich bleibe lieber zu Hause

reach, *(= to arrive at)* erreichen

read, lesen (er liest, las, hat gelesen); **to read aloud,** vor'lesen; **to read silently,** für sich lesen

ready, fertig, bereit

really, wirklich

receive, bekommem (er bekommt, bekam, hat bekommen), an'nehmen (er nimmt an, nahm an, hat angenommen)

record, *(phonograph)* die (Schall)platte, -n; **record player,** der Plattenspieler, -

recover, sich erholen

red, rot

relative, der Verwandte (-n), -n

remain, bleiben (er bleibt, blieb, ist geblieben)

remember, sich erinnern an (A)

repeat, wiederholen

reply, antworten

report, der Bericht, -e; **to report,** berichten; **report card,** das Zeugnis, -se

rest, sich erholen

restaurant, das Restaurant, -s

return, *(= come back)* zurück'kommen; *(= give back)* zurück'geben; *(= ride back)* zurück'fahren; **to return home,** nach Hause kommen

rich, reich

ride, *(in a vehicle)* fahren (er fährt, fuhr, ist gefahren); *(on horseback)* reiten (er reitet, ritt, ist geritten)

right, *(= correct)* richtig; **the right hand,** die rechte Hand; **to the right,** rechts; **right away,** sofort; **to be right,** recht haben

ring, der Ring, -e

river, der Fluß *(pl.* Flüsse)

road, der Weg, -e

rock, der Stein, -e

roll, *(bread)* das Brötchen, -

roof, das Dach, ̈-er

room, das Zimmer, -

run, laufen (er läuft, lief, ist gelaufen)

sad, traurig

salesman, der Verkäufer, -; **saleslady,** die Verkäuferin, -nen

same, gleich; **the same,** derselbe, dieselbe, dasselbe; *pl.,* dieselben; **at the same time,** zur gleichen Zeit

satisfied, zufrieden

Saturday, der Sonnabend, der Samstag

sausage, die Wurst, ̈-e

say, sagen

school, die Schule, -n; **at (in) school,** in der Schule; **to school,** in die Schule, zur Schule

science, die Wissenschaft, -en

sea, die See, -n, das Meer, -e

search: to search for, suchen nach (D)

seashore: at the seashore, an der See; **to the seashore,** an die See

seat, der Platz, ̈-e; **to take a seat,** Platz nehmen

second: the second time, das zweite Mal

see, sehen (er sieht, sah, hat gesehen)

seek, suchen

seem, *(= look)* aus'sehen (er sieht aus, sah aus, hat ausgesehen); **he seems tired,** er sieht müde aus; **it seems to me that . . . ,** es scheint mir, daß . . .

seldom, selten

sell, verkaufen

send, schicken

sentence, der Satz, ̈-e

September, der September

set, setzen; **to set down,** legen

seven, sieben; **seventeen,** siebzehn

several, einige, ein paar, mehrere; **several times,** mehrmals

shake hands, (sich) die Hand geben

shall, *(aux. of fut. tense)* werden; **I shall read,** ich werde lesen

shatter, zerbrechen (er zerbricht, zerbrach, hat zerbrochen)

shave, sich rasieren

she, sie

sheet (of paper), das Blatt, ̈-er

ship, das Schiff, -e

shirt, das Hemd, -en

shoe, der Schuh, -e; **a pair of shoes,** ein Paar Schuhe

shop, der Laden, ̈-; **pastry shop,** die Konditorei, -en; **to go shopping,** einkaufen gehen

short (shorter, shortest), kurz (kürzer, kürzest-)

should, sollen; **he should stay,** er soll bleiben

shout, rufen (er ruft, rief, hat gerufen), schreien

show, *(= performance)* die Vorstellung; **to show,** zeigen

shut, schließen (er schließt, schloß, hat geschlossen), zu'machen

sick, krank

side, die Seite, -n

simple, einfach

since, *(= because)* da, weil; *(= ever since)* seit (D), seitdem *(conj.)*

sing, singen (er singt, sang, hat gesungen)

single, einzig-

sister, die Schwester, -n

sit, sitzen (er sitzt, saß, hat gesessen); **to sit down,** sich setzen

six, sechs; **sixty,** sechzig

sky, der Himmel

sleep, schlafen (er schläft, schlief, hat geschlafen); **to fall asleep,** ein'schlafen; **to go to sleep,** schlafen gehen

slow, langsam

small, klein

smart, klug

smoke, rauchen

snow, der Schnee; **it's snowing,** es schneit

so, *(= therefore)* also

soap, die Seife, -n

sock, der Strumpf, ̈-e

soccer, der Fußball

sofa, das Sofa, -s

some, *(= a little)* etwas; *(= a few)* einige; *(often omitted)* **do you have some matches?,** haben Sie Streichhölzer?; **some day,** eines Tages

someone, jemand

something, etwas

sometimes, manchmal

somewhere, irgendwo

son, der Sohn, ̈-e

song, das Lied, -er; **popular song,** der Schlager, -

soon, bald

sorry: I'm sorry, es tut mir leid

sort: what sort of?, was für (ein)?; **all sorts of,** allerlei

south, der Süden; **southern,** südlich

speak, sprechen (er spricht, sprach, hat gesprochen), reden

special, besonder-

spend, *(money)* aus'geben (er gibt aus, gab aus, hat ausgegeben); *(time)* verbringen (er verbringt, verbrachte, hat verbracht); **to spend the night,** übernachten

sports, der Sport

spring, der Frühling; **in the spring(time),** im Frühling

stairs, die Treppe, -n

stand, stehen (er steht, stand, hat gestanden); **to stand up,** auf'stehen (ist aufgestanden)

state, der Staat, -en; **the state of Texas,** der Staat Texas

station: railway station, der Bahnhof, ̈-e; **at the station,** auf dem Bahnhof; **to the station,** zum Bahnhof

stay, bleiben (er bleibt, blieb, ist geblieben); **to stay with,** bleiben bei (D)

still, *(= yet)* noch; *(= quiet)* ruhig

stocking, der Strumpf, ̈-e

stone, der Stein, -e

stop, *(= halt)* an'halten (er hält an, hielt an, hat angehalten); *(= cease)* auf'hören (mit); *(at a place)* sich auf'halten; **he stops reading,** er hört auf zu lesen (*or* mit Lesen); **it has stopped raining,** es hat aufgehört zu regnen; **to stop in,** vorbei'kommen (er kommt vorbei, kam vorbei, ist vorbeigekommen)

store, der Laden, ̈-; **department store,** das Warenhaus, ̈-er

story, die Geschichte, -n; *(of a building)* der Stock, ̈-e

stove, der Herd, -e

straight, gerade; **straight ahead,** geradeaus

street, die Straße, -n; **in the**

street, auf der Straße; **streetcar,** die Straßenbahn, -en

strike, schlagen (er schlägt, schlug, hat geschlagen); *(stop work)* streiken

stroll, der Spaziergang, ̈-e; **to stroll,** spazieren'gehen (er geht spazieren, ging spazieren, ist spazierengegangen)

strong (stronger, strongest), stark (stärker, stärkst-)

struggle, der Kampf, ̈-e

student, *(college)* m., der Student (-en), -en; f., die Studentin, -nen

study, *(one's lesson, assignment, etc.)* lernen; *(a college subject)* studieren

such (a), solcher, so ein; **such a house,** so ein Haus; **such a pretty girl,** so ein hübsches Mädchen

suggest, vor'schlagen (er schlägt vor, schlug vor, hat vorgeschlagen)

suit, der Anzug, ̈-e; **to suit,** *(= satisfy)* passen (D); *(= look nice on, be suitable for)* stehen (D) (er steht, stand, hat gestanden); **the dress suits (looks nice on) you,** das Kleid steht dir gut

summer, der Sommer; **in summer,** im Sommer

Sunday, der Sonntag; **on Sunday,** am Sonntag

supper, das Abendessen; **for supper,** zum Abendessen

supposed: he is supposed to, er soll

surprise, überraschen

swim, schwimmen (er schwimmt, schwamm, ist geschwommen); **we're going swimming,** wir gehen schwimmen

table, der Tisch, -e

take, nehmen (er nimmt, nahm, hat genommen), bringen (er bringt, brachte, hat gebracht); **to take along,** mit'nehmen; **to take off** *(a garment),* ab'legen; **to take place,** statt'finden (es findet statt, fand statt, hat stattgefunden); **to take a walk,** einen Spaziergang machen; **to take care of,** sorgen für (A); **I'll take you to the station,** ich bringe dich zum Bahnhof

talk, sprechen (er spricht, sprach, hat gesprochen), reden; **to talk about,** sprechen über (A) *or* von (D)

tall, *(person)* groß; *(= high)* hoch; **a tall tree,** ein hoher Baum

tea, der Tee

teach, lehren, unterrichten

teacher, *m.,* der Lehrer, -; *f.,* die Lehrerin, -nen

telephone, das Telefon, -e; **to telephone,** telefonieren an (A), an'rufen (er ruft an, rief an, hat angerufen)

television set, der Fernsehapparat, -e

tell, sagen; **to tell about,** erzählen von (D); **tell me,** sag mir

terrible, furchtbar

test, die Prüfung, -en; **to flunk a test,** in einer Prüfung durch'fallen; **to pass a test,** eine Prüfung bestehen

than, als

thank, danken (D); **thank you very much,** danke schön, vielen Dank

that, das, jener; *(conj.)* daß; **that one,** jener, der; **about that,** darüber; **everything that he needs,** alles, was er braucht

the, der, die, das; *pl.,* die

theater, das Theater, -; **at the theater,** im Theater; **to go to the theater,** ins Theater gehen; **movie theater,** das Kino, -s

their, ihr

them, (D) ihnen; (A) sie

then, dann

there, dort, da; *(= to there)* dorthin; **there is, there are,** es gibt; **there are,** es sind; **there was,** es war

therefore, darum, also

these, diese

they, sie

thief, der Dieb, -e

thing, das Ding, -e, die Sache, -n

think, denken (er denkt, dachte, hat gedacht); *(= believe)* glauben, meinen; **to think of (about),** denken an (A); **what do you think of my new hat?,** was hältest du von meinem neuen Hut?; **I'll think it over,** ich werde mir die Sache überlegen

this, dieser; **this morning,** heute morgen; **whose pencil is this?,** wessen Bleistift ist dies?

those, jene

thousand: a thousand, tausend; **two thousand,** zweitausend; **thousands,** Tausende

through, durch (A); *(= finished)* fertig

throw, werfen (er wirft, warf, hat geworfen); **to throw away,** weg'werfen

Thursday, der Donnerstag

ticket, die Karte, -n; *(train, bus)* die Fahrkarte, -n

time, die Zeit, -en; **on time,** rechtzeitig; **at what time?,** um wieviel Uhr?; **what time is it?,** wieviel Uhr ist es? *(or* wie spät ist es?); **spare time,** die Freizeit; **this time,** diesmal; **the third time,** das dritte Mal

tired, müde

to, *(with dat.)* zu, nach; *(with acc.)* an, auf, in; **to school (to the station),** zur Schule (zum Bahnhof) *or* in die Schule (auf den Bahnhof); **to Berlin,** nach Berlin; **he goes to the door (to the kitchen),** er geht an die Tür (in die Küche); **to college,** auf die Universität; **to the movies,** ins Kino

today, heute

together, zusammen

toilet, der Abort, -e, die Toilette, -n

tomorrow, morgen; **tomorrow morning,** morgen früh

tonight, heute abend

too, *(adv.)* zu; *(= also)* auch; **too much,** zuviel

towards, gegen (A), nach (D)

town, die Stadt, ⸚e

traffic, der Verkehr

train, der Zug, ⸚e; **by train,** mit dem Zug

translate: to translate into, übersetzen in (A); **translate into German,** Übersetzen Sie ins Deutsche!

travel, fahren (er fährt, fuhr, ist gefahren), reisen (ist gereist)

tree, der Baum, ⸚e

trip, die Fahrt, -en, die Reise, -n; **to take a trip,** eine Reise machen

true, wahr

try, versuchen

Tuesday, der Dienstag

turn: to turn on the light, das Licht an'machen; **to turn off,** aus'machen

twelve, zwölf

twenty, zwanzig

twice, zweimal; **twice a week,** zweimal die Woche

two, zwei

uncle, der Onkel, -

under, unter (D/A)

understand, verstehen (er versteht, verstand, hat verstanden)

undress, sich aus'ziehen (er zieht sich aus, zog sich aus, hat sich ausgezogen)

unfortunately, leider

United States, die Vereinigten Staaten *(pl.)*

university, die Universität, -en; **to the university,** auf die Universität

until, bis (A); **not until,** erst;

not until 3 o'clock, erst um 3 Uhr

upstairs, oben

us, uns

use, gebrauchen; **used to +** *verb, use past tense with adverb :* **I used to go there often,** ich bin oft dorthin gegangen

usual(ly), gewöhnlich

vacation, die Ferien *(pl.);* **summer vacation,** die Sommerferien

very, sehr; **very much,** sehr viel

vicinity, die Nähe, die Gegend

village, das Dorf, ⸚er

visit, der Besuch, -e; **for a visit,** zu Besuch; **to visit,** besuchen; **visitor,** der Besucher, -

voice, die Stimme, -n

wait, warten; **to wait for,** warten auf (A)

waiter, der Kellner, -

walk, der Spaziergang, ⸚e; **to walk,** (zu Fuß) gehen; **to take a walk,** einen Spaziergang machen, spazieren'-gehen (er geht spazieren, ging spazieren, ist spazierengegangen)

wall, *(indoors)* die Wand, ⸚e; *(outdoors)* die Mauer, -en

want, wollen (er will, wollte, hat gewollt)

war, der Krieg, -e; **World War,** der Weltkrieg

warm, warm; **I'm warm,** mir ist warm

wash, waschen (er wäscht, wusch, hat gewaschen); **to wash oneself, "wash up,"** sich waschen; **I wash myself,** ich wasche mich; **I wash my face,** ich wasche mir das Gesicht

watch, die Uhr, -en; **to watch,** zu'schauen (D); **watch out!,** passen Sie auf!

water, das Wasser

way, der Weg, -e; **on the way home,** auf dem Wege nach Hause

we, wir

wear, tragen (er trägt, trug, hat getragen)

weather, das Wetter

Wednesday, der Mittwoch

week, die Woche, -n; **a week ago,** vor einer Woche; **a week from today,** heute in acht Tagen

weekend, das Wochenende, -; **for the weekend,** übers Wochenende

welcome: you're welcome, bitte (schön)!

well, *(adv.)* gut, wohl; *(interj.)* denn; **I am well,** es geht mir gut; **he doesn't feel well,** er fühlt sich nicht gut; **sleep well** *(= good night!),* schlafen Sie wohl!; **well, what's the matter?,** was ist denn los?

well-known, bekannt

west, der Westen; **western,** westlich

what, was; **what's your name?,** wie heißen Sie?; **what sort of?,** was für ein?; **what time is it?,** wieviel Uhr ist es?

when, *(interrog.)* wann; *(with the past tense except in the sense of "whenever")* als; *(= whenever)* wenn

where, wo; *(= from where)* woher; *(= to where)* wohin; **where do you come from?,** woher kommen Sie? (wo kommen Sie her?); **where are you going?,** wohin gehen Sie? (wo gehen Sie hin?)

whether, ob

which, welcher; *(rel. pron.)* der, die, das; **which one?,** welcher?; **the film which I saw,** der Film, den ich sah

while, *(conj.)* während

white, weiß

who, *(interrog.)* wer; *(rel. pron.)* der, die, das; **the man who came,** der Mann, der gekommen ist

whole, ganz; **the whole night,** die ganze Nacht

whom, *(interrog.)* wem, wen; *(rel. pron.)* (D) dem, der, dem; (A) den, die, das; **to whom?,** wem?; **with whom?,** mit wem?; **the man whom I saw (with whom I spoke),** der Mann, den ich sah (mit dem ich sprach)

whose?, *(interrog.)* wessen?; *(rel. pron.)* dessen, deren, dessen; *pl.,* deren

why?, warum?

wife, die Frau, -en

will, *(aux. in fut. tense)* werden (er wird)

wind, der Wind, -e

window, das Fenster, -; **shop window,** das Schaufenster, -; **at (by) the window,** am Fenster

winter, der Winter; **in winter,** im Winter

wish, wünschen

with, mit (D); *(= at the house of)* bei (D)

without, ohne (A)

woman, die Frau, -en, die Dame, -n

wood, das Holz, ⸚er; **woods,** der Wald, ⸚er

word, das Wort; **words,** *(in a list)* Wörter; *(in a sentence)* Worte

work, die Arbeit, -en; *(of literature, etc.)* das Werk, -e; **to work,** arbeiten; **to work hard,** schwer arbeiten

world, die Welt

would like, möchte(n) (gern); **I would like to go,** ich möchte (gern) gehen; **would you like a cup of coffee?,** möchten Sie eine Tasse Kaffee?

write, schreiben (er schreibt, schrieb, hat geschrieben); **to write to,** schreiben (D) *or* schreiben an (A); **to write about,** schreiben von (D) *or* über (A)

wrong, falsch; **he's wrong,** er hat unrecht

yard, der Hof, ⸚e

year, das Jahr, -e; **he's six years old,** er ist sechs Jahre alt; **what year (in school) are you in?,** in welcher Klasse sind Sie?

yell, schreien (er schreit, schrie, hat geschrien)

yellow, gelb

yes, ja

yesterday, gestern; **yesterday evening,** gestern abend; **day before yesterday,** vorgestern

yet, eben, noch; **not yet,** noch nicht

young, jung

your, *(fam. sing.)* dein; *(fam. pl.)* euer (eur-); *(formal sing. & pl.)* Ihr